DD677259

YALE STUDIES IN ECONOMICS: **6**

The
Evolution
of
Wage
Structure

by LLOYD G. REYNOLDS

and CYNTHIA H. TAFT

with a section by ROBERT M. MACDONALD

NEW HAVEN: *Yale University Press, 1956*

London: Oxford University Press

MAXWELL REPRINT COMPANY
Elmsford, New York
1970

The Yale Studies in Economics and the Yale Labor and Management Center join in sponsoring this book. From the point of view of the Yale Labor and Management Center, which supported the research leading to this volume, it is the twenty-first in a list of books and interim research reports issued by the Center and designed to study and appraise the facts and factors in industrial relations in the light of the terms and hypotheses of the social and psychological sciences.

Preface

THIS book has been gradually writing itself over the past ten years. Indeed, its ancestry can be traced back to 1939, when the Harvard University Committee on Research in the Social Sciences allocated funds to me for a study of the impact of collective bargaining on wage structure in the pulp and paper industry. This work was interrupted by the war and was never resumed. In 1953, however, I interested Robert Macdonald in doing a doctoral dissertation on this subject. His skillful analysis, based on extended field work in the industry, will eventually be published in book form. Meanwhile, some of the principal findings are presented as Chapters 5 and 6 of this volume.

A large body of material on the wage structure of the United States was assembled during the late forties with research assistance provided by the Yale Labor and Management Center. In 1951 a travel grant made it possible to spend time in Europe examining French, British, and Swedish wage data. A second travel grant and a Guggenheim fellowship in 1954 made possible work in Canada, a follow-up trip to Europe, and the free time necessary for completion of the manuscript.

The book would still not have gotten off the ground had I not persuaded Cynthia Taft, who had worked at the London School of Economics and in Paris, to come to New Haven in 1952. Miss Taft, with a sure grasp of British and French as well as American wage materials, supervised all the statistical work for the volume and wrote drafts of Chapters 2–4 and 8–12. I rewrote these chapters, wrote Chapters 1, 7, and 13, and must take responsibility for the general orientation and conclusions of the book. But it was Miss Taft's energetic and competent aid which got the material out of the file case and into a manuscript. She has also borne the tedious work of writing notes on the wage data of the various countries, as well as preparing a selected bibliography. I am happy to acknowledge my obligation to a gifted collaborator and friend.

The list of additional acknowledgments is a long one. The project was supported at various stages by the Yale Labor and Management Center, the Rockefeller Foundation, the Carnegie Foundation, and the John Simon Guggenheim Memorial Foundation. It is impossible to name individually the union and management officials in the United States, and the private and public officials in other countries, who gave so freely of time and information for the study. Their help was obviously indispensable, and the authors are greatly in their debt. We are also grateful to Jane Metzger Schilling, Shirley Miller Buttrick, and Tsung-Yuen Shen for research assistance at various points; and to Dorothy Loucks Badger and Joanne Taylor for typing successive versions of the manuscript.

Various chapters of the manuscript were read and criticized by the following: Chapter 2 by Kent T. Healy of Yale University and Donald S. Beattie of the Brotherhood of Locomotive Engineers; Chapter 3 by Otis Brubaker of the United Steelworkers of America and by Leo Teplow and Bert Jody of the American Iron and Steel Institute; Chapter 4 by Solomon Barkin of the Textile Workers' Union of America; Chapters 7 and 13 by William J. Fellner, Edward C. Budd, and Mark W. Leiserson of Yale University; Chapter 8 by Georges Rottier of the French Institute of Applied Economics and Raymond Lévy-Bruhl of the French Ministry of Labor; Chapter 9 by Gösta Rehn of the Confederation of Swedish Trade Unions and by members of the Swedish Employers Confederation; Chapter 10 by Henry Phelps Brown of the London School of Economics and K. G. J. C. Knowles of the University of Oxford Institute of Statistics; Chapter 11 by the Economics and Research Branch of the Canadian Department of Labour and by George V. Haythorne of the Canadian Department of Labour; and Chapter 12 by Edward C. Budd and Mark W. Leiserson of Yale University. These comments were of great assistance in correcting errors and omissions in the manuscript. It is only fair to add that I did not invariably agree with the commentators, and that they should in no way be held responsible for any defects which may remain in the book.

The body of wage theory which satisfied most economists before 1930 has been outdated by institutional changes and the accumulation of knowledge. No equally coherent and accepted body of principles has yet arisen in its place. May this book serve as a steppingstone toward that reconstruction of wage theory which all economists so strongly desire.

L.G.R.

Taormina
March 1955

Contents

PART 1

Trade Unionism and Wage Structure
in the United States

PART 2

Studies in National Wage Structure

List of Tables

CHAPTER 1 The Problem of Relative Wage Rates

RECENT work on wages has been on the one hand very microscopic, on the other hand highly aggregative in character. The onset of the Great Depression produced controversy over the efficacy of wage reduction as a depression remedy. During the early New Deal period in the United States, a general increase in wages and prices was widely advocated as a recovery measure. Publication of Keynes's *General Theory* induced a spate of aggregative models—"improved" Keynesian, anti-Keynesian, and eventually post-Keynesian—in which the role of the money wage level differed basically from its role in neoclassical theory. The outbreak of war posed the problem of stabilizing the general wage and price level as part of a broader program of economic mobilization. Postwar inflation, which continued in many countries through 1952 or so, stimulated a running discussion of the role of wages in an inflationary movement, and of whether trade unionism strengthens inflationary tendencies. Thus for a generation the attention of economists has been focused on the behavior of the money wage level.

While general economists were thus engaged, specialists in labor economics and industrial relations were making detailed investigations into the determination of particular wage rates. The forces determining the wage level of the individual firm were debated at length. Studies were undertaken of rates and earnings on particular jobs within a plant, including the operation of incentive wage systems and job-evaluation plans, and the changes produced in management practices by the growth of collective bargaining. It was demonstrated that, in modern large-scale industry, all wage rates are administered wage rates; and that the influence of economic forces is mediated through administrative decisions rather than expressed directly in the market place. It was also asserted with a good show of evidence that, in many situations, economic forces determine only a range of possible wage rates rather than a specific wage rate. The location of the actual wage within this range will be influenced by custom, conventional yardsticks, management preferences and judgments, trade union pressures, and government wage regulations.

Amidst all this there was a tendency to lose sight of that intermediate level of analysis which classical and neoclassical economists had regarded as the proper province of wage theory. This has to do with the

1

movement of relative wage rates for different occupational levels, industrial categories, and geographical areas over substantial periods of time. It involves the use of what may be termed semiaggregative wage indexes, indexes which relate to a broad category of workers, yet which are more detailed and realistic than a single index of all money wages. It relates to Marshallian intermediate and long periods rather than to short periods—not to what happens in a month or a year, but to what happens over ten, twenty, or more years.

It is curious that the most recent treatise on wage theory in this sense is Professor Hicks's study published in 1931. The problems have not become obsolete. They have simply been neglected. This is all the more unfortunate in that the study of relative wage rates, or what it is now fashionable to term "wage structure," provides a natural meeting ground for labor economists and general economists. The neglect by both groups of this potential meeting ground is a major reason why their inquiries have drifted so far apart and why they have tended to take notice of each other only at a polemical level.

Within the last decade, however, there has been a heartening renaissance of interest in the determination of relative wage rates. A substantial body of articles has accumulated in the United States, concerned mainly with interindustry differentials but with some attention to other aspects of wage structure. The Oxford Institute of Statistics and other groups in Britain have been analyzing the wage structure of leading British industries. Exploratory work has been done in Sweden, France, Holland, Australia, and a number of other countries. The International Labor Office and the U. N. Economic Commission for Europe have given an impetus to comparative studies of national wage structure. The 1954 conference of the International Economic Association, which was devoted to papers on wage determination, gave a prominent place to structural analysis.

The importance of the theoretical and practical problems in this area surely requires little demonstration. In a market economy, we rely heavily on relative wage rates to distribute labor among a multitude of occupations, industries, and localities. In a purely competitive system, the wage structure would be shaped by the relative strength of specific demands for labor and the relative attractiveness of various jobs to workers. Any shifts in these underlying conditions would produce both a change in relative wage rates and a reallocation of the labor force. A change in wage differentials would both signal the need for a transfer of labor and help to bring it about. The strength and effectiveness of competition in actual labor markets has been questioned by some economists and reasserted by others, decade after decade, and we seem no nearer an agreed solution of the dispute today than we were two or three generations ago. An examination of the behavior of relative wage rates over time, in the light of what can be learned about changes in demand and supply conditions, may at least clarify the issues in dispute.

The behavior of relative wage rates is important also for problems of income distribution and social welfare. In industrialized nations much the greater part of personal income is labor income, either paid out as wages and salaries or retained by self-employed persons as an imputed wage. There is still some room for transfers between property income and labor income, and the desirability of such transfers will continue to be a subject of political controversy. To an extent not generally realized, however, the possibilities of income redistribution in the future lie within the labor sector. To what extent is it feasible and desirable to redistribute income by raising low wages and salaries relative to higher ones? At what point does this begin to interfere with incentives to enter, and to perform efficiently in, the higher occupations? May it be desirable to bring about transfers mainly through the government budget, leaving a large measure of inequality in wage rates and pretax incomes? These are issues on which we may learn something by analyzing the actual evolution of relative wage rates, and particularly by an analysis which extends over several countries. Leveling of wage differentials, while it appears to be a world-wide tendency, has progressed at varying speeds in different countries. The developments which are debated and feared in one country have usually occurred somewhere else in the world, and comparative analysis lends a desirable perspective to a view of domestic affairs.

The growing strength of trade unionism throughout the western world poses additional problems. Does unionism tend to warp the wage structure away from its "normal" or "competitive" shape? Or does it, on the contrary, serve to correct deficiencies and inequities in the preunion wage structure? These questions must be answered before one can appraise the consequences of collective bargaining and judge whether it should be encouraged as a matter of public policy.

A theory of the determination of relative wage rates is necessary also in order to understand the movement of the general wage level. "General" wage movements are not in fact general, but involve systematic differences in the rate of movement of particular wage rates. It is the separate but articulated movement of a multitude of particular rates which moves the general index upward or downward. An adequate appreciation of labor market structure, including trade union reactions and behavior, is essential to the construction of useful aggregative models.

Each of these lines of inquiry leads back to the central problem of how relative wage rates are determined. This question becomes more amenable to empirical study with the introduction of a time dimension:

what are the determinants of *changes* in relative wage rates in a national economy over substantial periods of time? What forces guide the evolution of wage structures?

It has become customary in discussing this question to set against each other "market" or "economic" forces, on the one hand, and "power" or "institutional" forces on the other. This dichotomy, however, does not stand up under close scrutiny.[1] Trade unions, employer associations, and government agencies cannot be treated as noneconomic bodies, for their power may be used largely for economic ends. The operation of organized groups may also considerably alter the structure of the labor market.

A more tenable distinction is that between "individual responses" and "organizational behavior." The former category includes the behavior of workers in choosing and changing jobs, and in negotiating with employers over terms of employment. It includes also the behavior of employers in hiring, promoting, and discharging employees, and in establishing wage schedules. Granted, the term "individual" is not strictly accurate. In a large business, wage and employment policies are a matter of group rather than individual decision. Workers' responses are not purely individualistic, but are shaped by a social matrix. "Individual responses" is still a useful way of denoting how hiring and wage determination would go on if workers and employers were left to deal with each other in a market uninfluenced by group organization. One need not assume that the market is perfectly competitive or that workers' and employers' behavior is oriented entirely toward pecuniary gain. It is clear from recent studies that a more complicated model is required to approximate the operation of actual labor markets.

"Organizational behavior" comprises the efforts of workers and employers to alter the wage structure by working through quasi-political bodies with coercive authority. The most important bodies of this sort are the trade union, the employers' association, and the various levels of national and local government. The types of activity include direct regulation of wage rates, indirect effects on wage structure through manipulation of labor demand and supply, and efforts to change the market mechanism itself.

Neither type of response should be regarded as more "natural" or "economic" than the other. It is natural for individuals to pursue their objectives through group organization as well as through market decisions. The behavior of people in the market may have a higher economic

1. See in this connection the comments of Clark Kerr in "Trade Unionism and Wage Structures," to be published in the forthcoming report of the 1954 International Economic Association conference on wage determination.

content than their behavior in organized groups; but this is not certain, and in any case, the difference is one of degree only. The attraction of workers to trade unions, their behavior in trying to influence union policy, their attitude toward economic legislation, and their allegiance to one political party rather than another are certainly influenced by economic self-interest. The same is true of employers' group behavior. Introduction of the terms "economic" and "political" tends simply to arouse emotion and to befuddle the argument. The alternative terminology suggested here is both more neutral and more accurate.

Our problem thus becomes to determine how far, in a particular economy, the results of individual responses in the labor market have been modified by group behavior. The answer will obviously differ from one case to the next. In Canada and the United States organizational behavior has thus far had only a moderate effect on wage structure. In France, Sweden, and Australia it has had a more substantial effect. In Russia the effects of central regulation are still more pronounced. National economies may be arrayed in a spectrum, ranging from the most individualistic or "liberal" at one end to the most highly regulated at the other.

This is still not the heart of the matter. The existence of a large body of union-management agreements or government wage regulations in a country does not prove that these regulations have had any effect on wage structure. It may be that the wage structure is still being molded *au fond* by shifts in labor demand and supply, and that group regulations serve only to ratify the adjustments brought about by market forces. Any independent influence of organizational behavior must be demonstrated, not simply taken for granted.

If the problem in regulated economies is the *actual* influence of organizational behavior, the problem in liberal economies is one of *potential* influence. The statement that trade unionism and legislation have thus far had little influence on the American wage structure is not very interesting. The important question is how much influence they may come to have if the trend toward organized intervention in the economy continues to gather force. Is organizational behavior potentially powerful enough to produce marked deviations from the wage structure which would otherwise be indicated by individual responses? If so, what is the probable direction of these deviations, and what are the likely economic consequences?

These twin questions of actual influence in some economies and potential influence in others reduce to a single analytical problem. Do individual responses in an unregulated labor market produce a determinate wage structure, any alteration in which must cause shifts in labor supply and labor allocation? Or does the unregulated labor market leave considerable ranges of indeterminacy, within which wage rates may be adjusted without causing serious economic dislocation? What happens when a union or a government attempts to establish a rate outside the range of indeterminacy? Does this produce individual responses which cancel out the attempted regulation and force the wage rate back within the limits of the "market range"?

We are speaking here of large wage adjustments and of substantial time periods. It may well be true that a union can raise the earnings of a widget-machine operator in the XYZ Company by 5 cents per hour and that there will be no consequences whatever—at least during the short period until the observer gets bored and turns his eyes elsewhere. It is more interesting to ask what will happen over a period of ten or twenty years if the wage level of an entire industry is raised 20 per cent relative to that of other industries, or if the wage differential between craftsmen and laborers is reduced by one-third throughout the economy.

The strategy of the book is to approach this nest of problems in two stages. Part 1 is limited to the influence of collective bargaining on wage structure in the United States. The phenomenal growth of trade unionism during the past twenty years has naturally produced a backwash of speculation and controversy over its economic consequences. This growth fortunately coincides with a marked improvement of wage data since 1930, which makes it possible in many industries to trace the impact of unionism from the beginning. Chapters 2–6 present case studies of four industries which differ in economic structure and in type of union organization. In Chapter 7 we draw not only on these studies but on the large secondary literature in an effort to appraise the impact of American trade unionism as a whole.

In Part 2 the focus is broadened to include the wage structures of four additional countries, with main emphasis on the last two decades but with some reference also to earlier periods. These countries represent a range of institutional situations, from a low degree of central wage regulation in Canada to a rather high degree in France and Sweden, with Britain occupying an intermediate position. In each case, after summarizing the evidence on what has happened to the main dimensions of wage structure, we raise the ticklish question of causation. How much of what has happened can reasonably be interpreted as a result of individual responses in the labor market? How much must be attributed to collective bargaining and, in some countries, to government wage regulation? Has the impact of organizational behavior actually been as great as appears on the surface? In Chapter 13 we attempt to draw this material together into an analysis of the evolution of national wage structures.

Chapters 7 and 13 contain the main findings and the theoretical contribution of the book, and these chapters may commend themselves to the general economist as well as to the specialist in labor matters.

Before entering on the main argument, it is desirable to clear out of the way some preliminary questions concerning data, definitions, and methodology. To some of these questions there is no "correct" answer, and one's preference is bound to depend on the purpose in hand and on personal judgment about what is important in the economy.

THEORETICAL AND STATISTICAL CONCEPTS OF "WAGES"

At the outset one encounters the difficulty that the definitions of wages which are most useful in theoretical reasoning cannot readily be approximated from existing wage statistics, while the wage measurements we do have frequently lack conceptual precision and significance. There is unfortunately no remedy for this gap between theoretical and statistical techniques of wage analysis; but we can at least explore the nature of the problem, and bear it in mind as a qualification throughout the remainder of the book.

It is possible to define very simple conditions under which the problem would not arise, and these are the conditions usually envisaged in theories of wage determination. Suppose that all workers, at least within the occupational category being studied, are of uniform efficiency and will produce the same output under identical conditions. Suppose that they are paid by the hour (so that problems of piece-rate payment do not arise), and that hours of work are uniform in all establishments (so that it does not matter whether one works with hourly or weekly wages). It is necessary to specify that employers adhere strictly to the prescribed wage scale, so that there is no discrepancy between *rates* and *earnings*. Suppose further that "fringe" payments—vacations, paid holidays, medical benefits, pensions, and the like—are either absent, or are uniform for all establishments, or are correlated in a specified fashion with the basic wage rate. Suppose, finally, that working conditions and other nonwage terms of employment are either uniform among establishments or are uniquely correlated with the wage level.

Under these conditions one could define the price of labor in an unequivocal way; and the wage measures collected from surveys of individual establishments would correspond reasonably closely to this definition.

The actual situation, however, is far from this simplified case. The existence of payroll taxes, withholding of income tax at the source, pension systems, and other forms of deferred benefit means that "wages" to the employee (income currently received) differs substantially from "wages" to the employer (labor costs currently paid out); and the wage schedules and benefit systems which are bargained about by unions and employers introduce a third dimension into the wage concept. Workers tend to think in terms of weekly income, employers in terms of labor cost per hour or per unit of product. Hourly wage systems are conceptually quite different from piece-rate systems. We know that fringe benefits and working conditions are important, but we do not know how they are correlated with wage level, nor do we know much about workers' preference systems. We dare not ignore these things, we are a little ashamed of smuggling them into the labor supply curve by a subterfuge, yet we have no other technique for handling them at the present time.

These conceptual difficulties are compounded when one comes to examine statistical measurements of "wages." The commonest kind of wage measure in the United States consists of average hourly earnings and average weekly earnings for workers in an entire industry in a particular month. What a hodge-podge figure this is! It is affected by changes in the composition of the industry's labor force, by changes in production methods and skill-mix, by the appearance and disappearance of firms, by geographical shifts of production, by changes in weekly hours of work, by changes in the administration of incentive systems, and by a variety of other things in addition to wage rates per se. Rates and earnings tend to fluctuate together, but the relation is a rather loose one.

It would be interesting to try to devise a method of wage reporting which would have maximum significance for research workers. For the time being, however, we are limited by the data which governments have been in the habit of collecting. These data differ substantially from one country to the next. In some countries the material relates essentially to *rates,* in others to *earnings.* The industrial classification used is much more detailed in some countries than in others, and the categories never match precisely. The extent to which the data are broken down by occupational level, by geographical region, and by sex and other personal characteristics of the worker varies a good deal. One country may have good information on wage differences by occupation but little on differentials by age and sex, while in another country the opposite may be true. This means that for each country one can construct only a partial outline of the wage structure, with some pieces of the puzzle missing. Intercountry comparisons are extremely difficult, both because the missing pieces differ from one country to the next and because of differences in the treatment of the same subject.

These remarks are perhaps sufficient to warn the reader that the gap between measurement and theory remains essentially unbridged, and that efforts to test theoretical hypotheses about wage determination cannot be as rigorous as one would wish.

THE DIMENSIONS OF WAGE STRUCTURE

The concept of "wage structure" involves a considerable degree of abstraction. All that one finds in reality is hundreds of thousands of rates for specific jobs in particular establishments. (In plants which have not yet reached the stage of setting standard job rates, one is reduced to the ultimate unit of the individual.) Summary figures—averages for a factory, an industry, a region—are abstractions which are likely to be misleading in proportion to the breadth of their coverage. As one disaggregates the data more and more by areas, product classes, size of establishment, and occupational level, the material becomes increasingly meaningful yet at the same time more voluminous and unmanageable.

One is forced by the sheer mass of the material to summarize. It is this process of summarizing which gives rise, in a sense artificially, to the "wage structures" and "wage differentials" which are analyzed by statisticians and economists. This structuring of the raw data could be done in a great variety of ways. It becomes important, therefore, to consider what variables are most significant for purposes of classification, and also to make sure that the selected bases of classification are fairly independent of each other. One should aim at reasonable purity of concepts, even though the data themselves are not fully refined. Statistical measurements usually blend and confuse two or more types of "pure" wage differential, and it is well to be conscious of this fact even when we cannot do very much about it.

The most significant bases for classifying and summarizing wage data appear to be:

1. *Occupational differences:* the relative wage levels of different occupational groups in the same establishment. If one uses any broader grouping than this, the "pure" occupational differential becomes mixed with interplant, interindustry, and other types of wage difference. In practice, of course, we do speak of occupational differentials for an entire industry and even for larger units, but this usage must be recognized as imprecise.

2. *Geographical differences:* the relative wage level of workers in the same industry and occupation, but in different geographical areas. The commonest bases of classification are by broad regions of a country and by different sizes of community within the same region. There is some question whether one can define a "pure" geographical differential with quite the precision of our other definitions. One can require the workers

compared to be in the same occupation and industry, but one can scarcely require them to be in the same establishment, so that there is bound to be some mixture of interplant and geographical influences.

3. *Interindustry differences:* the relative wage levels of different industries for workers in the same occupational category and geographical area. In practice, we frequently compare average hourly earnings for all workers in each industry, but this is a very crude method, and more precise measures are desirable whenever they can be obtained.

4. *Interplant differences:* the relative wage levels of different establishments in the same industry and geographical area. The distinction between interplant comparisons and interfirm comparisons is important in some cases, but in general the two terms can be used interchangeably.

5. *Personal differences:* the relative wage levels of workers who are in the same establishment and occupation, but who differ in age, sex, race, or other personal characteristics. In addition to these categorical differences, many establishments without systematic rate structures show different rates for almost every individual, depending on the personal efficiency of the individual, the circumstances under which he was hired, and the judgment of the foreman or supervisor.

One can also analyze relative wage levels by size of establishment, by union or nonunion status, and in a variety of other ways. These five categories are basic, however, and each has been subjected to much statistical study. They are used, therefore, as the main frame of reference throughout this book.

Statistical surveys of wages rarely measure any of these "pure" differentials, but rather some combination of them. Differences in the wage rates paid by different employers in a locality for the same occupational title, for example, represent a combination of interindustry differences, interplant differences within each industry, and even occupational differences, since the same title rarely describes exactly the same work in each plant. Differences in average hourly earnings among industries represent a combination of true interindustry differences, geographical differences, occupational differences, and differences in personal characteristics of the labor force.

The pure differentials can sometimes be uncovered by getting hold of detailed returns from individual establishments and aggregating them in the desired way. One is usually faced, however, with a published statistical series aggregated in a way which blurs over and conceals the primary differentials. For this reason, one can rarely be completely certain how a particular differential has changed over the course of time. The movement of the composite figures may strongly suggest that certain changes have occurred in the underlying components, but this is an implication rather than a demonstration. Whenever the reader encounters a statement that "geographical differentials have narrowed in Sweden," or "interindustry differences have diminished in France," it should be read with this qualification in mind.

MEASUREMENT OF CHANGES IN WAGE STRUCTURE

One is usually interested not just in the size of a wage differential at a point in time but in the course of this differential over time. How does one measure whether a particular differential has narrowed or widened?

Suppose that in Period 1 the wage rate for occupation A is $2.00 per hour and that for occupation B is $1.00 per hour. In Period 2 one finds that these rates have risen to $3.00 for occupation A and $2.00 for occupation B. What has happened to the differential between the two occupations? In absolute terms it has remained unchanged at $1.00 per hour, but in percentage terms it has shrunk from 100 per cent to 50 per cent. Which is the more significant way of viewing the situation?

One can develop an attractive argument that the percentage basis is more significant, and that a "widening" or "narrowing" of wage differentials should always be defined in percentage terms. Most of our basic economic calculations—changes in price levels, wage levels, production levels—are made on a ratio or percentage basis. Beneath this practice lies the fact that, in a world of fluctuating price levels, only equal percentage changes in all prices and asset values will leave everyone in the same relative position as before. (This assumes, of course, the absence of money illusion. If money illusion is present it becomes difficult to define a "neutral" inflation which will leave the real situation unchanged.)

In our illustrative case, where the wage level of occupation A has increased by 50 per cent and that of occupation B by 100 per cent, it seems clear that group B has scored a relative advance. The gap in living standard between the two groups has been reduced.[2] Another way of viewing the situation is to say that the absolute differential between the two occupations, which has remained unchanged at a dollar per hour, represents less in real terms at a higher wage and price level. From any point of view, then, it seems logical to conclude that the wage differential has been narrowed.

Against this line of argument one must set the fact that many workers appear to think in terms of absolute or cents-per-hour differentials and

2. Not necessarily, however, in precise proportion to the narrowing of the wage differential. Different income groups have different patterns of consumption, and, since all retail prices never advance at the same rate, the cost of living for one group may have risen somewhat more rapidly than for the other. For the large shift in wage differentials which we have assumed here, one could be reasonably sure that relative living standards have changed in the same direction; but for a small shift one could not be so sure.

to be satisfied with maintenance of differentials in this sense even though percentage differentials may decline. Unions frequently demand and secure uniform cents-per-hour increases for their entire membership regardless of skill grade, a policy which narrows percentage differentials over the long run. During periods of rapid inflation one rarely finds percentage differentials maintained intact. On the contrary, the lower-paid workers typically receive increases which are larger in percentage terms, though smaller in absolute terms, than those received by the higher-paid groups. One can make a good argument that this is equitable, on the ground that the lowest-paid groups suffer most severely from inflation. In any event, it happened during the inflationary forties in every country which we have examined.

It is necessary, then, to measure changes in both absolute and percentage differentials in order to have a complete picture of what has occurred. The percentage calculation can still be regarded as primary in the sense that it indicates redistribution of real income and shifts in the relative living standards of different groups of workers. Percentage differentials should also come closest to indicating the relative attractiveness of different occupations, though this depends on worker attitudes about which we do not know very much. Recognition of the importance of percentage relationships, however, should not be confused with an expectation that these relationships either should be or will be maintained intact over the course of time. Such a view is certainly not warranted during periods of sharp inflation, and we shall argue in Chapter 13 that there is a natural tendency for percentage differentials to contract over the long run even with price stability.

When in subsequent chapters the term "differential" is used without qualification, it should be understood that we are speaking of percentage relationships. The statistical tables, however, will usually show the movement of absolute wage differences as well.

IMPUTING "CAUSES" FOR CHANGES IN WAGE STRUCTURE

After one has measured changes in wage structure over a period of time, there arises the problem of explaining how these changes have come about. One thinks immediately of at least four categories of cause: changes in demand and supply conditions for particular types of labor; general inflation, which appears to exert an independent influence on wage structure; trade union and employer policies in collective bargaining; and governmental control of wage rates. These factors do not operate independently but interact on each other in complicated ways. Several of them will frequently be found to have operated in the same direction, so that a particular change in differentials may be over-explained. That is to say, one could explain it quite plausibly on any of several alternative grounds—demand shifts, general inflation, collective bargaining policies. One suspects that in fact each of these things has contributed to the result. How unscramble these separate forces and assign to each its proper order of importance?

The problem of several independent variables impinging on a dependent variable is common enough in economics, and statistical techniques are available to deal with it. In this case, however, most of the independent variables either cannot be, or at any rate have not been, subjected to quantitative measurement. How does one measure the influence of a War Labor Board or the strength of trade union organization? Even to measure shifts in demand and supply curves for farm laborers or coal miners would be a formidable undertaking, which has not been attempted to date. We are forced back, therefore, onto qualitative appraisal of the forces at work and an intuitive "feel" of how the economy operates. Economists have been using intuition for a long time, and with some measure of success; but the results are not as satisfying as those of quantitative analysis and can readily be questioned by anyone of differing judgment.

This difficulty need not be labored further, since there is no apparent way out of it. It is necessary only to assure the reader that we have been very conscious of this problem at each stage of the argument. In later chapters we shall frequently have occasion to state that such-and-such causes appear to have been responsible for a particular change in relative wage rates. These statements are not meant to be more than tentative hypotheses, constructed in the light of the data, and sometimes with the aid of informed judgments by other scholars. Like any hypotheses, they are subject to error and to revision as additional evidence accumulates.

PART 1

Trade Unionism
and Wage Structure
in the United States

Introduction

THE rapid growth of trade union membership since 1933 has stimulated controversy over the economic consequences of collective bargaining, including its effect on wage structure. Unions have tended to take full credit for wage increases in unionized firms and industries, and to argue that unionism produces desirable changes in wage structure. Employers likewise assume that the impact on wage structure is substantial, though many of them deny its beneficent character. Economists have been drawn into the argument in various ways. Some, using deductive models of competitive wage structure and of economically motivated union behavior, have asserted that unionism necessarily has an undesirable influence on relative wage rates. Other economists have argued that the pre-union wage structure was too imperfect to be taken as a norm, and that in any case union wage behavior does not conform closely to economic models.

If the theoretical controversy is to be resolved, there is an obvious need for investigation of how the wage structures of various industries have evolved under collective bargaining. Granted, the net influence of unionism can never be conclusively demonstrated. The wage structure of an industry is always evolving, and the effects of union pressure are intermingled with those of economic change in a way which defies quantitative analysis. By combining information on union wage objectives with data on changes in industry wage structure, however, it is possible to draw reasonable inferences. If one finds that interplant differentials in an industry have diminished sharply while at the same time this has been a central objective of union policy, it is plausible to ascribe some of the reduction of differentials to union influence.

Chapters 2–6 undertake this kind of analysis for four industries which have unusually good wage data and which illustrate a variety of economic and organizational situations. Railroad transportation is a "natural monopoly" which for several decades has been declining and relatively unprofitable. Union organization, which is on a craft basis, goes back many decades and is now virtually complete. Iron and steel is a mature but still expanding industry, strongly concentrated in a few major companies and with a tradition of wage and price leadership. Union organization in basic steel is virtually complete, but has developed only within the past twenty years. Cotton textiles is a relatively small-scale and highly competitive industry, which has undergone a major locational shift from New England to the southeastern states. The leading industrial union, now almost twenty years old, has organized the tag end of the industry in New England but has been unable to establish a strong foothold in the South. This is representative of numerous other situations in light manufacturing, where the power of a union to manipulate wages in unionized establishments is limited by nonunion competition. Pulp and paper is an expanding and profitable industry which is unusually diversified in terms of geographical location and range of products. Two AFL unions, one craft and one industrial, work side by side in the industry. Virtually powerless in 1932, these unions are now strongly established in most parts of the country. They have followed an unusually pragmatic wage policy which affords a contrast to the tighter policies of some of the CIO industrial unions.

This is still a small sample of American industry, and if time had permitted it would have been desirable to explore a variety of other industries as well. Leading candidates for investigation would be clothing manufacture, hosiery, boots and shoes, printing and publishing, automobiles, heavy electrical equipment, coal mining, building construction, truck transportation, longshoring, and merchant shipping. Studies of wage structure have already been made in some of these industries, and in others there are general studies of collective bargaining which throw incidental light on the evolution of wage differentials.

Chapter 7 draws on the available literature as well as on our four case studies for an appraisal of the wage consequences of American trade unionism. With respect to each major dimension of wage structure, we raise the following questions: what pattern of differentials would exist in static equilibrium under conditions of perfect competition in the labor market? what kind of differentials develop in nonunion labor markets under actual conditions of imperfect competition and dynamic change? how is the nonunion pattern typically altered by the development of collective bargaining? does collective bargaining bring differentials closer to, or drive them farther away from, the hypothetical pattern which would prevail under perfect competition?

The argument leads to a finding that the wage structure is likely to come closer to competitive norms under collective bargaining than under nonunion conditions. This will doubtless seem implausible to many readers, who will wonder how "monopolistic" trade union organization can produce competitive results. Resolution of this paradox forms the substance of Part 1.

CHAPTER 2

Railroad Transportation

SOME ASPECTS OF COLLECTIVE BARGAINING

UNION AND EMPLOYER ORGANIZATION

THE railroads are a vital element in the American economic mechanism. A work stoppage on the railroads has an immediate effect on the national economy. The structure of occupations in the industry is such that a small minority of employees can bring about a general work stoppage. The result is that government is directly concerned with collective bargaining negotiations in the industry. There has been statutory provision for adjustment of railroad labor disputes for more than sixty years, and during the past twenty years almost every important wage determination in the industry has been arrived at through government procedures.

Railroad operations are centralized in a small group of large companies. While there were 464 railroads in the country in 1951, the twenty-five largest of these carried some two-thirds of all freight traffic.[1] Moreover, railroad traffic funnels through a limited number of major terminals. These two factors, plus the dependence of railroad operation on a few skilled trades, facilitate strategic control of labor supply by the unions.

Union organization on the railroads is characteristically along craft lines. The unions of train-operating employees are among the oldest and strongest labor organizations in the country. They were already negotiating collective agreements on a limited scale in the 1880's, and since World War I have had virtually complete control of their respective crafts throughout the country.[2]

The shop crafts and other nonoperating groups were slower to form effective unions in the face of vigorous employer opposition. Strength-

1. Jacob J. Kaufman, *Collective Bargaining in the Railroad Industry* (New York, King's Crown Press, 1954), p. 5.
2. For a discussion of the evolution of collective bargaining and wage structure in the railroad industry, see Kaufman, *Collective Bargaining;* Harry E. Jones, *Railroad Wages and Labor Relations, 1900–1952* (rev. ed., Washington, Bureau of Information of the Eastern Railways, 1953); and Harry D. Wolf, "Railroads," in Harry A. Millis, ed., *How Collective Bargaining Works* (New York, Twentieth Century Fund, 1942).

ened by government protection during World War I, they suffered a relapse when this protection was withdrawn. During the twenties and early thirties union membership declined, the coverage of collective agreements shrank, and company unions flourished on a considerable scale.

The final consolidation of union influence in the industry dates from the mid-thirties. Amendments to the Railway Labor Act in 1934 outlawed yellow-dog contracts, forbade the use of company funds by employee organizations, and protected the right of employees to join unions without punitive action by the employer. It was subsequently established through court decision that only national unions were entitled to use the grievance-adjustment provisions of the act, a step which obviously gave the "outside" unions an advantage over company unions.[3]

These provisions, plus rising economic activity and the general upsurge of unionism in other industries, brought a marked strengthening of railroad unionism. By the late thirties company unionism had virtually disappeared, and collective bargaining between the carriers and the national unions had been extended to the great bulk of railroad mileage in the country. Today some 80 per cent of all railroad workers, including white-collar workers, are union members. Virtually all manual workers are covered by collective agreements,[4] making this one of the most highly unionized industries in the United States.

The train-operating employees, referred to in industry parlance as the "ops," numbered in 1952 some 256,000 or about one-fifth of all railroad employees.[5] They are organized in the "big five" brotherhoods: engineers, firemen, trainmen, conductors, and switchmen. These unions are the most powerful in the industry because of their virtually complete coverage of their respective crafts and because of the essentiality of their members to train operations. They bargain independently of the nonoperating unions, and to a large extent independently of each other.

The clerical, maintenance, shop-crafts, train-dispatching, and other nonoperating employees—usually referred to as the "nonops"—belong to some fifteen national unions. About half of these are confined to the railroad industry, while the remainder have a substantial membership in other industries. The groups with largest railroad membership are the railway clerks, maintenance-of-way employees, railroad telegraphers, machinists, and railway carmen. These five groups in 1952 had about four-fifths of the total nonoperating membership of 800,000.[6] Most of

3. See Herbert R. Northrup, "The Railway Labor Act and Railway Labor Disputes," *American Economic Review, 36* (June 1946), 324–43.
4. Kaufman, *Collective Bargaining,* p. 45.
5. *Ibid.,* pp. 20–1.
6. *Ibid.,* pp. 53–4.

the nonoperating unions, unlike the major operating unions, are affiliated with the AFL. The machinists, carmen, boilermakers, blacksmiths, and other shop-crafts unions have banded together for joint action in the Railway Employees Department of the AFL. The nonops work more closely together in collective bargaining than do the ops, and typically serve joint demands on the employers. This is partly because the jurisdictions of the nonop unions are quite sharply defined, and they do not suffer from jurisdictional rivalry to the same extent as do the operating brotherhoods.

Employer organization for collective bargaining has developed as a parallel and counterweight to trade union organization. Collective bargaining began in the usual way with negotiations between a particular union and a particular railroad. The unions quickly encountered the contention that one railroad could not afford to raise wages without a similar increase being imposed on its competitors. In 1902 the conductors union in the West decided to meet this by making demands on all the western railroads at the same time. Employers at first refused to consider this joint demand, but the conductors held firm and were joined by the trainmen. After some months of discussion the employers finally conceded wage increases and other uniform concessions throughout the western territory. The success of this movement led the unions to institute regional bargaining in the eastern territory (east of Chicago and north of the Chesapeake and Ohio Railroad) in 1906. In 1909 a southern organization was established including all territory not covered in the eastern and western regions. Collective bargaining continued on a regional basis from this time until the thirties, except for an interlude of national negotiation arising from government operation of the railroads from 1917 to 1920.[7]

The tendency to consolidate regional wage movements into national movements and to move toward de facto national bargaining was a development of the 1930's. The reasons for this development probably included the following: 1. On several occasions—1931, 1932, 1933, and 1938—the employers took the initiative in demanding a general wage reduction. They apparently considered it advantageous to present a united front to the unions, and negotiations were on a national basis from the outset. 2. There has been a growing tendency for disputed issues to be referred to an emergency board or an arbitration board under the Railway Labor Act of 1926.[8] It is clear that a board decision affecting one regional association will be used as a precedent or "pattern" in

7. Jones, *Railroad Wages*, Chaps. 2–4.

8. See Herbert R. Northrup, "Emergency Disputes under the Railway Labor Act," *Proceedings of the First Annual Meeting, Industrial Relations Research Association . . . 1948*, pp. 78–88.

other regions, so that any important dispute is in effect a national dispute. Recognizing this fact, each union normally files the same demands at about the same time throughout the country. As these demands proceed through the various stages of negotiation and board hearings, they are typically consolidated into a single case and made the subject of a single award. 3. This tendency was strengthened during the war years 1941–45, when national settlements were invoked to ensure conformity with national wage-stabilization standards and to prevent work stoppages on the railroads. The wage controls imposed during the Korean war of 1950–53 had a similar effect.

National collective bargaining is now firmly established. As a matter of form, demands are still served on individual carriers throughout the country. Negotiation at the company level is largely perfunctory, however, and the issues are speedily passed on to higher levels on both sides. The upshot is a central conference, usually held in Chicago, at which officials of the western, eastern, and southern carriers associations meet with top officials of the union involved. From there the matter typically goes to an arbitration board or an emergency board, following procedures to be outlined below. The eventual settlement is a national settlement, and its terms are incorporated into union contracts with the great majority of railroad companies.

THE NATURE OF WAGE MOVEMENTS

The nonop unions tend to form a common front in collective bargaining and to present the same demands at the same time.[9] The operating unions, on the other hand, bargain separately from the nonops and very often separately from each other. In some years two or three of the ops will cooperate in presenting demands, but these combinations rarely include all the unions, and their composition changes from year to year. Instead of permanent alliances one finds a condition of permanent rivalry.

In 1945, for example, the firemen, conductors, and switchmen agreed to private arbitration of their wage demands, while the engineers and trainmen chose to go through the emergency-board procedure. In 1949 the conductors, trainmen, and switchmen served separate demands, while the engineers and firemen stood together. In 1950 the engineers and firemen once more bargained separately. In 1951–52 the trainmen settled separately while the engineers, firemen, and conductors settled together. In 1954 four of the five crafts signed agreements on substantially the same terms, but the engineers held out and went to arbitra-

9. See Kaufman, *Collective Bargaining*, Chap. 4.

tion in an effort to win a larger increase and widen their differential over the firemen.

This tactical maneuvering arises from conflicts of interest and jurisdictional rivalries among the operating unions. The engineers and firemen have frequently found themselves at odds on policy issues which affect the job opportunities of the two groups, such as limitations on the number of miles an engineer may run in a month. They are also rivals for membership. Every engineer is a promoted fireman, and because of fluctuating employment levels combined with the operation of the seniority system, a man at a certain stage of his career may move back and forth frequently between the two kinds of work. Should he belong to the engineers' union, or the firemen's union, or both? The railroad unions function as fraternal and insurance associations as well as bargaining agents, and a man frequently retains membership in both unions in order to retain insurance rights. A similar situation exists between the conductors and trainmen, who also form a promotional sequence based on seniority.

Each union, then, seeks to win greater increases than its rival as a demonstration of its superior strength and leadership, and as a basis for recruiting appeals to potential members. The contrary argument that all the unions might make larger gains by standing together is not very persuasive. Each of the operating brotherhoods is capable by itself of stopping train operations and bringing on governmental intervention. All five together could do no more. Joint action has therefore been rejected and bargaining strategy has become in part an instrument of interunion rivalry. The complicated shifts and maneuverings which go on during a wage movement are comprehensible only in political terms.

A wage movement begins with a straggling procession of demands filed at different times by various unions and combinations of unions. The demands may look quite different at the outset, partly because each craft has special problems which differ from those of other crafts, partly because of differing judgments as to what constitute the best "talking points" in a particular year. One union may prefer to demand increases in the basic wage schedule, another increases in fringe benefits, still another changes in working rules, which are highly complicated and offer a fertile field for bargaining.

The demands of a particular union, while served on individual employers in the first instance, are quickly consolidated into a single national movement. Representatives of the carriers and the union, fifty to a hundred in number, descend on Chicago and settle down to weeks or months of negotiation. If direct negotiation fails to produce agreement, as is normally the case, the National Mediation Board established under the Railway Labor Act may intervene and try to bring the parties closer together. If these efforts are unsuccessful the board is required to propose that the parties refer the dispute to private arbitration. This proposal is usually, though not invariably, refused by one or both parties. Thus the case may finally reach the stage of an "emergency board" consisting of public representatives appointed by the President to study the dispute and make recommendations concerning it.

Meanwhile the demands of other unions have been under discussion in separate conferences. Key representatives of the carriers typically participate in all negotiations, and the carriers adopt a uniform position vis-à-vis each union in turn. They are naturally unwilling to make concessions to one group which they are not prepared to extend to all the others. Both sides maneuver for position, watching for points of weakness on the other side, and seeking to reach a favorable settlement with one group which can later be urged as a pattern for others.

Over a period of months, a number of unsettled cases accumulate. As they reach the emergency-board stage there is a tendency to group and consolidate them. One emergency board may be appointed to hear all the nonop demands and another to hear the operating groups, though on occasion a single board has handled all outstanding cases. Or, if one or more unions have accepted arbitration, an arbitration board and one or more emergency boards may be sitting at about the same time.

The guidelines which emergency boards have used in reaching wage decisions need not be discussed in detail.[10] The main point is that both emergency and arbitration boards have shown a strong disposition toward parity of treatment for the various crafts. If a board has before it demands from five different unions, it will typically recommend comparable increases for all. The first awards or settlements during a particular movement tend to establish a pattern for later awards. Deviations from the pattern are rare, except where one group has lagged behind on a preceding movement and a catching-up adjustment can be justified, or where there is some special situation such as the conversion of the nonops from a forty-eight-hour to a forty-hour week in 1949.

The emergency-board recommendation is frequently not the end of the matter. Emergency-board findings were rejected by one or more unions in 1941, 1943, 1946, 1947, and 1951. This set off a typical sequence of events: a strike or threatened strike, seizure of the industry by the President under the emergency powers which he exercised during World War II and the Korean war, further negotiations between the White House and the parties, and a final settlement which was usually somewhat larger than the original board award. The formal procedures

10. See in this connection Kaufman, *Collective Bargaining*, Chap. 9.

of the Railway Labor Act have thus been supplemented by informal arbitration of major disputes at the White House level.

The final outcome, though it may be higher than the original award, is still uniform among crafts. In 1941 President Roosevelt secured 9½¢ for the ops, 10¢ plus paid vacations for the nonops. In 1943 he awarded 9¢–11¢ to the nonops, 9¢ plus a week's vacation to the ops. In 1946 President Truman arranged a uniform increase of 18½¢ for ops and nonops. In 1947 he persuaded three recalcitrant operating unions, after government seizure, to accept the 15½¢ increase which all other unions in the industry had accepted.[11]

National bargaining and government intervention thus reshape the diverse demands of individual unions and produce a uniform result at the end. Efforts of one union to obtain an advantage over its rivals are repeatedly frustrated by the wage-determining mechanism. Any advantage obtained by one group is apt to be temporary, being offset by catching-up adjustments for other groups within a few years. If one adds up the cents-per-hour increase in basic wage rates over the period 1937–54, as will be done in a later section, virtually the same total appears for every occupational group in the industry.[12]

WAGE DIFFERENTIALS WITHIN A CRAFT: THE CASE OF THE LOCOMOTIVE ENGINEERS

In appraising the impact of collective bargaining on the railroad wage structure, it is convenient to begin with the way in which contract rules affect the earnings opportunities of different members of the same craft. This analysis will deal with engineers' earnings, but a similar analysis could be made for firemen, conductors, or trainmen.

Engineers employed in different classes of service differ markedly in weekly and annual income, in hours worked per week, and in other job conditions. In 1953, for example, the range in weekly earnings was from $117.15 for yard service to $156.43 for road local and way

11. See the two articles by Northrup already cited; Jones, *Railroad Wages*, Pt. 1; and Kaufman, *Collective Bargaining*, Pt. 2.

12. This should not be interpreted as meaning that different crafts have not fared differently in *any* respect. Different groups have undoubtedly secured differential advantages from rules changes, changes in the basis of wage payment, and so forth. The engineers and firemen, as will be seen, have benefited substantially from the scale which relates their earnings to weight of engine. Differential advantages which are sufficiently complex to conceal them from the inexperienced eye can be awarded more easily than different cents-per-hour additions to wage scales, which are readily compared.

freight.[13] Since these are averages for large categories, the dispersion of earnings among individual engineers was considerably greater.

How has this situation come about? How is the rate of pay for a particular engineering job decided? How are opportunities for the highest-paid jobs rationed among those who want them? Elaborate regulations have been developed on these matters and, in view of the simple wage systems which existed in preunion days, it can be argued that the present structure has resulted mainly from union strength and union policies.

HOW ENGINEERS' WAGES ARE COMPUTED

A recent historical study of railway wages reports that ". . . the earliest basis of pay was a monthly wage . . . Another basis of pay, the daily wage, was originally applied on many railroads to trainmen. . . . A third method of pay was the so-called 'trip' system, under which the amount of work, number of hours, mileage and local conditions were separately valued for each specific assignment, and a rate established for the particular run or trip which was supposed to take these special factors into consideration . . ." [14] These were all time-rate or simple piece-rate systems. The more complicated mileage basis of pay was apparently an outgrowth of collective bargaining. Jones reports that "the mileage basis of pay was apparently first developed for engineers in the west and was embodied in agreements and understandings between many of the western railroads and their engineers as early as the 1880's." [15]

From these beginnings the method of wage payment has evolved through some seventy years of union-management negotiation. The earnings of a locomotive engineer presently are determined on a complicated basis, involving the following four factors: [16]

1. *The basic daily rate.* This term is somewhat misleading, because it does not correspond at all closely to engineers' actual daily earnings. The table of basic daily rates, however, is the starting point for computation of actual earnings. The table is graduated in two dimensions: a. The "weight-on-drivers" factor, i.e. the load which the locomotive is capable of pulling. A locomotive in passenger service with a weight-on-drivers of 200,000 pounds carried in 1953 a basic rate of $14.77, while one with a rating of 1,000,000 pounds paid $16.13. The rationale of this is that the larger locomotive hauls more cars and has a higher value

---

13. See Table 2-2.

14. Jones, *Railroad Wages*, pp. 36–7.

15. *Ibid.*, p. 37.

16. See Brotherhood of Locomotive Engineers, *The Wage Differentials of Railroad Engineers* (submitted to the Board of Arbitration, 1953 wage movement), pp. 1–23.

product. The union contends that the engineer should share in this higher productivity, and also that operation of the heavier equipment involves greater effort and responsibility. b. The second determinant is whether the engineer is employed in yard work, through freight, local and way freight, or passenger service. Yard service carries a somewhat higher basic rate than the various categories of road service. The reason is that the men in yard service receive little except the basic rate, while the road engineers receive mileage and other payments which bring them out with considerably higher earnings.

Much more important than these variations in the basic rate is the definition of the "day's work" for which the rate is paid. In yard service the day is eight hours, the basic daily rate being paid regardless of whether the full eight hours are worked. Freight engineers receive the basic daily rate for work of eight hours (or less) or 100 miles (or less). In the case of passenger engineers, the day is defined as five hours (or less) or 100 miles (or less). The basic rate, in short, is a guaranteed minimum which must be paid regardless of hours worked or miles run. It gives little indication of actual earnings, which are influenced by the other factors now to be described.

2. *Mileage pay.* Passenger and freight engineers receive payment on a *pro rata* basis for each mile run in a day above the 100-mile minimum. A passenger engineer whose regular run is 150 miles would receive one and a half times the daily rate, while a run of 200 miles would carry double the daily rate. This is an increasingly important source of compensation, particularly in passenger and through freight service, where the present speed of trains permits several hundred miles to be run in a few hours. Under this system, an increase in the average speed of trains produces higher earnings, or shorter hours, or both, quite apart from increases in the basic rate schedule.[17]

3. *"Constructive allowances."* These are payments made for special

---

17. Union contracts in the industry typically provide minimum and maximum limits for the average miles per month operated by engineers on each division. When actual mileage rises above the maximum, additional engineers are promoted from the firemen's roster, while if mileage falls below the minimum some engineers are sent back to firing. The level of these limits is always a rather controversial matter. A higher maximum means increased earnings for the senior engineers, but fewer jobs for men lower on the seniority roster.

Since the maximum is fixed at a given time, the immediate effect of an increase in train speeds is to produce shorter hours of work. Over a longer period, however, there is pressure for upward revision of mileage limits to keep them in a realistic relation to operating speeds. Thus if one considers several decades, one finds that the gains from increased speed are divided between higher earnings and shorter hours. Between 1922 and 1953 the average weekly hours of passenger engineers fell from 44.3 to 37.0, while the average hours of freight engineers fell from 54.7 to 47.3.

or extra work, such as switching, road work done by yard crews, and time lost in delay or waiting. For these activities (or lack of them) the worker is paid at the basic rate corresponding to his usual work classification.

4. *Overtime pay.* Yard engineers receive time and one-half for time worked over eight hours in a 24-hour period. For road engineers the system is more complicated. Freight engineers receive overtime for all time worked above that necessary to make the run at 12½ miles per hour. Example: A man is on duty for ten hours and only covers 100 miles, so that he gets no extra mileage pay. He will receive his daily rate plus two hours' overtime at time and one-half for the two hours above the eight which would have been required to make the run at an average speed of 12½ miles per hour. The system for passenger engineers is roughly the same, except that the average speed below which overtime payment begins is set at 20 miles per hour (100 miles divided by the basic five-hour day) to take account of the greater average speed of passenger trains. The rate of overtime payment to passenger engineers is five-eighths rather than one-half.

Table 2-1. *Per Cent of Earnings of Railroad Engineers Resulting from Specific Factors, 1950* * (*Class I railways*)

| | PER CENT OF EARNINGS RESULTING FROM | | | |
	DAILY RATE	MILEAGE PAY	CONSTRUCTIVE- ALLOWANCE PAY	OVERTIME PAY
Engineers				
Yard	82.6	3.4	5.6	8.4
Road through freight	56.1	24.8	13.1	5.9
Road local and way freight	64.3	7.7	7.3	20.7
Road passenger	55.8	32.0	9.1	3.2

* 1950 is the last year for which detailed information is shown in the ICC reports. Test calculations show that 1953 data, if fully available, would give approximately the same result.

Source: Brotherhood of Locomotive Engineers, *Wage Differentials of Railroad Engineers* (submitted to the Board of Arbitration, 1953 wage movement), p. 13

The relative importance of these components of earnings varies according to the class of service, as is suggested by Table 2-1. While this table might be subject to certain technical criticisms, arising mainly from the difficulty of making clear separation between related elements of compensation, the orders of magnitude shown can be taken as roughly correct. In yard service, basic rates are of dominant importance. In local and way freight, which typically involves low train speeds and long working hours, overtime pay is of considerable importance. Through freight and passenger engineers, operating relatively high-speed trains, typically exceed the hundred-mile definition of a day's work and thus benefit substantially from mileage pay. The upshot is that the ranking of different classes of engineer with respect to *earnings* is quite different from the ranking with respect to basic rates.

SOME CONSEQUENCES OF THE ENGINEERS' WAGE STRUCTURE

This method of calculating engineers' earnings has several consequences:

1. It introduces additional dimensions into wage negotiations. The union may demand an across-the-board increase in the schedule of basic rates, but it need not do anything so simple as this. It may argue for a change in the gradations in the rate table—for example, a steeper progression of basic rates with weight-on-drivers. It may argue that the definition of the basic day should be altered, or that overtime should be calculated on a more liberal formula. It may demand more generous payment for "constructive allowances," or provision for allowances hitherto unknown. Pressure by the union along certain lines may be countered by an employer pressure along others. There is wide scope for trading of demands *within* the wage sector of the agreement as well as between the wage and nonwage sectors. It becomes difficult to judge the cost effect of proposals from the two sides without long experience of the industry. A simple demand for addition of 5 cents an hour to basic rates will involve an earnings increase of substantially more than that, because of the cumulative effect of mileage and overtime payments, but just how much more requires expert calculation. This is one reason why handling of railroad labor disputes has tended to become a specialized skill.

2. The engineers' wage structure carries a built-in "improvement factor" which ensures that earnings will rise considerably faster than basic daily rates. The trend toward larger and more powerful locomotives, toward three-unit and even four-unit diesels, has meant that more and more engineers fall toward the upper end of the weight-on-drivers gradation. This has brought an increase in average earnings of engineers in addition to that produced by general increases in the rate table. Further, the general increase in train speeds, as was noted above, has tended to raise earnings and to reduce hours of work.

3. Engineers in different classes of service have progressed at different rates over the past twenty years. Wage increases since 1937 have been

made in the form of flat-rate additions to the schedule of basic daily rates, which might appear to yield equal benefits to all. The average hourly earnings of passenger and through freight engineers, however, have risen considerably more than those of local freight and yard engineers on both an absolute and a percentage basis. The reasons for this are inherent in the structure of the wage schedule. A rate increase of 5 cents an hour (40 cents a day) means an hourly earnings' increase of more than double this amount for the passenger engineer, and rather less than double for the freight engineer, because of the way in which the basic day is defined and because of the operation of the mileage system. Moreover, the passenger and through freight engineers have benefited automatically from faster trains and heavier engines, as described under point 2 above. Local freight engineers have benefited less substantially and yard engineers scarcely at all.

4. The system produces a considerable dispersion of earnings among engineers at a given time. The situation in 1953 in shown in Table 2-2. Firemen's earnings are included in the table to indicate that what has been said about engineers applies equally to the firemen, whose earnings are computed in precisely the same way. The average hourly earnings of passenger engineers in 1953 were almost double those of yard engineers. The spread in weekly earnings is not so great, because the groups which have low hourly earnings (yard and local freight) have a much longer work week than the passenger and through freight engineers. Even as regards weekly earnings, however, the highest group averages about one-third more than the lowest. Since these are group averages, the range in the earnings opportunities of individual engineers is considerably greater.

There is doubtless good reason for some differentiation of earnings among the various categories of engineer. Operating high-speed passenger equipment involves greater responsibility and nervous tension than shunting an engine around the yard. Road service also involves irregular hours and much time away from home, while the yard engineer goes to work each day like a factory worker. Weekly hours are perhaps necessarily shorter in road service, which might justify some premium in hourly earnings to equalize weekly take-home pay. Adding these things together, it is still questionable whether differentials of the present size are warranted in terms of job content. Their development must be attributed in large measure to collective bargaining, which has established a hierarchical arrangement under which the junior engineer begins at a relatively low level and has an opportunity to progress substantially in earning power by the end of his working life.

5. The individual engineer's range of choice among assignments depends on his seniority standing on a particular roster of a particular

railroad, seniority rosters typically being maintained on the basis of a division, a subdivision, or even an individual yard. The top engineer on the roster has his choice of any available job, and can displace ("bump") any man junior to him. Many of the long-service men occupy passenger runs, which combine short hours, high hourly earnings, and traditional prestige as the preferred type of service. The men at the bottom of the seniority roster have few options. The bulk of them are found in yard service and on the "extra board" from which men are drawn for spot replacements. In the event of a drop in railroad activity, they are the first to be demoted to firemen.

Table 2-2. Average Hourly Earnings, Average Weekly Earnings, Average Weekly Hours of Engineers and Firemen by Class of Service (Class I railways, 1953)

OCCUPATION	AVERAGE HOURLY EARNINGS *	AVERAGE WEEKLY EARNINGS †	AVERAGE WEEKLY HOURS ‡
Firemen			
Yard	$1.9958	$ 97.667	49.05
Road through freight	2.7074	93.128	34.41
Road local and way freight	2.1557	129.044	59.97
Road passenger	3.7843	130.843	34.62
Engineers			
Yard	2.2476	117.156	52.16
Road through freight	3.0762	118.835	38.64
Road local and way freight	2.4695	156.431	63.48
Road passenger	4.0261	148.872	37.03

* Calculated as follows: Total compensation, divided by straight time actually worked, plus constructive allowances, plus overtime paid for hours.

† Calculated as follows: Total compensation, divided by average number of employees (mid-month), divided by number of weeks.

‡ Calculated as follows: Straight time actually worked, plus constructive allowances, plus overtime paid for hours, divided by average number of employees (mid-month), divided by number of weeks.

Source: Brotherhood of Locomotive Engineers, *Wage Differentials of Railroad Engineers* (submitted to the Board of Arbitration, 1953 wage movement), pp. 15, 17. The data are based on Interstate Commerce Commission Statement M-300 (Jan.–Dec. 1953).

From inspection of the weekly earnings data in Table 2-2, it might be expected that a worker's normal order of progression with increasing seniority would be from the extra board to yard service to through freight to local freight to passenger service. This is probably the commonest pattern in practice, but there are many deviations from it. The long hours on local freight runs yield a high weekly income despite lower hourly earnings, and men who value income highly in comparison with leisure will prefer local freight; but men whose preference system gives heavier weight to leisure may opt for through freight instead. One also finds some men in yard service at every level of the seniority roster. The combination of regular hours, unbroken home life, and relaxed pace of work is sufficiently attractive that some men prefer it even when they could earn substantially more in road service.

As an engineer progresses in seniority, he has increasing opportunity to choose among different combinations of income, leisure, and working conditions. The nature of railroad workers' preference systems, as revealed by the choices actually made, presents intriguing opportunities for research. The seniority lists of railroads over the country provide a wealth of almost unexplored data which could be used for this purpose.

OCCUPATIONAL DIFFERENTIALS

Railroad wage adjustments since 1937 have typically taken the form of a uniform cents-per-hour addition to the daily wage in each occupation. This has produced a sharp compression of occupational differentials on a percentage basis. Manual workers have risen relative to office workers; the nonops have risen relative to the operating crafts; and within the op and nonop groups, the lowest-paid occupations have gained steadily on the highest paid.

The record of general wage increases in the industry since 1937 is shown in Table 2-3. While one group has sometimes gotten slightly ahead of the others in a particular movement, the discrepancy has usually been corrected within a year or two. Taking the period as a whole, and correcting for the forty-hour-week adjustment in 1949–50, the total increase was virtually identical for all groups.

This lock-step character of wage movements stems partly from the nature of union and employer strategies in the industry, partly from government intervention in wage determination. Occupational differentials have not shrunk because anyone in particular wished this result, but rather because there is no mechanism for orderly and simultaneous review of the whole wage structure of the industry. We have already noted that the unions, particularly the operating brotherhoods, stand at arm's length from each other. Far from striving for a united policy, each keeps a sharp eye on the others and is resolved not to be outdone in wage advances. The employers are also reluctant to follow any policy save that of giving the same amount to each occupational group. If they give the trainmen 5 cents an hour in 1954 and the conductors 10 cents, this may fan the fires of union rivalry and lead to an all-out effort by the trainmen to recover the extra 5 cents in 1955. The employers feel that they can avoid being whipsawed only by adhering strictly to "pattern" settlements which yield equivalent benefits to each group.

Table 2-3. *General Increases in Railroad Basic Wage Rates, 1937–52 (does not include increases due to rules changes nor cost-of-living adjustments)*

EFFECTIVE DATE	AMOUNT OF INCREASE PER HOUR		NONOPERATING EMPLOYEES
	ENGINE AND TRAIN SERVICE EMPLOYEES		
	ROAD SERVICE	YARD SERVICE	
August 1, 1937	$ —	$ —	$.05
October 1, 1937	.05½	.05½	—
December 1, 1941	.09½ *	.09½ *	.10 †
February 1, 1943	—	—	.04 to .10
April 1, 1943	.04	.04	—
December 27, 1943	.05	.05	.05 to .01
January 1, 1946	.16	.16	.16
May 22, 1946	.02½	.02½	.02½
September 1, 1947	—	—	.15½
November 1, 1947	.15½	.15½	—
October 1, 1948	—	—	.07
October 16, 1948	.10	.10	—
September 1, 1949	—	—	.23½ ‡
October 1, 1950	.05	.23 §	—
January 1, 1951	.05	.02	—
February 1, 1951	—	—	.12½
March 1, 1951	.02½	.02	—
When 5-day week is established	—	.04	—
Total amount of hourly increases 1937–51	.80½	.99	1.01 to 1.03

* Agreement also provided for a retroactive increase in compensation of 7½% for the period from Sept. 1, 1941 to Nov. 30, 1941.

† Agreement also provided for a retroactive increase in compensation at the rate of 9¢ per hour for the period from Sept. 1, 1941 to Nov. 30, 1941.

‡ 5-day-week adjustment.

§ Includes 18¢ for 5-day-week adjustment.

Source: Jones, *Railroad Wages,* p. 16

The tendency toward pattern settlements is reinforced by the importance of emergency boards and informal White House mediation in railroad wage adjustments. More often than not, wage decisions are reached through these channels rather than through collective bargaining or private arbitration. Emergency boards have been reluctant to grant differing amounts to different unions involved in the same proceeding. Where two or more boards have been appointed in connection with the same wage movement, the first board to reach a decision has typically been taken as a precedent by the second, and the awards have come out substantially uniform.[18] One finds frequent statements in board decisions that any other course of action would be impracticable and unsettling to labor relations.

On several occasions, to be sure, emergency boards have pointed out that it may not be wise to keep on making uniform cents-per-hour adjustments indefinitely, that occupational differentials can become undesirably narrow, and that various inequities and anomalies exist in the railroad wage structure. It has been suggested that the way to rectify these inequities would be for all unions in the industry to come into a joint bargaining conference, and for unions and employers jointly to undertake an evaluation of the various jobs. It has also been suggested that the government might convoke an independent commission similar to that which studied the wage structure of the industry during World War I. There has not yet been any strong disposition to act on these suggestions. Meanwhile, emergency boards continue to award flat-rate increases and to postpone the differential problem to future years. This problem is not confined to the United States. In June 1955, Britain suffered a railroad strike of several weeks arising from a claim by the engineers and firemen that their differential over lower crafts had been unduly reduced. The issue of differentials has also been acted on recently by a conciliation board in Canada and by an arbitration board in Australia.

Continuation of flat-rate increases has produced a sharp compression of percentage differentials between higher and lower job classifications. Wage developments in the nonop sector are indicated in Table 2-4. The differential of higher groups over the lowest (maintenance of way) classification did widen slightly in cents-per-hour terms, whether as a result of more numerous individual reclassifications or for other reasons. In percentage terms, differentials fell drastically. Shop-crafts employees, who had earned 65 per cent more than the track laborers in 1937, earned only 22 per cent more in 1952. Within the shop-crafts

---

18. The awards have been uniform in total cash value, not necessarily in direct addition to the daily wage. Part of the increase may consist in rules changes which lead to higher earnings, part may consist of fringe benefits. Union and company technicians have become very skilled in converting such adjustments into their hourly rate equivalents; and it is these equivalents which are expected to total out to the same value for different crafts during a particular wage movement.

group, machinists earned 107 per cent more than shop laborers in 1937; by 1953 they earned only 29 per cent more.

Table 2-4. *Average Hourly Earnings for Selected Railroad Nonoperating Groups (1937 and 1952)*

| | AVERAGE HOURLY EARNINGS | | INCREASE 1937–52 | | DIFFERENTIAL OVER MAINTENANCE OF WAY | | | |
| | | | | | ¢ per hour | | % | |
	1937	1952	cents	%	1937	1952	1937	1952
Maintenance of way	45.2	163.6	118	262	—	—	—	—
Clerical and station employees	67.5	189.9	122	181	22	26	49	16
Floating equipment (marine)	70.5	202.5	132	187	25	39	56	24
Telegraphers	71.3	196.1	125	175	26	33	58	20
Shop-crafts employees	74.6	199.6	125	168	29	36	65	22
Signalmen	79.6	202.7	123	155	34	39	76	24

Source: Jones, *Railroad Wages,* pp. 274–89

The course of events within the operating group is shown in Table 2-5, which includes both hourly and weekly earnings. In the case of the nonops, it makes little difference which of these measures one uses. Because of the intricate system of compensation for the operating crafts, however, hourly and weekly earnings move rather differently over the course of time and it seems desirable to look at the situation from both points of view.[19] The hourly earnings figures show a marked reduction of percentage differentials since 1937, while the weekly earnings figures show a smaller but still perceptible reduction.

The various crafts have fared rather differently. The conductors, who have received only the flat-rate increase in each wage movement, have suffered the sharpest relative decline. Next come the engineers, but in their case the drop in percentage differentials resulting from flat-rate increases has been partially offset by the effect of faster trains and heavier engines. These factors have increased the engineers' cents-per-hour differential considerably, but not enough to maintain their percentage position. The firemen have about held their own relative to the

19. It should be noted also that there are several possible methods of calculating average hourly earnings, and that there is considerable disagreement within the industry over their relative merit. The use of Mr. Jones's data at this point, and the use of data from union sources in an earlier table, is not meant to prejudice this technical dispute. The broad outlines of the picture remain substantially the same whatever method of calculation is used.

trainmen, and have gained relative to the conductors and the engineers. They have gained vis-à-vis the conductors because, like the engineers, they benefit from mileage pay and from the weight-on-drivers gradation, neither of which apply to the conductors. The firemen have gained vis-à-vis the engineers because flat-rate increases have yielded them more on a percentage basis, while the effects of mileage pay and heavier engines cancel out by affecting both crafts more or less equally.

The engineer-fireman relationship is particularly interesting. Comparing engineers with firemen *in the same class of service,* one notes a marked reduction in the engineers' percentage differential. In 1937 the engineer typically earned about 30 per cent more than the fireman riding in the same cab. By 1952 this advantage had shrunk to little more than 10 per cent.

This development cannot be explained in terms of changes in the relative content of the two jobs. The gap in job content between the two crafts is probably wider today than it was a generation ago. The development of the automatic stoker and later of the diesel locomotive has taken the "back labor" out of the fireman's job. Indeed, the carriers have argued in bargaining negotiations that there is scarcely anything left for the fireman to do. He has become in effect an apprentice engineer who learns the trade by riding in the cab with the engineer, perhaps relieving him occasionally and being prepared to take over in an emergency. The reduced differential between the two jobs must be attributed to the nature of collective bargaining in the industry and to the propensity of arbitration boards and emergency boards for uniform cents-per-hour increases.

A curious result of the present wage structure is that a man usually takes a considerable loss of income when he is promoted from being a senior fireman to a junior engineer. This is readily apparent if one looks back at Table 2-2. A man at the top of the fireman's roster will usually be able to secure a passenger run, which in 1953 yielded an average of $3.78 per hour and $130.84 per week. When a man is promoted to engineer, he normally serves some time on the "extra board" and then secures a regular assignment in yard service. Here his hourly earnings in 1953 would have been 40 per cent below his level as a top fireman, and even by working 17½ hours more per week he would have earned $13.70 less per week than before. When he acquires enough seniority for a freight run, he may be able to exceed his previous weekly earnings as a fireman by going onto local freight, but only at the expense of very long weekly hours. If he chooses the shorter week on through freight, he will still be earning less as engineer than he previously earned as fireman. Not until he rises toward the top of the engineers' roster and

Table 2-5. Wage Relationships among Train-operating Employees, 1937 and 1952

	AVERAGE HOURLY EARNINGS						AVERAGE WEEKLY EARNINGS					
	CENTS PER HOUR		ABSOLUTE DIFFERENTIAL OVER TRAINMEN		PERCENTAGE DIFFERENTIAL (TRAINMEN = 100)		DOLLARS PER WEEK		ABSOLUTE DIFFERENTIAL OVER TRAINMEN		PERCENTAGE DIFFERENTIAL (TRAINMEN = 100)	
	1937	1952	1937	1952	1937	1952	1937	1952	1937	1952	1937	1952
Road Passenger Service												
Engineers	181¢	388¢	71¢	111¢	165	140	$66.24	$145.92	$17.39	$38.96	136	136
Firemen	147	362	38	86	134	131	49.33	128.68	.48	11.72	101	120
Conductors	149	308	39	32	136	111	60.23	128.98	11.38	22.02	123	121
Trainmen	110	277	—	—	100	100	48.85	106.96	—	—	100	100
Through Freight Service												
Engineers	141	294	46	61	149	126	57.14	117.88	22.63	28.19	166	131
Firemen	108	257	13	24	114	110	37.22	92.55	2.71	2.86	108	103
Conductors	119	256	24	24	125	110	52.13	111.76	17.62	22.07	151	125
Trainmen	95	233	—	—	100	100	34.51	89.69	—	—	100	100
Local Freight Service												
Engineers	123	242	40	46	147	123	71.14	155.12	26.03	38.10	158	133
Firemen	93	210	10	14	112	107	49.41	128.06	4.30	11.04	110	109
Conductors	105	218	21	22	126	111	62.34	139.45	17.23	22.43	138	119
Trainmen	84	196	—	—	100	100	45.11	117.02	—	—	100	100
Yard Service												
Engineers	101	221	13	15	114	107	49.39	115.98	12.18	25.72	133	128
Firemen	79	196	−9	−11	89	95	35.20	96.44	7.99	6.18	95	107
Conductors	96	219	8	12	109	106	48.35	112.41	11.14	22.15	130	125
Trainmen	89	207	—	—	100	100	37.21	90.26	—	—	100	100

Source: Jones, *Railroad Wages*, pp. 178–224

secures a passenger run will he clearly be better off in terms of income plus leisure than he was as a top fireman.

How is it possible under these circumstances to persuade a top fireman to accept promotion? The answer is that almost all collective agreements on the railroads provide for compulsory promotion. When an additional engineer is needed, the senior fireman must accept promotion under penalty of losing his seniority and in some cases under penalty of discharge. This guaranteed supply of engineers cushions the effect of narrower differentials on recruitment, though it clearly raises problems of morale and of equity.

INTERCOMPANY AND GEOGRAPHICAL DIFFERENCES

The effort to achieve national uniformity in railroad wage rates goes back some forty years. Wages of the nonops were substantially standardized under federal operation of the railroads during World War I. One of the first acts of the federal director-general was to create a Board of Railroad Wages and Working Conditions, consisting of three carrier and three union representatives, to investigate wages and other terms of employment and make recommendations concerning them. Pursuant to these studies the director-general issued a wage order which effected a nation-wide standardization of pay for all shop-crafts workers. Succeeding orders installed standard minimum rates for the clerical and terminal forces, for maintenance-of-way employees, telegraphers, and station agents.[20] Since these orders applied to minimum rates only, it is not certain that they yielded complete standardization of hourly earnings; but they must have produced a sharp reduction of intercompany differentials.

This approach to uniformity during the war years was reversed with the decline of union strength during the twenties. In 1922 the shop crafts called a nation-wide strike against wage reductions and were supported by large numbers of clerical and maintenance-of-way workers. The strike was lost, the unions were forced to sign separate agreements with individual railroads, and on some roads the outside unions disappeared and were replaced by company unions. Differing degrees of wage reduction were achieved on various railroads, depending on their individual circumstances. Substantial intercompany differentials developed and continued through the twenties and early thirties.

With the recovery of union strength in the mid-thirties, the nonop unions were once more able to achieve effective coverage of the industry and to win uniform cents-per-hour increases for their members on dif-

20. Jones, *Railroad Wages*, p. 53.

ferent railroads. These increases, to be sure, have in most cases simply been superimposed on the nonuniform rate structure inherited from the past. The nonop unions have apparently not felt strong enough to insist on complete rate uniformity throughout the country. The large size of the flat-rate increases since 1937, however, has greatly reduced inter-company differentials on a percentage basis.

In the case of the operating crafts, the substantial uniformity of basic rates achieved under federal operation from 1918–20 was never lost. Minor differentials between the eastern, southeastern, and western ter-ritories continued into the 1940's, but even these were eliminated as an outcome of the 1943 diesel case. Since that time one can say that there has been a standard wage schedule throughout the industry. This does not mean that the standard scale is invariably enforced. Railroads in serious financial difficulty have sometimes been allowed to remain outside a national wage case and to settle subsequently for a smaller increase or even for no increase. Substandard rates are presently in ef-fect on a number of railroads and there are also cases in which one or more of the unions have established rates above the standard level.

The railroads also vary considerably in their working rules and con-sequently in the amounts paid as "constructive allowances." The size of intercompany earnings differentials arising from this cause cannot be established from existing statistics, but they are probably of substantial importance.

CONCLUDING OBSERVATIONS

Wage determination on the railroads takes place in a quasi-political context. The initial negotiations are carried on between powerful union and management organizations. The issues typically pass from their hands to an emergency board or arbitration board, and in recent years have tended to be passed on to the White House for final adjudication. The reasons for this are inherent in the structure of the industry: the fact that it is a public utility, which means that its rates and finances are subject to detailed governmental control; the presence of strong unions which work through political as well as economic channels; and the es-sentiality of continuous operation, which ensures Presidential inter-vention when all else fails. These factors produce a pattern of wage determination which differs from that of any other industry.

The main consequences of this system of wage determination seem to have been as follows:

1. It has probably not had any marked effect on the general level of railroad wages. The average weekly earnings of railroad workers rose somewhat less than those of manufacturing workers from 1937 to 1954.

The average hourly earnings of railroad workers also rose less if one deducts, as one probably should do, the special adjustment involved in shifting the nonops to a forty-hour week in 1950 (a change long since accomplished in manufacturing). There is of course no reason why railroad wages'should move precisely parallel to wages in manufacturing or any other industry. The comparison suggests, however, that railroad unionism has not wrenched the industry's wage level seriously out of line with the remainder of the economy.

2. Intercompany differentials in basic rates have been almost eliminated for the operating crafts and much reduced percentage-wise for the nonops. The unions have pressed for national negotiations and uniform settlements with all carriers, despite differences in their ability to pay. The carriers have favored national uniformity when pressing for a wage cut, but called it into question when wage increases were in order. The decisive factors have been union strength plus governmental dispute procedures which favor centralized settlements.

3. Occupational differentials have been sharply compressed over the past twenty years and are now narrower than in most other industries. Machinists in the railroad repair shops earn only about 25 per cent more than common laborers, and locomotive engineers earn only about 10 per cent more than firemen in the same class of service. The narrowing of differentials has occurred through a long succession of flat-rate increases for everyone in the industry. These uniform increases are not a direct result of union policy. They result rather from the craft basis of union organization, the severity of interunion rivalry, the determination of employers not to be whipsawed, and the tendency for negotiations to be consolidated into a single settlement under government auspices. This produces a matrix out of which uniform cents-per-hour increases emerge as a natural consequence, and efforts of individual unions to break out of the mold have thus far been unsuccessful.

4. Collective bargaining has sanctioned a wide dispersion of earnings opportunities within each of the operating crafts. This dispersion arises not so much from differences in basic daily rates as from supplementary provisions such as the weight-on-drivers gradation, mileage pay, and constructive allowances. The result is earnings for the top engineers or firemen which can easily be double those of the lowest ones. The unions follow the traditional principle of the "standard rate" as between men doing identical work on different railroads; but there is a systematic destandardization of earnings, an enforced inequality, among men in different assignments on the same road.

5. Collective bargaining controls the access of individual workers to the preferred jobs through a strict seniority system, favorable to the older men who tend to be regarded as leaders of the craft. The ar-

rangement is deliberately hierarchical and noncompetitive. While the younger men can make only slow progress upward, they at least know where they stand at any time, they are secure within the limits of overall employment fluctuations, and they can look forward to reaching the top of the ladder toward the close of their working lives. This is clearly very different from the hypothetical labor market of pure competition.

CHAPTER 3 *Iron and Steel*

INFLUENCES ON WAGE DETERMINATION

THE iron and steel industry is the core of the manufacturing economy. Wage changes in steel have repercussions throughout heavy industry and even beyond. Less than 10 per cent unionized in 1933, basic steel production is almost completely unionized at the present time.

The industry has been extensively studied, and its economic characteristics will be familiar to most readers. It is commonly divided into "basic steel," which will be our primary concern in this chapter, and "steel fabricating." The basic steel sector produces pig iron, steel ingots, and primary steel products such as rails, plates, sheet, bars, wire, and tubes. There are between 225 and 250 basic steel companies, but the various divisions of the United States Steel Corporation alone produce about one-third of basic steel output.[1] The next four companies in order of ingot capacity (Bethlehem, Republic, Youngstown, and Inland) produce an additional one-third, making this one of the more highly concentrated of American industries. These are integrated concerns which carry on all operations from smelting of iron ore to production of finished steel products. Most of the remaining producers in the industry are either semi-integrated companies, buying their pig iron but producing ingots and finished products; or nonintegrated companies, which produce neither pig iron nor steel ingots, but buy their steel and convert it into finished steel products. These companies are typically much smaller than the integrated concerns.

Steel fabricating or "nonbasic steel" includes several hundred miscellaneous metalworking concerns. This is not an industry, but a bundle of industries catering to distinct product markets, and having in common only the use of some primary steel product as a raw material. The companies in this group are heterogeneous in terms of size, profitability, wage level, type of product, and nature of product market competition. They are on the average considerably smaller than the basic steel units. Most of the basic steel companies, of course, are major fabricators as well.

The modern phase of unionism in the industry opens with the formation of the Steel Workers Organizing Committee in 1936 (later renamed the United Steelworkers of America) and negotiation of the first con-

1. George Seltzer, "Pattern Bargaining and the United Steelworkers," *Journal of Political Economy*, 59 (August 1951), 320.

tract with U. S. Steel in 1937.[2] The Little Steel companies held out for several years longer, and not until 1941 were collective bargaining relations established with most of the principal steel producers. The union grew steadily stronger during the war years and by 1945 was firmly established throughout the industry. Basic steel is now almost completely organized. The United Steelworkers estimated early in 1955 that it had under contract plants with 92.57 per cent of the steel ingot capacity of the country,[3] the remaining capacity being almost all organized by other international unions or by "independents." In steel fabricating the percentage of capacity which is unorganized or organized by other unions is considerably higher. About half of the membership of the United Steelworkers, however, is found in the fabricating end of the industry.

Wage policy is more highly centralized on both the union and management sides than in the other industries studied here. Centralization of control in the United Steelworkers is due partly to the fact that the union was organized from the top down. The original CIO unions, particularly the United Mine Workers, contributed organizers as well as money to the SWOC. The first national and district officials were appointed, not elected, and the rank-and-file steelworkers who had little experience of unionism naturally relied heavily on them for leadership. While elective procedures were installed at an early stage, and an indigenous steelworkers' leadership has gradually emerged, the imprint of the early days remains strong.

The focus of wage policy is the president and other national officers of the union. These men constantly have a finger held up to the wind to ascertain the drift of rank-and-file sentiment. They listen to reports brought in by district directors and by the organizers who are in constant circulation among the local unions. They observe the movement of wages in related industries and the tactics of the unions in those industries. They make short-term forecasts of economic conditions and particularly of steel demand. On the basis of such information, the national officers and their trusted confidential advisors construct "union policy" for the year. This policy is then submitted to the International Executive Board, which includes the thirty district directors as well as the national officers. In practice, the program is usually ratified as submitted by the president, though if there is serious opposition to certain items it may have to be modified and resubmitted.

The program is next submitted for discussion and approval to a larger Wage Policy Committee, consisting of representatives of the

2. See Frederick H. Harbison, "Steel," in Harry A. Millis, ed., *How Collective Bargaining Works* (New York, Twentieth Century Fund, 1942), pp. 508–70.

3. United Steelworkers of America, Research Department Memorandum, February 28, 1955.

various districts of the union,[4] but approval at this level is virtually certain. The Wage Policy Committee serves mainly as a sounding board for publicity concerning the union's demands and as a channel of communication to the membership, rather than as a decision-making body. It has, however, a potential veto power. Its members are consulted, formally and informally, at various stages of negotiations with the companies, and their opinions are given careful weight in the shaping of a final settlement.

On the employer side, wage policy frequently consists in following the lead of U. S. Steel, although there is no formal agreement on this, and from time to time other major companies take the lead. This was customary procedure even before the union came on the scene. On many occasions in preunion days a general wage increase or decrease announced by U. S. Steel was the signal for similar action by other major producers. Collective bargaining has, however, extended the area over which uniformity of action occurs. For example, a company survey in 1949 shows that uniform timing of wage changes became increasingly important following unionization. Ninety-six per cent of the wage adjustments effected in 1948 occurred within a single month, as compared with about 56 per cent in the early thirties.[5]

Wage leadership, however, is a more complicated relationship than appears at first glance. It is informal and cannot be arbitrary if it is to continue. The U. S. Steel Corporation, for instance, must consider the views and interests of other steel companies. Its course of action is effective and is followed only insofar as it reflects the general situation and outlook of the industry, since repeated disregard of this principle would cause any leader to be deserted in the long run. Furthermore the major steel companies are in close contact with each other both before and during wage negotiations through the Industrial Relations Committee of the American Iron and Steel Institute,[6] through special policy meetings, and through informal channels.

4. The members of the Wage Policy Committee from a particular district are elected by the delegates to the Union's District Conference, who in turn are elected by the members of the local lodges. Thus the committee operates, in a sense, at two removes from the membership. Because of the small number of members from each district, it is impossible to represent the smaller companies adequately, and even many locals in the large basic steel plants are without direct representation. The committee meets "whenever called into service" by the national officers, and its duties are confined to wage agreement problems exclusively. In practice it meets both before negotiations begin, to consider the program, and during or after the negotiations with major producers, to ratify the settlement terms proposed by the national officers.

5. John A. Stephens, "Statement Regarding the Emergence of Patterns in the Steel Industry, before the Steel Board (August 30, 1949)," Table 2.

6. This committee consists of top executives of all major companies and a selection from among the smaller ones. It meets once a month to discuss labor problems

Negotiations for a general wage change typically begin with discussions between the United Steelworkers and U. S. Steel. While these discussions are proceeding, the negotiating groups in other companies tend to mark time. Each company realizes that if it arrived at a settlement below that with U. S. Steel this would do it no good in the end, since the union would insist on the discrepancy being made up the following year. A more generous agreement than that in U. S. Steel, on the other hand, would be unpopular among the managements of other companies as an encouragement to whipsawing by the union. The safest course is to stall along until the pattern has been set. Once the logjam has been broken by a settlement in U. S. Steel, negotiations proceed in the smaller basic steel companies. Consistency of policy is secured on the union side through participation of district directors and other national representatives in these negotiations, and through a requirement that local contracts must have national approval to become effective.

While leadership by U. S. Steel is the general rule, it is not invariable. In 1942, for example, the wage pattern was established by a National War Labor Board award applicable to Bethlehem, Republic, Youngstown, and Inland. In 1949, when pensions and insurance were the central issues in negotiations, a settlement was reached first with Bethlehem. It would also be incorrect to suggest that there are no settlements with smaller companies until U. S. Steel has signed. Particularly in years when strikes have occurred, such as 1946, 1949, and 1952, there have been many settlements with smaller basic steel companies before the U. S. Steel settlement.

THE DEVELOPMENT OF A STANDARD WAGE SCALE IN BASIC STEEL

One of the clearest consequences of collective bargaining has been the development, for the first time, of a standard wage schedule throughout a large part of the basic steel industry. This required a great deal of work and negotiation and turned out to have far-reaching consequences.

The word "chaotic" is scarcely too strong for steel wages in pre-union days. An official of one company described the situation in his plant as follows:

There was no central department or authority responsible for fixing rates of pay. Such rates were fixed largely by supervisors of depart-

---

of common interest and conducts surveys of company practices within the industry. The committee has no formal power even to recommend uniformity of action on labor matters. Any votes taken are simply "public opinion polls." It provides a channel of communication and a discussion forum, however, which normally leads to consensus and a common course of action.

ments without relation to the rates in effect in other departments. There was no centralized control over the fixing of work standards which formed the basis of the employee's pay. Rates of pay were fixed largely on the basis of the opinion of individual foremen. . . . In consequence of the foregoing, many inequities in rates of pay developed and much inefficiency existed in the use of both labor and machines, causing gross wage inequalities within the plant.[7]

Along with these wage discrepancies *within* each plant, there were large discrepancies *among* plants in the industry, even when these were located in the same labor market area. The average wage level of some plants was substantially above that of others. Moreover, the ranking of jobs in different plants varied considerably. A job which yielded relatively high earnings in one plant might yield relatively low earnings in another. This was partly because close to half of all steelworkers are paid on an incentive basis, and also because of wide interplant variation in job content and production methods. A variety of methods of organizing production, a variety of systems of payment, frequent technological changes in work assignments—all contributed to wide dispersion of earnings among workers doing roughly the same kind of work in different plants.

The extent of interplant wage dispersion is well documented by a survey of twenty-seven plants of the larger basic steel companies carried out by the union's Production Engineering and Rate Analysis Department in 1945.[8] Average hourly earnings of first helpers in open-hearth departments varied from a low of $1.62 in one plant to a high of $2.51 in another. Corresponding figures for other standard production occupations were as follows: third helper, open hearth, 92¢ to $1.49; charging-floor craneman, open hearth, 89¢ to $1.55; stocker, open hearth, 81¢ to $1.18; soaking-pit craneman, rolling mill, $1.14 to $2.04; soaking-pit heater, rolling mill, $1.24 to $2.80; roller, plate mill, $2.03 to $3.85; roller, merchant mill, $2.31 to $5.05. Part of this variation can be explained by differences in job content and in the administration of incentive wage systems; but even maintenance machinist, first class, which is generally an hourly rated and relatively standardized occupation, showed a range of 97¢ to $1.49 per hour.

At the first wage and policy convention of the Steel Workers Organizing Committee in December 1937, resolutions were submitted calling for a uniform wage scale in the basic steel industry, and this has been

7. Quotations in this and the following sections are from interviews with union and management officials in the industry, conducted principally by Jane Metzger Schilling in 1946.

8. The results of this survey have not been published, but we were permitted to examine the raw data in the union files.

one of the professed objectives of union policy from the beginning. In practice, however, swoc leaders showed little concern about wage uniformity during the early organizing period. They were more concerned with pushing wages up for every individual and group in order to persuade workers to join the union. Inequities—i.e. any rates which workers complained about—were exploited as a weapon of organization rather than with a view to actually establishing equal pay for equal work. The depressed condition of the industry in the late thirties also made it unfeasible to press for substantial wage adjustments of any sort.

By the early forties, however, the union's attitude had begun to change. There seem to have been several reasons for this. First, the union was getting fed up with the heavy load of inequity grievances which had to be handled for political reasons regardless of their actual merit. The most obvious cases of inequity, which could be adjusted easily, had been brought up and settled. Local union officials and staff representatives were forced to spend an increasing amount of time on grievances for which there were no agreed principles of settlement. Under existing contract provisions, if no agreement could be reached, no more could be done.

Second, the union was stronger and better able to survive the antagonism which individual rate decreases (even relative ones) might arouse. The War Labor Board's directive permitting maintenance of membership and its check-off provisions in basic steel considerably strengthened the hands of union leaders. Third, the economic and political situation was favorable to an allowance for inequity adjustment sufficiently generous so that no rates would have to be lowered. Fourth, union officials had learned by the early forties to use job-evaluation systems to their own advantage. Though by no means sold on job evaluation, they realized the need for some systematic way of handling inequity grievances.

The steel companies by the early forties were also heartily tired of the flood of wage grievances and were ready to consider some kind of wage-rationalization program. A number of companies attempted unilaterally to introduce systems of job evaluation, and a few of them succeeded. There were two basic differences, however, between their outlook and that of the union. First, they hoped that the rationalization might be costless, with rate reductions just equaling rate increases in money value. The union naturally wanted all increases and no reductions. Second, while the companies favored systematization of wage structures within each plant, they objected to any effort to compare or equalize rates among plants. The union hoped to standardize the wage structures of all plants at a common level, and to secure equal pay for equal work throughout the industry. The history of union-management negotiations over a standard wage scale from 1942 to 1947 is the story of how these issues were resolved.

Discussions of the problem between the union and Carnegie-Illinois during 1942 and 1943 bogged down on these two points and on the method to be used to evaluate one job relative to another, and had to be abandoned. During the 1943 round of wage negotiations the union, in addition to demanding a general wage increase, demanded "equal pay for equal work," elimination of interplant and geographical wage differences, and simplified job classifications. No agreement being reached in direct negotiation, the issues were certified to the National War Labor Board. The board held hearings over a period of months, and on November 25, 1944 issued a directive order applying to eighty-six basic steel companies. It was this order which broke the impasse and led eventually to the establishment of both job classification and a standard wage schedule.

The board denied the union's demand for a general wage increase, but certain fringe benefits were liberalized, and the parties were permitted to use up to 5 cents per hour per employee for elimination of intra-plant wage inequities. It was provided that any rate reductions on out-of-line jobs were not to apply to the present incumbents of those jobs but only to new appointees in the future. The problem of developing a simplified job classification and a standard rate structure within each plant was referred back for further union-management negotiation, within the general framework of the directive order and under the supervision of a special tripartite Steel Wage Commission responsible to the board.

Without granting the union's demand for industry-wide uniformity of rates, the directive order provided for "taking into account" wage rates in comparable plants: "As an aid in determining the correct rate relationship between the jobs in a particular plant, the company and the union may take into account the wage-rate relationships existing in comparable plants in the industry. The contention [of the companies] that wage-rate relationships in other plants in the industry have no significance for this purpose is rejected."

Negotiations were undertaken first with the United States Steel Corporation, since this was the union's preference and since the industry's custom was to wait and see what U. S. Steel would do. It is not feasible to describe in detail the discussions which went on throughout 1945 and 1946, but a brief review of the main events may be helpful. As early as 1943 a Cooperative Wage Study had been established by twelve major steel companies to survey the existing wage situation and propose alterations. By the time of the 1944 NWLB case, complete proposals had been drawn up for determining inequities in steel plants. Following the

NWLB directive, the United Steelworkers set up an inequities negotiating committee to match a corresponding committee of U. S. Steel. The joint union-management committee proceeded to draw up detailed descriptions of over one thousand bench work jobs, using the companies' proposals as a starting point. The system of job evaluation and classification developed became known later as the CWS (Cooperative Wage Study) manual. The CWS manual differed from the companies' original proposals mainly in that it gave considerably less weight to skill and considerably greater weight to responsibility, thereby meeting previous union objections on this score. In further joint committee meetings and after much work, individual jobs were then rated and classified into the various labor grades. Originally thirty labor grades were set up and later two more grades were added. The wage schedule thus runs from grade 1 to grade 32.

A preliminary agreement reached in May 1946 provided that the rate scale for each plant should start at the existing plant minimum, which would become the rate for labor grade 1. The agreement further provided for systematic increments in rate for successively higher job classes, though the amount of such increments was not fixed. (The final agreement in January 1947 provided for a uniform increment between job classes, thereby establishing a straight-line progression from the minimum rate to the highest evaluated rate. This system has continued ever since, though the slope of the line has varied slightly.)

It is important to realize just what the new wage schedule did and did not accomplish. While it established a systematic basis for rating and compensating jobs *within* each plant, it did not alter wage differentials *between* plants. On the contrary, it left them unaffected in the first instance. The agreement provided only that the new scale should start at the former plant common-labor rate, whatever that happened to be, and should progress in uniform increments above this minimum. This meant that, if there was a 6-cent common-labor rate differential between two plants, all jobs in both plants which fell in the same labor grade would show the same 6-cent differential. The new schedule brought to light and systematized interplant differentials, but it did not by itself reduce them.

The question of establishing a uniform minimum rate, and thereby a uniform wage schedule, for all forty plants of the U. S. Steel Corporation was a central issue in the inequities negotiations. The management negotiators early agreed to establish a single minimum rate for each of the corporation's twelve geographical districts. The union continued, however, to press for national uniformity. Later, when full information was at hand, management negotiators discovered that there were no consistent geographical variations in plant minima outside the South.

The agreement finally reached in January 1947 provided a uniform minimum rate for every plant of the corporation except those in Duluth and Birmingham. The Duluth plant was subsequently brought up to the standard level in April 1947, and the Birmingham differential was reduced by 3 cents. By April 1947, then, a standard wage scale had been installed in all but one of the U. S. Steel plants, and the resulting manual of job classifications had been made available to the rest of the industry.[9]

While U. S. Steel bore the brunt of negotiations with the union over the inequities program, the views of other companies were by no means neglected. As early as 1943, twelve of the leading steel companies had created a committee for cooperative study of the wage problem. After the War Labor Board directive of 1944, the other basic steel companies were invited to join the discussions. In the end, fifty-one companies, employing some 87 per cent of basic steel workers, participated in the joint study. The committee employed a firm of engineering consultants, supplemented by engineers from the companies' own staffs. The committee made a careful examination of wage structures in the participating companies and went on to develop plans for a new job classification system. When U. S. Steel eventually proposed a classification plan to the union, it was the plan which the joint study had developed. Throughout these proceedings each company reserved its right of individual settlement with the union. As a practical matter, however, it was clear that whatever U. S. Steel did would become a pattern for the industry.

The conclusion of agreements with other major companies was held back until the results of the U. S. Steel negotiations were apparent. The final agreement in U. S. Steel, however, was the signal for rapid extension of the new standard scale throughout the basic steel industry. Within a year, about four-fifths of the industry's employees were covered by the CWS wage schedule. It should be reemphasized that this did not necessarily mean the elimination of interplant differentials, since the new schedule was simply hooked onto the existing common-labor rate in each plant. The process of bringing plant minimum rates to a common level has been a long one, and indeed is still continuing. This process is considered in the next section.

INTERPLANT AND GEOGRAPHICAL DIFFERENTIALS

BASIC STEEL

In discussing the intraindustry wage structure it is necessary to distinguish between basic steel and steel fabricating. It is also necessary to

9. See Robert Tilove, "The Wage Rationalization Program in United States Steel," *Monthly Labor Review, 64* (June 1947), 967–82.

distinguish between the *rate of change* of wages and the *wage level* of various companies at a given time. The uniform or "patterned" character of steel wage movements applies mainly to basic steel and, until recently, was a matter of uniform rates of change rather than of uniform wage levels.

The tradition of uniform wage movements in basic steel is a very old one. As early as 1916, all the leading steel companies in the Pittsburgh, Youngstown, and Wheeling districts were reported to be making simultaneous wage increases of 10 per cent.[10] The War Labor Board decision in the 1944 steel case emphasized this tradition in the following terms: "The evidence presented in both this case and in the Little Steel case has left no doubt in the minds of the Board that a policy of industry-wide uniformity is so well established that it has been the practice of the companies in the past to make wage adjustments retroactive to a common date."[11]

Although uniformity of wage changes has increased with the development of collective bargaining, it existed long before the appearance of the present union. It is inherent in the economic structure of the industry: the concentration of production in a few major companies; the tradition of price leadership by U. S. Steel; and integration of production with the consequent high ratio of wage costs to total costs, which necessarily causes wage changes and price changes to be considered together. The United Steelworkers, however, with its demand for uniformity as a matter of principle, has doubtless strengthened the forces working in this direction and has also extended the area of uniformity beyond its previous boundaries.

There is not complete uniformity of wage movements within basic steel even at the present time. The hard core of uniformity is found in the large, fully integrated companies which have the great bulk of steel-producing capacity.[12] The semi-integrated and nonintegrated companies tend to follow along, but in a somewhat straggling fashion. Seltzer has calculated that in the first three postwar rounds of wage increases (1946, 1947, 1948), at least 98 per cent of the workers in integrated steel firms got the same wage increase as workers in U. S. Steel. In non-

10. George Seltzer, "Pattern Bargaining and the United Steelworkers," p. 322.
11. Robert Tilove, *Collective Bargaining in the Steel Industry* (Philadelphia, University of Pennsylvania Press, 1948), p. 7.
12. Integrated companies conduct the full range of operations from ore mining through pig iron production, steel ingots, and finished steel products (primary shapes). Semi-integrated firms buy their pig iron but produce steel ingots and finished products. Nonintegrated firms produce finished steel products but no ingots. Seltzer calculates that as of 1948, integrated firms had 93% of the industry's pig iron capacity, 90% of the ingot capacity, and 88% of the capacity for hot rolled products—thus clearly being the decisive force in the industry. Seltzer, "Pattern Bargaining and the United Steelworkers," p. 320.

integrated firms, on the other hand, the proportion of workers receiving the standard increase was 94 per cent in 1946, 82 per cent in 1947, and 70 per cent in 1948. In 1949, when there was no general wage increase but fringe benefits were liberalized, almost all the integrated firms gave the same amount as U. S. Steel and Bethlehem (the "leader" in the pension settlement), but only 85 per cent of the semi-integrated firms and 55 per cent of the nonintegrated firms followed the pattern.[13]

The degree of uniformity in wage changes thus appears to diminish with a lower degree of integration, which means also smaller scale of plant and greater dispersion of geographical location. There is also some indication that the consistency of "wage following" has declined in recent years, as the enforced uniformity of the war years has receded into the past.

Uniformity of *wage changes* says nothing about the relative wage *levels* of different companies in an industry. Uniform changes may simply be added on to different levels of wages inherited from the past. This was the situation in the basic steel industry until the mid-forties. Wage levels differed not merely among companies but among plants in the same company, reflecting differences in community wage levels, in job content and titles and methods of wage payment, in administration of incentive rates, and a multitude of other factors. The magnitude of these differences was indicated in the previous section.

The attempt to equalize wage levels as well as rates of change was spearheaded by the United Steelworkers, and was pursued via the "inequities removal" program of 1944–47. It might have been possible to rationalize intraplant wage structures and install a uniform job classification system while leaving interplant differentials substantially unchanged. This would have been possible, at least, at a logical or technical level, but perhaps not in human and political terms. A uniform system of job titles and job classification brings to the surface and highlights interplant differences which until then have been hidden by differences in terminology and methods of wage administration. This is bound to set up a clamor among union members for interplant equalization. Rationalization of intraplant wage structures was perhaps bound in the end to produce interplant equalization as well. At any event, the union worked to combine the two objectives and succeeded eventually in overcoming employer resistance.

After the U. S. Steel agreement of 1947, companies employing about 80 per cent of all basic steel workers adopted the cws manual and system of labor grades, and the larger companies established plant minimum rates either identical with or very close to the U. S. Steel level. A considerable number of smaller companies were allowed to settle for less than the standard scale, while a few small and medium-sized com-

13. *Ibid.,* p. 321.

panies continued to pay rates above the scale. A study made by the union in late 1948 showed that, in the northern and western states, plants employing some 73 per cent of basic steel workers had common-labor rates identical with the cws rate of $1.23 per hour.[14] Plants employing 16 per cent of all employees had common-labor rates below this level, though rarely more than 5 cents an hour below. Plants employing some 11 per cent of employees had common-labor rates above the cws scale, though rarely more than 5 cents above. The plants paying above the scale were mainly plants located in high-wage communities such as Detroit, Toledo, Portland, and Seattle; or plants producing some highly profitable specialty—expensive alloys, electro-metallurgical products, seamless tubing.[15]

Some of the smaller companies, in addition to paying lower common-labor rates, also continued to graduate their wage schedules less steeply than the cws scale, so that their skilled workers remained even farther below the standard level. Since 1947 the union has made persistent efforts to bring substandard companies up to the cws scale. An examination of individual company wage structures year by year indicates that these efforts have met with considerable success. There are cases where little has been accomplished and even some cases in which a company has fallen still farther behind the cws scale. In most cases, however, the gap has been reduced, and a good many companies have been brought fully up to the standard level. A particularly large measure of success from the union's point of view was achieved in 1952, a prosperous year with substantial wage increases. The union estimates that the 1952 wage movement alone closed approximately half the gap between the substandard companies and the remainder of the industry.[16] Deviations below the standard scale were reduced in twenty-three companies, and in seventeen companies differentials in the production and maintenance units were eliminated entirely. Additional, though more limited, progress was made in 1953, when differentials were completely eliminated in four companies and reduced in fifteen. By the end of 1953 the gap had been reduced for most companies to only a few cents per hour; and for some of these elimination of the differential is clearly only a matter of time.

Some of the smaller, nonintegrated producers may never be brought

14. This is the rate for job class 2, which includes the lower grades of common labor under the cws system. Job class 1 is the plant minimum rate.

15. Statement filed with the Secretary of Labor by the United Steelworkers of America on February 23, 1949, in connection with proceedings under the Walsh-Healey Act (mimeographed), Appendix List C.

16. "A survey of the minimum rate and increment differentials in the Steelworker-organized plants in the basic steel, pig iron, and iron ore industries, pre-1952 and current." United Steelworkers of America, Research Department, June 11, 1953 (mimeographed).

fully up to the cws scale. The firms in question have relatively high costs due to obsolete equipment, poor marketing arrangements, poor management, or unfavorable location, and are no threat to the big companies. The union realizes that somewhat lower wage scales are necessary to keep them going. The attitude of local union officials is generally that it is up to the workers to decide whether they want to "subsidize" the firms in order to maintain their jobs, and the workers will usually vote to keep the plant going, particularly where it is located in a small town with few alternative sources of employment.

The national office of the Steelworkers is more reluctant to permit deviations, and opposes them unless the company can convince them that it is unable to meet the standard scale. The union is firmly committed in principle to elimination of all differentials. Within the framework of this position, however, it is able to tolerate the retention of a few differentials which in total are not significant to the industry. Where enforcement of the standard scale would involve the closing of a plant and loss of jobs for several hundred workers, the union tends to be more job conscious than wage conscious.

An important aspect of wage equalization among the major steel companies has been the elimination of the substantial geographical differences which existed in preunion days. In April 1938 the average hourly earnings of skilled workers in basic steel plants in the Pittsburgh-Youngstown area were 17 per cent above the average for the South. Semiskilled earnings were 31 per cent and unskilled earnings 47 per cent above the southern level. The general average for all employees showed Pittsburgh 30 per cent above the South. There were also substantial, though smaller, differentials outside the South. Mills along the Atlantic Coast averaged almost 10 per cent below the Pittsburgh level, while mills in the Pacific Coast states were almost 10 per cent above Pittsburgh.[17]

The union from the beginning regarded these differentials as undesirable, and set to work to eliminate them. At the time of the 1947 accord the union succeeded in eliminating base-rate differences in U. S. Steel plants outside the South, and the differential in favor of Birmingham was cut from 17½¢ to 14½¢. From this point on progress was quite rapid. The differential was reduced to 10¢ [18] in 1950, to 5¢ in 1952, and in 1953 an agreement was reached to eliminate it entirely as of July 1, 1954. Thus a differential in minimum rates which had existed for many decades

17. "Earnings and Hours in the Iron and Steel Industry, April, 1938, Part I," *Monthly Labor Review, 51* (August 1940), 431.

18. "Major contract economic gains, U. S. Steel Corporation, basic contracts 1937–1952," United Steelworkers of America, Research Department Memorandum (October 13, 1952), p. 2.

was completely eliminated within a period of seven years. Moreover, since the standard wage schedule graduates upward from the minimum rate in the same way in most plants, equalization of plant minimum rates means uniformity of wage schedules (though not necessarily of average plant-wide earnings, because of differences in incentive arrangements and skill composition in each plant).

The marked change since preunion days becomes apparent when one compares the 1951 BLS survey of steel wage rates with the 1938 survey. In 1951 the average hourly earnings of basic steel workers were virtually identical throughout the North and West. The average for the Middle Atlantic states was $1.78 per hour, for the Great Lakes states $1.81 per hour, and for the western states, $1.80 per hour. The South remained slightly below other regions at $1.68 per hour, because of the 10-cent Birmingham differential which was still in effect at that time.[19] A survey at the present time, however, would show the South almost equal with other regions.

The rapid wiping out of regional differences in wages can be traced to a number of factors: virtually complete union organization in all regions; the size of steel-producing units, which means that companies cannot readily shift their operations to take advantage of a wage differential; the fact that in a large part of the country no consistent geographical differentials existed previously; a long period of prosperity and price inflation which permitted wage increases sufficiently large that part of the increases could safely be allocated to removing regional differentials; the fact that the southern basic steel units are mostly subsidiaries of northern companies; and the tradition of wage leadership, which meant that when U. S. Steel agreed to reduce differentials there was strong pressure on other companies to do likewise. There are other cases in which a union, faced with less favorable circumstances, has been able to do little about regional wage differences. A leading case of this sort is the cotton textile industry, which will be considered in the next chapter.

STEEL FABRICATING

The companies generally lumped together as "steel fabricators" employ about half of all steelworkers. They fall into some twenty-five major product groups, and the number of individual products runs to many thousands. Almost every steel fabricator, then, has a somewhat different product market and a different group of competitors. In few, if any, cases are all firms in the same product group organized by the

19. U. S. Department of Labor, Bureau of Labor Statistics (BLS), *Wage Structure, Basic Iron and Steel, January 1951*, Series 2, No. 81, p. 8.

Steelworkers. Usually some plants are affiliated with other AFL or CIO unions, and some remain unorganized. For this reason many steel fabricators have protested strongly against being tied to the wage level established by the Steelworkers in basic steel. They point out that to follow the basic steel pattern may put them seriously out of line with their own industry and endanger their competitive position.

Union policy on this matter has become more flexible with increasing experience. In 1946 the union made the same demands on all the companies with which it had contracts and struck most of them when negotiations in basic steel bogged down. After a four-week strike, U. S. Steel granted an 18½-cent increase. The union then instructed its district directors to obtain the U. S. Steel terms from all other companies, and failing this to leave them on strike. This policy continued for another six weeks. Only after ten weeks of strike, as it became increasingly clear that many plants could not or would not grant the basic steel terms, did the union's policy committee vote that smaller settlements could be made if the district director certified that in his judgment the company could afford no more. In some plants the strike lasted for four or five months before agreement was reached. The reaction of union members in some of the fabricating plants was quite bitter. They felt that the national office had forced them to strike against their own judgment, that their employers actually could not afford the U. S. Steel terms, and that the strike had only lost them wages and endangered their jobs.

Since this experience the union has followed a policy of keeping the fabricating plants at work until the basic steel settlement has been reached. The district directors then set to work on the fabricators, using the basic steel settlement as a rough and flexible guide. Agreement may be reached with a fabricator to settle for less than the basic steel increase, provided he can make a convincing demonstration of inability to pay. The steel pattern sets a ceiling, but not a floor, for union demands.

Seltzer has made a detailed examination of District 31 of the United Steelworkers, which includes the metropolitan areas of Chicago, Gary, and South Bend. This district in 1950 included one-ninth of the union's membership, distributed about equally between basic steel and fabricating, and there were some 130 fabricating companies under union contract.[20] As regards rate of wage increase, the fabricators have shown a low degree of conformity to the terms of the U. S. Steel agreement, and the degree of conformity diminished steadily from 1946 to 1950. Some 75 per cent of the fabricators followed U. S. Steel in 1946, but only 40 per cent in 1947. In 1948 about 35 per cent of the fabricators signed up *before* agreement was reached with U. S. Steel, and the contracts

20. Seltzer, "Pattern Bargaining and the United Steelworkers," pp. 327–9.

signed after the U. S. Steel agreement showed considerable deviation from its terms. In 1949–50, when the large basic steel companies conceded substantial fringe benefits, about 60 per cent of the fabricators in District 31 made no change in their contracts; and of those which were revised only about half resembled the key bargain at all closely.

There is marked variation also in the absolute wage levels of the various companies, as indicated by plant minimum rates. In 1950 only 20 per cent of the fabricators were paying the same minimum as U. S. Steel, while 65 per cent had lower minimum rates. Seltzer notes that fabricators located closest to the large basic steel plants show the strongest tendency to follow their lead both in size of wage increases and in absolute wage level. Among steel fabricators located in East Chicago, Hammond, Whiting, and Indiana Harbor, about half were paying the U. S. Steel minimum in mid-1950. On the West Side of Chicago, which is more remote from the basic steel plants, only 5 per cent of the fabricators were paying the U. S. Steel rate. This suggests that geographical proximity remains an important influence even under collective bargaining.

Additional information on interplant wage dispersion is available from surveys of the Bureau of Labor Statistics. A study made in May 1950 of 583 structural steel-fabricating plants employing 52,000 workers, found common-labor entrance rates ranging from less than 75¢ an hour to $1.30 per hour. There was some clustering in the range $1.00 to $1.10, about one-third of the reporting plants having base rates within this range. The remaining plants, however, were well distributed over the entire range, with 10 per cent of them paying 75¢ per hour or less.[21] Another study of wage structure in steel foundries in December 1951 revealed minimum entrance rates ranging from 75¢ to $1.60 per hour, with a rather marked clustering between $1.25 and $1.35. The hourly earnings of men in selected semiskilled and skilled occupations also varied over a wide range.[22]

Interplant wage dispersion, in short, remains substantially greater than in basic steel. The commonest situation is one in which a fabricating plant, while paying high wages relative to its local labor market, is paying less than the basic steel level. Regional wage differentials remain substantial, in contrast to the situation in basic steel. The explanation is to be found in the wide variety of product markets in which steel fabricators operate, in the highly competitive character of some of these markets, and in the fact that many fabricating plants remain unorganized or are organized by unions from industries whose wage level is lower than basic steel. The United Steelworkers is frequently unable

21. BLS, mimeographed release, LS 51–3409.
22. BLS, *Wage Structure Steel Foundries, December 1951*, Series 2, No. 85.

to raise a plant all the way to the basic steel level without putting it in an untenable competitive position. Where the employer can make a case that enforcement of the cws scale would produce a plant shutdown, the union will usually make wage concessions.

OCCUPATIONAL DIFFERENTIALS

The steel industry has always shown a large differential between the earnings of the top occupations—blowers in the blast furnaces, melters and pourers in steel works, heaters and rollers in rolling mills—and the earnings of low-skilled men in the same department. The top jobs are highly skilled, involving major responsibility for both volume of output and quality of the product, and requiring some knowledge of metallurgy as well as of mechanical processes. The skilled men direct the work of the entire crew employed on the blast furnace, open-hearth furnace, rolling mill, or other major piece of equipment. The other members of the crew are assistants of various grades, some of whom are engaged in learning the trade and will succeed in working up to the top position. The less-skilled men doubtless accept large occupational differentials more readily because of the possibility that they may enjoy the top rate at some later time.

The history of union organization in the industry may also have had some effect. The AFL unions, which developed considerable strength in the industry during the eighties and nineties and again during World War I, were spearheaded by the skilled workers and were concerned mainly with protecting the upper layers of the wage structure. The skilled men again played a leading role in the organization of the United Steelworkers, in contradistinction to the situation in automobiles, textiles, and other mass-production industries.

The steel industry has proven highly resistant to the general tendency toward shrinkage of occupational differentials in American industry over the past fifty years. The course of events over the years 1907–38 is suggested by the data in Table 3-1. This material is by no means perfect. Both the number and identity of the mills covered in successive BLS surveys have varied, the recent surveys being considerably more complete than earlier ones. An effort has been made in Table 3-1 to avoid the omnibus term "common labor" by using a low-skilled job title which can be traced through the entire period. This still does not avoid all difficulties, because the content of the low-skilled and high-skilled jobs selected may have changed considerably over the period, and the differential between them may not fully represent the movement of skilled and unskilled rates in general. The data also relate to earnings, the movement of which does not coincide exactly with changes in wage rates.

There has been considerable fluctuation in differentials, including the normal tendency for differentials to narrow during the inflation of World War I and to widen during the subsequent deflation. Over the thirty-year period as a whole, however, there was no clear tendency for percentage differentials to widen or contract. The low-skilled improved their relative position on Bessemer converters and in puddling mills. On open-hearth furnaces, on the other hand, they lost ground substantially,

Table 3-1. Occupational Differentials in Selected Branches of Iron and Steel Production, 1907–38

	BLAST FURNACES (BLOWERS/STOCKERS)	BESSEMER CONVERTERS (POURERS/ CINDER PITMEN)	OPEN HEARTH FURNACES (MELTERS HELPERS, FIRST/ COMMON LABOR)	PUDDLING MILLS (PUDDLERS/ STOCKERS)
	PER CENT	PER CENT	PER CENT	PER CENT
1907	182	336	—	—
1910	180	292	265	—
1914	177	208	221	203
1920	165	224	207	260
1924	191	193	245	190
1929	203	209	288	149
1933	195	170	333	159
1938	185	186	322	153

Source: BLS, Bulletins 151, 168, 218, 305, 353, 377, 381, 442, 513, and 567; and Monthly Labor Review, 51 (August, Sept., and Oct. 1940), reprinted as Serial R 1168 (1941)

while on blast furnaces the differential in 1938 was almost identical with that in 1907. It seems reasonable to conclude that there was no sharp change in relative differentials for the industry as a whole. An important reason for this was doubtless the long-standing custom in the industry of making general wage increases and decreases on a percentage basis, which would tend to leave differentials unchanged.

With the entrance of the union on the scene in the late thirties one might have expected a marked change in wage behavior. With the low-skilled workers organized for the first time and constituting a substantial percentage of union membership, they might have been expected to press for flat-rate increases which would bring them much closer to the skilled men. In actuality, however, Table 3-2 indicates that the decline in occupational differentials between 1938 and 1951 was quite moderate. In only a limited number of groups did the percentage advantage over the laborers drop sharply. The most striking example is that of the rollers. Absolute differentials widened substantially, in many cases doubling between 1938 and 1951.

Such narrowing as has occurred in percentage differentials is due mainly to three rounds of flat-rate increases during the first decade of collective bargaining: a 10¢ increase in 1941, a 5½¢ award by the War Labor Board in 1942 in the Little Steel Case; and the 18½¢ increase of 1946, which also occurred under wage stabilization. The total amount of these increases was not large enough to narrow percentage differentials greatly, particularly since the skilled men are mainly on an incentive basis and have been able to keep their earnings well ahead of base rates.[23]

The inequities program and the standard wage schedule installed in 1947 produced no drastic change in occupational differentials. It was based on acceptance of traditional differentials by both union and management. The total cost of the inequities adjustments had been limited by the War Labor Board to 5 cents per hour, and all of this was needed to bring up individual jobs which were out of line and to bring up low-wage plants to the standard level. It was not feasible to do much with the general slope of the rate curve. Some jobs previously lumped together as "common labor" were now differentiated and pulled up into higher labor grades. This was done also for some of the lower semi-skilled jobs which had previously tended to "slump on the minimum." For the most part, however, the new schedule was a codification of existing occupational relationships and left the skilled-unskilled spread substantially intact.

Since 1947 general wage increases have been made in such a way as to widen the absolute differentials between the various labor grades, leaving percentage differentials virtually unchanged. In April 1947, for example, the minimum rate was increased by 12½¢ per hour. In addition, the increments between the thirty labor grades in the wage schedule were increased from 3½¢ to 4¢. This produced increases ranging from 12½¢ for workers in labor grade 1 to 27¢ for those in labor grade 30. Similar adjustments, tapered upward to provide larger absolute increases for the higher-paid workers, were made in 1948, 1950, and 1952.[24]

In 1953 and 1954 an equal flat-rate increase was given to all em-

23. See "Wage Chronology No. 3: U. S. Steel Corp., 1937–48," *Monthly Labor Review, 68* (February 1949), 194–200 for an account of the content of collective bargaining agreements over this period.

24. See "Wage Chronology No. 3: U. S. Steel Corp., Supplements 2, 3, and 4," *Monthly Labor Review, 71* (October 1950); *72* (May 1951); *76* (March 1953).

Table 3-2. Occupational Differentials in Basic Steel, 1938 and 1951

DEPARTMENT AND OCCUPATION	APRIL 1938			JANUARY 1951		
	AVERAGE HOURLY EARNINGS	PER CENT OF OPEN HEARTH LABORERS	CENTS PER HOUR ABOVE OPEN HEARTH LABORERS	AVERAGE HOURLY EARNINGS	PER CENT OF OPEN HEARTH LABORERS	CENTS PER HOUR ABOVE OPEN HEARTH LABORERS
Blast furnace						
Blowers	$1.19	214%	$ .63	$2.72	193%	$1.31
Keepers	.72	128	.16	1.95	138	.54
Stock unloaders	.64	115	.08	1.51	107	.10
Open hearth						
Melters	1.90	340	1.34	4.28	304	2.87
Pourers	1.04	186	.48	2.19	155	.78
Charging-machine operators	1.00	179	.44	2.30	163	.89
Laborers	.56	100	—	1.41	100	—
Blooming & slabbing mill						
Rollers	1.77	318	1.19	3.37	239	1.96
Heaters	1.38	247	.82	2.89	205	1.48
Soaking-pit cranemen	1.05	189	.49	2.33	165	.92
Merchant-bar Mills						
Stranders	.87	156	.31	2.15	152	.74
Hot-sheet mills						
Rollers	1.89	338	1.33	3.12	221	1.71
Matcher doublers	1.01	182	.45	2.02	143	.61
Maintenance						
Machinists, class A	.93	166	.37	2.06	146	.65
Welders, class A	.89	159	.32	1.95	138	.54

Source: "Earnings and Hours in the Iron and Steel Industry, April 1938, Part II," *Monthly Labor Review, 51* (September 1940), 709–26; BLS, *Wage Structure, Basic Iron and Steel, January, 1951,* Series 2, No. 81, pp. 9–12.

ployees, leaving the increments between labor grades unchanged. The reason for this was that the total increase agreed upon with the companies in these years was not large enough to permit an increase in increments. An increase of $\frac{1}{2}$¢ in the increment between job classes is estimated to cost about $3\frac{1}{2}$¢ per hour per employee. The total wage increase obtained in 1953 was $8\frac{1}{2}$¢ per hour, and the 1954 increase was 5¢. Had $3\frac{1}{2}$¢ of this been used for adjustment of increments in the latter case, workers in the lowest labor grade would have received an increase of only $1\frac{1}{2}$¢ per hour. This simply was not practical politics within the union. An adjustment of increments is politically feasible only when the total amount agreed upon with the companies is large enough to permit a substantial increase in the minimum rate as well.[25]

With this qualification, adjustment of increments so as to maintain percentage wage differentials appears to be the general practice. There is considerable difference of opinion on this point within the union, some members preferring to see differentials narrowed and others wanting to see them maintained. In most years, the policy of maintaining differentials prevails, but this is not invariably true. In 1952, for example, the union was strongly opposed to adjustment of increments and demanded a flat-rate increase. It was the companies which insisted on, and eventually succeeded in obtaining, an adjustment of increments.

As a result of successive increases in increments, the spread between the bottom and the top of the wage structure increased from $1.015 in 1947 to $1.705 in 1953, while percentage differentials remained almost constant. The rate for the lowest labor grade was 49 per cent of that for the highest grade in 1947, and 47 per cent in 1953.[26]

Occupational relationships at present are broadly similar, not merely to those existing in 1938, but to those existing at a much earlier period. In 1914, for example, the earnings of common labor relative to those of the top job were 53 per cent in blast furnace departments, 43 per cent on Bessemer converters, 44 per cent on open hearth furnaces, and 42 per cent in puddling mills. These data are not really comparable with those for 1953, since they relate to earnings rather than rates and to jobs which might not fall in the lowest and highest labor grades under the new rate schedule. It still seems safe to conclude that occupational differentials have declined only slightly over these forty years, and that there is no sharp difference between the preunion and postunion periods.

Why has steel behaved in this way when occupational differentials

25. For 1953 and 1954 wage-bargaining developments, see "Wage Chronology No. 3: U. S. Steel Corp., Supplement No. 5," *Monthly Labor Review*, 76 (October 1953), 1084.

26. See references in nn. 22–4.

have shrunk so sharply in many other industries? There are probably a number of reasons. The skilled men are mainly incentive workers, and their earnings may tend to pull ahead of those of the timeworkers as a result of technical progress. Larger base-rate increases may be necessary for them in order to keep base rates in sight of actual earnings. The top occupations in steel have probably been subject to less dilution of job content than has occurred in many other industries. The skilled men also have considerable responsibility to direct other employees. In earlier times they often operated as independent subcontractors, hiring and paying the men under them and receiving payment from the company on an output basis. Overtones of this earlier relationship continue even at the present time. The industry's custom of making general wage adjustments on a percentage basis is obviously important, but this should be regarded not as an independent causal factor but rather as a recognition by management of the weight of the other factors just noted. In the formation of union policy, too, the skilled men appear to have an influence disproportionate to their numbers.

Maintenance of occupational differentials in the steel industry is not confined to the United States. Differentials have been well maintained in Britain, although the industry is strongly unionized and although differentials in most other British industries have been sharply reduced since 1939. Turner attributes this partly to the fact that the low-skilled workers are assistants to a top craftsman and have reasonable opportunity to work up to his job over the course of time.[27] This may make them more willing to accept substantial wage differentials.

CONCLUDING OBSERVATIONS

The most important single accomplishment of collective bargaining to date has been the creation of an orderly occupational wage structure throughout the basic steel industry. Almost all the larger companies now use the same manual of job descriptions, the same method of classifying jobs into labor grades, and the same minimum hourly rate for each grade. This may seem like a prosaic job of industrial engineering. It was actually very important in cleaning up a multitude of grievances and potential grievances over specific rates of pay. Moreover, it laid the foundation for accurate information and systematic policies concerning occupational, interplant and regional differentials.

Installation of the cws scale did not by itself reduce interplant differences in wage level, since the new schedule was based on existing plant

27. See the more extensive discussion of this point on p. 274.

minimum rates which varied considerably even within the same company. Some leveling of plant minima was accomplished at the time the scale was introduced. In U. S. Steel, for example, plant minima outside the South were equalized in 1947. From a longer-run point of view, the CWS system provided an accurate yardstick for interplant comparisons, and this made it possible for the union and management to negotiate the union's demand for a uniform wage schedule. Reduction of interplant differentials has gone forward steadily since 1947, and the differentials remaining within basic steel are not of major importance.

The United Steelworkers has not been obstinate or inflexible in its effort to eliminate interplant differentials. Many of the semi-integrated and nonintegrated basic steel companies, and a majority of the fabricating companies, lag behind U. S. Steel. The ability of each company to pay has been carefully gauged. There are a considerable number of cases in which the union has made it possible for marginal firms to remain in operation by making wage concessions and by giving other types of assistance. National union headquarters in Pittsburgh has a staff of engineers who are available as consultants to local unions in marginal establishments, and work with them to improve production and personnel methods. Fears that a powerful national union may cause numerous business failures by enforcing a standard wage level under all circumstances do not seem warranted on the basis of experience in steel.

As part of the reduction of interplant differentials collective bargaining has resulted in the elimination of geographical differentials in basic steel, though not in the fabricating industries. Union pressure for regional uniformity was accompanied by certain favorable circumstances. The fact that many plants in the outlying regions are owned by the large integrated companies reduces the problem of interregional competition, which is a crucial difficulty in textiles and many other industries.

The standard rate schedule produced no marked change in the spread between the bottom and top of the wage structure, nor has any substantial change occurred since 1947. On the contrary, the union has made a deliberate effort to maintain percentage differentials by giving larger increases to the higher labor grades in each wage movement. It is an interesting paradox that in the steel industry, where industrial unionism might have been expected to produce a leveling of occupational differentials, this has not happened; while in the railroad industry, where the powerful craft unions might have been expected to maintain or widen occupational differentials, they have actually undergone a sharp contraction. This suggests the danger of simple hypotheses about the relation between union structure and wage policies.

Collective bargaining does not seem thus far to have had a marked effect on the level of average hourly earnings in steel relative to those in other industries.[28] The absolute increase in average hourly earnings in basic steel over the years 1939–54 was $1.36 as compared with $1.16 for all manufacturing. On a percentage basis, however, basic steel earnings rose by only 162 per cent, compared with 173 per cent for all durable goods and 184 per cent for all manufacturing.

The conclusion that collective bargaining has had little effect on the relative level of steel wages might be altered, however, if one took into account monetary benefits other than wages. The union estimates that contract gains in the northern subsidiaries of U. S. Steel from 1937 through 1952 totaled some $1.33 per hour. Of this total, general wage increases account for 91¢; other wage increases resulting from the inequities program and from adjustment of increments amount to 18¢; and various fringe benefits—vacations, paid holidays, shift differentials, group insurance, and pensions—account for some 24¢ per hour.[29] The rate of increase in fringe benefits has almost certainly been above the average for industry in general. It also seems certain that a larger proportion of the addition to the company's payroll costs during this fifteen-year period has been allocated to fringe benefits that would have been true in the absence of collective bargaining. Experience in steel supports the hypothesis that collective bargaining makes for diversification of the pattern of worker compensation and for allocation of a larger proportion of payroll cost to items other than direct wage payments.

In sum, the impact of collective bargaining on steel wages has been rather different from what one might have judged on the basis of newspaper reports and armchair speculation. The general level of steel wages has apparently not been greatly affected. Occupational differentials have been well maintained. The most important event of the period, the development of a uniform system of job classification and a standard wage schedule, occurred with no strike and little publicity, and involved a striking example of cooperative effort by union and management officials. The transfer of a growing percentage of payroll costs into indirect or supplementary income payments also foreshadows a trend of great long-run importance.

28. It is of course impossible to prove definitely that collective bargaining has or has not influenced the relative wage level of an industry, for reasons noted in previous chapters. The most thorough study which has been made in basic steel, however, concluded that collective bargaining was not a significant factor in the rate of wage increase over the period 1945–50. Albert Rees, "Postwar Wage Determination in the Basic Steel Industry," *American Economic Review, 41* (June 1951), 389–404.

29. "Major Contract Economic Gains, U. S. Steel Corporation, basic contracts 1937–52," United Steelworkers of America, Research Department Memorandum, October 13, 1952, p. 2.

CHAPTER 4 *Cotton Textiles*

INFLUENCES ON WAGE DETERMINATION

SOME CHARACTERISTICS OF THE INDUSTRY

COTTON textile production is one of the oldest and largest of American manufacturing industries and is a competitive one, characterized by numerous production units, lack of effective control over prices and production, and high mortality of firms. It corresponds more closely than most other branches of manufacturing to the theoretical concept of an "industry" because, while it produces hundreds of products ranging from fine lawn to coarse bagging, the machinery used and the skills required are standardized and highly transferable. Any cotton mill has potential access to a considerable range of products and shifts from one product to another with changes in their relative profitability. The industry is widely distributed throughout New England and the southeastern states. Almost all the New England mills, but only a small minority of the southern mills, are under union contract, and this fact has been of crucial importance for union wage strategy.

The basic processes of spinning yarn and weaving cloth are usually carried on in the same plant, though there are a considerable number of independent yarn mills and a smaller number of independent weaving mills. The machines used are standardized and relatively small, so that a small plant can obtain about as low unit labor costs as a large plant. The other major cost item, the price of raw cotton, is also virtually uniform to all buyers. Cost studies of the Federal Trade Commission indicate that, if one omits the very smallest plants, there is virtually no correlation between unit total cost of goods sold and size of plant.[1] This is true also of each of the major cost categories: raw material, labor, other mill expenses, and selling and administrative expenses. The long-run total cost curve thus appears to be virtually horizontal.

The industry in 1952 comprised some 715 establishments employing approximately 419,000 workers.[2] Because of product specialization, these plants are not all in direct competition with each other at a particular time. Most of them are in potential competition, however, because of

1. Federal Trade Commission, *Report on the Textile Industry* (Washington, Jan.–June, 1936).
2. BLS, *Wage Structure, Cotton and Synthetic Textiles, March, 1952*, Series 2, No. 89, p. 5.

the possibility of shifting equipment from one grade of cloth to another whenever it seems profitable to do so.

Most types of cotton cloth are sold on an effectively competitive market. Price and output are volatile, and the industry has its own cycles of profitability in addition to those induced by fluctuations in general business. These specific textile cycles seem to average only two to three years in length, and it is not uncommon to find textiles depressed when most other industries are prosperous.

Over the last several decades cotton textile producers have suffered from the expansion of rayon, nylon, and other synthetic yarns. Cotton-weaving equipment can within limits be converted to weaving synthetics, and the industry is now frequently termed the cotton and rayon industry. To a considerable extent, however, the new yarns and fabrics have been produced in new mills. As the price of synthetics has fallen and their production volume has expanded, cotton textile producers have been subjected to competitive pressure which has pushed many of the less efficient mills into bankruptcy. Cotton has enjoyed some periods of high profits, notably during the war and the postwar boom of the forties. Averaged over the last thirty years or so, however, the level of profits in cotton textiles has been a good deal below the general manufacturing average.

The industry has reacted in several ways to this competitive pressure. First, textile producers in the South discovered that unit costs could be lowered by operating on a two-shift or three-shift basis instead of the traditional one-shift system which had prevailed in New England. While this helped the individual mill, it intensified the problems of the industry. It amounted to an increase in the industry's productive capacity in the face of a shrinking market, and thus made still more certain the elimination of marginal producers. Second, many plants were shut down, particularly in the New England branch of the industry. The number of plants operating in New England declined from 506 in 1923 to 66 in 1954, and employment dropped from 196,000 to 42,000 over this period.[3]

Third, there was a considerable merger movement in the textile industry, particularly during and after World War II. In addition to horizontal and vertical integration within the cotton branch of the industry some of the mergers involved bringing together of cotton, woolen, and synthetic-textile operations under common management. These consolidations have probably involved little economy in production costs. They have made possible some escape from competitive pressure through trademarking of products, brand-name advertising, advantageous bar-

3. Bureau of Census, *Census of Manufactures, 1923* (Washington, 1926), pp. 201–2; BLS, *Wage Structure, Cotton and Synthetic Textiles, March, 1952*, p. 5.

gains with large buyers of fabrics, and other merchandising advantages.

The industry's struggle for survival has involved a dramatic shift of production from New England to the southeastern states. In addition to a substantial advantage in labor costs, the South has offered other cost advantages which will be enumerated below (pp. 84–92). The South had only 10 per cent of the industry's employment in 1870, and only one-third in 1900. During the twenties, however, it passed New England, and by 1954 had more than four-fifths of total employment in the industry. New England retains about 15 per cent of cotton textile production, while the remaining 5 per cent is distributed over the Middle Atlantic states and the Southwest.[4]

The shift was a complicated affair, involving partly the failure of New England producers and the establishment of entirely new firms in the South, and partly migration of New England producers to the South. It was accompanied by a running fire of criticism from political, civic, and union leaders in New England, but no effective method of reversing the movement was discovered. The mills remaining in New England are engaged mainly in fine-goods production, a specialty in which labor and managerial skills plus proximity to the New York market will doubtless enable some mills to continue indefinitely in competition with the South.

It is in this context of secular decline, low profitability, rapid geographical shifting of production, and general competitive turbulence that union leaders have struggled to organize the industry and to win wage advantages. The situation is analogous to that in hosiery, men's clothing, and other soft-goods industries, and stands in marked contrast to that in basic steel or automobiles. The inability of employers to bring competition under control, and the inability of the union to organize more than a minor part of the industry account for the union's limited accomplishments on the wage front.

THE GROWTH OF UNION ORGANIZATION

The history of cotton textile unionism goes back many decades. By 1900 there were already five national craft unions with jurisdiction over the loom fixers, mule spinners, weavers, carders, and slashers. In 1901 all these groups except the mule spinners combined to form the United Textile Workers of America (UTW), affiliated with the AFL. Over the next thirty years this union had a turbulent history marked by internal schism, pressure for craft autonomy, and secession of various crafts from time to time; by the incursion into the industry of more radical groups such as the IWW in 1910–15 and various Communist-led unions in the

4. Herbert J. Lahne, *The Cotton Mill Worker* (New York, Rinehart, 1944), p. 91; BLS, *Wage Structure, Cotton and Synthetic Textiles, March, 1952.*

twenties and early thirties; by determined employer resistance, and dramatic but frequently unsuccessful strikes; and by great fluctuations of union membership, from a peak of some 80,000 in 1920 to 6,000 or so in 1933. The South remained almost completely nonunion throughout this period, in spite of numerous efforts at organization and a brief period of progress from 1917 to 1920. The progress of unionism in New England was hampered by growing competitive pressure from the South, which caused New England producers to press for wage cuts and kept the northern mills in a constant turmoil of strikes and recriminations.[5]

The economic revival after 1933, the enactment of the NRA codes and the National Labor Relations Act, and the rise of the CIO brought a revival of union strength in textiles. In 1937 a contract was signed between the UTW and the CIO providing for CIO financing of an organizing campaign by a Textile Workers Organizing Committee. The UTW locals were permitted to keep their existing charters if they wished, but most of them decided to accept TWOC charters, and all new locals were chartered by the TWOC. The organizing campaign met with considerable success, and by 1939 the TWOC had 858 contracts covering some 235,000 workers in all branches of the textile industry.[6] In that year the organization was renamed the Textile Workers Union of America (TWUA) and became an independent national union.

The history of cotton textile unionism since 1939 is mainly the history of the TWUA-CIO. The UTW-AFL has remained in existence and has experienced a gradual growth, partly through new organization and partly through secession from the CIO union. It has never had more than a small fraction of the organized textile workers, however, and has tended to follow the lead of the TWUA in wage movements.

The TWUA made substantial progress from 1939 through the mid-forties. By 1943 it was reported to have some 131,000 members in the cotton textile industry.[7] The New England mills were almost completely organized, and there was a substantial beachhead in the South comprising 20 to 25 per cent of Southern cotton textile employment. In the late forties, however, the union's fortunes took a turn for the worse. Little new ground was gained in the South and some was lost. Total TWUA membership in all branches of textiles declined from 390,355 in 1947–48 to 361,970 in 1952.[8] While there are no separate figures for cotton textile membership, this doubtless declined as well.

5. For a thorough discussion of the history of cotton textile unionism through the early forties, see Lahne, *The Cotton Mill Worker*, Chaps. 14–19.

6. Lahne, *The Cotton Mill Worker*, Chap. 19.

7. *Ibid.*

8. BLS, *Directory of Labor Unions in the United States* (1947–48 and 1952), Bulletins 937 and 1127.

The decline was due partly to the return of normal competitive conditions in the industry after the wartime boom, which brought stronger employer resistance to wage increases and other union demands. An unsuccessful strike for wage increases in the South in 1951 contributed to the decline of southern membership. Another important factor was enactment of the Taft-Hartley Act in 1947. A TWUA official testifying in 1953 reported that in the five years preceding the Taft-Hartley Act the union had won 58 per cent of the NLRB elections in which it was involved. In the first five years after Taft-Hartley the union won only 37 per cent of the elections. In almost two-fifths of those cases where the union won an election no contract was ever signed and the union was subsequently wiped out, while in an additional one-fifth contracts were signed but the employer subsequently refused to deal with the union.[9]

The large amounts of money and organizing effort put into the South during the past twenty years have had a disappointing yield in terms of permanent local unions. Most of the larger textile companies in the South remain nonunion, and the organized sector is too small to give the union much influence on wage structure. Probably not more than 15 per cent of southern textile workers are covered by union contracts at the present time.[10] Union power even in the highly unionized New England region is severely limited by the presence of nonunion southern competition.

OTHER INFLUENCES ON WAGE STRUCTURE

Despite the growing importance of union and governmental action, the wage structure of the cotton textile industry is still mainly the outgrowth of employer decisions. One result is marked dispersion of plant wage levels within the industry. Cotton mills are widely distributed geographically, and the wage level of each mill tends to reflect that of the community in which it is located.

In many mill towns, of course, the cotton-mill wage level *is* the community wage level. In these cases the wage level has to be explained in terms of relative efficiency and competitive strength of the mill in question, modified by the abundance or scarcity of local labor supplies, the degree of parsimony or generosity on the part of the management, and other considerations. Whatever the reasons, there are substantial interplant differentials.

Employer associations are also of long-standing importance in the industry. As early as the 1850's there was an association of Massachu-

9. Statement of William Pollock, U. S. Congress, House of Representatives, Hearings before the Committee on Education and Labor, March 30, 1953, p. 1964.
10. Estimate by a TWUA official in 1950.

setts cotton spinners, which in 1865 became the New England Cotton Manufacturers Association and in 1906 the National Association of Cotton Manufacturers. The American Cotton Manufacturers Institute, which includes most of the southern producers, is also an old and powerful organization. These associations have typically aided their members in presenting a united front to union organizing campaigns, in resisting demands for general wage increases, and in pressing for wage cuts on occasion. Thus in 1922 the National Association of Cotton Manufacturers recommended to its members that "Those mills which could conveniently cut wages would have the full moral and financial backing of the Manufacturers' Association." [11]

Union-management negotiations are typically on a single-mill basis, except in a few of the oldest centers such as Fall River and New Bedford, where a single contract is signed with a local manufacturers' group. The regional and national employer associations are constantly in the background, however, furnishing their members with research services, moral and financial support, and advice on wage strategy. They also play a leading role in arbitration proceedings and in hearings before government bodies.

The federal government first entered prominently into wage determination in 1933, when the NRA cotton textile code set a minimum wage of 30¢ per hour in the South and 32½¢ in New England. In 1939, a uniform minimum of 32½¢ was set for both regions under the Fair Labor Standards Act. The legal minimum rose to 37½¢ in 1941, 40¢ in 1942, and 75¢ in 1950.[12] The wage level of the industry has risen so fast since 1940, however, that the legal minimum no longer has much coercive force. In 1955, some 85 per cent of cotton mill workers were earning $1.00 per hour or more.

The government also affected the textile wage structure considerably through wartime decisions of the National War Labor Board. In a 1944 decision the board, in addition to prescribing minimum common-labor rates for union mills in New England and the South, set standard rates for certain key jobs above the minimum. This was a major step forward in the union's campaign for a standard wage schedule throughout the industry.

THE GROWTH OF A UNION SCALE IN TEXTILES

The primary objective of the TWUA has been to establish a firm minimum wage in the industry, a floor below which a mill may not go no

11. Lahne, *The Cotton Mill Worker*, p. 208.

12. A further increase in the federal minimum wage to $1.00 per hour was enacted in 1955.

matter how severe the competitive pressure upon it. A minimum wage is not enough, however, because it applies only to the common-labor group in each mill. Some employers may pay substantial differentials to the higher occupations, others very small differentials. As the minimum is raised over the course of time, employers may respond by giving the higher occupational groups smaller increases or nothing at all, with a resulting compression of occupational differentials. One way to prevent this is to establish a standard schedule of job rates above the minimum, and to insist that increases in the plant minimum be reflected all the way up the line.

There are numerous other advantages in such a union scale. It provides a ready test of whether a particular job is fairly rated in a particular plant. It aids in the measurement and reduction of interplant differentials. It also provides a firm basis for industry-wide wage movements. It is one thing to secure a general 5-cent-per-hour increase which is added to a uniform rate schedule in each mill. It is vaguer and less satisfactory to secure a 5-cent increase which is added to whatever wage structure happens to exist in each mill. In any event, development of a standard scale of job rates has been a central objective of the TWUA, just as it has been of the United Steelworkers.

The effort to establish a standard rate for key textile occupations goes back several decades and stems from union activity in the New Bedford-Fall River area. The greater strength of unionism in this area apparently resulted from the fact that it was the center of print-cloth and later of fine-goods production. Fine goods required highly skilled workers and attracted from England many skilled men with a long tradition of unionism.

During the 1890's the craft unions of loom fixers, mule spinners, weavers, and cardroom operators organized the New Bedford Textile Council for joint action against employers in the area.[13] By 1914 six additional unions of lower-skilled crafts had affiliated with the council. On the employer side, the treasurers of the various mills were accustomed as early as 1903 to meet together and discuss strategy in countering union demands. In 1920 this loose organization was superseded by formation of the New Bedford Manufacturers Association.

Bargaining negotiations seem to have been on an individual mill basis until 1918. After that time there were central negotiations between representatives of the council and the association. There continued to be a separate agreement with each mill and any employer remained technically free to deviate from the terms approved by the association. Little use was made of this provision, however, and the terms arrived at in the

13. The following is based mainly on Lahne, *The Cotton Mill Worker*, and on interviews conducted by Jane Metzger Schilling in 1946.

central negotiations were normally written into all the individual contracts. A further step toward centralization was taken in 1933 when, apropos of the industry-wide NRA code, the New Bedford employers' association agreed to certain wage changes which became binding on all member mills. This remained an informal memorandum of understanding concerning changes in the separate mill contracts. Only in 1938, after the TWOC had entered the scene with a firm policy of written agreements, did the unions secure a full-dress written contract binding on all employers in the area. Centralized collective bargaining thus developed over a period of about forty years, and at the end of that time it still applied to only one area, albeit a key area, in the cotton textile industry.

Central negotiation with the employers originally meant only that wage increases and decreases would be applied uniformly in all mills. The New Bedford craft unions were naturally anxious to go beyond this and to establish "standard rates" which could be enforced uniformly throughout the area. Their success in doing this, however, seems to have varied with the strength of the individual union. The loom fixers succeeded in enforcing a standard scale from about 1900 on, but the mule spinners and slasher tenders had only partial success, while the poorly-organized weavers had scarcely any success. The central organization, the New Bedford Textile Council, was not able to bring about standardization of rates where the craft concerned was weakly organized.

A uniform city-wide rate schedule covering a substantial number of jobs was first established in 1933. The NRA code for the industry had established a minimum rate for the lowest-paid workers. The unions pointed out that this did nothing for the skilled and semiskilled groups, since employers could raise laborers to the new minimum, leaving higher rates unchanged. They urged the Code Authority to set three additional minimum rates for semiskilled, skilled, and highly skilled workers. This proposal, which would have applied to all mills in the industry, was denied by the Code Authority. In the New Bedford stronghold of unionism, however, the unions were able to persuade the Cotton Manufacturers Association to negotiate a uniform scale of rates applicable throughout the city.

This scale was determined after extensive statistical study by the unions and the employers association. It was agreed that the goal should be to establish, for each major occupation, a wage rate which was approximately the average wage for the top half of all New England cotton mills. In the case of hourly-paid workers, this was to constitute a minimum wage. In the case of pieceworkers, it was to be "the constant or controlling consideration" in determining piece rates. This "New Bedford scale," with numerous general increases and decreases since 1933, has remained in effect throughout the city since that time. It was extended soon afterward to the neighboring city of Fall River through a central agreement with the manufacturers association there.

In 1938 the TWOC appeared on the scene and, aided by governmental support and war prosperity, had within a few years organized virtually all cotton textile mills in New England. The development of collective bargaining in the New England industry as a whole shows an interesting parallel with the earlier development in New Bedford. Except in New Bedford and Fall River, negotiations are formally on a single-company basis, and the Union signs a separate agreement with each mill. At the beginning of each wage movement there is a meeting in Boston to which representatives of the various mills and of the Cotton Manufacturers Association are invited. Here the union explains and defends the (uniform) demands which it proposes to make on each mill in the months ahead. Employers are thus in a position to form a central strategy, and, while each mill is free to settle on any terms it may choose, there is strong pressure for a united front. If a wage dispute reaches the stage of arbitration, as has happened several times in recent years, this becomes in effect an arbitration between the union and the Manufacturers Association. This may be described as semicentralized collective bargaining, similar to the situation which existed in New Bedford from 1918 to 1933.

Under this system general wage adjustments are substantially uniform throughout the New England region; but this does not ensure interplant uniformity of wage levels. The TWUA, like the New Bedford craft unions before it, has made wage standardization a major objective from the beginning. After examining the experience of other industries, the TWUA concluded that uniform occupational hourly rates provided the most workable administrative device for establishing competitive parity. It favored this method to uniformity of piece rates or of labor costs because of the diversity of the industry and the rapidity of technological change. The stabilized wage structure had to combine several characteristics: it had to be applicable to all plants, irrespective of product and methods of operation; it must not be administratively possible to apply or to check; it must be comprehensible to the workers; and it must not be a bar to technological change. On these grounds a uniform occupational rate structure seemed generally preferable.[14]

The New Bedford scale provided an obvious starting point, and the union set to work to bring the wage structures of other New England mills into conformity with this scale. By 1944 the scale was in effect in thirty-three mills, twenty-two in New Bedford–Fall River and eleven in other

14. The union's Director of Research, Solomon Barkin, played a key role in the statistical and economic analysis leading to development of this policy. See his article in *Labor and Nation* (Feb.–March 1946).

areas, which employed about half the cotton and rayon workers in New England. An additional step forward was taken in connection with a wage demand initiated by the union in 1943 and adjudicated by the National War Labor Board in 1944. This decision, which had a stronger impact in the South than in New England, will be examined in more detail in a moment. In its application to New England, it required the unionized mills to establish specified hourly rates for certain key jobs ranging from laborer at the bottom to loom fixer at the top. Rates for other classifications lying between these "peg points" were referred back to the parties for collective bargaining under the guidance of a New England Textile Commission set up by the War Labor Board. Moreover, the board order provided that "the structure of rates set forth in agreements between the union and the Fall River Textile Manufacturers Association shall be used as a guide. This does not, however, preclude minor modifications of this structure by collective bargaining."

After much additional negotiation, standard rates were agreed on by late 1945 for some forty occupations, which included the bulk of cotton mill employees. The new standard wage scale was patterned closely on the New Bedford–Fall River scale. The board decision thus helped the union to bring mills throughout New England into general conformity with the New Bedford scale, though the process involved a strike in a number of Maine mills to bring them into line. Since 1945 the union's task has been limited to bringing a few stragglers into line, interpolating rates for jobs not included in the original list, making sure that piece-rate earnings in each mill bear a proper relation to the prescribed base rates, and general tidying up of the wage structure.

It is ironical that the long struggle to establish a standard wage scale in New England came to fruition just at the time when New England was sinking to a minor position in the industry. The main task of wage standardization obviously lies in the South, and it is in the South that the union's efforts have been least effective. The TWUA had by 1944 organized a hundred or so southern mills employing about 25 per cent of all cotton mill workers, but it had not yet had much effect on their wage levels or wage structures. Studies made in connection with the 1944 War Labor Board case indicated that the average wage level of the union mills was almost identical with that of the nonunion mills. Both the union and nonunion groups showed a remarkable dispersion of plant wage levels and great diversity of occupational wage structure from mill to mill. Some mills had a substantial wage spread between laborers and loom fixers, others a very small spread. Semiskilled jobs rated high in one mill were rated much lower in another. The union's description of the southern cotton wage structure as "chaotic" seems fully justified.

It was against this background that the union in 1943 launched a number of wage demands against unionized mills in both the South and New England. The demands included a 10-cent general increase, a 60-cent minimum wage in both regions, and a uniform schedule of job rates above the minimum patterned closely on the New Bedford scale. Adoption of this scale would have had, and was intended to have, a much more drastic effect in the South than in New England. Table 4-1 indicates that occupational differentials in the South at this time were considerably smaller than in New England, and this was a major factor contributing to the North-South differential in textile wage levels. Installation of what amounted to the New Bedford scale would thus have meant substantially larger wage increases in the South than in the North and would have narrowed the North-South differential drastically. For this reason the northern manufacturers offered only token resistance to the union's proposal. The southern mills, on the other hand, condemned it in strong terms and accused the union of conspiring with the northern manufacturers to undermine southern industry.

After extended hearings before two special textile panels and before the board itself, a decision was announced in October 1944 which, while it did not go as far as the union had proposed, did accept the principle of a standard wage scale and the desirability of wider occupational differentials in the South. The minimum wage in the South was set at 55¢ instead of the 60¢ which the union had demanded. The laborer-loom fixer spread was increased, though not up to the northern level. A modest North-South differential was permitted, ranging from 2¢ an hour at the minimum to 3¢ or 4¢ an hour in some of the semiskilled classifications.

Even this compromise order cost the southern mills considerably more than the northern ones, as is indicated by the last two columns of Table 4-1. The occupational structures of the New England mills were already in general accord with the New Bedford scale, which was put forward by the union and accepted by the board as a general guide to correct differentials. They came out, therefore, with close to a uniform 5¢ increase, although larger increases were provided for a few occupations and an especially large increase was granted to loom fixers, who were critically scarce during the war. The southern mills, in addition to a substantial increase in minimum rates, had to give even larger increases to almost all the semiskilled and skilled workers. The total cost of the settlement to them thus averaged out at about double the cost to the New England mills.

The full repercussions of the 1944 decision were more complicated than a brief summary can suggest. In the South, as in New England, the board order itself established only a few key rates. Rates for other jobs were returned to the parties for collective bargaining, under the general supervision of a Southern Cotton Textile Commission, and with a proviso that the total cost of installing a balanced wage structure was not to exceed 5 cents per hour in any mill. Collective bargaining over this issue bogged down in many southern mills, and the Southern Textile Commission ended by making most of the crucial decisions. Standard rates for some forty jobs were eventually established as a result of commission studies and hearings. The occupational differentials established

Table 4-1. Impact of 1944 National War Labor Board Decision on Cotton Textile Wage Structure

OCCUPATIONAL GROUP (MALE ONLY)	NEW BEDFORD SCALE, 1943	ASTHE * SOUTHERN COTTON MILLS 1943	NWLB PEG POINTS, 1944		WAGE INCREASE	
			SOUTH	NEW ENGLAND	SOUTH	NEW ENGLAND
Sweepers	.520	.454	.550	.570	.096	.050
Card tenders	.589	.500	.615	.640	.115	.051
Spinning doffers	.667	.576	.685	.720	.109	.053
Weavers, plain	.692	.614	.750	.750	.136	.058
Loom fixers, plain loom	.891	.746	.900	1.020	.154	.129

* Average straight-time hourly earnings.

Source: Survey conducted by the Southern Cotton Manufacturers Association, submitted in testimony before the Southern Cotton Textile Panel of the NWLB

by these decisions were usually in close accord with those provided in the New Bedford scale and ratified by the Northern Textile Commission.

One difficult problem was how the new base rates were to be applied to incentive jobs. Many southern mills took the attitude that they were under no obligation to bring incentive workers' earnings above the basic hourly minimum, and the Textile Commission did not feel that it had authority to require more than this. The union insisted that earnings should exceed the hourly minimum by a sufficient margin to provide an incentive to superior performance, but it was frequently unable to carry this point in the face of employer resistance. In New England employers were more accustomed to a premium for incentive workers and more willing to accept the union's reasoning on this point. The result was that the North-South differential was not reduced as much as might have been expected from the terms of the board order. The differential in *earnings*, at least for incentive workers, remained considerably larger than the differential in base rates.

The NWLB decision was a major strategic victory for the union, because it produced for the first time a standard wage schedule in the South. This could be used as a test of the adequacy of occupational structures in all the unionized southern mills, as a point of departure in demanding and applying general wage increases, and as a powerful organizing argument in the nonunion mills. The position of the union nevertheless remained precarious. The board order directly affected only the small unionized sector of the industry, and its immediate effect was to pull the wage levels and occupational structures of the union mills out of line with those of most nonunion mills.[15] The new wage structure could be defended over the long run only if the union could organize a major portion of the southern industry and bring many more mills into line with the new scale.

For several years after 1945 it looked as though the union might be able to do this. Nonunion employers in the South, plagued by labor shortages and fearful of union organization, tended to adopt certain features of the union scale and to match or anticipate the union on general wage increases. By 1950, however, with boom conditions receding, the Taft-Hartley Act in effect, and the union's inability to organize the industry increasingly clear, employers began to follow a more independent line. The traditional diversity of wage structures in the southern mills reasserted itself, and the prospect of effective wage standardization became more and more remote.

INTERPLANT DIFFERENTIALS

The union's effort to establish a standard wage schedule for the industry has been examined in some detail. What evidence is there concerning the effectiveness of this campaign in reducing interplant wage differences?

If one goes back to the mid-thirties one finds substantial interplant differentials both in New England and in the southern states. Data for selected occupations in 1937 are shown in Table 4-2. Dispersion of earnings was particularly great for semiskilled incentive workers and for common laborers. Dispersion was consistently lower in the North than in the South, reflecting the substantial standardization of wages in the Fall River–New Bedford area which had already been accomplished by 1937, and possibly also the greater compactness of the New England region.

15. Though not of all nonunion mills. The large, profitable, and nonunion Cannon chain, for example, already had in 1944 a wage level and a set of occupational rates very similar to those prescribed by the directive order of the NWLB. Indeed, the board supported its directive on the ground that it was in accord with the "best practice" already prevailing in the South.

Over the next fifteen years the union was to achieve a high degree of wage standardization in New England, but much less success in the southern states. The earliest standardization of wages was achieved in the New Bedford–Fall River area, which had been the scene of the first efforts to establish a union scale. Table 4-3 compares the New Bedford scale with average straight-time hourly earnings in New Bedford mills for selected occupations in 1943 and 1952. It will be noted that there was close conformity to the scale in both years, particularly for skilled timeworkers such as loom fixers and card grinders, and for unskilled timeworkers such as battery hands.

Table 4-2. *Wage Variation within Selected Cotton Textile Occupations, 1937*

	COEFFICIENT OF AVERAGE DEVIATION (PER CENT)	
OCCUPATION	SOUTH	NORTHEAST
Skilled		
Loom fixers	9.3	7.1
Semiskilled		
Doffers (male)	14.9	11.2
Frame spinners (female)	12.0	8.7
Unskilled		
Battery hands (male)	9.9	5.7
Battery hands (female)	8.0	4.4
Laborers (male)	14.5	8.4

Source: Richard A. Lester, "Diversity in North-South Differentials," *Southern Economic Journal, 12* (January 1946), 238–62.

The case of incentive workers is more complicated. It is normal for the average hourly earnings of pieceworkers to exceed the hourly base rate by a considerable amount. Moreover, because of differences in skill requirements, job conditions, tightness of piece-rate administration, and other factors, incentive earnings in an occupation may differ considerably from mill to mill even when base rates are the same. Thus in 1943 the basic rate for spinners was 60.7¢ per hour. Straight-time hourly earnings of male spinners in the lowest New Bedford mill were 63¢, in the highest mill 91¢, and the area average was 76¢. Male weavers on plain automatic looms had a base rate of 69.2¢. Actual earnings ranged from 72¢ in the lowest mill to 78¢ in the highest, and averaged 75¢. These deviations do not indicate departures from the standard wage schedule, but arise from the other factors that have just been mentioned.

Looking at the New England industry as a whole, one finds a greater dispersion of plant wage levels, but the degree of conformity to the New Bedford scale is still striking. The situation in 1952 is shown in

Table 4-3. *Comparison of New Bedford Scale with Average Straight-time Hourly Earnings, Selected Occupations, New Bedford Mills, 1943 and 1952*
(*cents per hour*)

		APRIL 1943			MARCH 1952		
		NEW BEDFORD SCALE	ASTHE *	EXCESS OF EARNINGS OVER SCALE	NEW BEDFORD SCALE	ASTHE *	EXCESS OF EARNINGS OVER SCALE
Battery Hand	(F)	—	—	—	117	120	3
Card Tender	(M)	59	63	4	123	132	9
Winder, non-auto	(M)	59	68	9	123	—	—
	(F)	59	67	8	123	—	—
Winder, auto		64	—	—	129	132	3
Spinner (ring frame)	(M)	61	76	15	125	—	—
	(F)	61	—	—	125	130	5
Spinning doffer	(M)	67	76	9	133	145	12
	(F)	67	67	0	133	—	—
Slubber tender		76	—	—	145	154	9
Weaver, plain auto	(M)	69	75	6	137	152	15
	(F)	69	75	6	137	157	20
Card grinder	(M)	73	73	0	150	154	4
Loom fixer	(M)	97	97	0	172	178	6

* Average straight-time hourly earnings.

Source: Data are from BLS surveys covering 10 New Bedford mills in 1943, 15 New Bedford and Fall River mills in 1952

Table 4-4. For timeworkers, both skilled and unskilled, hourly earnings in the three major areas are very close together and within a few cents of the minima prescribed by the union scale. For incentive occupations, there is typically more interarea variation and a larger premium over the minimum hourly rate for the reasons just mentioned. The average for male weavers, however, is almost identical in the three areas.

The present degree of wage standardization among the New England mills is probably close to the maximum which can be achieved. There will always be some payment over the standard rates, particularly during periods of high prosperity, because a particular mill has a difficult recruitment problem or needs a somewhat higher grade of skill. There is considerable difference in the content of the same occupational title from mill to mill, which may justify some variation in earnings. These considerations, which apply to time and incentive jobs alike, are augmented in the case of incentive jobs by additional reasons for variation in earnings from mill to mill. In view of these things, the TWUA appears to have done a remarkable job of wage equalization.

Table 4-4. Comparison of New Bedford Scale with Average Straight-time Hourly Earnings, Selected Occupations, Three New England Areas, March 1952 (cents per hour)

		AVERAGE STRAIGHT-TIME HOURLY EARNINGS		
OCCUPATION	NEW BEDFORD SCALE	NEW BEDFORD-FALL RIVER	NORTHERN NEW ENGLAND	CONNECTICUT AND RHODE ISLAND
Battery hand (F)	117	120	122	121
Card tender (M)	123	132	130	134
Winder, nonauto (F)	123	—	123	133
Winder, auto	129	132	137	135
Spinner, ring (F)	125	130	—	135
Spinning doffer (M)	133	145	136	147
Slubber tender	145	154	155	150
Weaver, plain auto (M)	137	152	153	153
(F)	137	157	151	153
Card grinder (M)	150	154	153	153
Loom fixer (M)	172	178	178	176

Source: Data from BLS wage survey covering 43 out of 51 cotton textile mills in the 3 areas; BLS, Wage Structure, Cotton and Synthetic Textiles, March 1952, Series 2, No. 89

In the southeastern states, in contrast to New England, interplant differentials have continued quite wide. The results of a BLS survey in 1943 are shown in Table 4-5. For almost all occupations the level of earnings in the highest plant was at least 50 per cent above the level in the lowest plant. For some of the most important semiskilled occupations (spinners, doffers, winders, plain-loom weavers), the top mill was almost 100 per cent above the lowest one. Moreover, most mills tend to be low or high across the board, so that the dispersion of average plant wage levels is also large.

Dispersion of plant wage levels in the South arises partly from the fact that the industry is spread over a large number of communities with differing wage levels; but there is also wide dispersion *within* each community. An analysis by Richard Lester, reproduced in Table 4-6, suggests that the dispersion of textile wages in most communities in 1943 was almost as great as the dispersion for the South as a whole.

Table 4-5. Average Straight-time Hourly Earnings of Plants with Lowest and with Highest Plant Average Hourly Earnings, in Five Southeastern States, Cotton Textile Industry, Selected Occupations, July 1943

STRAIGHT-TIME HOURLY EARNINGS
(CENTS PER HOUR)

OCCUPATION	LOWEST PLANT AVERAGE	HIGHEST PLANT AVERAGE	DIFFERENCE BETWEEN HIGH AND LOW PLANT
Card tender and stripper	$ .40	$ .62	$ .22
Card grinder	.47	.75	.28
Spinners, frame	.40	.77	.37
Doffers, frame	.41	.78	.37
Winders	.40	.80	.40
Weavers—other than jacquard loom	.41	.77	.36
Weavers—jacquard	.53	.82	.29
Loom fixer—other than jacquard loom	.50	.88	.38
Loom fixer—jacquard	.68	1.00	.32
Inspector, cloth-hand	.40	.65	.25
-machine	.44	.75	.31
Second hand	.46	1.19	.73
Stock clerk	.42	.88	.46
Trucker hand	.40	.51	.11
Janitor	.40	.54	.14
Watchmen	.40	.61	.21
Carpenter maintenance—class A	.54	.81	.27
—class B	.45	.86	.41
Electrician maintenance—class A	.65	1.08	.43
—class B	.50	1.05	.55
Machinist maintenance—class A	.55	1.25	.70
—class B	.45	.88	.43

Source: Calculated from BLS, "Cotton Broad Woven Goods and Yarn Mills: Five Southeastern States, Straight-Time Average Hourly Earnings, Selected Occupations" (July 1943), Serial IV-3

An explanation of this intracommunity variation must be sought in differences in products manufactured and skills required, in plant efficiency and profitability, in tightness of incentive wage administration, and in other aspects of company wage policy.

A comparison of the last column of Table 4-6 with the first column of Table 4-2 suggests that there may have been a slight reduction of interplant dispersion in the South between 1937 and 1943. The coverage of the two surveys is not identical; but the fact that the coefficients of deviation in 1943 run consistently below those for 1937 is probably significant.

Table 4-6. Variation in Occupational Wage Levels Among Southern Cotton Textile Plants in July 1943 (coefficients of average deviation calculated from plant averages of straight-time hourly earnings)

OCCUPATION	STATES-VILLE AREA	BURLINGTON-WINSTON SALEM AREA	CHARLOTTE AREA	GREENVILLE-SPARTAN-BURG AREA	183 MILLS 15 LABOR-MARKET AREAS IN SOUTH
	(PER CENT)	(PER CENT)	(PER CENT)	(PER CENT)	(PER CENT)
Janitors	6.5	5.5	3.0	4.1	5.7
Card tenders	10.9	6.1	6.6	3.0	7.4
Spinners	10.8	7.4	6.2	5.6	7.7
Doffers	14.0	9.7	11.9	6.7	12.5
Weavers	11.3	9.1	8.8	8.2	12.7
Loom fixers	11.4	7.6	6.1	4.6	7.9
Average	10.8	7.6	7.1	5.4	9.0

Source: Richard A. Lester, "Wage Diversity and Its Theoretical Implications," Review of Economics and Statistics, 28 (August 1946), 157. Basic data from BLS 1943 wage survey

There seems to have been a further reduction of interplant dispersion in the South between 1943 and 1952. Coefficients of average deviation calculated from a BLS wage survey in March 1952 run substantially below Lester's calculation for 1943. One can say with some confidence, then, that interplant differentials shrank over the period 1937–52 as a whole. This was probably due mainly to the great rise in the industry's wage level during this period, which tended to shrink all differentials on a percentage basis; and to the combination of labor shortages and high profits during the forties, which both permitted and compelled the low-wage firms to come up closer to the industry average. The installation of a union scale in the South in 1944–45 brought a marked reduction of wage dispersion among the unionized southern mills, and doubtless had some impact also on the nonunion sector, but this seems to have been secondary to the effect of economic developments.

While interplant dispersion in the South has diminished, it remains above the New England level, particularly among timeworkers. The

1952 BLS survey found that virtually all New England loom fixers, for example, were earning between $1.65 and $1.70 per hour. In South Carolina, however, substantial numbers of loom fixers were to be found over the entire range from $1.30 to $1.70. In North Carolina, the great majority fell within the range $1.40 to $1.70, though a few received as low as $1.20 and as high as $1.95.

It does not follow that the whole of the difference between the two regions is due to union influence. The New England mills lie closer to each other geographically, and might for this reason show smaller dispersion of wage levels even under nonunion conditions. They are also more homogeneous in terms of product than are the southern mills, being strongly oriented toward fine-goods production. Allowing for these factors, it still seems reasonable to conclude that union strength and policy is the main reason for the difference in dispersion within the two regions. If the southern branch of the industry were to be fully unionized it seems likely that interplant differentials would be brought much closer to the New England level.

GEOGRAPHICAL DIFFERENTIALS

Since the beginning of cotton textile production in the South the wage level of the southern mills has been consistently below the New England level. This is, indeed, the best known illustration of North-South wage differentials in the United States, and its causes and justifiability have been debated for decades. The facts of the case are complicated. There are substantial interplant differences within the South, as was noted in the previous section. In recent years the range of plant wage levels in the South has been considerably larger than the average difference between the South and New England. The North-South differential does vary considerably from one occupational level to another. For many years the differential was larger for common labor than for semiskilled and skilled occupations, while more recently the reverse has been true.

The gross differential between the two regions also results partly from differences in type of product. Almost all the nonintegrated yarn mills are located in the South, and since wages are lower in spinning than in weaving, this tends to pull down the Southern wage level. The New England mills which have survived in the industry have done so partly by concentrating on fine-goods production, which requires greater skill and has traditionally paid more than the coarser grades of cloth. Regional differentials between mills engaged on the same kind of product are typically less than the gross differential between all mills. In November 1954 the average hourly earnings of all cotton textile workers in New England were $1.32, compared with $1.17 in the southeastern states. Among mills producing combed-yarn products (fine goods), however, the spread in earnings was only from $1.31 in New England to $1.27 in the South.[16]

The trend of the differential has been generally downward over the past fifty years. During the 1890's, the northern wage level averaged roughly 80 per cent above that of the South. Soon after 1900 the differential began to decline as textile production expanded in the South. From 1908 to 1914, and again in 1920 at the peak of the postwar boom, the advantage of New England was only about one-third.[17] The differential widened once more with the collapse of the boom, wages being cut more severely in the nonunion South than in the partially unionized North. The New England premium rose to a peak of 64 per cent in 1924, but it proved impossible to maintain a differential of this size for very long. Partly in consequence of the large wage spread, the migration of the industry to the South gained momentum rapidly during the twenties. This tended to depress wages in New England and to raise them in the South. The depression of 1929–32 placed the New England mills in a critical position, and the unions were forced to take general wage cuts of 30 per cent. Wage cuts in the South during these years were somewhat smaller. Southern textile wages were sustained by a strong secular expansion of the industry in that region, the favorable competitive position of the southern mills vis-à-vis New England, and the lighter incidence of general depression in the southern states. Thus by early 1933 the New England premium had narrowed once more to 39 per cent.

The course of events since 1933 is summarized in Table 4-7. Between 1933 and 1934 the differential was cut in half by the NRA code for the industry, which raised wages in the South much more sharply than in New England. The code, issued in August 1933, established a minimum wage of 30¢ an hour in the South and 32.5¢ in New England. The impact of this can be judged from the fact that, in the month before the code was introduced, 89.5 per cent of southern cotton textile employees were earning less than 30¢ per hour, and almost one-third were bunched in the vicinity of 15¢.[18] A year after the code was introduced, only 6.9 per cent of employees were receiving less than 30¢

16. BLS, *Earnings of Cotton Textile Workers, November, 1954* (mimeographed, Washington, 1955), 4 pages.

17. For data extending back almost continuously to 1890, see Table 12-9. See also A. F. Hinrichs and Ruth Clem, "Historical Review of Wage Rates in the Cotton-Textile Industry," *Monthly Labor Review, 40* (May 1935), 1170–80.

18. U. S. Dept. of Labor, Wages and Hours Division, Bulletin No. R-422a (mimeographed, September 1939), p. 50.

and more than 20 per cent were earning 40¢ or better. The median wage in the southern mills had risen from less than 20¢ to about 35¢.[19] In the northern mills a much larger percentage of employees was already above the new minimum, so that the forced increase in wages was smaller.

Table 4-7. Average Hourly Earnings by Region, Cotton Textile Industry, 1934–54

	AVERAGE HOURLY EARNINGS *			NORTH AS PER CENT
	U.S.	NORTH †	SOUTH ‡	OF SOUTH
1934 §	$ .381	$ .422	$ .356	119%
1937 §	.411	.489	.383	128
1940	.403	.469	.385	122
1946	.75	.82	.74	111
1952	1.19	1.38	1.17	118
1954	1.19	1.32	1.17	113

* Gross average hourly earnings in 1934, 1937, 1940; straight-time AHE in 1946, 1952, and 1954.

† North in 1934, 1937, 1940; Northeast in 1946, 1952, and 1954.

‡ South in 1934, 1937, 1940; Southeast in 1946, and 1952, and 1954.

§ Excluding Arkansas, Oklahoma, Mississippi.

Source: BLS surveys of wages in cotton textiles for 1934, 1937, 1940, 1952, and 1954

When the NRA was declared unconstitutional and the textile code became inoperative, the southern mills tended to revert to their previous standards. The percentage of southern textile workers receiving less than 30¢ an hour was twice as high in 1937 as in 1934. Wages were better maintained in New England, partly because of more effective union activity, and the differential widened from 19 per cent to 28 per cent. The differential shrank once more after the passage of the Fair Labor Standards Act in 1938. The first industry order under this act, issued in 1939, established a uniform minimum of 32.5¢ per hour for both the northern and the southern branches of the industry, and this was subsequently raised to 35¢ and then to 37.5¢ in 1941. These orders forced larger wage increases in the South than in New England and narrowed the interregional spread.[20]

The differential was further reduced during World War II, and had fallen to 11 per cent by 1946. A gross differential of only this amount

19. BLS, *Average Hourly Earnings in the Cotton-Goods Industry, 1937,* Serial Reprint 747 (Washington, 1938), p. 23.

20. See N. A. Tolles, "Regional Differences in Cotton-Textile Wages, 1928 to 1937," *Monthly Labor Review, 46* (January 1938), 36–47.

meant that true differentials between comparable grades of labor working on comparable products had become negligible, and the union seemed at last to be in sight of its goal of wage uniformity throughout the industry. The reasons for the greater percentage increase in southern than in northern wages during the war were primarily economic. The textile industry, faced with an insatiable military demand, was extremely profitable and could afford substantial wage increases. With the location of numerous war industries in the South, the southern mills were forced for the first time to compete strenuously for labor supplies, and this raised their wages more rapidly than those of New England mills long accustomed to such competition. In part, the narrowing of differentials was a byproduct of rapid wage and price inflation. The *absolute* increase in average hourly earnings between 1940 and 1946 was almost identical in the two regions, 35.5 cents in the South, 35.1 cents in New England. Since the South was starting from a lower base, its *percentage* increase was greater and the percentage differential between the two regions diminished. The War Labor Board policy of granting uniform cents-per-hour increases in the textile industry during the war, and the fact that the TWUA's wartime demands were framed in these terms contributed to this uniform absolute rate of increase in the two regions.

For some years after the war, the union continued to demand and secure the same general wage increases in both regions. The nonunion mills in the South, still enjoying good profits and apprehensive about possible unionization, proved willing to match or even anticipate increases in the union mills. The North-South differential continued to decline, and reached an all-time low of between 7 and 8 per cent in 1950.

With the diminished threat of unionization after 1947, and the diminished profitability of the industry after 1949, many of the southern mills began to drag their heels on wage advances. There were increases of 8 per cent in late 1950 and 2 per cent in early 1951, during the inflationary upsurge which followed the outbreak of the Korean war, but there was no further advance in the southern wage level through mid-1955. Meanwhile, the union continued its efforts to push up wages in New England. In 1951 it won a general increase of 6.5 per cent, plus a cost-of-living escalator clause, plus various fringe benefits, the total addition to the labor cost of the New England mills being about 14 cents per hour. The North-South differential jumped to 18 per cent.

The union mills in the South refused to follow this increase, a strike to force them to do so was unsuccessful, and it consequently proved impossible to maintain the higher wage level in New England. The New England mills, arguing that they were in an untenable competitive position, demanded wage reductions, and in July 1952 an arbitrator awarded a general reduction of 6.5 per cent, which brought basic wage rates back to the 1950 level. There was no further change until early 1955 when the New England employers, contending that the differential was still too large, demanded a reopening of their contracts and a further wage reduction. A strike ensued, the outcome of which is still uncertain at this writing. Experience since 1950 clearly demonstrates the dependence of the New England wage level on wage movements in the South, and the impossibility of pushing the New England mills ahead faster than southern firms are willing to go.

The long-run downward tendency of the differential is clear. During the 1920's it ranged between 50 and 60 per cent. As late as 1933 it stood at 39 per cent. Between 1934 and 1940 it fluctuated between 20 and 30 per cent. Since 1940 it has ranged between 10 and 20 per cent, and it does not seem likely to rise much above 10 per cent within the visible future. A 10 per cent gross differential, as already noted, means a much smaller differential between mills producing the same type of product.

The North-South differential varies considerably from one occupational level to the next, and these relationships have changed substantially over the course of time. The course of events from July 1933 (immediately before installation of the NRA code) to November 1954, is shown in Table 4-8. The position of the laborers has changed especially sharply over the past generation. Before 1933 the differential of northern over southern laborers was substantially larger than for the skilled and semiskilled occupations. This is the normal situation in many American industries, as will be seen in Chapter 12. It arises from high birth rates, excess of rural population, and consequent abundance of unskilled labor in the South. In the southern mills, moreover, cleaning, sweeping, and similar occupations are frequently done by Negro laborers, so that the North-South differential is in part a white-Negro differential.

This situation was changed by the minimum wages established under the NRA and the Fair Labor Standards Act, which forced up the rates for southern laborers very sharply. The southern mills were obliged to give increases to the higher occupational groups as well, but these were typically on a less-than-proportionate basis. In the North, on the other hand, the union insisted that increases be granted uniformly across the board. Thus the North-South differential was relatively well maintained for the skilled and semiskilled, but shrank markedly for the laborers. During the war years the uniform cents-per-hour increases awarded by the National War Labor Board narrowed the laborers' differential still further. The 1944 NWLB decision established plant base rates of 55 cents in the South and 57½ cents in the North. While this was not binding on nonunion mills in the South, most of them must have followed it, as is shown by the remarkably small variation in laborers' rates in 1946.

Since the end of the postwar boom the laborers' differential has widened once more and is now about the same as for other occupational groups. In 1954 the differential was consistently in the neighborhood of 10 per cent for all major occupations.

Table 4-8. *Average Hourly Earnings of Male Workers by Region, Selected Cotton Textile Occupations, 1933–54 (North as per cent of South)* *

DATE	LOOM FIXERS	WEAVERS: PLAIN, AUTOMATIC	SPINNING DOFFERS	CARD TENDERS	COMMON LABOR †
July 1933	143%	128%	132%	146%	157%
August 1934	128	112	118	126	127
April 1937	136	122	124	132	137
Sept. 1940	137	120	121	126	113
1943	131	—	130	124	118
1946	115	106	110	110	106
March 1952	116	116	121	122	118
Nov. 1954	109	111	113	114	112

* "North" divided by "South" from 1933 through 1943: "Northeast" divided by "Southeast" in 1946, 1952, and 1954.

† Common labor in 1933 and 1934; scrubbers and sweepers in 1937 and 1940; janitors, sweepers, and cleaners in 1943; janitors in 1946, 1952, and 1954. Definition identical for the two regions in any given year.

Source: BLS wage surveys for respective years

The complicated history of the North-South differential suggests a number of questions. To what extent has the differential been responsible for migration of the industry to the South? What are the main reasons for the persistence of the differential over the course of time? What has been the general strategy of the TWUA toward the differential? Has the decline of the differential since the twenties been due mainly to union and governmental actions or to economic forces? What is the probable future of the differential?

There have been numerous inducements to location of new textile mills in the South, and students of the industry are by no means agreed on their relative importance. The list includes: loans and subsidies offered by local communities anxious to attract new industries; lower local tax rates than in the North, and remission of taxes for new industries in many cases; closeness of raw material supplies, with a consequent saving in transportation; somewhat lower power costs; lower building and heating costs because of the milder climate; an abundant supply of labor, which is an important consideration apart from relative wage rates; the possibility (before 1933) of employing women and young people without the legal restrictions existing in New England; the consequent ease of two-shift and three-shift operation in the South, which means a saving in unit overhead costs; freedom from union restrictions and fixed worker attitudes concerning work loads, work speeds, and output rates; and, finally, the substantial difference in hourly wage rates.

It seems unlikely that the hourly wage differential has been the decisive factor. Other inducements to location in the South are sufficiently strong that the industry would probably have moved in that direction even at equal wage rates. The wage differential obviously reinforced these other considerations, however, and probably speeded up the migration. It is significant that a peak North-South differential in the early twenties was followed by an unusually rapid southward movement.

The development of a substantial wage differential must be attributed mainly to the labor supply situation in the South. It is sometimes argued that southern cotton workers are less efficient and productive than New England workers, and that a wage differential is necessary on this account. In actuality, however, southern workers using identical equipment, with equivalent supervision and other attendant conditions, seem to be fully as productive as northern workers.[21] Nor does it seem that the southern mills have been unable to pay the New England wage level. Operating with newer buildings and machinery, and with the other cost advantages enumerated above, they could probably have achieved lower unit costs than the North even at equal wage rates. With the favorable differential the southern industry has been remarkably profitable, and it is this profitability which has led to its steady expansion.

The reasons for lower southern wages, then, must be sought on the supply rather than the demand side of the labor market. The southern mills, located in rural areas where they were usually the first industry and often remained the only one, have had to compete mainly with the low income levels in agriculture. They have been able to attract plenty of labor by establishing a wage level intermediate between agricultural wages in the South and textile wages in the North. The New England mills, on the other hand, are located in a crowded manufacturing complex with a large proportion of metalworking and other high-wage industries.

The existence of competitive pressure from the South has been a major problem for all unions in the textile industry, and a problem with which they have never been able to deal successfully. The obvious answer is unionization of the southern mills, but failing this neither the TWUA nor its predecessors have been able to have much effect on the

21. See in this connection Lester, "Effectiveness of Factory Labor, South-North Comparisons," *Journal of Political Economy, 54* (February 1946), 60–75.

southern wage level. During the 1940's unionism appeared more effective than it actually was. The TWUA normally filed similar demands at about the same time on union mills both in New England and the South. Filing of these demands was usually the signal for a wave of "voluntary" wage increases by nonunion mills in the South. After settlements were arrived at in the union mills, the remainder of the industry came into line. It appeared, therefore, that the union was the dynamic influence controlling the rate of wage advance throughout the industry as a whole. Actually, however, the willingness of the nonunion mills to raise wages was the controlling factor, and when this diminished the apparent influence of the union disappeared.

The level of southern textile wages at present is determined by decisions of the large nonunion producers. Cannon Mills, in particular, which is a large, progressive, and profitable concern, has long paid close to the highest wages in the South and has had special influence as a wage leader. Without putting the union mills out of competition, the TWUA cannot demand much more in the South than the nonunion mills are willing to give. Even at the peak of union strength in 1946, the wage level of the union mills in the South was only 2 or 3 per cent above that of the nonunion mills.[22] Nor can the unionized mills in New England be pushed too far above the southern level without causing shutdowns and unemployment. The nonunion southern producers, in short, have the whip hand. Their decisions determine the southern wage level and this in turn sets an effective ceiling on the New England wage level.

The professed objective of the TWUA has been elimination of the North-South differential. Lacking power to accomplish this, the union has fallen back on the pragmatic policy of securing as much as possible in each region. It has not been willing to eliminate the differential by holding New England wages constant while pushing up the South. On the contrary it has made the New England mills pay as much above the South as they are able to pay and remain in competition. In the early fifties it was overoptimistic in this regard, pushed New England rates to an untenable level, and was forced to step down again.

The decline in regional differentials over the past thirty years can be explained mainly on economic grounds: the great expansion of the

22. The 1946 BLS survey shows average hourly earnings by occupation and by union or nonunion status of the mill, for New England and the South. In New England the very few nonunion mills were almost exactly at the union level, as might have been expected. In the South the union mills were slightly above for most occupations, the advantage of the union mills ranging from 0 for weavers to 1% for spinning doffers, 3% for janitors and loom fixers, and a top of 5.7% for card grinders. BLS, *Occupational Wage Relationships, Cotton Textiles, 1946*, Series 1, No. 9, p. 11.

industry in the South and the shrinkage of textile employment in New England; the movement of new high-wage industries into the South, forcing textile producers to compete more strenuously for labor; and the general wage-price inflation, which tends to reduce all wage differentials on a percentage basis. Federal regulation contributed to raising southern textile wages more rapidly than northern rates in 1933–34 (NRA), 1939–41 (FLSA), and in 1942–46 (NWLB). Such effect as the union has had on regional differentials has been achieved mainly through exploiting governmental agencies and procedures rather than through collective bargaining.

The question of the future of the differential has diminished in importance as the industry has become basically a southern one, leaving only a fringe of fine-goods production in New England. It seems likely that the New England mills can continue to pay something like 10 per cent above the southern average, this being mainly a type-of-product differential rather than a geographical differential proper. The margin of tolerance can be measured by watching the actual movement of New England and southern rates over the years to come, for it can be assumed that the union will exploit the wage paying ability of the northern mills as fully as possible.

OCCUPATIONAL DIFFERENTIALS

The movement of occupational differentials in the industry from 1920 to 1934 is shown in Table 4-9. Except for a narrowing of differentials at the peak of the postwar boom in 1920 and a slight widening during the 1929–32 depression, the loom fixer-laborer spread remained stable over this period. It was also virtually the same in New England as in the southern states. Scattered data for earlier years back to 1900 suggest that the industry tended to maintain occupational differentials intact by making general wage adjustments on a uniform percentage basis.

Beginning in 1933, collective bargaining and government policy began to affect wage structure to a significant extent. The evolution of the New Bedford scale, traced in Table 4-10, is of interest as a reflection of union policy and a general guide to wage developments in New England. This table shows the differential of the most highly skilled job (loom fixer) and of three semiskilled jobs of varying grades over the lowest jobs in the wage structure. The wage increases resulting from NRA were applied in such a way as to leave occupational differentials unchanged. Indeed, all wage changes in New England from 1933 through 1941 were applied on a uniform percentage basis. This included a 10 per cent increase in 1937, a 12½ per cent cut in 1938, a 7 per cent increase in 1939, and two 10 per cent increases in 1941. This policy left occupational differentials virtually constant except for rerating of individual jobs, the improved position of spinning differs in 1941 being one example of this.

Table 4-9. *Average Hourly Earnings of Loom Fixers as Percentage of Four Lowest-paid Male Occupations, Cotton Textile Industry, 1920–34*

YEAR	NEW ENGLAND	SOUTH ATLANTIC AND ALABAMA
1920	144%	143%
1922	155	154
1924	155	152
1926	157	150
1928	154	149
1930	153	154
1932	157	158
1934	154	150

Source: Hinrichs and Clem, "Historical Review of Wage Rates in the Cotton-Textile Industry" p. 1179

Table 4-10. *Evolution of the New Bedford Scale (base rates for selected occupations as percentage of rate for sweepers)*

DATE	LOOM FIXERS	WEAVERS: PLAIN, AUTOMATIC	SPINNING DOFFERS	CARD TENDERS
July 1933	200%	138%	123%	115%
Nov. 1936	200	138	123	115
Sept. 1941	200	139	133	116
August 1947	151	120	117	108
July 1952	152	121	118	108
March 1955	152	121	118	108

Source: BLS, *Northern Cotton Textile Association*, Series 4, No. 2

In 1942 the National War Labor Board, following a policy of orienting wage increases toward the lowest-paid workers, ordered a general increase of 7½¢ per hour instead of a percentage increase. Additional general increases of 5¢ per hour in 1944, 8¢ in 1945, and 8¢ in 1946 were awarded before the expiration of wage controls. This succession of flat-rate increases necessarily reduced differentials on a percentage basis. Table 4-10 shows that the differentials provided in the New Bedford scale were cut in half between 1941 and 1947.

After the war the TWUA, responding to pressure from employers and perhaps also from skilled groups within its membership, reverted to percentage wage demands. All wage changes in the South since 1946, and in New England since 1947, have been on a percentage basis.[23] Differentials in 1954 thus stood at almost exactly the ′1947 level.

Table 4-10 shows rates only. Table 4-11 shows the course of average hourly earnings in New England for the same key occupations. Earnings have not always moved in close accord with base rates, particularly for the semiskilled workers who are normally paid on an incentive basis. Under the depressed conditions of 1933, the earnings differentials of the skilled and semiskilled workers were considerably less than the rate differentials prescribed by the New Bedford scale. Most New England mills, of course, were not yet covered by the scale at that time. By 1937, with the recovery of production and the extension of the standard scale to other areas, differentials were somewhat wider than the scale required. Earnings differentials shrank somewhat from 1940 to 1946, reflecting the shrinkage in rate differentials, and have remained fairly stable since that time.

Table 4-11. Evolution of Occupational Wage Structure in the New England Cotton Textile Industry, 1933–54 (average hourly earnings of male workers in selected occupations as percentage of sweepers' earnings)

DATE	LOOM FIXERS	WEAVERS: PLAIN, AUTOMATIC	SPINNING DOFFERS	CARD TENDERS
July 1933	189%	120%	105%	116%
August 1934	183	124	116	115
April 1937	207	145	128	124
Sept. 1940	201	141	127	120
1946	167	134	125	113
March 1952	150	130	126	114
Nov. 1954	151	133	115	114

Source: BLS wage surveys. Janitors used in lieu of sweepers in 1946, 1952, and 1954

Over the entire period 1933–54, the only group which has taken an appreciable drop in relative earnings is the loom fixers. The semiskilled machine operatives actually had a larger earnings differential in 1954 than in 1933, despite their reduced differential in base rates. The explanation is that these are piecework occupations, in which the gap between base rate and average hourly earnings is considerably larger than it was twenty years ago. This is a common phenomenon during

23. See BLS, Northern Cotton Textile Association, Series 4, No. 2.

a period of prosperity and labor shortages, which makes for maintenance of piece rates despite technical improvements and a rising level of worker output. It probably also reflects the growing strength of the union in New England, its insistence on a substantial premium for incentive workers, and its ability to prevent rate cuts.

The main effect of the union on the New England wage structure has been to improve the position of the semiskilled pieceworkers, relative to both the laborers and the skilled loom fixers. Some semiskilled jobs previously rated very close to the laboring level have been upgraded substantially over the course of time. Examples of this tendency are the occupations of spinner, spinning doffer, and winder tender. The general level of pieceworkers' *earnings* has also risen relative to the level of base rates, and this is probably due in part to union influence.

The decline in the standing of the loom fixers may be due in part to the fact that this is a highly specialized skill, with little transfer value or bargaining power outside the textile industry. The policy of cents-per-hour increases followed by the NWLB from 1942–46 contributed to a shrinkage of the loom-fixers' differential. The fact that in earlier decades the loom fixers had special protection through craft organization, while more recently they have been only a small component of an industrial union, may also be of some importance. It should be noted that the TWUA sought an unusually large increase for the loom fixers at the time of the 1944 peg-point adjustments, however, and its return to percentage wage adjustments after 1947 has protected the skilled workers' position since that time.

Table 4-12 presents corresponding data for the southern states. The present level of occupational differentials in the South is strikingly similar to that in New England. This was also the case in 1933, as Table 4-9 suggests. The similarity of the 1933 wage structures is veiled in Tables 4-11 and 4-12 by using sweepers, commonly a Negro occupation in the South, as the basis of calculation. If we had used instead the lowest-paid white occupation, the pattern of southern differentials in 1933 would have looked much like that in New England.

The two main developments in the South since 1933 have been the marked decline in the relative position of the skilled loom-fixers and the sharp increase in the relative position of common labor. The laborers' position was first improved by the NRA code, but this proved to be only temporary. The code lapsed after a short time, and by 1937 differentials were wider than they had been before it was adopted. The permanent decline in differentials dates from 1939, when a minimum wage of 32.5 cents per hour was ordered under the Fair Labor Standards Act. Southern employers held down the addition to their wage bills by giving the upper occupational groups much smaller percentage increases than they were compelled to give the lowest groups. The result was a sharp compression of differentials, which is reflected in the 1940 figures. There was a further decline in *rate* differentials as a result of the NWLB's policy of encouraging flat-rate increases during the war years. This accounts for the drop in the loom-fixer ratio between 1940 and 1946. In the case of the incentive occupations, however, any reduced differential in base rates was more than offset by a loosening up of piece rates, and the differential in earnings actually increased slightly between 1940 and 1954.

Table 4-12. Evolution of Occupational Wage Structure in the Southern Cotton Textile Industry, 1933–54 (average hourly earnings of male workers in selected occupations as percentage of sweepers' earnings)

DATE	LOOM FIXERS	WEAVERS: PLAIN, AUTOMATIC	SPINNING DOFFERS	CARD TENDERS
July 1933	230%	163%	138%	138%
August 1934	191	149	132	123
April 1937	232	181	157	143
Sept. 1940	165	132	117	107
1946	154	135	122	110
March 1952	153	135	124	110
Nov. 1954	155	135	123	110

Source: From BLS wage surveys. Janitors used in lieu of sweepers in 1946, 1952, and 1954

The relative improvement of unskilled wage rates in the South was due mainly to economic factors reinforced by government wage policies. The union was influential mainly through its role in shaping government policies, rather than through collective bargaining. It can be argued that both the similarity between the occupational wage structure in New England and the South and the marked similarity between union and nonunion mills within the South are due to nonunion imitation of the union scale, and that the union has actually had more influence than its numerical weakness in the South would suggest. An equally plausible interpretation, however, is that the occupational structure in both regions is normal in terms of the past history of the industry and that the union has not had a marked effect on these historic relationships.

CONCLUDING OBSERVATIONS

Collective bargaining has clearly had a substantial effect on wage relationships in New England. The development and general adoption of the New Bedford scale has provided a yardstick for use in collective bargaining and in wage administration. The ranking of individual occupations has been changed somewhat, and has been made uniform from mill to mill. The relative standing of the semiskilled machine tenders, who form the bulk of the industry's employees, has been improved by lifting their hourly earnings farther above the plant minimum. The large differential of the loom fixers has diminished considerably. The wage levels of different mills throughout New England have been substantially equalized, and without producing the dire consequences which many employers had predicted. The union was fortunate, of course, in being able to carry through its wage-rationalization program during a ten-year boom which enabled even the weaker firms to adjust to higher cost levels.

In the South collective bargaining has had much less effect on the wage structure. The extension of a modified New Bedford scale to many union mills in the South in 1944–45 provided a yardstick for occupational wage relationships and also brought the wage levels of these mills closer together. There was also some imitation of the union scale by nonunion mills, though this tapered off rapidly after 1949 or so. The main way in which the union has influenced the southern wage structure, however, has been by promoting government wage regulation. Successive increases in minimum wage standards, of which the TWUA has been one of the most vigorous proponents, have caused important changes in occupational and interplant differentials within the South.

In the matter of the North-South differential, too, the influence of collective bargaining has been secondary to that of government action. Minimum wage regulations, sponsored by the union, have contributed appreciably to a narrowing of the differential since 1933. On the collective bargaining side, unionism may well have operated to widen the differential because it is able to exact the maximum feasible wage in New England, but unable to do so in the South. In the absence of unionism, New England textile wages would probably sink closer to the southern level than they now are.

The limited effect of collective bargaining on textile wages reflects the weakness of union organization in the South. It is interesting to speculate about what might happen if the southern mills were ever to become fully unionized. The major effect would doubtless be the installation of something like the New Bedford scale throughout the South and a sharp reduction of interplant wage dispersion. This would be upsetting to the lower-wage mills for the time being. Experience in New England textiles and in other industries suggests, however, that the southern mills could adapt to a standard wage level, particularly if the transition were made at a time of high prosperity. While occupational relationships would be standardized from mill to mill, there is no reason to think that the average level of occupational differentials would be very much changed. The union has shown itself willing to go along with the traditional practice of uniform percentage increases, which maintain occupational differentials intact over time. The North-South differential would probably be narrowed but it is unlikely that it would be eliminated, for the union would doubtless continue to exploit the wage paying ability of each region as fully as possible. The New England fine-goods mills can probably stand a wage level slightly above the South and still survive.

The effects of full unionization, in short, would probably be less spectacular than either its friends or its critics maintain. An opportunity to test this hypothesis, however, probably lies a good many years in the future.

CHAPTER 5 *Pulp and Paper*

BY ROBERT M. MACDONALD [1]

THE INDUSTRY AND THE UNIONS

THE pulp and paper industry comprises all plants engaged in the manufacture of pulp from materials yielding cellulose fiber, and of paper and board from this pulp. The industry so defined covers the manufacture of five different kinds of wood pulp and a wide variety of papers and boards. The wood pulps are distinguished according to their method of production: groundwood pulp is produced by a mechanical (grinding) process; sulphite, sulphate, and soda pulps are produced by a chemical process, the difference being in the type of cooking liquor used to prepare the fibers; and semichemical pulp is produced by a combination of chemical and mechanical processes. In addition, a small amount of pulp is manufactured for special uses from rag, straw, jute, and cotton lintners.

Thousands of grades of paper and board can be distinguished as to character and quality, but the vast majority can be classified under a few broad categories. Thus newsprint, groundwood, book, tissue, writing, and wrapping papers constitute the basic types of paper produced, while container, bending, and building boards are the principal types of board. Newsprint and groundwood papers are made primarily from groundwood pulp mixed with a relatively small amount of sulphite pulp, the proportions used varying with the quality of paper desired. Coarse wrapping and bag papers and container board—often referred to as "kraft" products—use large quantities of sulphate pulp as raw material, though certain grades of wrapping paper (principally the finer qualities such as glassine and greaseproof) have a high sulphite-pulp content. Book and tissue papers and the lower grades of writing paper are manufactured from sulphite pulp, but with varying proportions of bleached sulphate, soda, and groundwood pulp added to the mixture. Rag pulp is used mainly in the production of fine, high-quality writing papers, while substantial quantities of wastepaper and other

1. Mr. Macdonald is Assistant Professor in the Department of Economics and Assistant Research Economist in the Institute of Industrial Relations, University of California, Los Angeles. Chapter 6, which is a continuation of Chapter 5, was also written by Mr. Macdonald. The study is part of a dissertation presented for the degree of Doctor of Philosophy in Yale University (1955).

fibrous materials are combined with varying amounts of new wood pulp in the manufacture of most types of board.

This brief and oversimplified description of the products manufactured in pulp and paper plants suggests that the industry is in reality a group of related industries. The essential similarity of production techniques and basic raw materials, however, together with the prevalence of multi-product producers and the possibilities of grade shifting, justifies treatment of these several "branch" industries as an interrelated whole.

The pulp and paper industry is the sixth largest manufacturing industry in the United States measured either by value of shipments or by value added in manufacture. In 1951 it was estimated to have total assets in excess of 6.5 billion dollars, an annual productive capacity of 25.3 million tons, and an employment force of 223,000 workers.[2] The typical work force in the industry's mills is of only moderate size. The average paper mill in 1947 employed only 223 workers, and few mills had a labor force exceeding 1,000 employees.[3] The industry, moreover, is widely dispersed geographically and the majority of its production units are located in small, semirural communities. In 1952 there were 766 paper mills and 260 pulp mills in operation, and these were distributed throughout 39 of the 48 states.[4] No community-size data are available for recent years, but in 1940, 83 per cent of the mills were located in communities with populations of less than 50,000 and 58 per cent were in communities below 10,000.[5]

Essential to an understanding of industry operations, problems, and policies is a knowledge of the characteristics of demand for and supply of the industry's products. These characteristics are discussed briefly below.

The demand for pulp and most types of paper is relatively inelastic in the short run. While demand varies directly with fluctuations in business activity, cyclical fluctuations in paper consumption are moderate compared with those in many other industries. Most studies of the industry have emphasized the relatively high degree of stability which characterizes demand (and output).[6] The consumption of paper has

2. Estimates of assets and capacity are from American Paper and Pulp Association (APPA), *A Capital and Income Survey of the United States Pulp and Paper Industry, 1939–1951* (New York, 1952); and of employment from BLS, *Employment, Hours, and Earnings, 1951.*

3. *Census of Manufactures* (1947), 2, 315.

4. Post's *Paper Mill Directory* (New York, 1952 edition).

5. APPA, *Presentation of the United States Pulp and Paper Manufacturers before the Senate Subcommittee on Trade Policies* (New York, Nov. 30, 1948), Appendix 1, p. 1.

6. See, e.g., Geo. S. Armstrong & Co., Inc., "The Pulp and Board Industry," in *An Engineering Interpretation of the Economic and Financial Aspects of American*

shown spectacular growth in recent decades as a result of population increase, the development and exploitation of new markets, and the more widespread adoption of paper in its manifold uses. In other words, demand in the industry is characterized by low price elasticity, moderate sensitivity to cyclical fluctuations, and a rising growth trend.

On the supply side, several important characteristics should be noted. Prior to World War II, the outstanding problems of the industry were excess capacity and grade shifting. Between 1919 and 1939 the industry operated at an average level of production which was only 75 per cent of capacity, and in no single year did the production-capacity ratio exceed 84 per cent.[7] Since the war this situation has improved markedly, but excess capacity is still regarded as the normal condition in most branches of the industry. As a consequence, supply is usually quite elastic in the short run, though it becomes very inelastic once excess capacity has been absorbed. An important point to note in this connection, however, is the possibility of grade shifting. In the short run, excess capacity in one branch of the industry may be transferred to the production of another grade or type of paper that is experiencing a more favorable demand. There are of course limits to this shifting process, but generally speaking the possibilities are sufficiently great to require that paper producers take account of potential as well as actual competition in the formulation of their price policies.[8]

Relative price movements arising from changes in demand are not the only inducement to grade shifting. The latter also occurs in response to technological developments. Thus grade shifting appears as part of a gradual and continuous process of adjustment to normal progress and expansion. As new mills, incorporating the latest improvements in method and design, are put into operation in the mass-production fields (e.g. newsprint, wrapping, and board), the older marginal mills—unless they can raise their efficiency—are forced into the production of other types and grades of paper where the premium on machine size and speed is lower and markets are less suited to large-scale production. In this way the older, high-cost mills have been crowded gradually into the fine-paper and specialty-paper branches of the industry. Since paper machines are practically indestructible and cannot be transferred to other uses, many of these old mills remain in operation for very long intervals, continuing to produce so long as they can reap a return in excess of variable costs.

Industry, 9 (New York, 1951), 16; BLS, *Report on the Pulp and Primary Paper Industry* (March 18, 1940), p. 27; and Spurgeon Bell, *Productivity, Wages and National Income* (Washington, D.C., The Brookings Institution, 1940), p. 122.

7. APPA, *The Statistics of Paper* (New York, 1952), p. 55.

8. Louis T. Stevenson, *The Background and Economics of American Papermaking* (New York, Harper, 1940), p. 142.

Pulp and paper production requires a heavy capital investment in buildings and equipment—and, frequently, in timber reserves. In 1944, for example, it was estimated to require an investment of nearly $20,-000 of total assets to put an employee to work; and the average investment per ton of daily capacity ranged from $27,000 for market-pulp mills to $44,000 for integrated-paper mills.[9] This large investment in fixed assets, together with relatively low capital-turnover rates,[10] means that fixed costs constitute a substantial part of total costs. Consequently there is constant pressure upon individual producers to operate their mills close to capacity because of the large unit cost reductions to be gained through expansion of output and sales.

In an industry faced with an inelastic product demand, high fixed costs, and a tendency toward overexpansion, it is not surprising that producers should have sought means to restrain competition and stabilize prices. This has taken the form of price leadership, zone-delivered pricing, open-price filing, and quota restrictions.[11] Studies of price policies during the last few decades indicate, however, that while the tendency toward cutthroat price competition in periods of declining activity has been fairly successfully curbed, along with the opposite tendency toward runaway price inflation in times of excessive demand,[12] most attempts to regulate prices closely "have proved unsuccessful because of the vigorous opposition shown by consumers and federal anti-trust agencies, and also because of inherent characteristics of the industry which make difficult the successful restriction of price competition."[13]

The implications of these structural characteristics of the industry for wages and employment will be dealt with in later sections, but one or two points are worth noting here. In the first place, relative stability of output and the phenomenal growth of consumption in recent decades have combined to create a favorable employment situation in the industry. The effect of these factors is revealed in the comparative employment indices (1923–25 = 100) that follow.[14]

9. APPA, *A Capital and Income Survey of the United States Pulp and Paper Industry, 1934–1944* (New York, 1946), pp. 3, 11, 15–18.

10. APPA, *A Capital and Income Survey of the United States Pulp and Paper Industry, 1939–1951*, pp. 6–7.

11. Cf. John A. Guthrie, "Price Regulation in the Paper Industry," *Quarterly Journal of Economics, 60,* No. 2 (Feb. 1946), 194–218; and Guthrie, *The Economics of Pulp and Paper* (Pullman, Washington, The State College of Washington Press, 1950), pp. 111–14.

12. U. S. Dept. of Commerce, *Transportation Factors in the Marketing of Newsprint,* Transportation Series No. 2 (Washington, 1952), pp. 93–4.

13. Guthrie, *The Economics of Pulp and Paper,* p. 114.

14. U. S. Department of Commerce, *Supplement to the Survey of Current Business* (1940–50).

Year	Pulp and Paper	All Manufacturing	Nondurable Manufacturing
1929	106.1	106.0	105.9
1932	81.9	66.3	79.2
1937	114.3	108.8	112.6
1938	106.1	92.6	103.8
1943	132.7	188.6	133.4
1946	154.8	152.0	139.6
1948	175.0	159.7	142.2
1949	164.2	145.7	134.6
1950	170.0	154.0	138.1

It is clear that employment in the pulp and paper industry has been stable and expanding compared with employment in general.

Secondly, consideration of the part played by labor in the production of pulp and paper suggests that the demand for most types of labor is quite inelastic. Several factors point in this direction: the demand for the industry's products is relatively inelastic; labor requirements are largely fixed by the nature and size of mill equipment; and labor costs are a relatively small proportion of total costs—10 to 25 per cent, depending on the type of mill. The demand for common labor is perhaps less inelastic than that for other types of labor because of the possibilities of substitution. It is at this level—the handling of materials in woodyards and pulp mills—that the greatest opportunities would seem to exist for the installation of labor-saving devices. To the extent that substitution does occur, however, it is a long-run rather than short-run process; and any displacement of labor is likely to be more than offset by the expansion of job opportunities due to increasing product demand.

The above conditions underlying the demand for labor in the industry suggest that the unions are in a strong bargaining position with respect to wage matters. This view is essentially correct; though, as shown in subsequent sections, it requires some modification in the light of other considerations.

Trade unionism made its first appearance in the paper industry in 1893 when the AFL issued a charter to the United Brotherhood of Paper Makers, an organization for skilled paper-machine operators only. When this membership base proved too narrow for effective organization, jurisdiction was extended to cover all workers on paper machines and, eventually, all workers in the industry. The skilled papermakers continued to dominate the union, however, and their craft-conscious policies soon resulted in a serious conflict of interest within the organization. This culminated in the withdrawal of the pulpworkers in 1906 and the formation of a rival organization, the International Brotherhood of Pulp and Sulphite Workers, which claimed jurisdiction over all pulpworkers and such paper-mill workers as were not paper-machine operators. Three years of bitter warfare ensued before it was finally realized that further jurisdictional strife would simply destroy all organization in the industry. Accordingly, peace was declared and an agreement entered into in 1909 which defined respective jurisdictions of the two unions—the International Brotherhood of Paper Makers (IBPM) and the International Brotherhood of Pulp, Sulphite, and Paper Mill Workers (IBPSPMW)—and established the basis for their joint and harmonious functioning in the industry.

Both organizations prospered under this arrangement and made impressive gains in membership, particularly during the boom years 1917-20. They suffered severe setbacks in the postwar depression of 1921–22 and were only beginning to recover when depression again struck in 1929–30. It is difficult to obtain accurate estimates of the extent of organization in pulp and paper mills at this time, but total U.S. membership in the two unions could not have been much in excess of 9,000 —or less than 10 per cent of industry employment.

The depression years were sad ones for the unions: membership was low and declining, finances were poor, and there was widespread fear that organization could not survive. These lean years were brought to an abrupt halt with the enactment of the NRA and the NLRA. The reaction of the paper unions to this favorable legislation was immediate. New locals sprang up rapidly not only in the older papermaking regions of the Northeast and Lake states but also in the newer regions of the Pacific Coast and the South. By 1935 the proportion of the industry's workers in labor unions had nearly doubled; and by 1938 it approached 35 per cent.[15] This expansion was not to go unchallenged, however, for the year 1937–38 saw the entry of other organizations into the industry in direct competition with incumbent unions. The vigorous organizing campaigns conducted by these rivals—particularly the United Paper Workers of America (CIO)[16] and District 50 of the United Mine Workers—presented a serious threat to the stability and growth of the two AFL brotherhoods, forcing a change in tactics, a relaxation of juris-

15. This ratio is based on estimates made by the writer. Total membership figures, as reported in convention proceedings, were adjusted to eliminate membership outside the United States or in the paper products industry. The adjusted figure for the two unions was 45,000. This figure understates over-all union membership in one important respect in that no allowance is made for employees represented by other unions.

16. This title was conferred only in 1946, the year in which the CIO issued a national charter to the Paperworkers Organizing Committee.

dictional lines, and a renewal of efforts to consolidate the two organizations into a single industrial union.

By the end of the war, however, any immediate danger from these aggressive rivals appeared to have passed. Both AFL unions had made remarkable progress as separate, though closely cooperating, organizations and had regained confidence in their ability to contain the activities of rival groups. The idea of amalgamation was consequently shelved in the late forties before any definite plans had been formulated. In recent years the AFL paper unions have concerned themselves mainly with the activities of the UPA-CIO. This union gained sizable representation rights during the early years of its existence—particularly in the CIO industrial belt running westward from New York to Chicago—and though at present it poses no imminent threat to AFL dominance, it remains nevertheless a dangerous potential aggressor.

Estimates of the present strength of trade unionism in the industry are necessarily little more than approximations. The number of unions in the industry and the fact that part of their reported membership lies outside the United States or in industries other than pulp and paper precludes accurate measurement. On the basis of available evidence, however, U.S. membership in the "big four" unions in 1951 may be conservatively estimated at 158,000.[17] Allowing an additional 15 per cent for workers belonging to craft unions, independent unions, and federal locals, this estimate is raised to 181,000, which was approximately four-fifths of the industry's labor force in 1951. Union membership has thus grown from 10 per cent to more than 80 per cent of industry employment in the period since the depression.

Union-management relations in the industry have been for the most part highly satisfactory, measured by any of the customary standards of performance. The two AFL paper unions, which represent the vast ma-

17. This figure is made up as follows:

IBPM-AFL	58,500
IBPSPMW-AFL	62,000
UPA-CIO	25,000
District 50, UMW	12,500
TOTAL	158,000

The basic membership statistics were drawn from the following sources: *Proceedings of the Twentieth Convention,* IBPM (March 1952), p. 16; *Proceedings of the Twenty-Second Convention,* IBPSPMW (August 1950), Report to the Executive Board; A. E. Greening, *Paper Makers in Canada: A Record of Fifty Years' Achievement* (Cornwall, Ontario, IBPM, 1952), p. 78; and BLS, *Directory of Labor Unions in the United States,* Bulletin 1127, pp. 14, 24, and 26. Additional data supplied by officials of the three major unions.

jority of employees in union mills, bargain with most employers under circumstances of mutual trust and confidence. They accept the capitalist system of private ownership and operation of business and recognize management's "right to manage." In turn, the majority of employers have accepted the principle of trade unionism, and many have played a constructive role in the development of a cooperative program. The quality of these relations is reflected in union-management agreements, which are characteristically short and straightforward and are comparatively free of detailed and encumbering protective clauses.

Most collective agreements in the industry are negotiated separately between the unions and individual plant managements; there are, however, several important agreements which extend beyond the boundaries of the single plant and which significantly influence labor policy. Some of these cover a number of companies in the same area. Thus a single agreement covers over 90 per cent of the plants (and employees) on the Pacific Coast, while two other agreements cover respectively a group of eight "rag" writing-paper companies in the Holyoke district of Massachusetts and a group of four "rag" writing-paper companies in Wisconsin. Other important agreements cover a number of plants belonging to the same company. Indeed, the multi-plant bargaining unit is the prevalent unit among companies with more than one plant in the same region. Altogether perhaps a fifth to a quarter of the industry's work force is covered by some form of multi-company, company-wide, or multi-plant agreement.

There may be one, two, or several unions party to these collective agreements. The two AFL paper unions negotiate jointly and sign a single contract in all mills where bargaining rights are shared. They may be joined in this agreement by any of the several craft unions which have managed to secure representation rights over part or all of the maintenance force. These craft unions may also choose to execute their own agreements with employers, either individually or jointly. Thus a wide variety of agreements are to be found in the industry not only with respect to the area covered but also with respect to the number and type of unions involved.

The pulp and paper industry, like most industries, has had its share of labor-management disputes, but it has remained relatively free of strikes during the last two decades. Such strikes as have occurred have been of relatively short duration and have involved only a few workers. A number of factors help to explain this record. In the first place, the period of union strength has been, for the most part, a period during which the industry was expanding and papermaking was a relatively profitable undertaking. It has been possible for most employers to grant improvements in wages and working conditions without seriously imperiling their sales and profit positions. Secondly, leaders of the major unions have followed a conservative and cautious program, based on a thorough knowledge of how the industry operates under widely varying conditions. This experience has taught them the limitations as well as the uses of the strike weapon. The devastating effects of strike activities in the twenties, when the membership and finances of both unions (particularly the Pulp Workers) were nearly destroyed, are well remembered and have led to the adoption of a more flexible and realistic policy, which recognizes the need for occasional strategic retreats in the matter of wage negotiations. Finally, since most mills are located in small, isolated, dependent communities, there are few if any alternative job opportunities for striking workers, and shutdown of the mills often threatens the livelihood of an entire community. Union officials have therefore been careful to exhaust all possible means of peaceful settlement before granting official recognition to strike requests.[18]

The essential elements of wage policy are discussed below in sections dealing with the wage structure, but a few preliminary remarks about policy formulation are in order at this point. Union wage policy in the pulp and paper industry is centralized in that the international unions exercise a fairly large measure of control over the formulation of policy and the conduct of negotiations. This centralization, however, has not led to uniform wage demands for the industry as a whole. On the contrary, union officials are firmly convinced that in an industry as diversified as pulp and paper, demands cannot be set at the national level. While the executive boards of the two major unions are empowered to call national wage conferences for the purpose of formulating policy, it is probably correct to say that essential decisions are made at international headquarters in consultation with international and regional staff members. These staff officials are constantly in touch with local unions and thus are able to represent the views and sentiments of rank-and-file members. At the same time they attend all regional conferences of local unions and all negotiating sessions, where, under general instructions from headquarters, they are able to influence agreements along lines consistent with over-all union policy. A balance of authority is maintained in part by the requirement that all agreements must be approved by the local unions concerned and by the international union, but disciplinary powers rest exclusively with the latter and strikes are forbidden unless authorized by the executive board.

While the unions have avoided promulgating a uniform wage policy for the industry as a whole, they have shown a tendency to establish fairly uniform policies for the mills within each major producing region.

18. Legislation of the mid-thirties and diminishing employer opposition (partly as a result of this legislation) removed, of course, some of the causes of strike action.

Practices differ somewhat between the various regions, but the general strategy is for leaders of the two internationals to supervise (or conduct) negotiations with certain key companies in each region where individual bargaining prevails. The terms so arrived at become the standard or pattern for negotiations in other plants, though international field officers and local officials are allowed some discretion with respect to actual settlements.

The position of employers on wage matters, though governed primarily by economic considerations, is quite complex. Generally speaking, employers are industry oriented in the formulation of their wage policies. Because of the competitive nature of the industry they tend to stress the wage position of competitors and the wage concessions granted in competing mills. Indeed, equalization of wage competition has played an important role in the development of multi-company bargaining; and similar interests have encouraged many companies to participate in studies and surveys of wages and working conditions within particular areas and regions and within particular competing groups.

OCCUPATIONAL DIFFERENTIALS

In the pulp and paper industry, the appropriate measure of wage level is the hourly wage rate.[19] Analysis of occupational differentials and of the impact of collective bargaining upon these differentials can therefore be confined to the issues involved in determining relative hourly wage rates.

The evolution of the occupational wage rate structure in pulp and paper mills during the period 1934–51 is summarized in Table 5-1. It will be noted that the data are weighted average hourly rates for key occupations within each major producing region rather than actual hourly wage rates in individual plants. The broad changes revealed in the movement of these regional averages reflect, however, the developments characteristic of virtually all mills for which separate wage rate data are available. Moreover, it is evident from a study of individual plant wage structures that the most important source of variation in occupational differentials among plants is regional location. The use of regional rather than national averages removes the danger of distortions arising from this source.

---

19. Incentive earnings are received by less than 10% of employees in the industry and are limited for the most part to specific occupation groups—primarily finishing-room personnel. Moreover, the vast majority of plants have formally established "single-rate" wage structures based on job requirements rather than on individual qualifications. Consequently, problems of incentive payments, individually determined rates, and rate ranges are of little importance in the industry.

The most significant developments in the occupational wage structure during the period in question can be summarized briefly. First, there
has been a very marked decrease in differentials in all the subperiods
considered, and particularly after the late 1930's.[20] The average wage
rate for the skilled machine tender in northern regions was twice as
high as that for common labor in 1934, but only two-fifths to one-half
higher by 1952. Similarly, in the South, the average machine tender's
rate was three-and-a-half times as high as the average common-labor
rate in 1934, but only twice as high in 1952.[21] In other words, in less
than two decades the relative spread between the lowest and highest
wage rates in the mills has been reduced by more than half through
successive improvements in the relative wage position of the unskilled
worker.

Secondly, the wage levels of skilled maintenance workers have suffered less in the general narrowing of the structure than the wage levels
of the skilled paperworkers. Indeed, the differential between maintenance-
craftsmen's rates and common-labor rates has been reduced only during the forties, primarily in the postwar years. A comparison of trends
in Table 5-1 shows that while millwrights' rates have fallen relative to
unskilled rates, they have risen relative to the rates for the highly skilled,
highly paid machine tenders and back tenders. These are the general
developments for which an explanation is sought in the following analysis.

The primary objective of this study is to examine the impact of
unions and collective bargaining upon the wage structure. Consequently
it is well to begin by examining the objectives of union and company
wage policies and the manner in which these policies interact to determine the relative wage rates for the different occupations. This will
be followed by a brief discussion of other factors which may be expected
to play a part in the shaping of differentials.

Union wage policy since the depression of the early thirties has generally favored the improvement of relative wage levels for the lower-
paid, unskilled workers in the industry. In order to appreciate fully
the role of unionism during this period, however, it is necessary to consider briefly the course of events prior to the depression. There is every
indication that the impact of the unions in earlier years may have been

20. One exception worth noting was the very substantial reduction that occurred
in Pacific Coast mills between 1934 and 1938.
21. The trend was similar in Central Zone mills. Plant wage structures in this
area appear to follow either the northern or the southern pattern, depending largely
on the type of product manufactured. (See section on interplant differentials, below,
pp. 129–48.

Table 5-1. *Average Hourly Wage Rates for Selected Pulp and Paper Occupations and Relative Wage Rate Levels, by Region,** 1934–52*

OCCUPATION	AVERAGE HOURLY WAGE RATES † (DOLLARS)					RELATIVE WAGE RATE LEVELS (COMMON LABOR = 100)				
	1934	1938	1941	1945	1952	1934	1938	1941	1945	1952
NEW ENGLAND										
Common labor	.422	.521	.569	.689	1.27	100	100	100	100	100
Beatermen	.459	.607	.638	.755	1.35	109	117	112	109	106
Third hands	.544	.586	.695	.821	1.44	129	112	122	119	113
Millwrights	.580	.690	.801	.940	1.58	137	132	141	136	124
Back tenders	.617	.743	.778	.919	1.54	146	143	137	133	121
Machine tenders	.843	.983	.988	1.103	1.75	200	189	174	160	138
MIDDLE ATLANTIC STATES										
Common labor	.415	.506	.575	.701	1.30	100	100	100	100	100
Beatermen	.444	.605	.652	.768	1.45	107	120	113	110	112
Third hands	.532	.531	.700	.816	1.48	128	105	122	116	114
Millwrights	.577	.723	.821	.965	1.63	139	143	143	138	125
Back tenders	.626	.749	.791	.922	1.62	151	148	138	132	125
Machine tenders	.813	.948	.977	1.131	1.88	196	187	168	161	145
LAKE AND CENTRAL STATES										
Common labor	.424	.520	.591	.722	1.35	100	100	100	100	100
Beatermen	.462	.601	.675	.813	1.54	109	116	114	113	114
Third hands	.519	.633	.681	.873	1.57	122	122	115	121	116
Millwrights	.579	.715	.819	.978	1.76	137	137	137	135	130
Back tenders	.613	.764	.836	.996	1.73	145	147	141	138	128
Machine tenders	.818	.975	1.048	1.209	1.99	193	187	176	167	147

	PACIFIC COAST									
Common labor	.459	.639	.759	.909	1.67	100	100	100	100	100
Beatermen	.483	.672	.801	.953	1.75	105	105	106	105	105
Third hands	.625	.739	.931	1.086	1.92	136	116	123	119	115
Millwrights	.650	.865	1.068	1.233	2.10	142	135	141	136	126
Back tenders	.764	.958	1.078	1.221	2.14	166	150	142	134	128
Machine tenders	.928	1.122	1.255	1.399	2.39	202	176	165	154	143
	CENTRAL ZONE ‡									
Common labor	.364	.403		.655	1.22	100	100		100	100
Beatermen	.405	.715		.930	1.27	111	177		142	104
Third hands	.473	.478		.838	1.41	130	119		128	116
Millwrights	—	.709		1.031	1.74	—	176		157	143
Back tenders	.600	.746		1.002	1.61	165	185		153	132
Machine tenders	.820	1.006		1.253	1.85	225	250		191	152
	SOUTHERN ZONE ‡									
Common labor	.307	.379	.496	.628	1.23	100	100	100	100	100
Beatermen	.360	.556	.631	.746	1.39	117	147	127	119	113
Third hands	.696	.626	.962	1.117	1.92	227	165	193	178	156
Millwrights	.592	.794	.949	1.213	2.02	193	209	190	193	164
Back tenders	.855	.983	.979	1.246	2.11	279	259	194	198	172
Machine tenders	1.070	1.253	1.246	1.526	2.41	349	331	251	243	196

* New England: Conn., Me., Mass., N.H., R.I., and Vt.; Middle Atlantic: N.J., N.Y., and Pa.; Lake and Central States: Ill., Ind., Ia., Mich., Minn., O., and Wis.; Pacific Coast: Cal., Ore., and Wash.; Central Zone: Del., D.C., Ky., Md., N.C., Tenn., Va., and W.Va.; Southern Zone: Ala., Ark., Fla., Ga., La., Miss., S.C., and Tex.

† Wage data are for Sept. 1934, Jan. 1938, Nov. 1941, Nov. 1945, and April 1952. Data for this last year are average straight-time hourly earnings rather than average hourly wage rates.

‡ Southern and Central zones are combined for Nov. 1941.

Source: 1934-45 data: APPA, Survey of Occupational Wage Rates in the Pulp and Paper Industry (1934, 1938, 1941, 1945); 1952 data: BLS, Wage Structure, Series 2, No. 91, Table 6

quite different—namely, in the direction of maintaining, and even increasing, occupational differentials.

When unionism first entered the industry, membership was confined exclusively to the highly paid and experienced machine tenders and beater engineers. The former had the power to hire and fire the unskilled members of the machine crew, and there is ample evidence that they thought only in terms of their own interests in negotiations with employers.[22] Nor was this attitude much affected by extension of the union's constitution to other categories of workers in the early part of the century, as witness the withdrawal of the pulp and sulphite workers in 1906. Although no wage data are available for these early years, it would seem reasonable to assume that differentials were actually widened in union mills.

Following the accord of 1909, both unions gained in strength and secured substantial wage improvements, particularly during the sharp inflation of the postwar years. When business activity declined in 1921, however, prices fell off drastically and employers immediately sought a 30 per cent reduction in wage rates. The unions fought this wage cut vigorously, with the result that two-thirds of their membership were on strike by the middle of the year.[23] In order to break the deadlock, a large group of Canadian and American companies finally agreed to arbitrate the wage issue. The award of the arbitration board, handed down in August 1921, called for a reduction of only 10 per cent in the wage rates of workers receiving 60 cents or more an hour compared with a reduction of $16\frac{2}{3}$ per cent for those receiving less than 60 cents. Furthermore, as Greening points out, "the final settlement was even worse for the unskilled and lower paid workers, since the wages of all employees who received less than 50 cents an hour were to be cut by 8 cents an hour." [24] These wage reductions, which were based on the findings of a union-management committee, certainly served to increase differentials in union mills.

A year later, at the time of the 1922 negotiations, this same group of mills offered to renew contracts with the skilled employees but refused to sign agreements for common labor on the grounds that such labor could be hired more cheaply at the "market price." According to the president of the Pulp Workers (the union representing the bulk of unskilled labor in the mills), the skilled trades, principally the Paper Makers, accepted this proposal and signed agreements for their membership, leaving the unskilled groups to their own devices.[25] This action also tended to widen the gap in differentials.

22. See Greening, *Paper Makers in Canada*, pp. 7–8.
23. IBPSPMW, *Proceedings of the Sixteenth Convention* (March 1935), pp. 2–3.
24. *Paper Makers in Canada*, p. 20.
25. IBPSPMW, *Proceedings of the Sixteenth Convention*, pp. 3–4.

Such evidence of the course of events up to the early twenties, although suggestive, is too fragmentary to yield definitive conclusions. The complete absence of wage statistics for the years preceding the depression prevents the testing of any hypothesis concerning relative wage movements. Some data are available for union mills in Ontario, and these reveal that the differential between the average rates for skilled machine tenders and unskilled fifth hands (expressed as a per cent of the fifth hands' rate) rose from 113 per cent in 1922 to 129 per cent in 1930 and thereafter declined fairly steadily to 77 per cent in 1950.[26] While it is not unreasonable to assume that developments in union mills in the northeastern United States were roughly parallel—since, after all, mills in these two areas manufacture the same product, compete in the same market, are organized by the same unions, and may be owned (or financed) by the same companies—the lack of specific wage data for individual mills not only prevents comparisons between the two groups but leaves in doubt the precise nature of relative wage rate movements in the Ontario mills. The twenties witnessed a great expansion of newsprint capacity in lower eastern Canada, and this in itself may have brought about a rise in the relative wage levels of skilled papermakers, either through the need for attracting such workers from other areas (mostly, the United States) or through progressive increases in the average size and speed of machines, which normally lead to greater proportionate increases for skilled than for unskilled machine-crew workers.[27] On this last point, however, it is important to note that machine improvements were also a feature of the postdepression years, and yet machine-crew differentials decreased markedly during this period. All in all, therefore, despite the flimsy nature of the evidence it would appear that unionism certainly did not contribute to any narrowing of differentials in predepression decades, and may in fact have tended to increase them.

The depression of the early thirties witnessed a dramatic shift in overall union policy and in the impact of collective bargaining upon plant wage structures. The skilled papermakers—for reasons explained below—aligned themselves with the less skilled pulpworkers to protect wage levels at the lower end of the scale. Widespread unemployment and the threat of still further joblessness eventually forced the unions to accept successive wage cuts of 7 to 10 per cent in 1931, 10 per cent in 1932, and approximately 7 per cent in 1933; but, in contrast to the situation in 1921, the largest part of these reductions was borne by the highest-paid workers. Thus the president of the Pulp Workers reported that "in most union mills, there was only a 10 per cent reduc-

26. Greening, *Paper Makers in Canada*, pp. 25, 31, 77.
27. See the discussion below of the Paper Makers' Standard Minimum Wage Schedule.

tion off the base rate" during this period; [28] and this report was confirmed in a statement by the secretary of the Paper Makers that, throughout the depression, "the manipulation of reductions was handled in such a way that the minimum of the low-paid workers in the industry . . . dropped from forty cents down to thirty-five cents per hour." [29]

The change in attitude on the part of the Paper Makers was not motivated solely by an altruistic concern for the plight of the lower-paid worker. Self-interest and expediency were also involved. Many papermakers were beginning to accept the view that high common-labor or base rates were a necessary foundation for high wage structures at the same time that workers in the lower-skilled categories were demanding a wage policy more conducive to their interests. The Executive Board of the IBPM recognized this new situation in its report to the 1935 convention:

> The Paper Makers' Organization is primarily a skilled workers' organization. Throughout the years of its existence it has dealt with the wage structure of the paper industry in terms of craftsmanship. We established the rates for the skilled men first and then by creating differentials downward between the varying degrees of skill and responsibilities attendant to each job or class of work we succeeded in building a good rate for the man at the bottom of the group.
>
> In recent months, or since we moved into new divisions of the industry, we find that the base rate now fixed by law has a tendency to pull down all the semi-skilled rates to the base rate and this situation makes it difficult for us to establish our traditional rates for the men who man the paper machines. The opposition comes mostly from the men at the bottom of the group.[30]

To understand how these new attitudes and pressures affected the wage policy of the IBPM, it is necessary to consider them in conjunction with the union's Standard Minimum Wage Schedule. This schedule, which represents in a sense an "ideal" structure of wage rates from the union's point of view, can be presumed to reflect the basic orientation of the Paper Makers toward relative wage levels. It was designed originally (in 1915) as a wage scale for skilled paper-machine operators in the newsprint branch of the industry. The wage rates for machine tenders, back tenders, and third hands were graduated according to the width and speed of the paper machines, so that the larger and/or faster the machine, the higher the rates for these three occupations. Any increase in wire width or operating speed which placed a machine

28. IBPSPMW, *Proceedings of the Sixteenth Convention*, p. 16.
29. IBPM, *Proceedings of the Fourteenth Convention* (March 1935), p. 126.
30. *Ibid.*, pp. 53–4.

in a higher classification was grounds for an upward adjustment of wage rates. During the depression, however, it became quite evident that other workers under the Paper Makers' jurisdiction were dissatisfied with an arrangement which awarded efficiency increases to skilled machine operators only. As a consequence, a flood of resolutions were presented at the 1935 convention which resulted in extension of the "graduation" principle to the wage rates for unskilled machine-crew members. Subsequent revisions gradually brought other occupations under the scale, and recent developments indicate that the process is continuing.[31]

The most interesting feature of the schedule as it has developed in recent years, however, is the manner in which it appears to reflect a compromise between old and new attitudes toward occupational differentials. The basic structure of the schedule continues to emphasize the interests of the highly skilled worker, while revisions of the schedule over time reveal acceptance of the principle of higher relative rates for the unskilled. The data in Table 5-2 summarize the essential elements

Table 5-2. Rate Ranges and Relative Wage Rate Levels in the Paper Makers' Standard Minimum Wage Schedule, 1949

| OCCUPATION | RANGE OF WAGE RATES (LOWEST TO HIGHEST) | | MACHINE CLASSIFICATION (MACHINE TENDER'S RATE = 100) | |
	DOLLARS	AS PER CENT OF LOWEST RATE	LOWEST	HIGHEST
Machine tender	$1.30	90%	100	100
Back tender	1.25	98	88	92
Third hand	.88	77	79	74
Fourth hand	.52	50	72	57
Fifth hand	.41	41	69	52
Sixth hand	.15	15	— *	42

* Rates for sixth hands are not given for the lowest machine classes.

Source: IBPM, Standard Minimum Wage Schedule, 1949 edition

of the schedule's structure by comparing, first, the range of rates (from lowest to highest) for each machine-crew occupation, and, second, the relative wage rate levels for these same occupations on machines in the lowest and highest machine classifications. It is apparent from these comparisons that more favorable treatment is accorded the highly skilled members of the machine crew: for while it is true that the benefits of greater machine productivity are spread among the six occupations, there

31. IBPM, Conference on Wage Scale and Working Conditions (March 29, 1952), pp. 5–7.

is a disproportionate sharing of the reward in that skill differentials increase rapidly, both absolutely and relatively, as the width and speed of machines increase.[32]

Although the structure of the schedule retains the basic features of a strongly craft-conscious policy, a comparison of recent and earlier versions of the schedule indicates that revision of wage rates (to bring the scale into line with higher current levels) has been accomplished simply by adding approximately the same number of cents per hour to all rates, thus leading to a vast improvement in the relative wage position of the unskilled and semiskilled machine-crew members. The effect of these revisions is shown in Table 5-3 by a comparison of relative wage-rate increases for the various occupations in the period 1939–49. These data show that the relative increase in unskilled rates was substantial on all classes of machines.[33]

Table 5-3. *Per Cent Increases in Wage Rates for Machine Crew Occupations in the Period 1939–49, Pulp and Paper Industry*

| | PER CENT INCREASE IN WAGE RATES, 1939 TO 1949 | |
OCCUPATION	LOW MACHINE CLASS	HIGH MACHINE CLASS
Machine tender	48%	26%
Back tender	61	27
Third hand	56	40
Fourth hand	66	54
Fifth hand	75	51

Source: IBPM, *Standard Minimum Wage Schedule,* 1939 and 1949 editions

A final point worth noting in the development of the wage schedule was the decision in the mid-forties to tie the entire rate structure for machine-crew and other occupations under the Paper Makers' jurisdiction to the base rate prevailing in each mill. This was accomplished through a provision requiring that all schedule rates be raised or lowered by the amount necessary to equate the lowest sixth-hand rate on the

32. Since the back tender is a highly skilled paperworker responsible for supervising operations at the "dry" end of the paper machine, his rate is maintained at a more or less constant number of cents per hour below the rate for the machine tender. This explains why the back tender's rate actually rises relative to the machine tender's rate as machine size and speed increase.

33. The same comparison cannot be made between the 1934 and 1939 schedules, since the former provided rates for machine tenders, back tenders, and third hands only. Nevertheless, consideration of the wage rate ranges for and between these occupations in the 1934 schedule suggests a similar, if somewhat less marked, trend in the earlier years.

scale with the common-labor or base rate in the mill. This decision gave recognition not only to the reality of interplant wage differences but also to the strategic role of the base rate as the foundation of the plant wage structure.

So far, attention has been centered on the mechanics of the Paper Makers' schedule, and nothing has been said about its application. In practice, the scale has not received universal recognition either from local unions or from employers. On the other hand, the notion that wage rates should be higher on larger, faster machines is widely accepted, and virtually all employers agree that an increase in the size or speed of a machine justifies upward rate adjustments. Thus the principle of the scale is conceded, but views diverge on what constitute proper wage rate levels or differentials.

The schedule has been applied most successfully in the newsprint mills for which it was originally intended. When the schedule was first introduced, it was structured on rates then prevailing in union mills engaged in the manufacture of newsprint. Consequently the scale was geared more closely to the current wage practices of producers in this branch of the industry. Of more importance in explaining its limited use in other mills, however, is the fact that while newsprint machines run for long periods of time at fairly uniform speeds, machines engaged in the production of other papers, especially the fine and specialty grades, are often required to operate at widely varying speeds within relatively short intervals because of frequent changes in the weight of paper manufactured. Under the latter conditions it is clearly not feasible to maintain a close relationship between wage rates and machine size and speed. In spite of these and other limitations, however, the scale has still proved useful (if not actually indispensable) as a standard for the negotiator in dealing with management and as a source of authority for the union official in dealing with the membership.

Examination of the wage-rate structure for machine-crew members in 159 mills reporting wage data for December 1951 reveals that, while a large number of mills appear to pay rates roughly in line with the wage schedule, newsprint mills are the only ones which follow a policy of fairly strict adherence.[34] A few companies (for example, the "rag" writing group) have adopted a modified version of the scale where machine width alone is made the determining factor. Other companies (20 to 25 per cent of those surveyed) tend to pay uniform wage rates on all machines located in the same mill regardless of width and speed differences. That the schedule has had a pervasive influence on the general structure of machine-crew rates is suggested, however, by the data in Table 5-4. A comparison of these average machine-crew differentials

34. APPA, *Current Wage Survey, 1951.*

in 1951 with the structure of differentials proposed by the Paper Makers in 1949 (the limits of this structure are given in Table 5-2) indicates some measure of consistency between the over-all *actual* and *schedule* structure of wage rates, especially if allowance is made for the reduction in *actual* differentials which occurred as a result of wage increases between 1949 and 1951.[35]

Table 5-4. Relative Average Wage Levels for Paper-Machine Occupations, by Region,* December 31, 1951 (average machine tender's rate = 100)

OCCUPATION	NEW ENGLAND	MIDDLE ATLANTIC	LAKE STATES	CENTRAL STATES	CENTRAL REGION	PACIFIC COAST	SOUTH
Machine tender	100.0	100.0	100.0	100.0	100.0	100.0	100.0
Back tender	99.1	86.8	88.7	85.8	85.5	89.1	87.6
Third hand	80.1	78.9	79.6	78.5	76.7	78.1	79.9
Fourth hand	73.5	75.6	72.9	74.5	69.1	69.6	68.8
Fifth hand	72.0	75.8	69.7	73.8	66.4	66.9	60.1

* *Lake states:* Mich., Minn., and Wis.; *Central states:* Ill., Ind., and O. Other regions as in Table 5-1.

Source: APPA, *Current Wage Survey, 1951*

It would be a mistake, of course, to overlook the fact that the schedule itself responds to the type of general wage increases negotiated. This raises the question of the extent to which the IBPM itself actively promoted such a policy of narrower differentials as against merely accepting the results of such a policy originating elsewhere. In the preceding discussion it has been shown that there was in fact a fundamental shift in the policy of this organization in the early thirties which was favorable to the interests of the unskilled worker; but it appears unlikely that narrowing of the structure would have progressed as far or as rapidly in the absence of other strong pressures originating outside this particular union. These pressures will be examined in the analysis of general wage increases which follows.

The most compelling evidence of how the unions have affected occupational wage differences is found in a comparison of union and management attitudes on the subject of general wage increases. On the whole, the unions have favored cents-per-hour increases which serve only to preserve the absolute spread in wage rates, whereas employers

35. It is not necessary to emphasize that this general relationship refers to relative, and not actual, wage-rate levels.

have shown a distinct preference for per cent increases which are intended to maintain relative differentials. In neither case, however, is the formulation of demands a simple matter, susceptible to sweeping generalizations without regard to time and circumstance. It is necessary therefore to examine carefully the position of both parties, especially that of the unions, before turning to actual wage developments in recent years.

The two important unions in the industry at the time of the depression were the IBPM and IBPSPMW. These organizations had in the past sought somewhat different objectives, the former focusing primarily on the interests of the skilled worker and the latter devoting its energies to improving the lot of the unskilled worker. These separate objectives were best served by promoting different types of general wage increases; but since the two organizations bargained jointly with the majority of unionized employers, some compromise was clearly necessary. In the last two decades, this compromise has proved favorable to the establishment of higher relative wage levels for the low-skilled groups. This outcome was scarcely predictable on the basis of organizational structure alone, but was rather the product of a particular set of circumstances affecting the industry at the time.[36]

The shift of emphasis in the Paper Makers' wage policy has already been explained. It meant that the skilled papermakers supported the efforts of the less skilled pulpworkers to establish a floor under base rates during the depression and to raise these rates in the early years of recovery. It is quite unlikely that this represented a willingness on the part of the IBPM to endorse the notion that wage demands should be phrased in cents-per-hour terms, though it did signify that the union might be content with something less than the strict maintenance of relative differentials.[37] Indeed, during the mid-thirties the Pulp Workers' union itself was wont to follow a fairly flexible policy in this respect. While it placed great stress on the desirability of cents-per-hour increases, it nevertheless permitted local unions to negotiate percentage increases in those plants where employers simply refused to consider adjustments of any other kind. It is evident, therefore, that while both unions (es-

36. Where multiple unionism exists, it is notoriously difficult to predict the net effect of union wage policies on occupational differentials. How, for example, does one weigh the numerical preponderance of unskilled and semiskilled workers against the more strategic position of the skilled groups; or take account of the fact that neither union represents skilled or unskilled workers exclusively, so that conflict of interest may occur within as well as between organizations?

37. The ability of the IBPM to secure special wage adjustments for its skilled members when larger, faster machines were installed or when improvements permitted the speeding up of existing machines may have helped to meet some of the objections of the skilled papermakers to this new policy.

pecially the Pulp Workers) tended to emphasize the need for raising base rates during the mid-1930's, the problems of securing any increases at all and of extending organization to nonunion mills overshadowed to some extent considerations involving the precise nature of the increases granted.

The latter issue was brought into sharper focus, however, in the year 1937–38, when a new competitive force entered the industry in the form of industrial unionism. The new rival unions—the United Paper Workers of America–CIO, and District 50–UMW—made their appeal primarily to the large groups of unskilled and semiskilled workers in the industry; and the early successes of their aggressive organizing campaigns strengthened concern on the part of incumbent unions for the interests of the low-skilled, low-paid worker. These new unions favored the negotiation of cents-per-hour increases and were willing to fight vigorously to bring about settlements of this type. Whatever else they may have accomplished, they exposed the weaknesses of dual organization and forced the two AFL unions to cooperate closely in common defense of their membership. This meant, among other things, that wage policies had to meet the interests of all groups, particularly the unskilled and semiskilled. How wage gains were to be distributed was now, more than ever before, a major issue; and from the standpoint of organized labor it was clearly resolved in favor of cents-per-hour increases.

The position of the unions on general wage increases contrasts sharply with the views of employers. Prior to the depression, some employers had shown a willingness to negotiate agreements for skilled workers only, and there is even evidence of efforts to woo these groups away from their support of the unskilled.[38] The counterpart of this policy since the depression has been a strong preference for wage increases which at least preserve relative differentials. The overwhelming majority of employers are convinced that no other form of increase is as equitable or desirable. They deplore the narrowing of plant wage structures brought about by union pressures to raise base rates, and their firm and persistent opposition to cents-per-hour increases is attested to by the leaders of all three major unions—particularly the IBPSPMW and the UPA.[39]

38. The following comment by an official of the IBPM is relevant here: "Hundreds of times in this paper industry have manufacturers come to the officers of the Paper Makers' organization and cited to them that there was nothing they could not get in the way of wage rates if they would only break away from the desire to protect the lower-paid man in the industry." *Proceedings of the Fourteenth Convention*, p. 126.

39. A few employers support a somewhat different point of view, primarily because their mills are located in high-wage areas. Since recruitment and turnover problems are to a large extent confined to the common-labor level, these employers are less critical of cents-per-hour increases, and may even prefer them.

Employers offer a number of reasons in support of their position. The majority recognize the strategic position of the skilled worker: he is more difficult to replace, is responsible for very expensive and delicate machinery and equipment, and is really the person who "gets the paper out and earns the profits." Moreover, it is felt that if skilled rates are allowed to lag through failure to maintain adequate differentials (which, in reality, means traditional differentials), skilled workers will become dissatisfied, and workers in lower skill classifications will be reluctant to accept promotions, with consequent deterioration in the over-all levels of morale, incentive, and efficiency. This raises a special problem in the case of maintenance craftsmen who comprise a substantial part of the work force in most mills. Failure to maintain adequate skill differentials for this group is regarded as an open invitation to the craft unions to enter the mill.[40] Finally, there is the general argument that the plant wage structure simply is not maintained unless the percentage spread in wage rates is preserved. Underlying all of these reasons to some extent is the notion that too narrow a wage structure is dangerous and difficult to maintain. Employers fear—and not without reason—that cents-per-hour increases will lead to further demands for special individual rate adjustments for workers of higher skill. They naturally prefer to avoid these internal stresses and strains which may result in upward "see-sawing" of the wage structure and in year-round negotiations.

It would be an oversimplification to suppose that the conflicting objectives of unions and employers on the subject of general wage increases remain unchanged in relative strength over time. It is significant, however, that there has been a persistent struggle throughout the last twenty years over the form that increases should take. An appraisal of the increases actually negotiated permits us to say something about the part played by the unions in the evolution of a narrower wage structure.

Evidence of the type of general wage increases negotiated since 1934 is presented in Table 5-5 for a large leading northeastern company, a large leading southern company, and companies party to the West Coast region-wide agreement. The Pacific Coast mills represented by these data were unionized throughout the period, whereas those in the Northeast were organized only in 1937–38 and those in the South in 1938–40. It is interesting to note, therefore, that cents-per-hour increases were granted only after unionization, and that at no time did the nonunion mills grant other than percentage increases. This evidence itself suggests the role of unionism, for while it is true that the unions did negotiate

---

40. As the APPA informed its membership on Nov. 19, 1947 (*Weekly Bulletin*): "The Taft-Hartley Law allows craft groups now incorporated in a union to withdraw and have their own Union . . . and the thing that would influence them to do this would be dissatisfaction over wages, since the difference between the wages of the skilled and the unskilled is sometimes quite small."

a number of per cent increases during the mid-thirties, the Pulp Workers' reports show that probably the majority of settlements took the form of cents-per-hour increases.[41]

The drive on the part of the unions to obtain the latter type of wage adjustment was strengthened, of course, by the entry of rival industrial unions into the industry in the late 1930's. From that time until the end of the war, wage settlements in nearly all union mills called for uniform cents-per-hour additions to all wage rates. As a result, by V-J Day unskilled rates had been raised substantially above the levels prevailing in the thirties, and skill differentials had been very much reduced. Employer resistance to further cents-per-hour increases was therefore very strong in the postwar period. There were occasional reports of unrest among skilled workers and of a tendency for employees to refuse promotions on the grounds that the extra earnings failed to compensate for added responsibilities. Many skilled workers who had accepted union policies designed to gain relatively greater wage advances for the unskilled worker as long as the latter's rate was "low" now felt that the position of the low-paid worker had been sufficiently improved to justify programs which would give more attention to restoring proper and adequate skill differentials. In spite of the strength of these pressures, however, the outcome of negotiations in the postwar period represented little more than a compromise: net wage changes between V-J Day and late 1951 permitted some increase in absolute differentials but still with substantial reductions in percentage differentials.[42]

The wage increases shown in Table 5-5 are relevant here for they represent the settlements negotiated with "wage leaders" in each region.[43] Compression of the wage structure was especially marked in the older regions where the vast majority of mills are located. It is quite clear, however, that the postwar adjustments in all regions consisted of a mixture of types of increase—straight cents-per-hour increases, per cent increases with and without a fixed minimum, and bracket increases—the net result of which was a further narrowing of plant wage structures. It is worth noting that even the negotiation of per cent increases

41. IBPSPMW, *Proceedings of the Seventeenth Convention* (March 1937), pp. 40ff.

42. Unfortunately the high level of unionization in the industry at this time and the fact that many nonunion mills simply followed union patterns prevent comparison of wage developments by union status. It does appear, however, that the few mills in the Northeast which granted mainly percentage increases in the postwar years were nonunion.

43. Postwar wage changes in West Coast and southern mills followed precisely the patterns shown in Table 5-5. Pattern setting was less strong in the older papermaking regions from the standpoint of timing and amount of increases, but there was very little variation between mills with respect to type of increases negotiated.

when accompanied by a fixed minimum proved something less than satisfactory to a number of employers.

Table 5-5. Representative Wage Increases (and Decreases) in the Northeast, South, and Pacific Northwest, Pulp and Paper Industry, 1934-51

	NORTHEAST		SOUTH		PACIFIC COAST	
DATE	INCREASE	BASE RATE	INCREASE	BASE RATE	INCREASE	BASE RATE
August 1934	—	$.40	—	$.34	—	$.45
November	5%	.42	—	—	—	—
February 1935	—	—	*	.36	—	—
June	—	—	—	—	2.5¢	.475
June 1936	—	—	—	—	5.0¢	.525
November	—	—	10%	.40	—	—
December	5%	.45	—	—	—	—
February 1937	5%	.47	—	—	—	—
June	5.0¢	.52	10%	.44	10.0¢	.625
September 1938	−5%	.49	−5%	.42	—	—
March 1939	—	—	5%	.44	—	—
January 1940	5.5%	.52	—	—	—	—
June	2.0¢	.54	3¢	.47	2.5¢	.65
June 1941	5.0¢	.59	7¢	.54	10.0¢	.75
November	—	—	7%	.58	—	—
December	5.0¢	.64	—	—	—	—
June 1942	3.0¢	.67	4¢	.62	10.0¢	.85
June 1943	—	—	—	—	5.0¢	.90
June 1944	—	—	1.5¢	.635	—	—
June 1945	3.0¢	.70	—	—	—	—
November	5.0¢	.75	—	—	—	—
December	—	—	2.5¢ + 13%	.75	15% (15) †	1.05
February 1946	10.0¢	.85	—	—	—	—
June	—	—	10¢–6¢	.85	4%	1.09
September	5.0¢	.90	—	—	—	—
January 1947	—	—	—	—	10%	1.20
June	13% (14) †	1.04	15.0¢	1.00	7.5¢	1.275
April 1948	11.0¢	1.15	—	—	—	—
June	—	—	5¢–13¢	1.05	9% (15) †	1.425
June 1950	5%	1.21	7¢–10¢	1.12	3%	1.47
October	5%	1.27	4% (5) †	1.17	—	—
November	—	—	—	—	4%	1.53
June 1951	3.0¢	1.30	8¢	1.25	12.5¢	1.655
December	2.0¢	1.32	—	—	—	—

* Adjustments only.

† Figures in parentheses denote fixed cents-per-hour minima.

Source: Confidential data supplied by individual companies and unions

The reduction of occupational wage differences in pulp and paper mills is almost entirely attributable to these general wage changes which, under collective bargaining, have led to progressive improvement in the relative wage position of the low-skilled worker. It is in this area that the influence of the unions is most clearly distinguished. Yet unionism has had certain other effects which deserve brief comment.

One important consequence of widespread unionism has been the strengthening and systematizing of promotion procedures based on plant or departmental seniority. In the majority of plants where the union is installed, each worker is related to a particular line of job progression, and his seniority status determines his promotions (providing certain minimum standards of performance are met).[44] The vast majority of jobs in the skilled and semiskilled categories are thus insulated from direct competitive pressures. Paperworkers in these jobs in one mill cannot "compete" for positions in other mills, nor can unionized employers seek to induce movement of labor between mills by manipulation of particular wage rates, for, with the exception of maintenance craftsmen, workers entering a mill must start at the bottom of the occupational ladder and can only reach the higher positions through seniority promotions.[45] Thus market forces operate directly only at the common-labor and maintenance-craft levels where most labor supply and turnover problems occur.[46] This is a primary reason for the emphasis placed on rates for these two occupations in wage negotiations.

The development of stricter plant seniority systems has two important implications. First, wage rates for occupations other than common labor and the maintenance crafts are determined largely without reference to market conditions. Instead their adequacy is tested by their relationship to certain key rates, primarily the base rate in each mill. This suggests that in principle the only effective limits on the extent to which skill differentials can be reduced are, on the employer side, the threatened loss of production resulting from lowered incentive and efficiency, and, on the union side, the threatened loss of membership (or, perhaps, of leadership for incumbent officials) through disaffection

44. In mills where seniority is not the determining factor, it is nevertheless an important consideration, for management has to justify to the union such promotions as do not follow the seniority principle. See APPA, *Analysis of Union Agreements in the Primary Pulp and Paper Industry, 1948* (New York, March 1949), pp. 34–40.

45. The IBPM itself recognizes the difficulties inherent in strict plant seniority systems, and has sought ways to overcome, for example, the problem faced by skilled workers who are discharged from one mill but can only obtain employment in other mills at the unskilled level. IBPM, *Labor Unrest and Dissatisfaction* (Albany, N.Y., June 15, 1944), pp. 47–50; IBPM, *Proceedings of the Eighteenth Convention* (March 1947), pp. 137–47.

46. It might be noted that the majority of pulp and paper "skills" are unique and therefore not easily transferable.

of the skilled groups. One is tempted to speculate about the possible consequences of these plant seniority systems for occupational differentials, and even to conclude that in periods of rising wages they will foster a narrowing of the plant wage structure. This may be so, but, as observed above, the large majority of employers in the industry during the period studied continued to favor the distribution of any given increase in wage costs in a manner consistent with the preservation of traditional relative differentials. The important point to note, however, is that collective bargaining, by reason of this development alone, can alter the structure of occupational wage differences.

Secondly, the development or strengthening of these seniority plans may help to explain why skilled rates generally within the industry have suffered a much greater relative decline than maintenance-craft rates.[47] Journeymen machinists, millwrights, electricians, and other maintenance craftsmen can move freely between industries, and this easy access to alternative job opportunities exerts pressures upon mill operators and union leaders to keep craft rates more or less in line with "outside" rates. Sometimes this requirement has been met through normal, plant-wide general increases; frequently, however, it has been necessary to negotiate additional special rate adjustments.

Two other effects of unionism are worth noting. First, there is the elimination of differentials based on personal characteristics rather than on job content. Ordinarily this would simply entail individual rate adjustments within the wage structure. Occasionally, however, the range of rates itself is affected. This was the case, for example, when the color differential was eliminated from common-labor rates in southern mills in 1944. Other instances of a similar effect are found in union demands for "equal pay for equal work" on behalf of women and in union opposition to low or prolonged probationary rates for new workers. Secondly, there is the persistent drive by the unions to increase the number of job classifications in the mill. In this manner they have built up an elaborate job structure and corresponding rate structure which rewards all elements of skill and responsibility wherever the latter can be distinguished. This has resulted in a more or less steady decline in the proportion of workers employed at the common-labor level. The reduction in the spread of occupational wage rates has been accompanied by a decrease in the dispersion of employees within this spread.

It remains now to consider those factors other than unionism which may have influenced the behavior of occupational differentials during this period. Of particular interest are the ones which tended to operate in the same direction as unionism, and these can be listed as follows:

47. This relative decline was even more marked than the data in Table 5-1 suggest, for increases in average machine-crew rates are partly a consequence of the ever increasing size and speed of paper machines.

the halting of large-scale immigration in the twenties, the extension of public education, the increasing use of capital in combination with labor of low skills, minimum wage legislation and wartime wage regulations, full employment, and inflation.

It is difficult, if not impossible, to estimate with any accuracy the extent to which each of these forces may have contributed to the narrowing of plant wage structures in pulp and paper. In the writer's judgment, however, unionism has been the primary pressure in bringing about the reduction of differentials, while some of these other factors (principally full employment and inflation) have played an important secondary role by providing an environment favorable to the success of union wage demands. Limitations of space unfortunately permit no more than the briefest summary of the reasoning behind this conclusion.

The factors listed above might be expected to affect plant wage structures in the pulp and paper industry in two ways: first, by raising the supply price of unskilled labor relative to other types of labor for the economy as a whole; and second, by direct impact upon the wage structure of individual plants. All factors are relevant under the first consideration, but minimum wage impositions and perhaps changes in capital-labor ratios appear to be the only factors likely to have any significant direct impact upon individual plants' wage structures.

Changes in the relative supply of different grades of labor will certainly exercise a pervasive influence on relative wage levels in the economy. Just how effective these pressures will be and how large the adjustments they will bring about is a matter of judgment. It seems unlikely, however, that the effects would be other than gradual, working themselves out over a relatively long period of time. If account is taken of the fairly widespread unemployment existing throughout the thirties, it is questionable if such changes had any significant effect at all prior to World War II.

Experience within the paper industry itself tends to confirm this general impression. First, to the extent that employers' policies reflect fundamental changes in the supply price of different grades of labor in local markets, it is impossible to discount the implications of management's criticism of successful union efforts to negotiate cents-per-hour increases and its advocacy of wage adjustments which would preserve traditional differentials. Secondly, in the case of wage developments in the southern kraft branch of the industry—an extreme, but nevertheless useful, illustration—it is quite apparent that net market pressures have so far operated strongly to increase rather than diminish the spread of occupational rates.[48] In support of this conclusion, it is only necessary

48. This argument does not assert that the factors under discussion have had no effect upon general wage-rate relationships in the South, but simply that pressures

to cite the following facts: 1. the base rate in southern paper mills is approximately 50 per cent higher than the rate for equivalent labor in sawmilling and pulpwood cutting; 2. the high rate paid to common labor in paper mills has been under severe criticism by employers in other southern industries; and 3. the opposition of paper producers in the South to any further narrowing of differentials has been exceptionally strong throughout the postwar period.

It is possible to argue that the narrowing of differentials between common-labor and maintenance-craftsmen's rates, both subject to market pressures, is evidence that general market forces were operating to reduce the relative spread between skilled and unskilled wage rates. This argument gains in plausibility if the effect is attributed to full employment and the postwar inflation, for it was during the forties, particularly in the postwar years, that the relative wage position of maintenance craftsmen declined. Two points are worth noting on this issue, however. First, journeymen's rates suffered much less than other skilled rates during the period in question. Thus, even if a general trend is conceded on the basis of the relative behavior of maintenance-craft rates, compression of the structure for production workers proceeded well beyond this standard and was a feature, moreover, of the prewar years when no discernible decline took place in the common-labor–maintenance-craftsmen differential. Secondly, an alternative explanation can be offered for the behavior of maintenance-craft rates. The unions have relied upon special wage adjustments in conjunction with general increases to keep craft rates more or less in line with "outside" rates. In some cases no extra adjustments were required; in others such adjustments as proved necessary were not large enough to preserve the wage position of maintenance workers relative to common labor. This explanation of craft rate behavior is as plausible as the one suggested above. There is little point in debating their respective merits, however, for the narrowing of the differential is probably accounted for by both sets of forces.

The possible impact of minimum wage legislation and changes in capital-labor input ratios (at the various labor levels) upon individual plant wage structures can be dealt with more summarily. Apart from the fact that there is no evidence of any pronounced change in differentials following minimum wage enactments, a study of common-labor rates in the mills prior to the effective dates of these enactments reveals that only a few mills were affected, and most of these were located in the South. Among mills affected by the minimum wage, the adjustment

---

from this source insofar as they affect plant wage structures in pulp and paper have not been sufficiently strong to overcome other market influences tending to widen differentials.

required in nearly all cases was quite minor, so that the impact on differentials, if any, was very slight.[49]

The question of how changes in the amount of capital used in conjunction with the various labor grades affect relative wage levels within the plant raises difficult problems which can only be touched upon here. Technological improvements certainly provide the basis for permanent wage gains by raising labor productivity; but it is not easy to assert the precise nature of this relationship in pulp and paper mills or to assess its consequences for occupational differentials. In the first place, the introduction of labor-saving devices into woodyards and materials-handling operations has been an effect as well as a cause of high wage rates for common labor. Secondly, paper machines, upon which the productivity of skilled operators largely depends, have undergone steady and substantial improvement during the last twenty years, so that it would be dangerous to assume greater productivity increases for unskilled groups than for skilled machine-crew members. Thirdly, opportunities for altering capital-labor imput ratios are limited in the majority of mills by the already high level of mechanization and by the absence of woodyard and pulping operations where the bulk of unskilled labor is used. Finally, there are no significant differences in the wage-structure development of plants which have differed widely in the degree to which labor-saving devices and processes have been adopted. Apart from these, difficulties, the most important consideration is the practical one of the method of employee compensation. Workers in the mills are paid on an hourly rather than piece-rate basis, and increases in productivity, whatever the source, are normally reflected in reductions in total labor costs. The gains from these reductions are then distributed more or less evenly over the work force. The only employees benefiting regularly from specific productivity increases are those on the paper machines, and this arrangement tends to widen rather than narrow the plant wage structure.

Thus, even granting that certain factors such as full employment and inflation (and perhaps government wartime policy) were conducive to a narrowing of the occupational wage structure, it would still appear that unions have been the primary source of pressure to reduce differentials.

49. APPA, *Wage Survey* (Nov. 1–15, 1939), pp. 149–53; APPA, *Current Wage Survey, 1949–50;* BLS, *Report on the Pulp and Primary Paper Industry* (1940), p. 53; and BLS, *Earnings and Hours in the Paperboard Industry,* Bulletin 692 (Washington, 1941), pp. 7, 8, 14–23.

CHAPTER 6 *Pulp and Paper*

(continued)

INTERPLANT DIFFERENTIALS

JUST as the previous chapter was concerned with the impact of unions and collective bargaining upon relative wage rates *within* plants, so the present one is devoted to an examination of the effects of these same forces on relative wage levels *among* plants. The analysis of interplant differentials would be less than complete, however, without consideration of the influence of factors other than unionism. Consequently, a secondary objective is to discover the reasons for such interplant differentials as remain in the industry.

The range of hypotheses to be tested can be summarized in the following questions: First, have the unions sought through collective bargaining to standardize wage levels among rival or competing producers? If so, have their efforts been successful? Secondly, are union mills to be distinguished from nonunion mills by higher wage rates? Thirdly, to the extent that interplant wage differences remain, are they to be accounted for by such factors as differences in community size, size of plant, type of product manufactured, length of the scheduled work week, or ability to pay? [1]

The first problem is the choice of an appropriate measure for comparing the wage levels of different plants. In some industries it may be difficult to reach a decision on this crucial issue; but in pulp and paper, consideration of the adequacy of alternative measures of the plant wage level lends overwhelming support to the selection of the mill base rate as the most significant and meaningful basis for interplant wage comparisons. The case for using this measure rather than another can be stated briefly. The base rate is the most strategic rate in each plant. It is the foundation of the plant wage structure, other wage rates being judged adequate or inadequate largely in terms of their relationship to this base. It is the focal point in union-management negotiations and is used con-

1. It has proved convenient from the standpoint of exposition to consider differences in wage levels among plants in the same major producing region rather than in the same geographic area. This should not be allowed to obscure the fact that the intercommunity and interarea differences discussed below (pp. 129–48) and the interregional differences examined in the following section are all aspects of the same dimension of the wage structure—namely, geographic differentials.

sistently by both parties in measuring the relative wage position of the plant within the area or industry. The base rate is the most important rate from the standpoint of labor recruitment and turnover. It reflects most directly the interplay of competitive forces in the labor market. It is also the most common rate in each plant in the sense that more workers (approximately 15 per cent of the labor force on the average) are employed at this rate level than at any other level. Finally—and this is perhaps the most important reason—the base rate is the wage rate for common labor, one of the few occupational groups which meet the test of rough comparability among plants. Common labor involves only physical work, requires a minimum of skill and experience, imposes little responsibility, and is found in all mills primarily in the handling of materials. For these reasons, the mill base rate is the most useful single statistic for analysis of interplant wage differences.

In tracing the development of interplant differentials, it would be desirable to show for a large group of plants in the industry how wage levels were dispersed about the average at different times throughout the period. Unfortunately, this "ideal" cannot be realized due to the lack of adequate wage rate data for individual plants in the early postdepression years. The trend since the late thirties is shown, however, in Table 6-1, which presents intraregional measures of the absolute and relative dispersion of mill base rates for specified years during the period 1938–51. These measures are not strictly comparable, since several of the mills in the 1938 and 1941 samples failed to report data during the postwar period. Nevertheless, the fundamental trend revealed in the table is confirmed by other data. Thus, an examination of base-rate behavior in sixty northeastern mills for which wage information was available in both 1940 and 1951 shows that the relative dispersion of base rates about the mean fell from 11.3 per cent to 6.0 per cent during this eleven-year period.[2] It is safe to conclude, therefore, that the intraregional structure of plant wage levels has narrowed by approximately 40 to 50 per cent since the late 1930's.

The lack of an adequate sample of mill base rates for the early thirties is particularly unfortunate in that it prevents, among other things, the testing of Maclaurin's finding that the influence of unionism in the paper industry during the thirties was "in the direction of increasing differentials."[3] This particular finding will be examined below, but it

2. Absolute dispersion of base rates (measured by the standard deviation) rose from $0.057 in 1940 to $0.074 in 1951, while the mean base rate increased from $0.505 to $1.241. Wage rate data from APPA, *Survey of Occupational Wage Rates, November 1940;* and APPA, *Current Wage Survey, 1951.*

3. W. Rupert Maclaurin, "Wages and Profits in the Paper Industry, 1929–39," *Quarterly Journal of Economics, 58* (Feb. 1944), 228.

Table 6-1. Dispersion of Base Rates in Pulp and Paper Mills, by Region, 1938–51

REGION	OCTOBER 1938			NOVEMBER 1941			DECEMBER 1947			DECEMBER 1951		
	x*	s*	v*	x	s	v	x	s	v	x	s	v
New England	$.463	$.056	12.1 (74) †	$.550	$.058	10.5 (95)	$ .945	$.076	8.4 (44)	$1.219	$.078	6.4 (43)
Middle Atlantic	.475	.063	13.3 (61)	.551	.063	11.5 (60)	.961	.091	9.5 (62)	1.227	.097	7.9 (59)
Lake States	.496	.060	12.1 (60)				1.025	.081	7.9 (49)	1.333	.069	5.2 (44)
Southern States	.367	.031	8.4 (13)				1.000	.059	5.9 (18)	1.244	.072	5.7 (21)
Central States	.491	.042	8.6 (19)				.980	.062	6.3 (16)	1.225	.057	4.7 (17)
Central Zone	.415	.054	13.0 (15)				.899	.109	12.1 (12)	1.194	.139	11.6 (11)
Pacific Coast	.620	.000	— (22)				1.275	.000	— (14)	1.655	.000	— (14)

* x = mean; s = standard deviation; v = coefficient of variation.

† Figures in parentheses denote number of mills in sample.

Source: Computed from data in APPA, Survey of Occupational Wage Rates (Oct. 1938 and Nov. 1941); and APPA, Current Wage Survey (Dec. 1947 and Dec. 1951)

may be well to note at this point that the only available information (admittedly quite unsatisfactory) suggests that there was probably little change in the dispersion of plant wage levels during this period.[4]

The reduction of interplant wage differences, which appears to have occurred for the most part after the late 1930's, coincides with the period of rapid union growth. This suggests a causal relationship between the expansion of collective bargaining and the leveling of wage rates among plants, though it does not constitute proof. The latter must be sought in the objectives of union wage policies and in the evidence of how these policies have operated.

The policies of the major unions in the industry have been characterized as opportunistic. This does not mean that the elimination of wage competition between rival producers has been abandoned, but simply that the unions recognize, in practice, severe limitations surrounding the attainment of this goal and are willing to adapt their policies to the economic and political needs of the moment. They strive for substantial uniformity (if not of wage rates, at least of wage rate increases) within each region, but are prepared to make fairly numerous concessions to the less efficient plants in order to keep them in operation. One cannot be certain how many of these concessions below the standard represent a proven lack of ability to pay on the part of the employer and how many are simply the result of either strong employer opposition to wage increases or a lack of union aggressiveness; but it would appear that the majority are in the former category. The precise nature of the policies pursued by unions and their effectiveness in bringing about a uniform interplant wage structure will depend to a large extent on the economic characteristics of the industry in question. The more important aspects of industry structure as they impinge on policy are therefore examined below.

In the pulp and paper industry, the area of competition over which the union might be presumed to enforce uniform wage standards cannot be defined simply by reference to the market areas and production units for each product. Just as the possibility (and occurrence) of grade shifting leads to an interrelated structure of prices, so it tends to interrelate the wage levels of plants in the various product lines. This tendency is strengthened, moreover, by the prevalence of multi-product plants in the industry and by the fact that many of the larger companies manufacture different kinds of paper in their several mills. In a situation of this sort, where the majority of producers are confronted with competitors in more than one branch of the industry and must often be

4. In 1933 the relative dispersion of plant base rates in 36 northeastern mills was 13.2%. Wage rate data from APPA, *Employment, Wage Rates and Hours of Work in the Paper and Pulp Industry,* Bulletin 2 (Oct. 1933).

concerned with the potential competition inherent in grade shifting as much as with actual competition, it is not difficult to see why the major unions approach the problem of wage standards not simply from the standpoint of "competitive" producers but also from that of "comparable" producers.[5] The simplest course for the unions, and perhaps the only realistic one, is to strive for a broad measure of intraregional uniformity in plant wage levels regardless of particular product lines.

One important case of noncomparability derives from grade shifting in an effort to forestall normal obsolescence. Since paper machines are practically indestructible, and since technological improvements in the way of larger and faster machines are usually introduced in the production of standard tonnage grades, the older and narrower machines have gradually been forced into the manufacture of fine and specialty papers. Many of the mills engaged in the production of these latter grades are on the way out. They are low-efficiency mills operating obsolete plant and equipment, and they continue to produce just as long as they can reap returns in excess of variable costs. Mills in these branches of the industry are certainly not comparable with those in other branches, and it is reasonable to expect that their wage rates will tend to be depressed. The fact that fine- and specialty-paper production is concentrated in the older paper-producing regions means that the problem is largely confined to those areas.

The leaders of the two AFL paper unions have long recognized the difficulties posed by this latter situation and the necessity for compromise between the "standard-rate" principle and the principle of ability to pay in the formulation of their wage policies. They have emphasized at conventions that standardization at a wage level which the less efficient firms can afford to pay will simply hold down wages in the industry as a whole, whereas standardization at higher levels will result in loss of jobs for a part of the membership through the shutdown of submarginal mills. Officials have been careful to avoid committing the unions to any program of strict interplant uniformity. Standardization has been sought where feasible (i.e. among comparable mills), but through policies sufficiently flexible to meet the needs of individual plants and branches of the industry which are especially inefficient or unfortunate. The unions, in short, have embraced a limited and long-range version of the standard-rate principle applied to "comparable" rather than "competing" mills.

In any study of the wage consequences of trade unionism and collec-

5. Normally mills are considered comparable if equipment, processes, raw materials, and products (broadly defined as, for example, tonnage grades, fine grades, or specialties) are roughly similar. A major criterion in judging comparability, however, is often "ability to pay."

tive bafgaining, it is obviously desirable to distinguish between the various phases of union growth. With sufficient data this could be accomplished by comparing successive cross-sections of the interplant wage structure, beginning in the preunion period. Adequate wage statistics are available, however, only for recent years. In the analysis which follows, the questions posed at the beginning of this section will be considered with reference to the structure of wage levels in 1940 and 1951. The data for these years permit appraisal of interplant wage differences under conditions of both partial and virtually complete unionization. Since the information on individual plants is much more comprehensive for the year 1951, the reasons for continued differences in plant wage levels will be discussed in relation to the data for that year.

The question of the impact of unionism upon plant wage levels in the partially unionized industry is best introduced by considering the findings of an earlier study by Maclaurin. In this study, which covered 217 paper mills in eleven northern states in 1939, union and nonunion mills were separated into three wage-level categories—high, medium, and low. The measure of the mill wage level was a composite of unskilled, semiskilled, and skilled rates, and the resulting distribution within each group was as follows: [6]

Mill Wage-Rate Level	Union Mills Number	Per Cent	Nonunion Mills Number	Per Cent
High	40	54	43	30
Medium	16	22	25	18
Low	18	24	75	52
TOTAL	74	100	143	100

On the basis of these data, Maclaurin concluded that union mills tended to have higher wage rates on the average than nonunion mills, and that this suggested "the unions had concentrated initial attention on, and had been most successful in organizing, the larger and more profitable companies." The following statement appeared in the summary of the study:

Under present conditions, with the industry only half organized, the union influence has been in the direction of increasing differentials. The larger, more profitable and higher-paying companies have been the ones that have been organized first and have yielded to requests for still higher wages. However, as the unions succeed in organizing

6. Maclaurin, "Wages and Profits in the Paper Industry," p. 222.

an increasing proportion of the industry, their influence is likely to iron out many of the intra-regional differentials in wage rates that now exist.[7]

While this statement of the effects of unionism appears plausible, there are several reasons for doubting its adequacy. It is difficult, for example, to reconcile the conclusion that the unions were successful in organizing first "the more profitable and higher-paying companies" with another finding in the same study to the effect that there was little difference in profitability between union and nonunion firms.[8] Secondly, no explanation is offered for the large number of high-wage plants in the nonunion group or for the low- and medium-wage plants in the union group. Thirdly, no evidence is presented in support of the conclusion that differentials have indeed increased, nor is it quite certain whether "increasing differentials" means an increase in dispersion or simply a widening of the gap between the highest and lowest plant wage levels. These points are not raised simply to highlight shortcomings in an otherwise careful and useful study: they are intended rather to illustrate the dangers involved in drawing inferences about the influence of unionism, and, at the same time, to prepare the way for further examination of the same topic. The analysis which follows attempts to offer a more satisfactory explanation of how collective bargaining affects plant wage levels in a partially unionized industry.

When a union first enters an industry it is confronted with a great diversity of plant wage levels, reflecting differences in market conditions, financial position and profitability, and management policy. In the process of organizing plants in the industry the union is likely to find itself representing workers in both low- and high-wage plants. In an industry such as paper and pulp, with a large number of small and medium-sized companies, it is undoubtedly true that the union will seek to organize the larger and more influential firms first; but these are not necessarily the high-wage firms, nor the most profitable, nor the easiest to organize. Thus, while larger firms are likely to predominate in the unionized sector, the union will nevertheless find itself with a variety of plants differing widely in their respective wage levels. What will be the effect of unionism in this situation?

A study of the base rates in November 1940 shows that union mills paid higher rates on the average than nonunion mills. (Table 6-2.) Of more interest than these average rates, however, is the distribution of union and nonunion mills by base-rate levels. It is clear from Table 6-2

7. *Ibid.*, p. 228.
8. *Ibid.*, p. 212.

that a major difference between the union and nonunion sectors is the tendency for union wage levels to cluster in the higher wage-rate classes. The marked difference between the two groups in this respect is shown by the following measures of absolute and relative dispersion of base rates for those mills located in the northeastern regions (New England and the Middle Atlantic states):

	Union	Nonunion
Number of mills	60	62
Average base rate (mean)	$.522	$.477
Standard deviation	$.038	$.057
Coefficient of variation	7.3%	12.0%

These data support the hypothesis that when the union enters the industry, it is effective in raising wage levels, but primarily those of already low-wage firms. In other words, wage differentials which in pre-union days were the result of factors other than ability to pay—about which more will be said later—become a target for the union. Thus, while unionism may well raise high wage rates still higher (as Maclaurin suggests), and, in addition, undoubtedly exerts an upward pressure on the wage levels of some nonunion firms anxious to prevent unionization, a most significant effect is the reduction of differentials within the union sector, brought about by raising the relative wage levels of low-wage plants.[9]

There is no way of estimating how successful the unions have been in raising the levels of high-wage plants still higher or to what extent the differential pull exerted by union negotiations has affected the range of nonunion wage levels. There is reason to believe, however, that these effects are often overestimated in the case of the partially organized industry. This matter cannot be discussed fully here, but it is well to remember that unions are by no means impervious to the pressures of nonunion wage competition. In an industry where less than half the production units are organized, nonunion rates exercise a strong restraining influence on union rates. This influence, moreover, is likely to limit gains most severely in the already high-wage plants, for it is undoubtedly easier to raise low rates to levels already existing in competing mills than to raise high rates still higher above the levels prevailing elsewhere. The combined effect of these various pressures dur-

9. In this connection, it is worth noting that the 3 union mills in the lowest wage bracket in the Central states and 3 of the 4 low-wage union mills in the Middle Atlantic states belonged to companies organized only in 1940, the year of the survey. (See Table 6-2.)

Table 6-2. Union and Nonunion Pulp and Paper Mills by Base-rate Class and by Region, November 1940

BASE-RATE CLASS	NEW ENGLAND		MIDDLE ATLANTIC		LAKE STATES		CENTRAL STATES		CENTRAL REGION		SOUTH		PACIFIC	
	U	N	U	N	U	N	U	N	U	N	U	N	U	N
40 cents		8		7	2	1			1	3	1	3		
41–43				2				1			9	2		
44–46		3	4	6	1			5		3				
47–49	2	7	3	5			3	2	2					
50–52	19	3	5	1	14	1	3	4	1					
53–55	8	8	14	7	8	1	3	6						
56–58	1	2	1	2	6		2						1	
59–61				1	6	1	1							
62–64			3											
65							1						17	
TOTAL	30	31	30	31	37	4	13	18	4	6	10	5	18	—
Average base rate (dollars)	.517	.477	.526	.476	.523	.515	.532	.496	.475	.423	.425	.410	.645	—

Source: APPA, *Survey of Occupational Wage Rates* (Nov. 1940)

ing the thirties may well have been to increase the *range* of plant wage levels within the industry, but wage-level *dispersion*—the more appropriate measure of the degree of uniformity—may have diminished at the same time.

The data for 1940 suggest that the main initial effect of unionism was to decrease dispersion through an upward leveling of wage rates in the union sector. It remains now to examine the structure of plant wage levels in late 1951 with a view to determining the extent of uniformity achieved by that date, and the forces responsible for such interplant wage differences as exist. The principal findings, for which evidence is presented below, can be summarized briefly. First, the unions, through collective bargaining, have established virtually complete uniformity in the newer papermaking regions of the Pacific Northwest and the South, and have been successful in securing a substantial degree of wage rate uniformity among significant groups of mills in the older regions, particularly the large producers of standard tonnage papers. Secondly, such base-rate differences as exist among mills in the older regions appear to be related to differences in the following: length of the scheduled work week, plant location, union status and affiliation, type of product manufactured, and ability to pay. It is convenient to examine the effect of each of these factors before presenting evidence of the degree of uniformity achieved in recent years.

Table 6-3. *Average Plant Base Rates by Length of Scheduled Work Week, Pulp and Paper Industry, December 1951*

| | LENGTH OF THE SCHEDULED WORK WEEK | |
REGION	40 HOURS	48 HOURS
New England	$1.220 (36) *	$1.129 (9)
Middle Atlantic States	1.293 (23)	1.173 (20)
Lake States	1.366 (33)	1.220 (8)
Central States	1.220 (4)	1.247 (7)
Central Region	1.308 (6)	1.070 (3)

*Figures in parentheses denote number of mills in sample. All mills in the South and Pacific Northwest are on a 40-hour work week.

Source: APPA, *Current Wage Survey, 1951*

The length of the scheduled work week is an important consideration in wage determination, for the vast majority of workers judge the adequacy of wages not only in terms of hourly rates of compensation but also in terms of weekly take-home pay. This fact has long been recognized in the policies of unions and employers. Thus when unions seek a reduction in the length of the work week, their demands invariably include the provision that hourly rates be adjusted in order to maintain the level of weekly earnings. Similarly, employers paying relatively low wage rates frequently find it to their advantage to offer a longer work week as an inducement to recruiting and maintaining an adequate work force. This device is particularly effective when it can be shown that the longer work week at the lower rate will yield much higher weekly earnings. The effect of this relationship on the structure of interplant wage levels in pulp and paper is shown in Table 6-3.

It is clear that mills operating a forty-hour week tend to pay substantially higher base rates than those offering forty-eight hours a week. These data measure differences in average rates only, but plant-by-plant comparisons reveal a fairly consistent pattern of differentials ranging from 8 to 14 cents. In addition, a few mills actually employed common labor on both the short and the long work week. These mills also allowed a differential of 10 to 12 cents between the rates for the two groups.[10]

Part of this development can be traced to experience in the postwar years. Up to V-J Day, the majority of mills were operating on a forty-eight-hour basis because of acute labor shortages. With the cessation of hostilities, and the release of labor from wartime industries and from the armed services, many of the mills returned to the forty-hour week. Some· of these firms announced that wage increases granted in late 1945 and early 1946 were in full compensation for the cutback in hours. This is open to dispute, for the unions were seeking—and would have obtained—substantial wage improvements in any case. That they were at least in partial compensation for the reduction in hours seems to be indicated, however, by the larger net increases granted by mills with the forty-hour work week during the postwar period. The average increases granted within each group between V-J Day and December 1951 were as follows:

	40 Hours	48 Hours
New England	$.58	$.52
Middle Atlantic	.60	.53
Lake States	.66	.56
Central States	.56	.56
Central Region	.66	.53

10. Further evidence that wage rate decisions are not independent of decisions on hours of work is supplied in the following statement by a union official: "The base rates in most organized mills [in the Middle Atlantic states] now range from ninety cents per hour to one dollar and two cents per hour, depending greatly on the number of hours of scheduled operation. Many of our mills are still working 48 or more hours per week." IBPM, *Proceedings of the Eighteenth Convention,* p. 21.

Again, these averages are representative of the situation existing in the vast majority of individual plants.

It is doubtful whether there is any simple explanation for the development of this relationship between wage levels and the number of hours worked. The most plausible hypothesis is that the unions, in seeking the shorter work week in combination with compensating rate adjustments, have not been uniformly successful in pressing these conditions upon employers, either because some employers could not afford (or refused to pay) higher wage rates or because local members were unwilling to pursue claims to the point of strike action. This explanation certainly would account for the fact that a minority of union mills continue to pay rates below prevailing levels but meet market conditions by offering a longer work week. It would also be consistent with the finding that a majority of nonunion mills pay low rates and operate on a forty-eight-hour basis.[11] (See Table 6-5 below.)

A second factor accounting for differences in wage levels is plant location. The role played by location is a limited one, however, in that it provides for variations above, but seldom below, the prevailing pattern. The typical wage-setting environment in pulp and paper is the relatively small, semirural community. Such communities are usually low- or medium-wage areas. Thus, even though pulp and paper mills frequently pay the highest wage rates in their localities, the industry itself is perhaps most aptly described as a medium-wage industry. Location is a factor, therefore, only in those mills located in high-wage areas where the prevailing regional level for pulp and paper is insufficient to ensure retention of an adequate work force. While the unions are not averse to variations of this sort, they will seldom approve on the same basis wage rates below the prevailing pattern, because wage concessions granted for any reason other than lack of ability to pay represent a threat to the stability of the wage-price structure and are difficult to defend before competing producers and the local membership. It is important to note that the relevant consideration in appraising the influence of location on plant wage levels is not community size per se, but rather the presence of other high-wage plants (such as metalworking, automobile, steel, chemical, and rubber) in sufficient concentration to

11. If allowance is made for overtime compensation, however, it would appear that average hourly earnings for common labor are as high in some of the union mills with the longer work week as in those with the shorter week, despite the wide discrepancy in actual hourly wage rates. This suggests that either a shortage of labor in a particular locality or a preference on the part of the employer for the 6-day week (which is, after all, the normal running schedule for mills) may be a contributing factor in certain mills. A more likely explanation, however, stems from the fact that wage costs tend to be more flexible (downward) in mills operating on a 48-hour work week, for unit labor costs can be reduced by simply curtailing the number of hours worked.

raise the minimum supply price of labor to the paper mill above prevailing levels for the paper industry.

A study of intraregional wage levels in pulp and paper reveals that the influence of plant location is confined largely to mills in the northern industrial belt running westward from the Middle Atlantic states through the Midwest. There was no evidence in forty-four New England mills or thirty-three Lake states mills that differences in local labor market conditions were a cause of wage-level variation. On the other hand, in a few mills in the Middle Atlantic states and in Michigan, wage levels were clearly affected by location in abnormally high-wage areas. To facilitate the comparison of these high-wage mills with other mills in their respective regions, base rates have been listed in Table 6-4 below.

The prevailing wage levels for mills in both of these regions are between $1.28 and $1.32.[12] These rates represent the pattern established in negotiations with the leading northeastern companies. It will be observed that there were three mills in each region which paid base rates clearly above the pattern. Examination of the characteristics of these mills and interviews with union and company officials provided ample evidence that the high rates paid in each case were the result of location in a very high wage market. Thus the three Middle Atlantic states book mills, two of which paid $1.37 and the third $1.47, were located in the Niagara Falls area, close to a number of large chemical, metallurgical, and abrasive plants. It is interesting to note, however, that despite the high-wage structure and acute labor shortages existing in this area,[13] intraindustry standards were still a powerful force in determining wage levels. This was shown by the small differential (of only 5¢) established between the rates in these three mills and in other mills owned by the same "wage-leader" companies,[14] and by the low wage levels of paper plants relative to other plants in the Niagara Falls area.[15] In the Michigan area, the three high-wage mills were situated very close to the large

12. A number of mills pay slightly lower rates. These are discussed below in connection with the influence of differences in ability to pay.

13. The majority of the large plants were advertising for labor as far south as Tennessee.

14. The mill with the high base rate ($1.47) was owned by a company in the Lake states where wage levels tend to be 7¢ or 8¢ above northeastern levels.

15. This can be shown by a comparison of the rates paid in Niagara Falls during mid-1953 by the principal competitors for labor in the manufacturing field:

Type of Plant	Common-Labor Rate	Class A Machinist's Rate
Paper (2 plants)	$1.50–1.55	$1.96–1.99
Abrasive	1.62	2.17
Carbon	1.71	2.23
Metallurgical (3 plants)	1.70–1.75	2.04–2.19
Chemical (7 plants)	1.66–1.82	2.12–2.34
Business forms	1.82	—

Table 6-4. Base Rates in 25 Middle Atlantic States Mills and 9 Michigan Mills by Type of Product, Mill Capacity and Union Status and Affiliation, Pulp and Paper Industry, December 1951

PRODUCT	CAPACITY (TONS DAILY)	BASE RATE	UNION STATUS & AFFILIATION
	MIDDLE ATLANTIC STATES		
Groundwood	180	$1.32	AFL
	450 (1) *	1.32	AFL
Book	85 (2)	1.315	UPA-CIO
	113 (1)	1.32	AFL
	145 (2)	1.315	Nonunion
	163 (3)	1.28	District 50
	180	1.47	District 50
	200 (1)	1.37	AFL
	200 (1)	1.37	AFL
	225 (3)	1.28	District 50
	250 (2)	1.30	District 50
	300 (3)	1.28	District 50
	310 (4)	1.25	AFL
Writing (sulphite)	150	1.24	Independent
	350	1.30	AFL
Tissue	17	1.305	AFL
	80	1.255	AFL
Sulphite wrapping	75 (4)	1.25	AFL
	85 (1)	1.29	AFL
	n.a.	1.17 †	AFL
Kraft wrapping	25 (4)	1.25	AFL
	38 (4)	1.25	AFL
	40 (4)	1.25	AFL
Miscellaneous	88	1.28	AFL
	200	1.31	CIO
	CENTRAL AND LOWER MICHIGAN		
Book	225	$1.26	AFL
	350	1.31	AFL
Writing	40	1.43	UAW-AFL
	75	1.28	District 50
Tissue	150	1.46	AFL
Sulphite wrapping	40	1.31	UPA-CIO
	65	1.31	AFL
Paperboard	140	1.28	District 50
Miscellaneous	15	1.385	CIO

* Figures in parentheses identify mills belonging to multi-plant companies.

† Nonproduction incentive bonus raises rate 10–13%.

Source: APPA, *Current Wage Survey, 1951*

automobile plants in the southeastern section of the state. The tissue mill paying $1.46 to common labor was located in Detroit, the high-wage city of the nation; the writing mill paying $1.43 (and organized by the UAW-AFL) was in Ypsilanti, a relatively small town but the home of the Kaiser-Frazer Corporation; while the mill manufacturing miscellaneous papers and paying $1.385 was in Rochester, a small community north of Detroit and only a few miles east of Pontiac. The wage levels in these mills were high primarily because they were competing for labor in markets dominated by the automobile industry.

There is evidence that several other mills experienced the pull of area wage levels. In virtually all these cases, however, local market pressures were not sufficiently strong to pull rates above the paper industry standard but led rather to greater recruitment problems for these mills at wage levels equal to, and often below, the prevailing pattern. Preoccupation with the problems posed by area or local wage levels is found most frequently among employers operating low-wage mills. Consequently, local labor market pressures may operate to reduce as well as to widen the intraindustry spread in plant wage levels.

A third factor which accounts for wage-level differences among plants is union status. The effect of this factor was discussed at some length in the analysis of the 1940 data, and findings for late 1951 tend to confirm these earlier conclusions. Comparisons between union and non-union mills for recent years are limited by the relatively small number of unorganized mills remaining in the industry and by underrepresentation of this group in APPA samples. Such information as is available for late 1951 indicates that while a number of nonunion mills pay base rates on a par with prevailing union levels, there is a tendency for wage rates to be lower in the nonunion sector. These lower rates are only partially offset, moreover, by provisions for the longer work week. If the structure of plant wage levels is considered as a whole, one finds high- and low-wage plants in both the organized and unorganized sectors. The distribution of plants by wage levels within each group, however, is strikingly different;[16] for whereas the union plants are concentrated in the higher wage brackets, the nonunion plants tend to cluster at the bottom of the rate range. Thus, for the nineteen nonunion plants in New England, the Middle Atlantic states and the Lake states, it was found that only three paid rates equivalent to the union pattern, while the remaining sixteen paid rates which were among the lowest in each region. With only minor exceptions, the lowest base rate within each product division was paid by a nonunion mill.[17]

16. See Table 6-5.
17. Union affiliation is a potential source of plant wage differences, since both the UPA and District 50 tend to give greater stress in negotiations to area than to industry

The final, and perhaps most important, cause of interplant wage differences is ability to pay. The major unions in the industry have long been willing to make wage concessions to particularly inefficient mills in order to keep such mills in operation. They realize that where profitability is low the imposition of too high rates will simply result in unemployment and the loss of a local union. It is important to note in this connection, however, that it is the threat of shutdowns rather than capital-labor substitution which underlies the unions' willingness to make concessions below the pattern. The unions are aware that high-wage policies for the industry as a whole can lead to increased mechanization, but due to the steady growth of the industry and the gradual manner in which most substitution takes place, labor displacement from this source has not been a serious problem. Indeed, substitution has been welcomed in recent years as an avenue to still higher wage rates.[18] The unions face a different problem, however, in the case of a fairly large number of the older, high-cost firms located in the Northeast and manufacturing fine and specialty papers. Attempts to follow a high-wage policy in these mills will not encourage additional investment to increase efficiency but will simply close down production. Long-run profit expectations in these areas are poor, and the companies cease to operate as soon as they can no longer cover variable costs. In the older regions, therefore, where few facilities are being constructed and where there are even signs of secular decline in particular groups, the unions have no alternative but to permit low wage rates in the less efficient mills.

It may be argued that such a policy on the part of the unions makes little sense in an expanding industry, since labor displaced in shutdowns can be absorbed easily elsewhere. It should be remembered, however, that workers, and hence the unions, seek security of employment not simply in terms of a sufficient over-all demand for labor but also in terms of specific demands in particular localities and plants. Thus, while shifts in location are an inevitable part of the process of economic change, unions often pursue policies which aim to preserve existing plant locations. This problem in the paper industry is particularly

wage levels. This arises because these unions, especially District 50, have limited representation rights, a relative lack of experience in the industry, and jurisdictions which extend beyond pulp and paper into other industries. So far, however, these differences appear to have had no great effect on the interplant wage structure, perhaps because of the competitive pressures operating through employers, who may be expected to insist on wage settlements in line with negotiations in the dominant AFL mills.

18. IBPSPMW, *Proceedings of the Twenty-Second Convention* (August 1950), p. vi.

serious, since the bulk of the expansion is occurring in the newer regions and since many of the threatened plants are located in small and relatively isolated communities which afford few alternative opportunities for the employment of discharged workers.

As a consequence of the wide differences in ability to pay among northern mills, the unions have been forced to adopt a compromise approach to wage policy. Through wage leadership, they have sought to establish wage levels which the vast majority of tonnage producers can afford to pay and to spread this pattern as far as possible to other mills, permitting agreements below the standard in mills which are inefficient or where the local members are unwilling to risk strike action.[19] On the whole, this technique would seem to raise the wage level of the least efficient firm close to the maximum wage which it can pay; while the wage level of the most efficient firm remains further below the maximum it can pay, even though it is paying higher wages than the less efficient firm.

In the absence of comprehensive cost data for individual mills, it is impossible to give any quantitative estimate of the effect of differences in ability to pay upon the interplant wage structure. It seems certain, however, that a large number of the organized mills with low base rates simply cannot pay the rates negotiated in the more profitable mills. Employer resistance and lack of union aggressiveness are considerations not to be discounted: but the fact that all these low-wage mills are located in the older papermaking regions and, with minor exceptions, are engaged in the production of fine and specialty papers suggests that ability to pay is a primary influence. This tends to confirm our original hypothesis, based on industry characteristics and development, that wage levels would be lower and dispersion greater in the nontonnage mills of the Northeast.

One striking illustration of how low wage-paying ability has led to lower wage levels in the fine-papers group is found in the mills manufacturing high-quality rag writing papers. None of these mills paid base rates as high as $1.20 in late 1951, when the unions had established patterns of approximately $1.30 in the Northeast and $1.37 in the Lake states. Examination of these mills reveals that plant and equipment are old, machines small and narrow, and labor requirements relatively high because of the many operations performed by hand. These mills are finding it difficult to obtain sufficient labor at going rates, yet both employers and unions admit the difficulty of raising these rates any higher, since for several of them it would simply mean suspension of operations. A number of the older mills which have been crowded into specialty production are undoubtedly in a similar position.

19. This applies to wage increases and wage levels alike.

With the reasons for wage-level differences disposed of, the question of the degree of uniformity in late 1951 may be examined. Interplant wage uniformity is an accomplished fact in the Pacific Northwest and in the South. In the former region, this has been achieved through the development of a region-wide bargaining system, first established in 1934 to cover eighteen West Coast mills and extending in the postwar years to thirty-four mills or over 90 per cent of primary producers. An integral part of this agreement has been a thoroughgoing job-classification system expressly designed to eliminate interplant inequities by standardizing hourly wage rates for all occupations in all mills party to the agreement. The APPA *Current Wage Survey* contains information for only twelve mills in this region, but the identical rate structure found in these mills (with a base rate of $1.655 an hour) applies to all mills belonging to the region-wide bargaining system.

In the South, key wage rates have been equalized through quasi-regional bargaining. The mills in this region, with few exceptions, were organized only in the late thirties and early forties. Since the end of the war, however, the base rates set in the mills of the largest southern kraft producer have become the pattern for all other kraft mills in the region. Thus, of the nineteen mills in the South reporting wage data to the Survey in December 1951, sixteen paid a base rate of $1.25; and the only mill remaining clearly outside the pattern was independently organized and located in Texas. A more comprehensive survey of the mills in this region for December 1952 yields even clearer evidence of the degree of uniformity achieved through strong wage leadership.[20] At this time, there were forty mills in the South, thirty-three of which were organized by the IBPM and IBPSPMW. Base rates were reported for thirty of these AFL mills: twenty-seven at $1.32; two at $1.33, and the remaining one, located in Texas and the sole producer of newsprint, at $1.23.

In the older regions, for reasons already discussed, there is much less uniformity in plant wage levels. Some success has been achieved, however, within particular groups. This is illustrated in Table 6-5, which shows the distribution of mills within each region according to base-rate levels and also identifies such wage-level differences as can be attributed to differences in the length of the scheduled work week, plant location, and union status. Considering those mills operating on a forty-hour basis, it is apparent that substantial uniformity existed in northern New England, the Middle Atlantic states, the Lake states, and even perhaps in Massachusetts. There was, moreover, a close similarity in the pattern of base rates (and of postwar wage adjustments) *between*

20. IBPSPMW, Dept. of Research and Education, *Field Manual* (Feb. 1953), Sections 6.10 and 6.14.

the first two areas. Wage levels in the Lake states were somewhat higher than those prevailing in the Northeast primarily because of the larger increases negotiated in this region in the years immediately following V-J Day. In Massachusetts, on the other hand, base rates were considerably lower, for the reason that the mills in this state, with the exception of the two high-wage mills (which, incidentally, belonged to the same company), were concentrated in the fine-writing and specialty

Table 6-5. Mills in the Northern Regions by Base-rate Class, Pulp and Paper Industry, December 1951

BASE-RATE CLASS (DOLLARS)	NEW ENGLAND		LAKE STATES		MIDDLE ATLANTIC	CENTRAL STATES	CENTRAL REGION
	NORTHERN AREA *	SOUTHERN AREA †	MICHIGAN AREA ‡	WESTERN AREA §			
40 hours							
1.12–1.14		3 (2) **					
1.15–1.17		12 (1)					
1.18–1.20		2 (1)					
1.21–1.23		2				3 (2)	
1.24–1.26		1	1		7	1	2
1.27–1.29	8 (1)		1		5		
1.30–1.32	7 (1)	1	3	2	9 (1)		1 (1)
1.33–1.35				3			2
1.36–1.38				15	2 ††		1
1.39–1.41			1 ††	4			
1.42–1.44			1 ††	1			
1.45–1.47			1 ††		1 ††		
48 hours							
Below 1.00		1 (1)			1 (1)		1
1.01–1.14	1	2 (2)			2 (1)		1
1.15–1.17					3 (2)		
1.18–1.20				4 (1)	9 (4)	2 (1)	
1.21–1.23		2		1	4	2 (1)	1
1.24–1.26		1		2		2	
1.27–1.29				1	3 (1)		

* Maine and New Hampshire.

† Massachusetts.

‡ Central and Lower Michigan.

§ Wisconsin, Minnesota, and Upper Michigan.

** Figures in parentheses denote the number of nonunion mills included in the totals.

†† High rates due to plant location.

Source: APPA, Current Wage Survey, 1951

branches of production. In the Central Region, there is little evidence of strong central tendency toward any particular wage level. It is important to note, however, that wage differences in this area are due primarily to the overlap of northern and southern patterns. Kraft mills in this region tend to follow the negotiations of southern competitors, while nonkraft mills look toward the standards set by northern competitors. Thus the two kraft mills represented in the sample paid the southern base rate of $1.25 and followed the postwar pattern of increases negotiated in that branch of the industry. The nonkraft mills, on the other hand, tended to pay rates in line with those in comparable mills in the North. This tendency was no doubt strengthened by the fact that the two book mills with a base rate of $1.34 belonged to a large northeastern company, the other book mill with a rate of $1.30 to a large midwestern company, and the mill manufacturing miscellaneous papers and paying $1.37 to a large Lake states company. As far as can be judged from the present small sample, therefore, the Central Region is little more than the meeting place of North and South.

In summary, it appears that collective bargaining has led to a uniform structure of plant wage levels in the Pacific Northwest and in the South and has brought about a rough standardization of wage levels in certain areas and for certain product groups, especially the producers of standard tonnage papers, in the North. Despite this tendency toward particular concentrations of wage levels it is evident that interplant differences are still a feature of the older regions.

INTERREGIONAL DIFFERENTIALS

In this section attention will be focused on wage developments in three major regions—the Northeast, the South, and the Pacific Coast—and upon the forces responsible for these developments, particularly the influence of unions and collective bargaining. Since the unions can be expected to strive for standardization of wage levels among rival (comparable) producers, a primary consideration will be the nature and extent of interregional competition. This entails, among other things, an examination of the economic characteristics of the industry within each of the major producing regions.

The behavior of interregional wage differences over the period 1934–51 is shown in Table 6-6. As with interplant differences, the best measure for comparative purposes is the mill base rate. Since intraplant structures differ considerably between North and South, however, it is useful and even necessary to consider certain additional measures of the interregional wage structure. Accordingly, movements in the relative levels of skilled maintenance workers' rates and of average hourly earnings for all employees are also shown.[21]

The major development since 1934 has been the more rapid rise of wage levels in the newer papermaking regions of the South and Pacific Coast. The North-South differential has narrowed not only in relative terms but also in absolute terms. Thus, base rates in the South rose from only 71 per cent of the northern level in 1934 to 96 per cent by 1951, while the absolute differential declined from 12 to 7 cents. The East-West differential, on the other hand, has widened considerably during this period, though there are indications of a reversal of the trend in the postwar years. While in 1934 base rates on the Pacific Coast

Table 6-6. Interregional Wage Differences in the Pulp and Paper Industry, 1934–51

	NORTH-EAST *	SOUTH	PACIFIC COAST	NORTH-EAST *	SOUTH	PACIFIC COAST
		(DOLLARS)			(NORTHEAST = 100)	
Common-Labor Rates						
August 1934	.42	.30	.45	100	71	107
December 1940	.54	.43	.65	100	80	120
July 1945	.70	.635	.90	100	91	129
December 1951	1.32	1.25	1.655	100	96	127
Maintenance Craft Rates						
August 1934	.65	.70	.75	100	108	115
December 1940	.85	.94	.95	100	111	112
July 1945	1.06	1.265	1.25	100	119	118
December 1951	1.76	2.11	2.135	100	120	121
Average Hourly Earnings						
4th Quarter, 1934	.533	.425	.590	100	85	111
4th Quarter, 1940	.673	.617	.839	100	92	123
4th Quarter, 1945	.972	.976	1.196	100	100	123
4th Quarter, 1951	1.670	1.751	1.997	100	105	120

* Middle Atlantic states.

Source: Wage-rate data from confidential records of leading companies; average hourly earnings from APPA, Quarterly Labor Review, 5, No. 1 (1944), 7; and 12, No. 4 (1952), 7

21. The wage rate data in Table 6-6 are drawn from confidential records of individual companies that are the acknowledged wage leaders within each region. The wage developments reflected in these data are consistent with the wage reports made by unions to convention delegates. Their adequacy is confirmed, moreover, by a comparison of net changes in these *individual* rates over the period with net changes in *average* rates for common labor and maintenance craftsmen as shown in Table 5-1.

were only 7 per cent higher than those in the Northeast, they were 29 per cent higher by the end of the war and 27 per cent higher in late 1951. The spectacular increase in Pacific Coast rates during the prewar period prevented any narrowing of the West-South differential prior to the forties. Between 1940 and 1951, however, southern base rates advanced very rapidly, so that the differential between these two regions was reduced from 51 per cent to 32 per cent of the southern level.

The movement of skilled rates has been somewhat similar, though the relative position of the three regions differs. In 1934 skilled rates were highest on the West Coast and lowest in the Northeast. During the thirties, however, the West Coast suffered a relative decline while the South advanced rapidly. As a result, wage rates for skilled maintenance workers were more or less equalized between these two regions by 1940 —and at a level approximately 11 per cent above that of the Northeast. During the forties, rates in these two newer regions advanced together relative to the northeastern level and were 20 per cent higher by 1951.

In summary, wage rates in southern and western mills have risen relative to those in northeastern mills, the greatest increases being recorded in the South. Throughout most of the period, the South has been the low-wage region in the industry, but only because of the low wage rates paid to unskilled and semiskilled labor. The West Coast, on the other hand, has been the high-wage region by virtue of high wage rates for all types of labor. Developments since the mid-thirties have raised the relative wage levels of southern mills so rapidly, however, that in recent years the North-South differential in base rates has been well-nigh eliminated, and skilled rates in the South have been placed on a par with West Coast levels. These changes are reflected in the behavior of average hourly earnings. Thus between 1934 and 1951 the level of earnings of southern paperworkers rose from 85 per cent to 105 per cent of the northeastern level and from 72 per cent to 88 per cent of the West Coast level. The East-West differential in earnings increased from 11 per cent to 20 per cent during the same period.

The movement of interregional differentials in pulp and paper cannot be explained without reference to differences in the character of the industry in the various regions. Unless the distinctive features of each region are understood, it is difficult to account for the policies of the unions or to determine the impact of these policies on relative wage levels. Consequently the first step in the analysis is to compare industry conditions in the three regions in question.

The development of the pulp and paper industry in the United States has led, among other things, to a certain amount of regional specialization.[22] The earliest paper mills were located in Pennsylvania and Massachusetts, and used rags as raw material. Mill sites were found on streams and rivers close to population centers, and industry growth tended to follow in the wake of population expansion. The growing scarcity of rags, however, stimulated research on other materials; and, with the development of the wood-pulp processes in the latter part of the nineteenth century, the modern phase of expansion into the timber areas began.

The first areas to be exploited were in northern New England and New York. As increasing demand raised pulpwood prices, the industry spread westward into the Lake states and, following the Canadian Reciprocity Act of 1911, into the abundant timber lands of eastern Canada. At the same time, pulp and paper production was growing on the Pacific Coast where there was a natural market for local producers, expanding constantly as population shifted westward. The abundant supplies of cheap wood and power in the northwestern states and the availability of water transportation made for ideal mill locations. Concurrent with the expansion of West Coast production, attempts were being made to develop techniques for utilizing the great stands of southern pine in the manufacture of coarse wrapping paper and board. By the early thirties these efforts had met with success; and, with abundant cheap wood and power and an adequate supply of unskilled labor, the great southern kraft branch of the industry sprang into being.

The expansion of production in the South was more spectacular than on the West Coast, but, as the following figures indicate, both these newer regions have grown rapidly relative to the country as a whole: [23]

		Per Cent of U. S. Output Produced in:	
		South	*Pacific Coast*
Pulp:	1924	12%	8%
	1929	17	15
	1951	54	18
Paper:	1925	3	5
	1929	4	8
	1950	25	8

22. The growth of the industry is discussed in detail in Stevenson, *The Background and Economics of American Papermaking*, Chap. 1.

23. U. S. Pulp Producers Association, Inc. (USPPA), *Wood Pulp Statistics* (New York, August 1952), pp. 38–9; *Census of Manufactures*, 1927, pp. 554–6, and 1931, p. 493; and APPA, *Statistics of Paper*, 1952, pp. 25–6.

The major reasons for the more rapid expansion of production in the newer regions have already been suggested—namely, cheap raw materials and, to a lesser extent, cheap fuel and adequate water transport facilities. That abundant, cheap wood supplies were the major attraction can scarcely be disputed,[24] for pulpwood costs are the most important single cost item in the production of pulp and of a number of types of paper. Since more than half the commercial timber available in the United States is located in the Pacific Northwest and the South, these two regions enjoy a substantial price advantage in the purchase of pulpwood.[25] These lower raw material prices are reflected in the costs of producing wood pulp. This is shown in the following comparisons of manufacturing costs per ton: [26]

		Northeast	Lake and Central	Pacific	South
Groundwood:	1934	$20.33	$24.78	$19.44	
	1946	33.83	35.78	23.48	
Unbleached sulphite:	1934	40.78	40.24	28.12	
	1946	75.24	64.21	46.45	
Unbleached sulphate:	1934		37.80	27.66	$23.64
	1946		61.99	39.39	42.55

The Pacific Coast has considerably lower costs than the older regions in the production of groundwood and sulphite pulps and shares the low-cost position with the southern states as regards the production of sulphate pulp.

Low wood-pulp costs are in turn reflected, but to a lesser degree, in the production costs of paper.[27] Thus newsprint is produced at lowest

24. C. W. Boyce, executive secretary of the APPA, testified in 1939 that there was no tendency to seek low-wage areas in expansion since other locational factors (principally timber supplies) were of much more importance. U. S. Department of Labor, "The Determination of the Prevailing Minimum Wage in the Paper and Pulp Industry," *Report of Proceedings before the Division of Public Contracts* (Washington, March 27, 1939), pp. 91–2.

25. USPPA, *Wood Pulp Statistics, 1952,* p. 117. In 1947, for example, the average cost of pulpwood per cord was $14.42 for southern pine, $18.28 for western hemlock, and $24.58 for northern spruce and fir.

26. 1934 data from U. S. Tariff Commission, *Wood Pulp and Pulpwood,* Report No. 126, Second Series (Washington, 1938), pp. 208, 229, and 243; and 1946 data from Guthrie, *The Economics of Pulp and Paper,* pp. 146–8.

27. This discussion of interregional cost differentials is based primarily on Guthrie, *The Economics of Pulp and Paper,* Chaps. 5, 6, and 11.

cost on the Pacific Coast. This is revealed in the following estimates of average costs per ton: [28]

	Pacific Coast	Maine	Lake States
1940	$32.45	$34.35	$40.00
1942	39.59	37.36	46.30
1946	50.85	54.25	

No data are available for the new southern newsprint mills, but it is generally believed that newsprint production costs in the South approximate those in the Northeast.[29] It will be noted that the advantage enjoyed by Pacific Coast producers over northern New England producers is slight. The latter, with mills located in Maine, have extensive timber holdings and are therefore still able to manufacture newsprint at relatively low cost. Since there is little difference in production costs between the three producing areas of the Pacific Northwest, northern New England, and the South, and since these areas are widely separated and transportation costs are high, it is not surprising that there is little interregional competition in newsprint.[30] Each producer competes rather with others in the same region and with Canadian producers.

In the production of kraft wrapping and bag papers, the primary raw material is sulphate pulp. This pulp is produced most cheaply in the Pacific Northwest and the South, and producers in these two regions therefore enjoy a considerable advantage over others in the manufacture of kraft papers. In 1942, for example, the average cost of producing a hundredweight of standard kraft wrapping was $2.65 on the West Coast, $3.00 in the South, and $3.80 in the Lake states.[31] West Coast producers appear to have slightly lower manufacturing costs than even southern producers; but the cost of transporting wrapping paper to principal consuming centers in the eastern and midwestern states is

28. *Ibid.*, pp. 152–3. It is interesting to note that newsprint production was discontinued in Lake states mills in the postwar years.

29. See, e.g., U. S. Tariff Commission, "Newsprint," *War Changes in Industry Series*, Report No. 22, Revised (Washington, 1951), p. 23.

30. In 1948 newsprint produced in Maine was sold in markets east of the Mississippi and principally in neighboring states. Washington and Oregon newsprint was consumed in the western states, principally California, and Texas-originating newsprint was sold in Texas and neighboring Oklahoma. See U. S. Department of Commerce, *Transportation Factors in the Marketing of Newsprint* (Washington, 1952), pp. 27–9.

31. Guthrie, *The Economics of Pulp and Paper*, p. 156.

greater for western mills, and this tends to offset the slight cost advantage enjoyed by the latter.

Relatively high production costs have placed mills in the older regions at a serious competitive disadvantage in the manufacture of standard kraft grades, and gradually such mills have been forced to retreat into specialty production.[32] This competition comes mainly from southern producers; for since the war West Coast production of kraft papers has been required to satisfy regional demand. Profit positions in recent years suggest, moreover, that southern mills will continue to dominate markets outside the western region.[33]

The production of tissue, writing, and book papers is concentrated in the older regions of the Northeast, Lake states, and Midwest, though most regions manufacture a certain portion of the total. Regional cost data for these grades are even more fragmentary than for others, but it is possible to draw some general conclusions.[34] None of these papers is produced in large quantity on the Pacific Coast or in the South, and indications are that while the former region may enjoy in some instances certain production advantages because of low pulp costs, these are generally not sufficient to encourage expansion of capacity beyond the requirements of the western market. There is some cross-shipment of these grades between East and West, but in general the flow of trade is to, rather than from, the Pacific Coast.

Paperboard covers a wide variety of types, only one or two of which need be considered here. Kraft boards are manufactured primarily from sulphate pulp, and production tends to be concentrated therefore in the South and Pacific Northwest where pulp costs are lowest. Pacific Coast producers have a slight cost advantage over southern producers in the manufacture of these boards,[35] but again freight expenses are a significant item in the delivered price, and it is doubtful therefore if West Coast producers have any advantage over southern producers outside the western market. Jute board, on the other hand, is made primarily from wastepaper stock which is available in quantity near all large consuming centers. Thus, even though the Pacific Coast appears to have a small cost advantage in manufacturing this product also,

32. BLS, "The Coarse Paper Industry, 1949 and 1950: Capital Requirements and Operating Ratios," *Report No. 24* (Washington, 1953), p. 3.

33. Thus in 1950 profits averaged 26% of net sales in 4 southern kraft mills compared with 15% in 5 northern kraft mills. On an individual mill basis, profit ratios ranged from 20% to 35% in the South against 11% to 20% in the North. One of the 5 northern mills was located in the Pacific Northwest. *Ibid.*, p. 34.

34. See Guthrie, *The Economics of Pulp and Paper*, pp. 86–9, 157–60.

35. *Ibid.*, p. 161. In 1941 the cost of producing a ton of kraft liner board was $35.50 on the West Coast and $37.00 in the South. The relative production costs per ton of kraft corrugating board were almost the same.

any net advantage is probably confined to sales in the western states.[36]

In summary, it would appear that West Coast producers have lowest costs in the production of most grades of pulp and paper. Freight costs limit the profitability of bulk selling in eastern and midwestern markets, however, save in the case of sulphite pulp (extensive shipments of which are made to eastern and midwestern markets) and perhaps such tonnage grades of paper as kraft wrapping and board. There appears to be some cross-shipment of most types of paper; but for the most part West Coast mills produce for the expanding western market. In the South there is less diversification of production than on the West Coast. By virtue of its raw material resources, the South enjoys a great comparative advantage in the manufacture of kraft pulp and papers. The majority of its mills consequently specialize in the production of these grades. The privileged position of the South is evidenced not only in the relative profitability of southern mills and the continuing shift of northern competitors into specialty and other grades of paper, but also in the fact that recent construction of new papermaking facilities has tended to be concentrated in this region.

Lower raw material costs are not the only advantage enjoyed by producers in the Pacific Northwest and the South. Labor costs also tend to be relatively low in these two regions, as the following comparisons of direct labor costs per ton show: [37]

		April 1942	April 1946
Unbleached sulphate:	Lake and Central	$6.00	$6.83
	Pacific	3.11	3.73
	South	2.84	5.04
Unbleached sulphite:	Northeast	4.16	7.11
	Lake and Central	3.09	4.05
	Pacific	2.82	4.69
		1942	1946
Newsprint:	Maine and New York	$4.27	$5.80
	Pacific	4.24	6.60

Labor costs are relatively low in Pacific Coast mills despite the fact that wage rates in this region are approximately 20 per cent above the levels prevailing elsewhere. This can be attributed to the very high

36. *Ibid.*, p. 162. The manufacturing costs of jute liner board in 1941 were $39.00 per ton in the Pacific Northwest, $42.70 in the Lake and Central states, and $44.40 in the Northeast.

37. Pulp data from OPA, "Survey of Paper and Paper Products Manufacturers," pp. 11–12; newsprint data from Guthrie, *The Economics of Pulp and Paper*, p. 140.

level of investment per worker, the efficiency of management and equipment, and the use in pulping of larger logs which involve less wastage and require less labor to handle. Less marked, but nevertheless significant, are the relatively low labor cost levels in the South compared with the older regions.

In view of the interregional cost structure, which has promoted a fair degree of regional specialization, it is not surprising to find that union policies are directed more toward intraregional than interregional uniformity of wage rates. No union official denies the desirability of uniform job rates in all plants throughout the country, but few advocate uniformity as a practical objective. The goal set by the unions is simply the highest wage level obtainable for each region, spread more or less uniformly over plants within each region. It is true that wage levels in the Northeast (and, more recently, in the Pacific Northwest) have been used as a lever to raise base rates in the South, but such tactics are purely opportunistic. As long as differentials exist they make a good talking point in negotiations. As they do within regions, however, so among regions the unions recognize and accept—or are forced to accept—differences in resource availability, in prevailing wage levels, and in productive efficiency. Their objective is to establish a pattern (for comparable mills) within each region based largely on regional capacity to pay.

The more rapid wage advances made in the Pacific Northwest and the South since the depression are entirely consistent with this sort of policy. Mills in these two regions are in a superior competitive position, particularly in those lines of production where wood-pulp costs represent a high proportion of the total cost of the finished product. In addition, both regions are characterized by a greater degree of concentration of production, less heterogeneity among mills, and a very high level of unionization. These conditions establish the basis for greater relative wage increases in Pacific Coast and southern mills. In order to understand the part played by collective bargaining, however, it is necessary to examine in a little more detail the particular forces which have helped shape wage developments within each region.

Since unionism in the industry was very weak during the depression, it is not unreasonable to assume that the structure of interregional differentials in 1934 (see Table 6-6) conformed approximately to the structure that would have developed in the absence of collective bargaining. With this in mind, and using the Northeast as a base for comparison, it is possible to trace the forces responsible for wage-level developments in the Pacific Northwest and the South.

The Pacific Coast branch of the pulp and paper industry has been the subject of extensive investigations in recent years. From the findings of these investigations and from other sources (including interviews with union and company officials), it is clear that the principal forces influencing wage levels within this region have been the wage-paying capacity of plants, competition for labor from other industries, and trade unionism.

In the discussion of interplant differentials it was shown that plants located in high-wage communities may be forced to pay wage rates above prevailing industry levels in order to ensure an adequate labor force. Similarly, plants located in a high-wage region may be compelled to offer rates higher than those in other regions in order to compete successfully against other industries for the available labor supply. This is the case on the West Coast. Location in a labor-scarce, high-wage region is the fundamental reason for higher wage rates in Pacific Coast pulp and paper mills. As Kerr and Randall point out:

> For the majority of pulp and paper workers, employment in the sawmills has been the major alternative. Pulp and paper mills in Everett, Hoquiam, and Longview, for example, are virtually next door to lumber mills. The common labor rate in the sawmills has been well known and, in fact, has served as the key rate in the Pacific Northwest. If wages in pulp and paper were to fall significantly below those in the sawmills, many workers would be tempted to change jobs.[38]

Wages in the lumber industry, especially in sawmills, have been a primary factor in determining base rates in Pacific Coast pulp and paper mills.

The relationship between base rates in pulp and paper mills and common-labor rates in sawmills is closer, however, than market forces alone would normally dictate. Trade unionism has had the effect of defining more narrowly the extent to which base rates in the industry may deviate from sawmill levels. The International Woodworkers of America (CIO), which represents the sawmill workers, has long been a strong rival for representation rights over pulp and paper mill workers (especially in Washington), and this rivalry has compelled the incumbent AFL unions to match closely the wage levels and wage gains secured by the IWA. Failure on the part of the paper unions to measure up to the standards set by this powerful and aggressive opponent would

38. Clark Kerr and Roger Randall, "Crown Zellerbach and the Pacific Coast Pulp and Paper Industry," *Causes of Industrial Peace under Collective Bargaining,* Case Study No. 1 (Washington, National Planning Association, Sept. 1948), pp. 51–2.

threaten the security of the unions and the stability of the collective bargaining relationship—a fact well recognized by mill operators as well as union officials. The data in Table 6-7 show that sawmill negotiations have dominated the pattern of wage movements in Pacific Coast pulp and paper mills. This comparison of base rates in sawmilling and papermaking for the

Table 6-7. *Increases in Common-Labor Rates for Pacific Northwest Sawmills and Pulp and Paper Mills, 1937–48*

	ENTRANCE RATE SAWMILLS	COMMON-LABOR RATE PULP AND PAPER MILLS
January 1937	$ .50	$ .525
April 1937	.625	
June 1937		.625
June 1940		.65
December 1940	.675	
April 1941	.75	
June 1941		.75
April 1942	.825	
June 1942		.85
September 1942	.90	
June 1943		.90
November 1945	1.05	
January 1946		1.05
April 1946	1.10	
June 1946		1.09
November 1946	1.25	
January 1947		1.20
April 1947	1.325	
June 1947		1.275
April 1948	1.45	
June 1948		1.425

Source: Kerr and Randall, "Crown Zellerbach and the Pacific Coast Pulp and Paper Industry," p. 59

period 1937–48 leaves little doubt as to the leadership of the IWA. Additional evidence to this effect is found in the fact that employers reopened the pulp and paper contract voluntarily on January 1, 1947 to grant a wage increase of 10 per cent which brought the base rate to within 5 cents of the rate negotiated in sawmills in November of the previous year. As Kerr and Randall observed, "This was done unilaterally, although with union knowledge and encouragement." [39] Wages have

39. *Ibid.*, p. 60.

been set for the most part in the lumber industry, and both employers and the unions in pulp and paper have been compelled to match these standards.[40]

Primary influences in the development of southern wage levels have similarly been the wage-paying capacity of plants, trade unionism, and interindustry competition for labor. Unlike the situation on the West Coast, however, competition for labor in the South has tended to limit rather than encourage advances in the wage level. Labor market pressures have operated against the pressures for higher relative wage rates arising out of the profitability of operations and widespread union organization.

The remarkable expansion of southern kraft production in recent decades could be expected to produce a rise in base rates in southern mills relative to the levels in northern mills and in the South generally. The enormous increase in demand for labor and the need for offering very high wage rates to skilled paperworkers to induce immigration from other areas were certainly influences tending in this direction. These pressures alone, however, can offer no more than a partial explanation for the extremely rapid wage advances secured for unskilled labor in southern mills. A more complete explanation would have to take account of the independent (and powerful) influence of unionism.

A number of considerations lend support to the role of the unions in raising the relative level of base rates in southern mills. In the first place, the unions' efforts to eliminate the difference in base rates between North and South have met with vigorous opposition from paper producers in the latter region. This opposition arises from the firm belief that economic differences between the two regions justify, and even make desirable, the maintenance of an adequate wage differential. Secondly, to this already strong opposition on the part of southern paper producers is added the persistent and growing protests of employers in other southern industries, who see in the high wage rates secured by the unions for common labor in southern kraft the undermining or destruction of prevailing (low) wage patterns for unskilled labor in the South. Thirdly, it is abundantly clear that southern kraft producers could have secured an adequate supply of common labor at wage rates substantially below those actually negotiated. In this connection, it should be noted that the unions established a necessary condition for raising wage rates in southern kraft mills above prevailing wage levels in the South; for by spreading organization to virtually all producers in the region and by standardizing wage rates among these rival producers, they removed

40. General plant-wide wage increases in Pacific Coast paper mills appear to have maintained craft rates at a satisfactory level. Thus, special craft-rate adjustments have been negligible in this region compared with other regions.

the threat of price competition based on differing wage standards. Since southern producers of kraft papers have enjoyed considerable labor and nonlabor cost advantages over northern competitors, it is not surprising that the unions have therefore been able to reduce the North-South differential to negligible proportions.

In summary, union wage policy with regard to interregional differentials appears to have been highly opportunistic. The unions are aware of substantial differences in the character and profitability of the industry in different regions and tend therefore to pursue policies which are sufficiently flexible to take account of these differences. Any alteration of interregional differentials has been largely incidental to the primary objective of securing the highest wage level possible within each region consistent with a fair degree of intraregional uniformity. The unions are of course anxious to eliminate low-wage pockets in the industry, but normally not at the expense of foregoing any increases obtainable in already high-wage areas or regions. Indeed, they may have no choice in the matter, as witness the situation in the Pacific Northwest.

This is not to argue that the unions have abandoned the notion of standardizing wages throughout the industry, for it is clear that the standard rate remains a cardinal principle of trade union philosophy.[41] It is, however, a long-run objective which may well be overshadowed by other needs of a more urgent and immediate character. It should also be noted that, as long as substantial nonlabor cost differences exist among regions, a rational wage policy for the unions might well include the preservation (and even widening) of interregional differentials. Insofar as the unions are interested in protecting employment opportunities for their membership in *existing* locations or in cushioning the effects of readjustments between areas, it is total unit costs rather

41. The situation *within* the West Coast region affords an excellent illustration of the strength of this principle. Wage levels in West Coast mills are set primarily by forces outside the industry: employers and the unions alike are compelled to match standards set in the lumber industry, and particularly in sawmills. These pressures are felt most acutely in mills in the state of Washington where lumber operations are concentrated and rival unionism is strong. Notwithstanding the difficulties faced in this area, however, the unions (with the approval of northern producers) have insisted on region-wide uniformity even though wage gains for the region as a whole are limited by the normally lower wage-paying capacity of Southern California mills. Had the unions chosen to follow a discriminatory wage policy, their ability to meet the challenge of the IWA in Washington might well have been considerably enhanced and the friction between local and international unions thereby reduced. So far, however, they have preferred to follow a policy of intraregional uniformity, though this has required at times the use of rather severe measures to discipline dissenting locals in the Washington area. See Kerr and Randall, "Crown Zellerbach and the Pacific Coast Pulp and Paper Industry," pp. 64–5.

than simply wage rates which are the relevant consideration. By reducing the cost advantages enjoyed in developing regions through the manipulation of wage differentials, the unions may "dampen" their rate of expansion and thus afford a measure of protection to members in the less favored areas.

Union leaders probably have in mind considerations of this sort in their approach to interregional differentials. These differentials are the product of a multitude of influences, however, over which the unions may have little or no control. The behavior of the East-West differential appears to fall within this category. How the East-West differential behaves is determined solely by the relationship between negotiated wage increases in the East and minimum required increases on the West Coast. It is the forces operating to set wage levels within each region which determine the nature of the differential rather than any coordinated wage policy on the part of the unions.

The effect of union policy is more clearly distinguished when wage-level developments in northern and southern mills are compared. There seems little basis for disputing either the unions' intention to narrow the North-South differential or their contribution to its reduction (and even elimination). This does not deny the influence of other factors in raising relative wage levels in the South. The enormous expansion in demand for pulpworkers and paperworkers, the high profitability of southern producers in relation to northern competitors, and the tendency for southern wages in general to rise relative to northern levels were certainly forces operating in the same direction. Notwithstanding such influences, however, it is clear that North-South differentials have been narrowed further and more rapidly under the pressure of unionism.

SUMMARY OF FINDINGS

The principal findings of Chapters 5 and 6 can be summarized briefly in terms of the effects of collective bargaining upon occupational, interplant, and geographic differentials.

Unionism has been a primary force in bringing about a substantial narrowing of occupational differentials in the industry. This is not to argue that unions alone have been responsible for this effect, for other factors—particularly full employment and the inflation of the postwar years—obviously contributed, if only in the sense that they set the stage for general wage increases. These other forces did in fact make a positive contribution toward a narrower structure of wage levels; but the success of the unions in protecting the wage standards of unskilled workers in the early thirties and in negotiating cents-per-hour increases in the face of strong employer opposition offers convincing evidence of the independent and powerful influence exercised by unionism upon the structure of skill differentials.

One of the most interesting aspects of this development was the modification of policy on the part of the IBPM during the late twenties and early thirties. The nature of this change in policy was illustrated by examining the evolution of the Standard Minimum Wage Schedule, the basic wage document of this essentially craft-type organization. It appears that while the original structure of this schedule, which reflects the orientation of a skill-dominated union, has been retained, revisions over time mirror the union's responsiveness and accommodation to needs which are distinctly "noncraft" in nature—the needs of unskilled and semiskilled workers. Evidence of this transformation is found not only in the successive uniform cents-per-hour adjustments made to all schedule wage rates, but also in the extension of the graduation principle to the majority of occupations included in the union's jurisdiction. The evolution of this schedule demonstrates the flexible and adaptable nature of union policy in adjusting to the political needs of organization and also to the economic needs of the industry, as witness the union's acceptance of interplant differentials and its linking of the wage schedule to the base rate in individual mills.

Although the primary influence of unionism upon the occupational wage structure has been the reduction of skill differentials, certain other effects are worth noting. The unions have worked toward the elimination of wage differentials based on personal characteristics (e.g. sex and color) rather than on job content. They have also sought to increase the number of job classifications by distinguishing all elements of skill, responsibility, and conditions of work. As a result, most plants have a fairly elaborate job structure and corresponding rate structure developed through collective bargaining. In a few instances (e.g. the West Coast agreement), these job classifications have been established through formal programs of job analysis and evaluation. Whether formally or informally developed, however, the pressure toward increase in the number of job titles and job rates has come from the unions. The most striking feature of this development has been the gradual but steady reduction in the number of employees compensated at the common-labor or base-rate level. There has been a marked reduction in the dispersion of employees within the range of plant wage rates as well as a decrease in the range itself.

Finally, while the unions did not establish the seniority principle, they have considerably strengthened and systematized its application to promotions and transfers. As a result, the wage rates for common labor and maintenance craftsmen are the only rates which remain fully subject to the pressure of market forces. The majority of semiskilled and skilled rates, on the other hand, are insulated against these pressures, except indirectly through the transmission of impulses from movements in the two key rates. This development suggests at least two reasons for anticipating a narrowing of skill differentials: first, the institutional barrier to movement between plants may permit reductions which could not otherwise have occurred; and second, promotions on a seniority (rather than efficiency) basis may result in a general lowering of the productivity of the skilled groups. Against these possibilities, however, must be weighed the employers' preference for maintenance of differentials, the machine-paced nature of production, and the fact that the majority of these occupations have a very narrow market in any one locality so that their rates have always been set as much by administrative action as by market forces.

Investigation of the impact of unionism upon interplant differentials reveals that the unions have met with considerable success in their efforts to standardize the wage levels of rival producers—or, perhaps more correctly, comparable and potentially rival producers. The clearest evidence of achievement is found in the uniform wage standards negotiated for Pacific Coast mills under a region-wide agreement, and in the equalization of key rates in the South under a system of quasi-regional bargaining. The unions have met with less success in the older regions of the Northeast and Midwest—and for obvious reasons. Here they have been faced with a combination of unfavorable economic and institutional factors, of which the more important are the greater heterogeneity of mills (in terms of products manufactured, raw materials used, and levels of efficiency and profitability), less widespread organization, the existence of strong union rivalry, and less concentration of production. Nevertheless, even in those regions the unions have made some progress toward establishing and maintaining a rough uniformity of wage levels within particular groups—notably the tonnage producers of northern New England and New York, the larger companies of Wisconsin and upper Michigan, and the fine writing-paper manufacturers of the East. In all, therefore, the unions' drive to standardize plant wage levels has met with a large measure of success.

Analysis of union efforts to eliminate interplant wage differences raises a number of related issues which were examined in the study and deserve brief mention here. These are the reasons for continuing differences in plant wage levels, and the manner in which the reduction in dispersion of plant wage levels is accomplished. The findings in each case are presented below.

Such wage-level differences as currently exist among plants in the industry are related primarily to differences in the length of the work week, union status, and ability to pay.[42] Differences in ability to pay are probably the principal source of interplant differentials, though conclusions on this score remain tentative in the absence of more data. It should be noted that, even while the negative correlation between wage rates and length of the scheduled work week emphasizes the interrelatedness of decisions on hourly rates of compensation and the number of hours worked, it is possible that these wage-level differences also reflect variations in the wage-paying capacity of plants. Some employers may simply be unable to meet prevailing union wage standards but may nevertheless find it necessary to offer large earnings on a weekly basis in order to attract and hold the necessary work force. However, the most persuasive argument in support of the contention that ability to pay is the primary determinant of plant wage differences within the unionized sector is that no other explanation is consistent with the objectives of union policy. Unions will sanction differences in ability to pay as a legitimate though limited source of wage differentials partly because low-wage, high-cost plants pose no threat to the stability of the price-wage structure and partly because the only alternative to a wage concession is shutdown and loss of employment.

The structure of plant wage levels in the older papermaking regions demonstrates how the conflict between the standard-rate principle and the principle of ability to pay is normally resolved. Where differences in the wage-paying capacity of plants are moderate, it is usually to the unions' advantage to seek uniformity. If differences are substantial, however, the cost of uniformity runs high: the unions must choose either to forego large wage benefits in the more efficient mills or to accept major disruptions in established employment patterns. The solution to this problem in pulp and paper represents perhaps the typical compromise: union policy has been modified to secure a reasonable degree of uniformity for the majority of firms, with wage concessions granted to the least efficient.

The present study has little, if anything, to say about the extent to which unions have affected the general level of wages in the industry. A comparison of wage levels in union and nonunion mills suggests that wage rates have advanced more rapidly in the union sector; and it is further possible that nonunion wage levels reflect the influence of union negotiations. Unfortunately the precise nature and extent of these effects cannot be measured from current statistics; the answers must be sought within a somewhat different framework of analysis.

One significant effect of unionization which can be identified is the manner in which interplant differentials have been narrowed within

42. Wage differentials due to plant location are considered under the heading of geographic differentials.

the union sector through an upward leveling of wage rates in low-wage mills. This compressive effect of collective bargaining is deserving of further study, for it may well be that much of the unexplained wage behavior revealed in interindustry studies can only be accounted for by changes occurring *within* the wage structure of individual industries. One might speculate, for example, on the extent to which influences of this sort help to explain why unionism tends to yield more appreciable gains in the early stages of organization than in later periods.[43] Indeed, it might well be argued that a knowledge of intraindustry wage patterns and changes in these patterns is essential to an understanding of trends in interindustry earnings, for summary statistics relating to the industry as a whole conceal those dynamic changes which are most meaningful in the analysis of wage problems. One need only consider the effect on industry earnings of changes in geographical location, structure of occupations, or output-mix of the industry to realize the serious shortcomings of statistical averages of such wide coverage.

The impact of unionism upon geographic differentials can be dealt with more summarily. In the case of interregional differentials, it is probably correct to say that union leaders harbor a deep-seated desire eventually to reduce them.[44] It is clear, however, that union policy is quite flexible on this issue. In practice, the unions recognize the reasons for such interregional differentials as exist, and they are not unaware of differences in the economic potential of the various regions. Moreover, they are often faced with considerations of a more urgent and vital nature, such as the security of the organization itself. These considerations may well overshadow the objective of uniformity and may actually lead to wage movements in the opposite direction. This does not signify that the goal of greater standardization has been abandoned, but rather that other needs claim a higher priority. It is in this sense that union wage policy appears flexible and opportunistic.

The fact that the East-West differential widened up to the mid-1940's and has only recently shown signs of declining has been in large part an incidental outgrowth of policies designed to meet the needs of both unions and employers within each region. Mills on the West Coast have a higher wage-paying capacity than those in the East and are located in a high-wage region. Consequently they have traditionally been the high-wage mills in the industry. Moreover, the needs of unions and employers

---

43. This tendency has been observed by Arthur M. Ross and William Goldner, "Forces Affecting the Interindustry Wage Structure," *Quarterly Journal of Economics,* 64 (May 1950), 267; and Paul H. Douglas, *Real Wages in the United States, 1890–1926* (Boston, Houghton Mifflin, 1930), p. 562.

44. Leaders of the IBPM, IBPSPMW, and UPA-CIO have always opposed, for example, the recognition of regional differences in minimum wage legislation.

in the Pacific Northwest are closely defined by the trend of negotiations in the lumber industry. Any reduction in the East-West differential will depend therefore on the unions' ability to secure wage gains in eastern mills which exceed minimum wage requirements on the West Coast.

The behavior of the North-South differential has, for obvious reasons, been quite different. Broad regional forces have been operating in recent decades to improve the relative wage position of the South. In addition, it is apparent that southern papermaking has been highly profitable and expanding compared with papermaking in the North. These factors alone suggest that some narrowing of the North-South differential would have occurred even in the absence of collective bargaining. With unions present in strength in the South, however, this reduction has proceeded further and more rapidly, so that for all practical purposes the traditional differential no longer exists.

Within regions, the unions have successfully sought elimination of intercommunity and interarea differentials. The only wage differences of this type which have been given the stamp of union approval are found in plants located in high-wage markets where the prevailing regional wage level for the industry is insufficient to ensure an adequate supply of labor to the plant. Needless to say, this policy is not reversible in the case of plants situated in low-wage communities, since wage concessions granted under these conditions would constitute a potential—if not actual—threat to the stability of the wage structure. Accordingly, if union mills located in low-wage markets are paying wage rates below the standard, the cause is more likely to relate to wage-paying capacity than to location.

CHAPTER 7 *The Impact of Unionism on Wage Structure*

ECONOMISTS have frequently viewed with alarm the rise of powerful labor syndicates able to influence the pricing and allocation of labor services. The apparent parallel with industrial monopoly, the interference with market pricing, and the possible limitation of free occupational choices provide a basis for legitimate apprehension. The great expansion of union strength in the United States during the thirties and forties has brought a new wave of critical comment [1] and of proposals for curtailing union power.

Recent discussion of the impact of unionism has focused on two principal issues. One controversy has to do with the effect of unionism on the general level of money wage rates. Does strong unionism increase the likelihood of a rapid advance of wages and prices during periods of high employment? Does it contribute to secular inflation? A much older controversy, which is the central concern of this chapter, has to do with the impact of unionism on relative wage rates. Does unionism distort the wage structure away from its "normal" pattern, with disruptive effects on relative prices, outputs, and resource allocation?

In addition to its direct impact on the wage structure, unionism has at least two possible indirect effects which can only be noted in passing. First, union rules undoubtedly alter workers' reaction patterns, employers' hiring and promotion practices, the channels through which labor moves into employment, and other features of the labor market. Seniority systems, for example, may reduce both the willingness and ability of workers to change employers, and may mean that interfirm competition for labor occurs principally at the bottom of the occupational structure. Discussion of these side effects is omitted here, partly for reasons of space, partly because research in this area is only in its infancy.

1. See Henry Simons, "Some Reflections on Syndicalism," *Journal of Political Economy, 52* (March 1944), 1–25; Fritz Machlup, "Monopolistic Wage Determination," paper read at Economic Institute on Wage Determination and the Economics of Liberalism, U. S. Chamber of Commerce, January 11, 1947; David McC. Wright, ed., *The Impact of the Union* (New York, Harcourt, Brace, 1951).

Second, unions might influence wages by controlling the number of workers admitted to particular occupations and industries. Indeed, it has sometimes been argued (or assumed) that this is the principal way in which unions influence the wage structure. Manipulation of wages via labor supply, however, implies a closed shop plus a policy of admitting to the union fewer workers than employers would be willing to hire at competitive wage rates. The closed shop has been used by only a minority of craft unions, while deliberate restriction of members is found in a still smaller number. Opinion is now shifting increasingly to the view that unions influence wage rates not by control of labor supply but by direct control of the employer. The sequence of events is not that supply is first reduced and then wages rise. Rather, wages are raised through direct negotiation with the employer under threat of strike action, and this limits the number of workers who can find employment at the bargained wage.

We shall confine ourselves in this chapter to direct effects on wage structure arising from union policies in collective bargaining. Before embarking on the main discussion, several methodological comments are in order.

First, it is necessary to take account of all the dimensions of wage structure. Theoretical discussion has tended to focus on interindustry differentials and on the problem of whether unionism alters these in an anti-competitive way. Equally important, however, are personal differentials among workers in the same type of work, occupational differentials, interfirm differentials within an industry, and geographical differentials. The effect of unionism on each of these things must be appraised before its total impact can be judged.

Second, there is no warrant for the assumption that unionism is the only thing preventing attainment of a perfectly competitive wage structure. There is a growing body of evidence that the labor market is by nature an imperfect instrument and that all kinds of wage distortions exist even under nonunion conditions. To compare the wage structure which develops under collective bargaining with a hypothetical wage structure which might exist under perfect competition is an arbitrary and unreal procedure. The significant comparison is between the bargained wage structure and that which actually exists in imperfect nonunion labor markets. It may turn out that the bargained wage structure lies closer to the hypothetical competitive pattern than does the nonunion structure. In any event, the inquiry should not be biased by taking a position on this point before the evidence has been examined.

Third, the consequences of unionism cannot be discovered simply by deduction. General reasoning must be checked by systematic observation of bargained wage structures in different industries, different countries, and different time periods. We know relatively little about the mainsprings of union wage policy, and students of the subject are at odds on many points. There would be widespread agreement among informed observers, however, that the analogy with business monopoly is seriously misleading. It is reasonable to take profit maximization as a first approximation to business behavior, because a concern for profit is a condition of survival and growth for the firm. The trade union, however, is not engaged in buying and selling. It does not make a profit if wages are set high, nor does it become bankrupt if wages are set low. It is a regulatory agency engaged in determining the minimum standards under which production may continue, and is more nearly comparable to a local government than to a business organization.

With respect to each main dimension of wage structure, then, it is proposed to raise the following questions: 1. What kind of differentials appear to develop in nonunion labor markets? 2. What evidence is available concerning the changes resulting from the growth of union organization and collective bargaining? 3. To the extent that evidence is available, does unionism seem to have improved or worsened the wage structure? Determination of what constitutes an "improvement" necessarily involves a large element of personal judgment. One might try to use as criterion the kind of wage structure which would exist in a perfectly competitive labor market, and the argument of this chapter was at one stage worked out in this way.[2] The difficulty is that the concept of a competitive wage structure cannot be reduced to quantitative terms. Any effort to use it as an operational yardstick thus seems bound to fail, though the reader may still detect the concept lurking in the background of the argument at various points.

The discussion of this chapter is in no way restricted to the data presented in Chapters 2–6, but draws also on the general research literature which has accumulated so rapidly in recent years. The focus is on experience in the United States over the past two decades. The experience of other countries will be cited occasionally, however, and the analysis may anticipate a few of the findings from the case studies in Part 2.

PERSONAL DIFFERENTIALS

THE NONUNION LABOR MARKET

IN A fully competitive system, the relative earnings of workers employed in the same occupation in the same establishment would correspond

2. In a paper presented by L. G. Reynolds to the 1954 conference on wage determination of the International Economic Association, which will be published in the forthcoming report of that conference. Where statements made in that paper differ from those made here, the present text should be taken as the later and more thoroughly revised version.

to their relative efficiencies. How far this actually happens under non-union conditions depends partly on the method of wage payment. An incentive system permits individual efficiency to be reflected in earnings. This is not to say that earnings actually do vary with (potential) efficiency, for there is a well-known tendency for pieceworkers to adhere to group norms and for the faster workers to adjust to the pace of the slower. Some of the incentive formulas in use also require earnings to rise less rapidly than output, which may mean that the more a worker produces the further does his wage fall below his value product.

Time payment is still the predominant form, particularly in non-manufacturing industries. Many nonunion employers, particularly the smaller ones, have not reached the stage of standard occupational wage rates but establish a separate personal rate for each employee. This permits adjustment of individual earnings to estimated efficiency, but does not ensure this result. A system of personal rates lends itself to favoritism, bribery, and other forms of malpractice by foremen and supervisors. There is no certainty that a man's rate will be closely related to his personal efficiency, and monopsonistic exploitation may occur on a considerable scale.

The larger employers normally have a centralized wage system which provides a standard hourly rate or range of rates for each occupation. This is accompanied by increased centralization of hiring and more careful selection and assignment of new employees. A system of standard rates reduces monopsonistic exploitation and also eliminates complaints of favoritism and inequity. On the other hand, it excludes from an occupation all workers whose value productivity in that occupation falls below the standard wage. How serious this is for resource allocation depends on the size of the gap between an excluded worker's productivity in this occupation and in his next best alternative. In many kinds of work the range of individual productivities is probably not wide and the impact of a standard rate not very serious. On the whole, a system of standard rates appears to have more advantages than disadvantages.

Employers are also able to temper the rigidity of a standard rate system in a variety of ways. Instead of a single rate for machinists one finds rates for machinists A, machinists B, and machinists C. The distinction between these grades is a distinction in terms of both job duties and individual proficiency, the less able workers falling into lower grades with a lower rate. An even more flexible device is that of "rate ranges," under which workers in a particular group may be paid anything from, say, $1.50 to $1.80 per hour. This has some of the earmarks of a personal rate system, but the outside limits of the range are clearly specified, formal criteria are usually set up for the location of individuals within the range, and decisions of lower supervisors are subject to some degree of central control. Carefully administered, and with major weight given to productive efficiency in setting individual rates, this arrangement doubtless comes closer than any other hourly rate system to meeting competitive tests of performance.

THE INFLUENCE OF UNIONISM

The union frequently has some effect on the choice between time payment and incentive payment. While some unions have a distinct preference for incentive payment, the general tendency of unionism has probably been to retard the spread of incentive wage systems. Unions have frequently blocked the installation of incentive payment, and in some cases, such as the automobile industry, have caused its abandonment where it had long been established.[3] Substitution of time payment for incentive payment makes it somewhat harder to relate individual earnings to output, but does not prevent this from being accomplished in a rough way through "measured day work" and other devices.

Where unions have accepted incentive payment, they have normally insisted on a voice in the structure and administration of the system. Unions have preferred systems under which earnings increase proportionately with output to decreasing piece-rate systems of the Bedaux or Gantt type. They have insisted that piece-rate earnings bear a consistent relation to a basic schedule of occupational hourly rates, usually termed "minimum," "guaranteed," or "fall-back" rates. By protecting workers against arbitrary cuts in piece rates, unionism may have encouraged them to work somewhat closer to their individual capacities than they feel safe in doing under nonunion conditions. Each of these effects appears desirable. The main thing to be set on the other side of the ledger is that some unions, where their strength is sufficient, have presented intransigent resistance to any adjustment of piece rates as production methods change. This tends over time to distort the earnings structure away from the structure of hourly base rates.

In the more common case of time payment, the union typically insists on a standard wage schedule which "rates the job, not the man." While for most large companies this is nothing new, in many smaller establishments union organization has forced the abandonment of personal rates and the development of a systematic wage structure. This is probably a net gain, for the reasons noted in the previous section.

Unions do not necessarily insist that every member of an occupational group receive the *same* wage. On the contrary, many unions prefer

3. On this whole subject see Van Dusen Kennedy, *Union Policy and Incentive Wage Methods* (New York, Columbia University Press, 1945).

a system of rate ranges rather than single job rates. This is more flexible, provides greater opportunity for personal advancement over the course of time, and provides greater opportunity for the union to demonstrate that it is giving service to its members by pressing for individual adjustments within the established range) Certain craft groups, as was noted in Chapters 2 and 5, have deliberately created a rate structure under which some members of the craft are able to earn much more than others. It seems unlikely that the dispersion of earnings among locomotive engineers, or among paper-machine tenders, would be as great under nonunion conditions as it has become under collective bargaining. Unionism may thus make for less equality, rather than greater equality, among members of the same occupational group.

As regards criteria for advancement of individual workers within an established rate range, or from one level to another of a craft hierarchy, unions attach major importance to length of service while employers typically prefer freedom to reward superior efficiency. If the dispersion of efficiency levels within the group is wide, and if one assumes no correlation between efficiency and seniority, a strict seniority system may have undesirable results. In many situations, however, one or both of these conditions is absent, and a seniority system will not produce very different results from a merit system. It is also an open question how far nonunion employers, uncontrolled by contract rules, do actually make wage increases and promotions on an efficiency basis rather than on other grounds. While the net effect of union seniority rules is probably to worsen the earnings structure, the strength of this effect should not be exaggerated.

APPRAISAL

The main ways in which unionism appears to improve the personal wage structure are:

1. Insistence on a uniform rate, or rate range, for each occupation in lieu of personal rates. This is standard union policy under either time or incentive payment. In the latter case, it takes the form of establishing standard hourly minimum or guaranteed rates.

2. Union influence on the administration of incentive wage systems has on the whole been in a favorable direction.

Against this must be set the following considerations:

1. Union insistence on time payment rather than incentive payment has sometimes made it more difficult to relate earnings to output.

2. The standard rate schedules established under collective bargaining do not always have the correct width and flexibility to permit recognition of efficiency differences within an occupational group. In-

sistence on a single rate instead of a rate range may be too restrictive. At the other extreme, creation of an unduly wide range of earnings opportunities within a craft may be undesirable.

3. The seniority principle seems to have an adverse effect on allocation of labor and on the earnings structure, despite its advantages on other counts.

Where the balance is struck depends on the relative weight given to each of these considerations. The balance sheet is clearly a mixed one, and unionism cannot be given a high positive or negative score on this count.

INTERPLANT DIFFERENTIALS

THE NONUNION LABOR MARKET

We abstract here from wage differences associated with geographical location, leaving these to the section on geographical differentials (pp. 180–4). This section is concerned with differences in the rates paid to the same occupational category by different plants in the same industry and community. Under perfect competition in the labor market, each plant would pay the same wage per efficiency unit of labor. This would be true regardless of the nature of competition in the product market and in other factor markets.

It is now well established that this situation is far from being realized in actual labor markets.[4] Different plants in the same industry and community often pay strikingly different wage rates for the same category of labor, and their average wage levels show a corresponding variation. This is so much the general rule that interplant uniformity of wages can be taken as prima facie evidence of trade union or government intervention in the labor market.

The difficulty is that there are several possible reasons for interplant wage dispersion. It is necessary to distinguish these and attempt to estimate their relative importance. The possibilities include:

1. The industry categories used in making wage surveys are probably never completely homogeneous. Plants classified in the same industry may actually be making different products, requiring different degrees and combinations of skill, which would account for some difference in plant wage levels.

---

4. See the studies cited in Richard A. Lester, "Wage Diversity and Its Theoretical Implications," *Review of Economics and Statistics, 28* (August 1946), 152–9, and Richard A. Lester, "A Range Theory of Wage Differentials," *Industrial and Labor Relations Review, 5* (July 1952), 483–500.

2. All plants in an industry are never in full equilibrium at the same time. Some are expanding and adding to their work force while others are contracting and laying off labor. This could account for moderate differences in wage level.

3. The workers in an occupation are never of uniform productive efficiency. Interplant variation in workers' hourly earnings could conceivably be due entirely to differences in ability and effort. Some firms have attracted a better than average labor force, others an inferior one, and these quality differences are just offset by wage differences. This would still leave unit labor costs uniform throughout the industry.

To this point there is nothing incompatible with competitive theory. It is quite unlikely, however, that observed interplant differentials can be explained entirely on these grounds; and one is obliged to fall back on additional considerations of a less orthodox sort.

4. The firms in any actual industry differ considerably in cost levels and in market position. In consequence, they may differ markedly in wage-paying ability. Under simple profit-maximization assumptions, this would not produce any difference in their wage levels. The more profitable firms would simply pay the prevailing rate of wages, pocket their profits, and expand their operations at the expense of marginal firms. In actuality, there seems to be a tendency for the more profitable firms to pay better than average wages.[5] This may be partly a method of recruiting a superior labor force, but it is probably influenced also by altruistic and prestige motives. At the other extreme, high-cost firms which are hard pressed for survival react by paying wages below the industry average.

In many industries then, one finds certain firms which are well managed, efficient, pay high wages, enjoy a superior labor force, have relatively low unit costs, and earn good profits. An opposite syndrome exists at the tail end of the industry: low efficiency, low wages, an inferior labor force, high unit costs, and low profits.

This kind of wage structure is not really dependent on peculiarities of labor supply. It would be quite stable even though the labor market were perfect in all respects. The high-wage firms can simply refuse to allow free competition for their jobs and decline to substitute cheap labor for dear. The number of jobs available in the top firms at a given time being limited, the remaining workers will be obliged willy-nilly to seek work in lower-wage firms. Those who have been strained through the recruiting sieves of all the higher firms, and have been found wanting, will end up in the plants at the bottom of the wage structure.

Such an open and stark system of interplant differentials would how-

5. See Sumner H. Slichter, "Notes on the Structure of Wages," *Review of Economics and Statistics*, 32 (February 1950), 80–91.

ever create considerable tension and ill feeling. The imperfection of actual labor markets is helpful in glossing over the true situation, allowing any worker to think that he works for the best plant in town and any employer to tell himself that he is paying prevailing wages. An employer is able, not only to offer lower wage rates than his competitors and still attract an adequate labor supply, but also to satisfy his workers' expectations and his own conscience at the same time.

The main positive factor accounting for interplant differentials, in short, is the substantial variation in the wage-paying ability of various firms, combined with refusal of the more profitable firms to maximize profits by paying as low wages as they could pay. The labor market imperfections which have been revealed so fully by recent research appear to have only a passive or permissive effect. They would not necessarily produce large interplant differentials in the first instance. Once these differentials have developed, however, the market mechanism does little to erode them and permits their continuance over an indefinite period.

THE INFLUENCE OF UNIONISM

Collective bargaining clearly makes for reduction of wage differentials among firms competing in the same product market. Several factors work in this direction. The maxims of "equal pay for equal work" and "the standard rate" are deeply embedded in union thinking. Departure from the principle of equality requires justification, while conformity to it does not. There is likely to be pressure from union members in low-wage companies to be brought up to the wage level which other members are receiving for the same work. High-wage companies are also likely to favor industry-wide standardization on competitive grounds. The decisive factor making for wage uniformity is the pressure of competition in the product market. A firm which is allowed to pay less than the prevailing rates may, by undercutting prices, become a threat to the entire wage and price structure of the industry. A standard wage scale thus comes to be viewed by union and employers alike as a method of "stabilizing the industry," of "putting a floor under competition."

It follows that the area over which a union attempts to impose a standard rate will be related to the area of competition in the product market. In retail trade, service industries, building construction, and other local industries, the union may be expected to establish a standard scale in each locality; but it will not be considered essential to bring different localities to a common level. In industries where competition is regional or national in scope, on the other hand, the union will be under pressure to develop a standard scale for all employers regardless of location. The struggle of unions to establish greater wage uniformity can be traced in the history of many American industries. The list includes railroading, coal mining, basic steel, most branches of the textile industry, men's clothing, pulp and paper on the Pacific Coast, hosiery, pottery, flat glass, pressed and blown glassware. In some industries, wage equalization has been pursued via centralized negotiation with employers' associations. This does not appear to be essential, for in other industries the union has continued to bargain separately with each employer and has tried in the course of successive annual negotiations to herd them in the direction of a common wage level.

Analysis of experience in these industries suggests that the concept of wage equalization or wage uniformity is more complicated than may appear at first glance. Precisely what is to be equalized? [6] The possibilities include:

1. Hourly rates for workers actually paid on a time basis. Equalization in this sense will equalize workers' hourly earnings, except for possible payment above the scale during periods of labor shortage. It will not equalize average direct labor cost per unit of output (referred to hereafter as unit labor cost), because of nonuniformity in both plant efficiency and in quality of labor.

2. Hourly minimum rates for workers paid on a piece-rate or other incentive basis. This will not equalize the average hourly earnings of workers on the same job in different companies, unless the companies follow identical standards of piece-rate determination. It is compatible with equalization of unit labor cost but will not by itself produce this result.

3. Piece rates per unit of output. This will not equalize workers' earnings, because of variations in both plant and worker efficiency. It will equalize unit labor cost but is compatible with wide variations in average total unit cost.

4. Earnings per unit of skill and effort required (Marshall's "efficiency earnings").[7] On this basis, piece rates in different plants would be so adjusted as precisely to offset variations in the quality of tools, materials, supervision, and other factors outside the worker's control. A worker putting forth a given amount of skill and effort would then earn the same amount regardless of the plant in which he was employed. Earnings of workers on the same job would not necessarily be equalized, but differences would reflect only differences in skill and effort among the workers themselves. Unit labor cost would of course not be equalized. Unit *total* costs would be more unequal than under method 3,

6. See on this matter Thomas Kennedy, *The Significance of Wage Uniformity* (Philadelphia, University of Pennsylvania Press, 1949).

7. Alfred Marshall, *Principles of Economics* (8th ed. London, Macmillan, 1938), pp. 548–9.

because the least efficient firms in an industry would be obliged to pay the highest piece rates. Marginal firms would receive an added penalty and efficient firms a bonus under this arrangement.

From the worker's standpoint, only method 4 will equalize earnings for workers of equal efficiency. From the employer's standpoint, only method 3 provides assurance of equal unit labor costs throughout the industry. In general, the methods which will ensure uniformity of earnings will destroy uniformity of labor costs, and vice versa. It is possible to work out hypothetical conditions under which the two objectives could be achieved simultaneously, but there is little likelihood of these conditions actually being realized. Faced with this dilemma, both employers and unions seem to give greatest weight to uniformity of labor cost. An effort is sometimes made to protect workers against abnormally poor plant conditions by prescribing higher piece rates, extra payments, and so on; but beyond this earnings are left to fall where they may.

The consequences of a union's wage-leveling activities depend on what it is that the union undertakes to equalize, and on what the reasons were for inequality of wages in preunion days. It was suggested in the previous section that two main elements can be distinguished; differences in the quality of the labor employed, normally a minor factor; and difference in firms' wage-paying ability, normally the major factor. It is necessary to separate these for analysis and to ask concerning each: if interfirm differentials in an industry were due entirely to this element, what would be the effect of eliminating them?

Suppose, first, that interfirm variation in workers' hourly earnings is due entirely to differences in ability and effort; and consider for simplicity only the case of time rates. Differences in labor efficiency, then, are precisely reflected in different levels of hourly rates in the various firms. If an effort is now made to raise the wage levels of the lowest firms and impose a standard scale on the industry, this clearly will have a disturbing effect. It will impose higher unit labor costs on the firms with an inferior labor force. These firms will begin to suffer losses and will face elimination unless they can raise the quality of their labor force *pari passu* with the rise in their wage level. If the process of wage leveling is sufficiently gradual, if employers are reasonably free to alter their labor force by discharges and new hirings, and if the industry in question is a small factor in the total labor market, it may be quite possible for firms to make the necessary adjustments. The outcome may be a new equilibrium with a uniform quality of labor in all firms corresponding to the uniform level of hourly wage rates. This implies that many workers will have been forced out of this industry into others whose wage structure is either not standardized at all or is standardized at a lower level. There is no insuperable difficulty in imposing uniform quality requirements *within* a single (relatively small) industry, provided there remains sufficient room for quality variation *among* industries.

The effect of imposing a uniform scale of minimum hourly rates, while earnings are computed on a piece-rate basis, will be more moderate. It will impose considerable pressure on the firms with the poorest labor force. The pressure will not be so serious as that of uniform time rates, however, because there remains an escape valve in the gap between the hourly minimum and actual hourly earnings. The firms with an inferior labor force may survive partly by holding this gap considerably below that which exists in the superior firms. If the union will not permit this and insists on a uniform gap throughout, the effect becomes identical with that of uniform time rates.

Suppose, second, that the quality of labor is uniform throughout the industry, and that interfirm variation is due solely to differences in ability to pay. What happens when a union enters the industry and tries to enforce a uniform level of wages? The severity of the impact will depend on the kind of wage standardization which is attempted. A uniform scale of time rates will put heaviest pressure on the low-wage firms. Uniform minimum hourly rates for pieceworkers will exert somewhat less pressure. Uniform piece rates will exert even less pressure, but will still exert some. In order fully to offset their higher unit overhead costs, it will have been necessary for the less efficient firms to pay their workers, not merely less per hour, but also less per piece. Establishment of uniform piece rates will thus work some hardship upon them. An attempt to equalize *efficiency earnings* of pieceworkers, by setting higher piece rates where production conditions are unfavorable, will of course bear still harder on the marginal firms.

Any type of wage standardization will thus worsen the position of the marginal firms and threaten their survival. Their first reaction will doubtless be to reexamine their costs and endeavor to reduce them. This is the "shock effect," which has frequently been observed as an aftermath of minimum wage legislation. Some of the inefficiency of the high-cost firms may turn out to be removable, and wage increases may force management to take remedial action. After everything possible has been done in this direction, continued pressure for wage equalization can result only in eventual elimination of the highest-cost firms.

Cases in which union wage pressure actually produces a plant shutdown are rare in practice. Where a marginal firm would be put out of operation by enforcement of the standard wage scale, local union leaders and members will usually be willing to make concessions in order to protect their jobs. National leaders are more reluctant to permit payment under the standard scale and more insistent that inability to pay be fully demonstrated; but if the facts are clear, even national headquarters will usually approve a lower wage scale. Numerous instances of this sort have been pointed out in cotton textiles, pulp and paper, basic steel, and steel fabricating, and many additional illustrations could be given from other industries. Exceptions to the standard scale are usually regarded as temporary, and are frequently accompanied by a requirement that the employer take steps to improve plant efficiency. In some industries the union itself maintains an engineering department which provides free assistance to marginal employers who must improve their efficiency in order to survive.

APPRAISAL

Imposition of a standard wage scale throughout an industry would appear, prima facie, to bring the industry closer to the situation which would prevail under perfect competition. We may grant that in actuality the firms in a competitive industry differ in technical efficiency and financial strength. The less profitable firms cannot, because of their unprofitability, pay less for bank loans, machinery, or raw materials. Why should they be permitted to pay less for labor?

The first effect of union pressure is to ensure that the low-wage firms are actually paying as much as they are able to pay. Allegations of inability to pay are not always well founded, and the union requires proof before making wage concessions. Second, union pressure frequently forces management to step up efficiency and increase the firm's ability to pay. It may be objected that this shock effect works only the first few times it is applied, but a few times may be sufficient to raise the firm's efficiency substantially.

Up to this point there can be little question that union influence is beneficial. But what happens when a firm has done all it can to improve efficiency, when it is paying all that it can afford to pay, and when further wage increases would cause a shutdown? The effect of a shutdown will depend on what happens to the displaced resources. One possibility is that the more efficient firms will expand to take over the market formerly served by the defunct firm, and that the displaced workers will be absorbed in these firms with an increase in their value productivity. Reabsorption may be difficult, however, if the defunct firm is in an isolated location; and it may also be blocked by union wage policies or management price policies in the surviving firms. One cannot, therefore, exclude the possibility that the displaced workers may be forced down into lower-productivity employments.

This issue is somewhat academic, because in practice union leaders are reluctant to throw their members out of employment. When the union is convinced that the firm has reached its limit, it will usually hold its hand and allow production to continue more or less indefinitely at a substandard wage level. The resulting wage structure is intermediate between the competitive pattern of complete equality and the previous nonunion structure; but the change produced by unionism is in the direction of competitive norms.

It should be recognized that a union may do harm if it insists on rapid wage leveling, particularly of a rigid type such as uniform time rates, in a situation where the quality of labor differs markedly from plant to plant. Under these circumstances a firm might face elimination, not because it was less efficient than other firms, but because it happened to enter the union era with an inferior labor force. Cases where the whole labor force of a plant is markedly inferior to those of other plants in the same industry and locality are probably unusual. Where they do exist, the impact of the union can be minimized by using a flexible type of wage uniformity, by moving only gradually toward full equalization, and by reasonable willingness to make concessions to obviously marginal producers.

On balance, the effect of union efforts to reduce wage differentials among rival producers appears to be moderately favorable—not so completely beneficial as unions sometimes allege, but sufficiently so to warrant a positive score for collective bargaining.

GEOGRAPHICAL DIFFERENTIALS

THE NONUNION LABOR MARKET

Geographical wage differences in the United States have historically been quite wide. While they have diminished slightly over the past fifty years, they are certainly wider than they would be in static equilibrium. The wage level of the southeastern states averages some 30 per cent below the level of the Pacific Coast. For common labor, regional differentials are considerably wider than this, while for most skilled occupations they are somewhat smaller.[8] There is also a marked relation between wage level and size of community within each region. While summary statistics are difficult to come by, the wage levels of small towns may average 15 to 20 per cent less than those of metropolitan centers in the same region. These money wage differentials are far from fully offset by differences in living costs, so that substantial differences remain in real wages.

What is the basis for these large and persistent geographical differ-

8. For a survey of what is known about geographical differentials, and also each of the other main types of wage differential in the United States, see Chap. 12 below.

ences? The answer lies partly in the fact that net additions to the labor supply now come mainly from the rural population. This has always been a major source of labor supply, and since the cessation of mass immigration to the United States in the early twenties it has been virtually the sole source. The relatively high birth rates in rural areas lead to an accumulation of population which cannot be absorbed in agriculture, and this excess population is drained off into urban occupations at a rate which varies with the level of urban employment. During periods of peak employment, there is heavy migration to towns and cities. There was a net migration from farms of about three million during less than four years of World War II. During a depression, on the other hand, the cityward movement slackens and may even reverse itself, as it did in 1932.

The small towns throughout the country are in the best position to tap this source of additional labor. A factory located in such a town can readily recruit new employees by spreading word through the surrounding countryside. With the growth of road systems and automobile transport it is no longer necessary for farm people to move to town in order to take urban jobs. Large numbers of them continue to live at home while driving ten or twenty miles to work each day. This ready availability of labor means that the small town need not offer as high a wage level as the metropolitan center which must draw its recruits from a wider area. Moreover, the lower level of living costs in small communities enables their workers to enjoy the same real wages as city workers at a significantly lower money wage.

Rural birth rates, while always higher than urban birth rates in the same region, themselves differ markedly from one region to another. They are highest of all in the southeastern states, and this has been an important factor depressing the relative wage level in that region.

A second important factor is the variation of value productivity in agriculture, and consequently of agricultural wage rates, from one region to another. All urban employments are ultimately in competition with agricultural employment, and the level of agricultural incomes in a region provides a sort of base from which the urban wage structure graduates upward. Farm wage rates in the southeastern states are only about half the level of farm wage rates in New England, and it is consequently not surprising that urban wage rates are lower—particularly wage rates for common labor, which stands in closest competitive relation to agriculture. On the Pacific Coast, on the other hand, farm wages are from 50 to 100 per cent above the level of the northeastern states, the percentage varying somewhat with the method of payment (by the day or the month, with or without board, etc.). This would alone be sufficient to account for higher urban wage rates in the Far West. It is interesting, however, that the very large geographical differentials which exist in agriculture are "weathered down," as it were, and reflected in more moderate differentials in urban occupations.

The North-South differential, while varying a good deal from one occupation and industry to another, is sufficiently large that one would expect it to have important economic consequences. Assuming that nonlabor costs are approximately equal in the two regions, which is probably not far from the truth, one would expect migration of capital from North to South so long as southern wages, adjusted for any difference in efficiency of labor, remain below the northern level. One would also expect labor migration from South to North as long as the difference in real wages remains sufficient to offset the costs of movement. For both reasons one would expect a gradual decline in the North-South differential over the course of time.

These processes have actually been going on over the past several decades. There has been a large volume of industrial investment in the southern states. There has also been heavy migration of workers from South to North. This migration is impeded, however, by ignorance and uncertainty, by local attachments, and by cyclical fluctuations in the availability of jobs in the North. Meanwhile, the pressure of high birth rates continues inexorably. The result is that cross-migration of labor and capital has not been sufficiently rapid to produce a sharp narrowing of North-South differentials. One can find numerous manufacturing industries in which differentials have narrowed in recent decades. One can find some manufacturing industries, however, and a number of important nonmanufacturing industries (agriculture, building construction) in which differentials have widened. On the whole, differentials remain considerably above the level one would expect them to reach in static equilibrium.

THE INFLUENCE OF UNIONISM

Unionism appears thus far to have had only a slight effect on geographical differentials; and this effect has not always been in the same direction. In manufacturing and other industries characterized by interregional competition, union efforts to place different firms on an equal competitive basis have often involved a reduction of geographical differentials. There are exceptions, however, such as the pulp and paper industry, where the unions have followed a pragmatic policy of exploiting the wage-paying ability of each region as fully as possible, leaving differentials to fall where they may. In other cases the organizing ability of the union has varied considerably from region to region. In textiles, hosiery, clothing, and light industry generally, union progress in the South has been slow, and this has limited what could be done in narrowing regional differentials. In some of these cases the union may have widened geographical differentials for the time being, because it could exploit fully the wage-paying ability of firms in the North but was unable to do so in the South.

In other manufacturing industries, geographical differentials have been reduced and in a few cases eliminated entirely. Where differentials have been eliminated, as in flat glass and basic steel, there has typically been a combination of favorable circumstances: a high degree of unionization, a high degree of industrial concentration, and a situation in which the southern plants were subsidiaries of northern companies. It is easier in such a situation for the union to force acceptance of wage equalization, and for the industry to adjust to it, than in an industry which has hundreds of small, independent producers and is only partially unionized.

There is a regrettable lack of evidence concerning the impact of unionism on geographical differentials in local industries. It may well be that unionism, by entrenching itself first in the high-wage regions and communities, has for the time being widened differentials in such industries. This may be one reason why building construction wages in the South today are further below the northern level than they were forty years ago. If and when unionism spreads evenly throughout the industry, geographical differentials may tend to narrow once more.

APPRAISAL

The *tendency* of unionism is certainly toward a narrowing of geographical differences, as will be apparent from the case studies of Britain and Sweden in Part 2. The limited impact in the United States to date is more a reflection of union weakness than of union intentions. Present geographical differentials in the United States appear wider than they need be on any functional basis; and union efforts to reduce them would thus seem to be beneficial in the first instance.

We should not overlook the possibility that unions may in time overshoot the mark and reduce differentials more than is desirable. Complete equalization of money wage rates throughout the country would mean real wages higher in the South than in the North and higher in small towns than in large cities. Such a wage structure would be undesirable both on grounds of equity and in terms of inducing necessary movements of capital and labor.

It may be desirable, indeed, to maintain money wage differentials somewhat wider than the equilibrium level in order to encourage location of new industrial investment in the southern states and in small towns rather than metropolitan centers. This policy of "bringing the job to the man rather than the man to the job" could be justified as a way of reducing the volume and costs of migration. One could also support it in terms of the social and political advantages of decentralizing the population from crowded metropolitan areas.

On this count, then, unionism should be given a positive score up to the present, with a reservation that this judgment may have to be altered several decades hence.

OCCUPATIONAL DIFFERENTIALS

THE NONUNION LABOR MARKET

Occupational differentials have in the past been strikingly wide in the United States. We would judge that they have been considerably wider than they would be in static competitive equilibrium. This opinion cannot be verified empirically, but it seems plausible on several grounds. Applying the Smithian concept of equalizing differentials, it does not seem that a skilled craftsman should earn double the wage of a laborer. The craftsman's work is more pleasant, more secure, and carries greater prestige than that of the laborer. While there is a certain learning period, this is not sufficient to justify a large premium in earnings. Nor can high earnings for craftsmen be explained satisfactorily as a rent for scarce talents, which can scarcely be a factor in many manual occupations. It is relevant to note also that occupational differentials in most European countries have long been narrower than in the United States, yet there has apparently been no difficulty in manning the skilled occupations.

Occupational differentials, to be sure, have been tending to diminish in the United States for at least fifty years. During the past two decades, in particular, there has been a substantial increase in manual wage rates relative to clerical salaries, and in laborers' rates relative to rates for skilled labor. The developments of the past twenty years can be explained reasonably well in supply-demand terms. The list of contributing factors includes: the cutting off of mass immigration; the steady extension of public education and the rapid increase in the percentage of young people who graduate from high school; the deskilling of many formerly skilled occupations through technical development; the prolonged period of virtually full employment since 1940; and the sharp rise of wages and prices since 1940, which has tended to narrow every type of wage differential on a percentage basis. The combination of these things seems adequate to account for most of what has happened to occupational differentials. Moreover, as will be explained in Part 2, the shrinkage of differentials in the United States is consistent with what has happened in other countries, and seems to be part of a world-wide development.

THE INFLUENCE OF UNIONISM

The effect of unionism on occupational differentials appears to have been slight, and rather different from what might have been expected from speculative reasoning. It seems logical that an industrial union, having a large percentage of low-skilled members, will favor a narrowing of occupational differentials, and that where the skilled men are organized separately in craft unions they will be able to widen their advantage over the unskilled. This hypothesis, however, does not stand up against the evidence. In the printing industry, differentials have been well maintained, the premium of compositors over bindery women having fallen by only about one-fifth between 1938 and 1952. Other cases can be found, however, in which differentials have been drastically reduced despite the prevalence of craft organization. The building construction and railroad industries are two leading examples.

Turning to the industrial unions, one finds a similar diversity of experience. In several major industries, including the automobile industry, occupational differentials have been sharply compressed. In basic steel, however, there has been little reduction. In the woolen and worsted textile industry, the percentage differential of loom fixers over laborers has actually increased since the mid-thirties.

It does not appear, then, that there is any marked correlation between type of union organization and rate of decline in occupational differentials. A more detailed analysis would be necessary to confirm this observation. If correct, it raises interesting questions. Are the skilled members of an industrial union much more influential than one might suppose from their numbers alone? Are the skilled craft unions less aggressive and self-interested than one might expect on economic grounds? Are they restrained by regard for public opinion or by other considerations from advancing their already high wage scales at a disproportionate rate? Are they interested in raising the rates of the unskilled, possibly as an underpinning to their own position and a platform for future wage demands?

To the extent that unionism has had any net effect on occupational differentials, this has almost certainly been in the direction of narrowing them. One can find numerous instances during the thirties and forties in which a union sought and won an equal cents-per-hour increase for all employees, whereas the employer would have preferred a uniform percentage increase. The pulp and paper industry appears to be a leading example. It is difficult to find cases of the opposite sort. The cost-of-living escalator systems which were installed in many companies at union insistence during the forties and early fifties were invariably constructed to yield uniform cents-per-hour increases to all employees. One can conclude, then, that there has been some tendency for unionism to increase the use of uniform cents-per-hour wage adjustments, which necessarily reduce occupational differentials on a percentage basis.

APPRAISAL

Occupational differentials in the United States have been, and probably still are, wider than they would be under static competitive equilibrium. The narrowing of differentials over the past twenty years, therefore, has brought the wage structure closer to what might be regarded as a normal competitive pattern. To the extent that trade unionism has accelerated this development, its influence has been beneficial and in accord with underlying economic tendencies. The indications are, however, that the influence of unionism has not been very strong relative to the influence of market forces.

INTERINDUSTRY DIFFERENTIALS

THE NONUNION LABOR MARKET

Given full competitive equilibrium, interindustry differentials proper would not exist. Each industry would pay the same wage for workers of uniform quality employed in the same occupation and locality. Interindustry differences in average hourly earnings would reflect mainly differences in the occupational composition of each industry, and perhaps to some extent locational differences.

It appears that in actuality substantial interindustry differentials do exist, but it is difficult to measure their magnitude. Comparisons of average hourly earnings are not necessarily significant because of the large differences in labor force composition. What one needs is interindustry comparisons of the earnings of male (or female) workers at the same occupational level in the same locality. Here one encounters the difficulty that most occupations are quite specialized and confined to a single industry. One cannot be certain that a particular semiskilled task in one industry is on precisely the same level as another semiskilled job in another industry. The occupations which come closest to cutting across industry lines are skilled maintenance jobs at the top and common labor at the bottom. But even "common labor" turns out not to be really common. It is light labor in some industries and heavy in others;

working conditions vary from pleasant to extremely unpleasant; elements of skill are usually present and vary from industry to industry; and the nature of the work done changes over the course of time. Any comparison of laboring wage rates, therefore, must be carefully scrutinized and an effort made to adjust for these factors.

The most careful analysis of interindustry differentials in labor rates has been made by Sumner Slichter.[9] He found substantial interindustry differences which seemed to have persisted with little change over the years 1923–46. In general, the level of rates for male common labor tended to be high where: 1. value added by manufacturing per wage-earner hour is high; 2. payrolls are a low percentage of income from sales; and 3. income after taxes is a high percentage of sales. Slichter concluded that "managerial policy is important in determining interindustry wage differences. . . . two important determinants of wage policy are the size of payrolls relative to gross income and profits per dollar of sales."

The commonest kind of interindustry analysis has to do with rates of change in average hourly earnings over the course of time.[10] The significance of these studies is difficult to appraise because shifts in average hourly earnings are due partly to changes in occupational composition and to other factors which cannot be isolated. For what they are worth, the studies show substantial differences in the rate of increase in industry wage levels over the past twenty or thirty years. In general, wage levels seem to have risen most rapidly in industries which are highly concentrated and which have experienced a rapid rate of increase in man-hour output, these two variables themselves being strongly correlated. The influence of other factors, including union organization, seems to have been minor.

The evidence suggests that interindustry differentials are both wider at any given time and more subject to change over the course of time than they would be in a fully competitive system. Much of the reasoning in the section on interplant differentials (above pp. 173–5) applies to interindustry differentials as well. Profitable industries, like profitable firms, seem to pay higher wages than they could get by with. This is only partially offset by differences in the quality of labor hired, so that the cost of an efficiency unit of labor varies positively with profits. This kind of behavior is facilitated by workers' lack of information and strong attachment to their present jobs, by employers' recruitment and promotion practices, and by other characteristics of our imperfect labor markets.

9. "Notes on the Structure of Wages," pp. 80–91.
10. For recent studies of this sort in the United States, see the references cited in Chap. 12, pp. 337–8.

THE INFLUENCE OF UNIONISM

Much of the theoretical criticism of trade unionism has rested on a presumed distorting effect on interindustry differentials. Assuming that all industries are unionized and that the union in each industry follows a "monopolistic" wage policy, one might expect wages to be set highest in industries where the demand for labor is rising most rapidly, whether because of rising demand for the product or a rapid increase in labor productivity. There is some tendency in this direction even in the absence of union organization. Expanding industries tend to bid up wages somewhat to attract an adequate labor force, while stationary or declining industries take advantage of the imperfection of the labor market to lag behind the general pace of wage advance. Trade unionism, however, might be expected to accentuate this tendency for the expanding industries to outpace the others. A larger part of any increase in labor demand will be translated into wage increases and a smaller part into employment increases than would be the case without collective bargaining.

What evidence is there that these disruptive potentialities of collective bargaining are actually realized? The statistical evidence is by no means conclusive but suggests that the actual impact of unionism is much less than might have been expected on theoretical grounds.

A serious difficulty in interpreting the evidence is that there is a marked intercorrelation among the variables of rate of increase in man-hour output, degree of concentration, and extent of unionization, and particularly between the last two. Garbarino found a "Z" of 0.89 for the relation between unionization and concentration, which is above the 1 per cent level of significance.[11] This is not surprising, for once the core of employer resistance has been penetrated, full unionization of a highly concentrated industry is simpler than unionization of an industry containing scores or hundreds of small concerns. The association of unionization with concentration seems mainly responsible for the fact that a simple correlation between rate of increase of earnings and degree of unionization yields a high positive coefficient. High concentration, in other words, tends to accompany *both* high unionization and a rapid rate of increase in earnings.

This still leaves the question of causation unsettled. It may be that highly concentrated industries show a rapid rate of wage increase *because* they are also highly unionized. It should be emphasized, however, that large, oligopolistic, and progressive firms seem in any event to

11. Joseph Garbarino, "A Theory of Interindustry Wage Structure Variation," *Quarterly Journal of Economics, 64* (May 1950), 283–305.

follow a high-wage policy. This tendency can be traced back to the early decades of this century when union organization was very weak.

Garbarino, working with manufacturing data for 1923–40, concluded that "the relationship between unionism and earnings for this period seems to be rather vague. This result may well be due to the fact that the influence of unionism entered the picture so late in the time period." [12] Ross and Goldner, after an examination of data for 1933–46, concluded that "New unionism (that is, unionization) has been a source of relative wage advantage during the 1933–46 period, whereas continuing unionism has not." [13] Lester and Robie, after a study of seven industries characterized by strong unionization and regional or national collective bargaining, reported: "Generally speaking, wage and earning levels do not appear to have risen more rapidly under national and regional bargaining than for manufacturing as a whole." [14] Dunlop found that economic variables have dominated the changes in interindustry differentials and that unionism has played a minor role.[15] Rees, in a study of the fully unionized basic steel and bituminous coal industries during the inflationary period 1946–50, concluded that their wage levels probably rose somewhat less rapidly than they would have risen under nonunion conditions.[16]

The only recent study which finds strong indications of union influence is that of Levinson,[17] who concludes:

For the period 1920 to 1933, there was a consistent positive correlation between the strength of unionism and the trend of money wages. Those groups of workers who were strongly unionized obtained much greater wage concessions than those who were not; furthermore, the wages of those groups of workers who became unionized during these years rose from the lower non-union level to the higher union level, while the wages of workers whose unionism was greatly weakened followed almost exactly the opposite pattern. For the remaining years, however—1914 to 1920, and 1933 to 1947—there was no signifi-

12. *Ibid.,* p. 302.
13. Arthur M. Ross and William Goldner, "Forces Affecting the Inter-Industry Wage Structure," *Quarterly Journal of Economics,* 64 (May 1950), 254–81.
14. Richard A. Lester and Edward A. Robie, *Wages under National and Regional Collective Bargaining* (Princeton, Princeton University Press, 1946), p. 93.
15. John T. Dunlop, "Productivity and the Wage Structure," in *Income, Employment and Public Policy,* Essays in Honor of Alvin H. Hansen (New York, Norton, 1948).
16. Albert E. Rees, "The Economic Impact of Collective Bargaining in the Steel and Coal Industries During the Postwar Period," *Proceedings of the Third Annual Meeting, Industrial Relations Research Association . . . 1950,* pp. 203–12.
17. Harold M. Levinson, *Unionism, Wage Trends and Income Distribution, 1914–1947* (Ann Arbor, University of Michigan Press, 1951), p. 110.

cant correlation between the strength of unionism and the trend of money wages in the manufacturing, extractive, construction, and public utility industries.[18]

Almost all studies except Levinson's have focused on manufacturing industries, and it is possible that one might find clearer indications of union influence by widening the focus to include construction, transportation, trade and service, and a variety of other industries. It would also be a rewarding task to try to reconcile the divergent methods and findings of the authors cited above. About all one can say at present is that the evidence is inconclusive. A few scholars believe that unionism has shown some tendency to widen interindustry differentials. The preponderant opinion is that union influence has been slight or even nonexistent.

If the preponderant view is correct, how can this result be explained? Why does unionism not wrench the interindustry wage structure apart as Simons and others anticipated? The answer appears to lie partly in the realities of union behavior and partly in the structure of labor markets. Wage bargaining is only one aspect of union activity, and in the case of old and secure unions it is by no means the most important aspect. As regards wage bargaining, there are indications that most union leaders function as "lazy monopolists." They are conservative institutional leaders who try to keep out of trouble both with employers and with their members, and to whom aggressive wage maximization would appear as a dangerous and quite unnecessary course.

Suppose, however, that this hypothesis about union behavior is wrong, and that one or more unions do endeavor to raise the wage levels of their industries at an abnormally rapid rate. The usual conclusion is that this will reduce employment in those industries, and that this will force the displaced workers to seek employment in other industries, whose wage level will then necessarily fall. This process can continue so long as the aggressiveness and power of the unions continues, and so long as there is any employment at all left for their members. The consequence must be an ever increasing gap between the bottom and top of the wage structure.

It is perhaps unfair to compare this essentially static argument with the dynamic movement of wages in actual labor markets. In actuality, however, it does not seem that the process just described could continue indefinitely. There appears to be at any given time a maximum feasible gap between the highest and lowest wages offered for compara-

18. The results for 1920–33 are doubtless influenced by the fact that these years include 2 periods of sharp deflation, during which organized workers were in a better position than the unorganized to protect their wage level.

ble labor in the same labor market.[19] To the extent that unions do work actively to force up the top strata of the wage structure, there are other forces working to push up the lower layers. These forces include the advance of legal minimum wage levels and of benefit rates under social insurance programs. They include employer fears of incipient or potential unionism in the unorganized industries. They include also employer and worker reactions expressed directly in the labor market.

Wage increases in some industries tend to influence the supply price of labor to other industries. The higher wages generate expectations among workers in the market and influence their conception of what is a reasonable or fair wage for a certain type of work. As the top of the wage structure rises, this minimum expectation also rises, and the lowest wage employers are under pressure to raise wages in order to recruit labor and to maintain the morale of their present work force. Nor do employers necessarily wait to be forced by supply pressures. They take it for granted that their wage levels should keep pace in a rough way with the movement of wages elsewhere in the market. They do not sit passively until an avalanche of displaced workers descends on them from the high-wage industries. The low-wage firms take positive action to keep within sight of the wage leaders; and the consequent increase in their wage (and price) levels may largely or even entirely prevent any displacement from occurring.[20]

Beyond a certain point, then, an effort by the more highly organized and strategically situated workers to increase their advantage over the low-paid workers must become a futile attempt to rise by pulling at their own bootstraps. The market reactions just described operate most strongly, to be sure, during periods of high employment and may be largely suspended during severe underemployment. What may happen, therefore, is a cyclical alternation of low employment periods during which the well-organized workers widen their advantage over the ill-organized ones, and of high employment periods during which the latter narrow the gap.

APPRAISAL

The influence of unionism on interindustry differentials appears to be quite weak—so weak, indeed, that its existence is called into question by some students of the problem. To the extent that unionism has

19. For a more extended argument on this point, see L. G. Reynolds, *The Structure of Labor Markets* (New York, Harper, 1951), Chap. 10.

20. This assumes a general absence of pure competition in product markets; and it of course assumes a dynamic economy marked by a secular increase in productivity as well as by cyclical fluctuations. There is nothing wrong with the static "wage distortion" argument on its own premises; but these premises are so far from actuality that the argument has little predictive value.

any influence, this is probably in the direction of widening interindustry differentials in the first instance. Unionism seems to establish itself first and most strongly in those industries which are already toward the top of the wage structure, and in which conditions for further wage increases are most favorable. Taking off from this advantageous position, unions may propel the high-wage industries forward at a (relatively) faster pace than they would have maintained otherwise. They may take fuller advantage, in other words, of the potential gap between the top and bottom of the wage structure.

Is this merely a transitional situation which exists in an economy in process of unionization? What is likely to happen if and when all industries are highly unionized? Unionization in the United States is still too fragmentary to provide much evidence on this point, and one could learn more from experience in the more highly unionized countries of Western Europe. It seems possible that, when unionism reaches the lowest-wage industries, these unions may press forward with sufficient vigor to narrow interindustry differentials once more. In this case the wage distortion produced by collective bargaining might reach a maximum at some point during the period of partial unionization and then begin to diminish.

The eventual outcome might be a narrower range of interindustry differentials than exists in nonunion labor markets. The experience of, countries such as Britain and Sweden, which will be examined in Chapters 9 and 10, suggests that this is a distinct possibility. In Sweden, which has a powerful and centralized labor movement, interindustry differentials have gradually been whittled down by deliberate union policy and have now fallen to a low level. In Britain unionism has been somewhat less important and minimum wage legislation a good deal more important, but here too the common-labor rates of various industries are much closer together than in the United States. The interindustry wage structure of both countries seems considerably closer to competitive norms than is the American structure; and this result has come about not through less but through more unionism.

CONCLUDING OBSERVATIONS

This chapter has been concerned with the impact of collective bargaining on relative wage rates. We have argued that the effects of trade unionism cannot be deduced from first principles, and that, on the contrary, simple economic models of union behavior are likely to be quite misleading. Patient empirical study is required, and any general judgment should be suspended until the results are in. Even in a single country such as the United States, unionism is far from a homogeneous phenomenon. Some unions have raised the relative wage levels of their industries, others have not. Some have maintained occupational differentials, others have narrowed them sharply. Some have had little effect on interfirm differentials, others have reduced them, and these wage-leveling activities have taken a wide variety of forms. All the dimensions of wage structure and all the complicated variety of union behavior must be brought under examination before an over-all judgment can be reached.

We have also argued that in evaluating the results of collective bargaining one must distinguish: 1. the equilibrium wage structure which would exist in a perfectly competitive labor market; 2. the wage structure which exists in actual labor markets under nonunion conditions; and 3. the wage structure which develops in actual labor markets under collective bargaining. There has been some tendency in theoretical writing to contrast situation 3 with situation 1 and to conclude that, since collective bargaining does not reproduce the results of perfect competition, it must have an adverse effect on the wage structure. Such a conclusion is untenable. The impact of collective bargaining must be appraised by comparing situation 3 with situation 2, and then forming a judgment as to whether the changes have been in a desirable direction.

We have essayed this sort of comparison for each of the major dimensions of wage structure, with the following results:

1. The impact on *personal* differentials has been substantial, and the effects have been desirable in some respects, undesirable in others. On balance the results appear moderately favorable, but this judgment cannot be asserted very strongly.

2. The impact on *interfirm* differentials within the same competitive group has also been substantial, and on the whole in a beneficial direction.

3. The impact on *geographical* differentials has thus far been slight, partly because of uneven regional development of union organization. The tendency of union policy is in the direction of narrowing both interregional and intraregional differentials. Since it appears that geographical differentials have heretofore been needlessly wide, we would regard this tendency as beneficial.

4. The impact on *occupational* differentials has also been slight. Such influence as unionism has exerted has been in the direction of narrower differentials. This appears beneficial in the sense of producing differentials which are more equitable and closer to those which would exist in competitive equilibrium, without (thus far) interfering with recruitment to the higher occupations.

5. The impact on *interindustry* differentials has certainly been minor, and its existence has been denied by some scholars. If there has been

any effect, it has probably been in the direction of widening inter-industry differentials. This is the one case in which the effects of unionism should probably be classified as harmful.

Summing up these diverse consequences of collective bargaining, one can make a strong case that unionism has at any rate not worsened the wage structure. We are inclined to be more venturesome than this, and to say that its net effect has been beneficial. This conclusion will doubtless strike many economists as surprising. Economists customarily regard trade unionism as intervening in a normal market process, and leap intuitively to the conclusion that a "monopolistic" institution of this sort must do harm. This habit of mind we regard as unfortunate and erroneous. It arises from idealization of the nonunion labor market, from undue concentration on interindustry differentials to the exclusion of other dimensions of wage structure, and from drawing a priori conclusions about the behavior of interindustry differentials under collective bargaining without an adequate empirical check, leading to an exaggerated estimate of the impact of unionism.

The friends of trade unionism as well as its critics have tended to overestimate its actual effects on wage structure. This may be due partly to the striking parallel between the evolution of wage differentials in recent decades and the tenor of union wage policies. Most types of wage differential have tended to narrow, not only in the United States but in other countries. Union wage policies also favor a narrowing of most types of differential. What more natural than to conclude that unionism has been responsible for the course of events? It will be argued in Part 2, particularly in Chapter 13, that there have been powerful economic forces working toward narrower differentials, and that it would be an error to ascribe more than a minor part of what has happened to union influence. Unionism seems to have had greatest effect on personal and interfirm differentials, and a considerably smaller impact on the other three types.[21] It happens that the two cases in which union influence has been strong are cases in which this influence can be classified as beneficial.

Even though the net effect of unionism has been beneficial in the past, will this necessarily be true in the future? In a partially unionized economy such as the United States it is particularly necessary to distinguish between the observed effects of partial unionization and the potential effects of full unionization at some later time. Speculation about the future is necessarily inconclusive. It seems likely, however, that the effects on personal, interfirm, and occupational differentials would not be very much changed by stronger union organization. They would be

21. Clark Kerr, in the IEA paper cited above, comes to the same conclusion and gives an interesting rationalization of this differential impact.

extended to a wider range of industries but would continue to operate in the same general direction as at present. In the case of personal and interfirm differentials the equilibrium level is at or near zero, so that unions are unlikely to overshoot the mark. In the case of occupational differentials the equilibrium level is above zero, and some unions might try to reduce differentials more than is desirable; but employers have a remedy for this in their freedom to raise earnings above the minimum contract rates where necessary to recruit skilled labor. This has actually happened on a limited scale in the United States, and on a larger scale in certain other countries, during the past decade.

The equilibrium level of geographical differentials is also well above zero. There is certainly a possibility that strong unions might reduce differentials below what is socially desirable, and in this case there is no prompt and effective competitive check. Thus one effect of unionism which has been beneficial up to now might in time become harmful. In the case of interindustry differentials, on the other hand, the past tendency of unionism to widen differentials in a monopolistic direction might be reversed, and this effect might be converted into a beneficial one. The eventual development of strong unions in the lowest-paid industries may enable these industries to pull up closer to those which now stand at the top of the wage structure.

Fears that complete unionization will bring seismic disruption of the wage structure do not seem to be well founded. The elaborate attempts to find ways by which the presumed catastrophe could be averted —by government wage regulation, by prohibiting national unionism, by sending all union leaders to graduate schools of economics—may turn out to have been academic exercises, shadow battles against a nonexistent enemy. The countries with the strongest union movements appear to have a wage structure which is more orderly and defensible than the wage structure of countries where unionism has been weak. After examining a variety of national wage structures in Part 2, this general issue will be reviewed once more in Chapter 13.

Studies in National Wage Structure

Introduction

THE first five chapters of Part 2 provide parallel case studies of wage determination and wage structure in France, Sweden, Great Britain, Canada, and the United States. The chapters are arranged in order of decreasing influence of government and trade unions on wage determination. France stands as the case in which wages are most nearly subject to deliberate and centralized control, Canada and the United States as the countries in which market responses come closest to having full sway.

These countries were selected because they represent a variety of institutional situations and because they have reasonably good wage data. It is not implied, however, that they are superior in these respects to other countries which have not been included. Interesting case studies could certainly be made of the remaining Scandinavian countries, Holland, West Germany, and Australia; and also, except for deficiencies in the data, of Italy, Russia, and India.

The time span covered in Part 2, like that in Part 1, is roughly the past two decades. Where information is available for earlier periods however, the analysis has been pushed back as far as the data permit Some of the British and American series carry back as far as 1900.

The purpose of each chapter is to explore what light experience in a particular country throws on the central problem stated in Chapter 1: the role of individual responses and of organizational behavior in the determination of relative wage rates. In each chapter we examine first the wage-determining mechanism of the country and then proceed to consider the behavior of occupational differentials, interindustry differentials, and geographical differentials. The concluding section of the chapter points up the significance of the observed wage behavior.

The final chapter of Part 2 is an essay on the evolution of national wage structures over long periods. While it draws on the factual findings of earlier chapters, it goes beyond them at certain points. The chapter begins with a discussion of how one might expect the various dimensions of wage structure to evolve in a progressive industrial economy subject only to market influences. Trade unionism and government wage regulation are then brought onto the stage and their impact on wage structures examined. This leads to an appraisal of the strength of these organizational influences, a discussion of whether they typically reinforce market processes or work contrary to them, and an examination of what

199

happens when market and organizational pressures conflict. The chapter makes no pretense at being a full theory of relative wage rates; but it does try to indicate the general direction in which an adequate theory might be found.

CHAPTER 8 *France*

INFLUENCES ON WAGE DETERMINATION

TRADE UNIONISM AND COLLECTIVE BARGAINING

A CENTRAL feature of the French case is the weakness of union organization and the imperfect development of collective bargaining procedures.[1] In the enthusiasm of the postliberation period, the membership of the General Confederation of Labor (CGT) rose to almost five million, or about half the nonagricultural wage earners of the country.[2] A rift soon developed, however, between the dominant Communist element in the CGT and the non-Communist groups. In 1947 and 1948 the rift became a rupture, following a series of strikes which the Communists were accused of exploiting for their own ends. The trade union leaders opposed to the Communists withdrew to form a new federation, the General Confederation of Labor-Workers' Force (CGT-FO), which was proclaimed to be "free from political domination." [3]

The failure of the strikes of 1947 and 1948 and the split in the trade union movement brought quick disillusionment to many workers, and union membership dropped sharply. More than half the CGT membership fell away, and the new CGT-FO gained only a small proportion of it, perhaps half a million.[4] Communist control of the old CGT was tightened, and it has remained the most aggressive and popular trade union in the eyes of the workers. The CGT-FO has most of its strength among white-collar and government employees and has failed to make important inroads among manual workers.

1. A selection of references on trade unionism and collective bargaining in France in recent years are the following: V. R. Lorwin, chapter on France in Walter Galenson, ed., *Comparative Labor Movements* (New York, Prentice-Hall, 1952), pp. 313–409; Lorwin, *The French Labor Movement* (Cambridge, Harvard University Press, 1954); Lorwin, "French Trade Unions since the Liberation, 1944–1951," *Industrial and Labor Relations Review,* 5 (July 1952), 524–39; Georges Lefranc, *Les Experiences syndicales en France de 1939 à 1950* (Paris, Editions Montaigne, 1950); Adolf Sturmthal, "Collective Bargaining in France," *Industrial and Labor Relations Review,* 4 (January 1951), pp. 236–48.

2. Lorwin, "French Trade Unions since the Liberation," p. 533.

3. J.-L. Guglielmi and M. Perrot, *Salaires et revendications sociales en France, 1944–1952* (Paris, Librairie Armand Colin, 1953), p. 90. This book is an interesting study of trade union attitudes toward diverse postwar problems, as revealed in the official trade union press.

4. Lorwin, "French Trade Unions since the Liberation," p. 533.

The third important trade union federation is the French Confederation of Catholic Workers (CFTC) whose membership has remained fairly steadily at slightly more than half a million.[5] The CFTC competes with CGT-FO among white-collar workers and has strength among wage earners in some localities. Among higher government officials and professional people, the most important union is the General Confederation of Technicians and Supervisory Employees, which at some levels is in competition with the CGT-FO and the CFTC.

The orientation of French unionism, particularly of the dominant CGT, is strongly political. The CGT is an instrument of revolution. Its purpose is to solidify workers' opposition to the existing regime, to harass and undermine the employer, and to prepare the way for a complete change in the social system. The compromises involved in collective bargaining are regarded as unnecessary and undesirable appeasement of the employer. This basic disbelief in the merit of collective bargaining is a major reason for its limited development in France.

Certain structural weaknesses of the French trade unions also limit their effectiveness in bargaining. The level of union dues is low and payment of them is erratic.[6] The concept of "union membership" lacks precision in France. Union attachment spreads out in concentric circles from the small nucleus of active dues-paying unionists to those who consider themselves union members but pay dues irregularly if at all, then to those whose participation consists solely in voting for one ticket or another in shop elections, and finally to the apathetic majority. None of the unions has been able to build up substantial strike funds, so that the cost of a strike comes mainly from the pockets of the strikers. In recent years even the CGT has rarely been able to persuade a majority of its members in any industry to go on strike. Weakness of union treasuries also means an inadequate staff of salaried union officials. At the regional and local levels one overworked official must often spread his energies over the problems of several different industries.

French employers are considerably better organized than their employees, more unified in their policies concerning wages and other terms of employment, and much better equipped with professional staffs. Most of the basic industries are organized into regional and national federations, which have considerable control over the wages set in individual establishments. At the top of the hierarchy stands the influential National Confederation of French Employers (CNPF), which helps to coordinate the employers' position on both the collective bargaining and political fronts.[7]

5. *Ibid.*
6. On this point see Lorwin, *The French Labor Movement*, pp. 171–5.
7. *Ibid.*, Chap. 11.

In the basic steel industry, for example, there is a national federation of regional employer associations. Wage agreements are made by the regional groups, but there is advance consultation with national headquarters in Paris and general agreement on the position which the industry will take. The regional associations are not free to diverge from national policy without the risk of the penalties which a strongly cartelized industry is able to inflict.

Collective bargaining procedures are governed by a basic law of February 11, 1950. This law provides that collective agreements may be concluded at the national, regional, or local levels. While the law establishes no order of priority, it seems to have been expected that national agreements would speedily be concluded in most industries, and that the terms of these agreements would then be adapted to varying conditions by supplementary regional and local agreements. The CNPF and other employer associations, however, have taken a strong stand against national bargaining, so that few national agreements have been concluded. A majority of collective agreements are on a regional basis, though there are also a considerable number of single-company agreements.[8]

Almost all of the agreements in force are simple wage agreements (*accords de salaire*) rather than complete collective agreements (*conventions collectives*). The law requires that a full collective agreement must cover many nonwage issues, including trade union rights, union activity in the plant, the powers of shop stewards and plant committees, hiring and firing, and conciliation procedures for disputes arising under the agreement. Employers have typically refused to bargain on these issues, and there is no legal requirement that they must bargain on them. The unions have thus been forced to settle for *accords de salaire* which, regarded by the drafters of the 1950 law as stop-gap measures pending conclusion of a full agreement, have instead become the normal form of collective contract. This situation obviously hampers the unions in establishing themselves firmly in the plant and extending their influence over nonwage conditions of employment.

In wage bargaining, the employees are handicapped by the fact that their delegation usually includes representatives of several unions, most commonly the CGT, CGT-FO, and CFTC. These groups are not only rivals on the industrial front but are also political enemies. They are often more concerned with embarrassing each other than with outmaneuver-

8. As regards collective bargaining procedures, see references in n. 1; also, "Les Conventions collectives et les accords de salaires intervenues en application de la loi du 11 fevrier 1950," *Revue française du travail* (March–April 1951), 188–217; Robert Salle, *Les Conventions collectives de travail* (Paris, La Documentation Economique et Syndicale, F.O., 1951).

ing the employer. The CGT representatives, in particular, frequently enter negotiations with extravagant demands which are clearly impossible of attainment. They also frequently walk out part-way through the negotiations, leaving the other groups to carry on the discussions and sign the eventual agreement. The CGT, which has not signed, is then free to denounce the agreement as a "sell-out" to the employer and to seek political advantage from it. This sort of interunion maneuvering is not compatible with driving a good bargain with the employer.

For all these reasons, the employers typically have the whip hand in collective bargaining. Direct union pressure on the industrial front is much less effective than in the United States, Britain, or the Scandinavian countries.

The largest single employer in the country, of course, is the French government. In addition to the regular civil service, the government owns and operates the railroads, coal mines, potash mines, aircraft plants, gas and electric power facilities, the Renault auto works, and numerous other enterprises.[9] Most of these industries are organized as semiautonomous public corporations, responsible to a cabinet minister but with their own board of directors, which normally includes several union representatives. In practice, in a number of industries such as coal, gas, and electricity, the power of decision has come to reside more and more with the government departments under whose jurisdiction they fall. Wage determination in these industries is a complicated and highly political process. There are discussions within the enterprise between union representatives and members of the salaried management. There is discussion within the board of directors, and the unions get a second crack at the problem through their representatives on the board. If there is no agreement at this level, which is almost invariably the case, the matter goes to the responsible minister. A wage increase in a major industry, which will have wage and price repercussions throughout the economy, usually becomes a matter for discussion in the full cabinet. At this stage the unions work through political channels to influence the key ministers in a favorable direction.

The preponderant opinion of French wage experts is that the unions have a more difficult time winning wage increases in the nationalized industries than in private industry. Most private industries are strongly cartelized, and a wage increase is normally offset by a simultaneous price increase. Such offsetting action has been particularly easy during the years of postwar inflation. It tends, of course, to sustain the pace of

9. On nationalization in France, see W. A. Robson, "Nationalized Industries in Britain and France," *American Political Science Review, 44* (June 1950), 299–322; and Adolf Sturmthal, "The Structure of Nationalized Enterprises in France," *Political Science Quarterly, 67* (September 1952), 357–77.

inflation, but no one private industry is responsible for holding inflation in check. The government, however, does have this responsibility. It must consider the fact that a wage increase in a nationalized industry will either 1. raise the price of coal, transportation, electric power, or what not, which will raise costs and prices in the private sector of the economy; or 2. increase the deficit of the industry in question and the size of its subsidy from the general budget, which will tend to increase the over-all budget deficit with obvious inflationary consequences.

While the nationalized industries are legally independent, they operate in practice under the surveillance of the Minister of Finance. If an industry is operating at a deficit, or if a proposed wage increase will lead to a deficit, the Minister of Finance will have to provide the necessary subsidy. This gives him, if not precisely a veto power, at least a prominent voice in wage decisions. In recent French experience, the Minister of Finance has typically tried to reduce proposed wage increases and to require that any increases be recovered by raising the price of public services. This has led the unions to complain that the government is "employer minded," and that it makes common cause with the CNPF in retarding wage movements. The government has certainly not acted as "wage leader" during the postwar years but has tended rather to lag behind the pace of private industry.

THE ROLE OF GOVERNMENT

In discussing collective bargaining in the nationalized industries we have already introduced a theme which must now be developed more thoroughly, viz. the central role of government in French wage determination.[10] There are several reasons why the influence of government is stronger in France than in other countries. There is a long tradition of *étatisme* in France. Unregulated private capitalism on the American model has never existed there. The weakness of the trade unions on the industrial front leads them to seek economic gains primarily through state action. The importance of the government as employer forces it to play an active part in wage determination. The unsettled situation in the first years after World War II led to extensive government regulation of economic affairs, and, while these regulations have now been relaxed, they effectively set the stage for the evolution of the postwar economy.

From the 1944 liberation until 1950, the national wage structure was regulated in detail by the government. After some preliminary experi-

10. The following discussion of the role of government in wage determination is based largely on interviews by L.G.R. in 1951. See also in this regard the chapter by Lorwin in Galenson, ed., *Comparative Labor Movements,* pp. 382–6, and Lorwin, *The French Labor Movement,* pp. 197–9.

mentation, an official wage structure was promulgated in 1945 with the following characteristics: [11]

1. A minimum basic wage rate for unskilled labor.

2. A graded job classification scale within each industry. Starting with the unskilled laborer's wage as 100, each job in the higher categories was assigned a coefficient which, when multiplied by the laborer's wage, yielded the minimum rate for the jobs in question. Heavy laborers generally received coefficients varying from 108–118, semiskilled operatives from 120–138, and skilled workers 140 and above. This *échelle hiérarchique* has remained a key feature of the postwar wage structure.

3. A third characteristic was the variation of wage rates by geographical region, to take account of cost-of-living differences and traditional differences in wage level. Taking the Paris wage rate for a particular job as 100, a series of zones were established within which wage rates were fixed at from 5 to 25 per cent below the Paris level.

4. All the above refers to minimum rates only. In a period of rapid inflation it was necessary to have some control over maximum wage rates as well. It was therefore provided that the actual average hourly earnings of workers in a particular establishment and category could not exceed the minimum for the category by more than 15 per cent, except for laborers in metallurgy and metal fabrication who were allowed a differential of 20 per cent. Pieceworkers were also allowed to average as much as 20 per cent above the minimum rate. The effectiveness of these maximum limitations is open to question. There is evidence of considerable overpayment by many employers during the rapid inflation of 1945–49.

The immediate impact of this official structure is difficult to determine from the imperfect statistics available. The new geographical and occupational differentials were considerably smaller than those which had existed in 1939; but it is not certain that they were smaller than those existing at the time the decrees were issued. A considerable leveling of wages had already occurred during the years of war and occupation. It is quite possible that the 1945 decrees did not reduce differentials further but simply codified existing wage relationships.

The wage relationships established in 1945 were subsequently modified by numerous decrees, almost all of which had a wage-leveling tendency. A decree of 1946 required "equal pay for equal work" by men and women. The width of the geographical wage spread was gradually reduced by a series of decrees over the next ten years. Today the lowest zone stands only 12.5 per cent below Paris instead of 25 per cent as in 1945. As we shall see in the next section, the spread in actual wage

11. For a description of the 1944 and 1945 wage regulations, see Louis Alvin, *Salaire et sécurité sociale* (Paris, Presses Universitaires de France, 1947).

rates remains somewhat greater than the spread in the legal minima; but the reduced spread in the minimum rates has had some effect, particularly as regards laborers whose rates stand very near the minimum.

In the matter of occupational differentials, policy has varied from time to time. "Policy" is perhaps too strong a word in this connection. There has been a series of unrelated actions, taken by different governments in the light of economic and political pressures at the moment, without any long-term goal or strategy. The first two large wage increases after the liberation were calculated on a percentage basis, so that occupational differentials were approximately maintained. Since 1947, however, most of the government's wage actions have raised the lowest-paid workers more rapidly than the higher-paid ones, on a percentage basis. In some cases a special "bonus" has been awarded to workers with "abnormally low" salaries, i.e. salaries below a prescribed level. The minimum wage for common labor has been raised on several occasions. Since 1950 government has had no direct control over adjustment of rates above the minimum in private industry; but it has frequently urged that an increase in the legal minimum be applied to the higher grades in a degressive fashion.

The tendency for government to cater to the low-paid and low-skilled workers is understandable. In part it has been a reaction to rapid inflation, which raised the wage and price level twentyfold between 1939 and 1954. The cost of food has risen even more rapidly than prices in general. The lowest-paid workers, who spend the largest proportion of their income on food, have been particularly hard pressed, and it has been a special concern of government to prevent their falling below a minimum level of subsistence. Social considerations are reinforced here by political considerations. The CGT and the Communist party direct their strongest appeals to the low-skilled workers, incessantly demanding large flat-rate additions to wage rates. The parties of the center and moderate right, which in shifting coalitions have formed the government of France since 1948, have been obliged to move in this direction to retain electoral support.

In 1950 wages were returned formally to private control, leaving in government hands only the minimum wage (*salaire minimum interprofessionel garanti,* typically abbreviated as SMIG). This legal minimum, however, has more profound significance for the national wage structure than is true in most other countries. Unlike the situation in the United States, the wage rates of the lowest grades of labor are typically very close to the legal minimum. An increase in the minimum, then, means an immediate and roughly proportional increase in wages for these grades. Further, the principle of the échelle hiérarchique, relating the rates of higher skill grades to the laborer's rate, is now firmly established in custom and in collective agreements. An increase in the base of the structure automatically brings demands for a general wage revision, which tends to occur quite rapidly despite governmental efforts to restrain it.

General wage movements in France appear to evolve in the following way.[12] First, retail prices creep up—sometimes gradually, sometimes with a rush. After a certain time, worker discontent and union agitation reach a point where employers must take account of them and offer concessions. There is some tendency for the metalworking industries in Paris to take the lead in wage movements. The 40,000 Parisian metalworkers form about one-third of the industry, the unions here are old and relatively strong, wage statistics for the industry are accurate and well publicized, and workers in other parts of the country look to Paris for leadership. A wage increase in this sector is transmitted to metalworking firms in the provinces, which in turn are closely linked to the basic steel industry. Since the steel industry operates throughout the North, the East, and the Loire Valley, its wage actions fan out into other industries in these regions. Some of the key public services, particularly in the Paris area, are apt to become involved in the movement at an early stage. One may have strikes on the Paris subways, the buses, the gas and electricity services, even the railroads.

When things have reached this state, the government examines the cost-of-living statistics and finds that the index has risen and that an adjustment of minimum wage scales is in order. (In 1952, the discretion of government on this point was limited by a law requiring that minimum wage levels *must* be adjusted whenever the retail price index rises by 5 per cent.) A new scale of minimum rates is promulgated for Paris and for each of the other geographic zones. Employers and unions throughout the country then proceed to conclude agreements based on the new minima, and within a few weeks the whole national wage structure moves to a new plateau. Through the operation of cartel arrangements, offsetting price increases are made at the manufacturing level, which are passed on rapidly to the consumer through fixed retail markups. At the end of the process, real wage rates are likely to emerge virtually unchanged.

The minimum wage system thus serves as a fulcrum, giving the government some leverage over the wage level. Changes in the wage *level* can also be used to exert considerable influence on the occupational wage structure.

12. This description applies mainly to periods of rapid inflation, such as 1945–51. During 1952–54 the price level remained quite stable, wage increases were moderate, and there was considerable divergence in the movement of particular rates.

An additional way in which government action affects workers' incomes is through the system of pensions, family allowances, and other social payments. These payments form a much larger percentage of the French workers' income than they did in prewar years, and also a larger percentage than in most other countries. They have brought about a substantial redistribution of income within the working class, particularly as between families of differing sizes, and a growing discrepancy between the *wage* income of a worker and his *total* income. Since some of the social payments, notably family allowances, are on a flat-rate basis unrelated to the worker's wage level, they produce a further narrowing of occupational differentials. Occupational *income* differentials become a good deal smaller than occupational *wage* differentials.

Through all these channels—the legal structure of minimum wages, the quasi-legal structure of regional and occupational differentials, direct control over wage schedules in nationalized industries, the extensive system of social payments—the government exercises a pervasive influence over the relative incomes of French workers. Trade union influence exerted through collective bargaining is of minor importance, and collective agreements tend to ride on the coattails of government decrees.

EVOLUTION OF THE NATIONAL WAGE STRUCTURE

THE ECONOMIC CONTEXT

We shall first comment briefly on the course of economic events in France over the past decade—the level of employment and production, changes in price levels, the behavior of money wages and real wages. This background information is helpful in understanding the sources of change in wage structure. The wage structure of a country is likely to develop differently under high employment than under serious unemployment. A rapid rise in the general wage and price level almost automatically narrows wage differentials of every sort. An economy in which per capita output and consumption are advancing rapidly may behave differently from one in which productivity is stationary.

For some years after the liberation in 1944, the French economy was engaged in repairing the ravages of war and occupation.[13] Labor was in great demand and unemployment remained at a very low level. Beginning in 1949, however, the labor market softened considerably. Unemployment, while still low in comparison with the 1930's, has since 1949 been about three times the 1946–48 level and has shown no

13. See BLS, *Wage Trends and Wage Policies in Various Foreign Countries*, Bulletin 934 (1948).

tendency to diminish.[14] There are also indications of considerable disguised unemployment in agriculture, trade, and other sectors.

The level of production rose rapidly from 1945 to 1950 and continued to increase gradually from 1950 to 1955. Industrial production in 1954 stood about 50 per cent above the 1937 level. Comparable measures of total output do not exist, and total output has doubtless advanced less rapidly than industrial production. Sauvy estimates that in 1953 French national income was 17 per cent above, and national income per capita 14 per cent above, the level of 1939.[15] The gain in per capita output has been less substantial than in the other countries which we are considering, and there has consequently been less room for improvement in real wages and living standards.

We have already had occasion to refer to the striking increase in price levels since 1939. In 1945 the index of retail prices was already about four times as high as in 1938.[16] Rapid inflation continued through 1948, prices quadrupling during the 1945–48 period. After a brief period of price stability, the devaluation of the franc in late 1949, followed by the Korean war in 1950, brought another 50 per cent increase in the price level. Prices stabilized at the beginning of 1952 and remained almost constant through early 1955.

Comparable wage data for prewar and postwar years do not exist. The movement of money wage rates since 1946 is shown in Table 8-1. These data, drawn from quarterly surveys of some 30,000 firms by the Ministry of Labor, are relatively reliable. The reported figures include, in addition to basic wage rates, certain kinds of fringe payment common to everyone in the plant. Piecework earnings, individual bonuses, and so on are not included, so that the index does not really represent the movement of hourly *earnings*. An index of earnings would undoubtedly run somewhat above the wage-rate index.

The figures in Table 8-1 follow a pattern which we shall find in later chapters to have been characteristic of other countries as well. Women's wage rates have risen more rapidly than men's rates, and common-labor rates have risen faster than rates for skilled workers. Low rates, in short, have risen faster than high rates on a percentage basis, and a general process of wage leveling has occurred.

The movement of real wages can be observed with accuracy only since 1948, because the postwar index of retail prices was first published in that year. The index is unfortunately limited to the Paris area, and the

14. Figures on registered unemployed in recent years are published in each issue of the *Revue française du travail*.

15. Alfred Sauvy, "Le Revenu national de 1901 a 1953" (Paris, Institut National de la Statistique et des Etudes Economiques [INSEE], 1954), mimeographed.

16. See Table 8-1.

movement of consumer prices in the provinces has doubtless been somewhat different. For what it is worth, we may note that this index rose by 70 per cent between mid-1948 and mid-1954, while the wage level of all male wage earners rose by 109 per cent.[17] The real wage level has thus risen appreciably, particularly during the period of price stability since 1952.

Table 8-1. Index of Hourly Wage Rates, France, 1946–54 (January 1946 = 100) *

| | MEN | | | WOMEN | | | TOTAL |
| | COMMON | SKILLED | | COMMON | SKILLED | | MEN- |
YEAR	LABOR	LABOR	TOTAL †	LABOR	LABOR	TOTAL †	WOMEN
1946	100	100	100	100	100	100	100
1947	163 ‡	152 ‡	152	156 ‡	165 ‡	165	156
1948	260 §	236 §	243	290 §	261 §	270	256
1949	301	271	282	331	298	311	291
1950	329	279	305	364	316	336	314
1951	417	364	385	469	399	429	398
1952	497	443	462	553	475	509	476
1953	508	456	475	560	486	516	487
1954 **	553	481	505	624	518	558	521

* Annual average of four quarters.

† Including semiskilled categories which are not included separately in this table.

‡ Average of April and October.

§ Average of only three quarters: February, May, and October.

** July 1954.

Source: Ministry of Labor, quarterly survey of wages and employment published quarterly in the Revue française du travail

Labor's share of national income appears to have risen somewhat relative to the prewar period. Wage and salary payments formed only 45 per cent of personal income in 1953, compared with 46 per cent in 1938. Family allowances, pensions, and other social transfers, however, were 18 per cent of personal income in 1953, compared with 7 per cent in 1938. Since the bulk of these transfers go to wage and salary earners, it seems safe to conclude that their participation in national income has increased. This has not been at the expense of profits, for entrepreneurial incomes have also risen from 16 per cent of personal income in 1938 to 19 per cent in 1953. These gains have come from

17. Calculated from quarterly data in the Revue française du travail.

a sharp decline in the share of rent, interest, and dividend payments (from 12 per cent to 3 per cent of personal income), and a moderate drop in the share of agriculture (from 19 to 15 per cent).[18]

Table 8-2. Real Wage Rates, France, 1948–54 (1949 = 100)

YEAR	COST OF LIVING *	HOURLY WAGE RATES †	REAL HOURLY WAGE RATES
1948	90.6	88	97
1949	100.0	100	100
1950	110.4	108	98
1951	130.1	137	105
1952	145.	163	105
1953	143.7	167	116
1954	143.3	177	123

* The cost-of-living index for 1948–54 is the Consumers Price Index for Paris based on a survey of working-class expenditures of 1948 and 1949.

† The index of hourly wage rates is based on the quarterly surveys of the Ministry of Labor.

Source: Ministry of Labor, quarterly survey of wages and employment; and INSEE.

The French situation since the war may be summarized, then, as one of reasonably full employment, substantial price inflation, moderate advance in per capita output and real wage rates over the 1939 level, and considerable redistribution of income within the wage-earning class as well as between wage earners and other groups.

All types of wage differential have shrunk considerably since 1945. Most of the reduction occurred during the sharp inflation of 1945–49. From 1949 through 1951 differentials remained almost stable despite a further moderate increase in the price level. During 1952 and 1953, with the price level stabilized, differentials widened somewhat, reversing the tendency of previous years. In 1954 and 1955 there was a renewed tendency toward narrowing of differentials as a result of three government decrees raising the earnings of the lowest-paid groups. The movement of the principal types of differential will now be examined in greater detail.

18. République Française, INSEE, Annuaire statistique de la France, 1953 (Paris, 1954), pp. 343–4.

OCCUPATIONAL DIFFERENTIALS

We have already noted that one of the key features of the system of wage control set up in 1944–45 concerned occupational differences. Following a tremendous task of job classification, percentage relationships between various degrees of skill were laid down. This échelle hiérarchique was worked out in consultation with union and employer representatives. The final scale was in reasonable accord with the existing wage structure, though it represented something of a reduction from the prewar occupational differences. Table 8-3 reproduces this scale. It involved considerable variation from one industry to the next, apparently in line with the differing wage structures then in existence.

Table 8-3. Average Coefficients in the Scale Fixed in 1945 for Different Categories of Workers in Each Sector of Industry, France

INDUSTRY	COMMON LABOR	SPECIALIZED LABOR	SEMI-SKILLED	SKILLED	HIGHLY SKILLED
Foodstuffs	100	115	130	140	170
Chemicals	100	115	125	135	160
Rubber	100	115	125	135	160
Paper and boxes	100	108	125	140	170
Printing	110	121	138	170	240
Textiles	100	110	120	135	170
Clothing	100	112	125	155	175
Leather and furs	100	115	132	145	170
Woodworking	100	115	130	155	180
Metallurgy ⎫ Metalworking ⎭	100	110	121	140	170
Fine metals	100	108	121	140	170
Construction	110	130	140	168	196
Stonecutting and pottery	110	128	140	168	196
Transportation	100	115	125	140	170
Trade	100	115	130	140	170
TOTAL	100	115	125	145	175

Source: Ministry of Labor

During the years since 1945 occupational differences have become noticeably less than those in the original scale. Table 8-4 gives the movement of wage rates for different categories of skill from January 1946–January 1955.

The premium of other grades over the common laborer has been markedly reduced, both relative to the original échelle hiérarchique and to the actual situation at the beginning of 1946. This narrowing occurred mainly during the years of rapid postwar inflation, 1945–49, as the minimum wage was raised without fully proportionate increases for the higher grades. Differentials narrowed a bit more in 1950 and 1951 during the price inflation associated with the Korean war, then widened somewhat under the price stability of 1952 and 1953. Between January 1952 and October 1953, the wages of skilled male workers rose by 5.9 per cent, while those of male common labor rose by 4.9 per cent.[19]

Table 8-4. *Movement of Average Wage Rates for Different Skill Grades, France, 1946–54* * (*January 1946 = 100*)

YEAR	COMMON LABOR	SPECIAL-IZED LABOR	SEMI-SKILLED	SKILLED	HIGHLY SKILLED	COMMON LABOR AS A PERCENTAGE OF SKILLED
1945 scale	100	115	125	145	175	69
1946 †	100	111	130	153	—	65
1947	100	110	125	149	—	67
1948 ‡	100	108	121	138	157	72
1949	100	107	117	132	154	76
1950	100	107	116	130	154	77
1951	100	107	115	128	152	78
1952	100	107	116	131	156	76
1953	100	107	117	131	158	76
1954	100	105	114	128	153	78
1955 §	100	105	113	125	150	80

* Annual average of four quarters.

† January 1946.

‡ Three-quarters average: February, May, July.

§ January 1955.

Source: Ministry of Labor, quarterly survey of wages and employment

Beginning in 1954, there was a renewed tendency toward shrinkage of differentials. Through three decrees (February 1954, October 1954, and April 1955) the government added a bonus of 26 francs to the 100-franc minimum wage in the Paris region, with correspondingly smaller bonuses in the lower geographical zones. This device was used in lieu of an increase in the minimum itself in order to avoid an auto-

19. For a detailed review of changes in wage structure over the past few years, see INSEE, "L'Evolution récente des revenus salariaux modestes en France," *Études et conjoncture*, 9 (August 1954), 754–79.

matic increase in family allowances and certain other social payments which are based on the minimum wage scale; and also to weaken the tendency for increases in the minimum to be extended automatically to higher grades of labor. Within the nationalized industries, the 1954–55 increases were applied in a tapered fashion which gave smaller percentage increases to the higher groups. It is not clear what has happened in the private sector, where wages above the minimum are not subject to government control. The narrowing of differentials shown in Table 8-4 suggests that private employers also gave smaller percentage increases to the higher occupational groups. This may be partly a lag in adjustment, however, and over the next year or two the skilled workers may gain ground as they did in 1952–53.

Table 8-4 is based on rates rather than on earnings, and this may exaggerate the actual compression of occupational differentials. The skilled men, who are sometimes able to bargain for wages above the established scale and who benefit from incentive systems and other production bonuses, may come out with better earnings than the rate schedules suggest. Limited evidence from the Paris metalworking industries points in this direction, but no comprehensive data on earnings are available.

Table 8-5 indicates that the narrowing of differentials has occurred not simply on an average basis, but within each individual industry. The extent of the narrowing has varied somewhat, but the direction of change has been the same in every industry for which comparisons can be made. An interesting feature of Table 8-5 is the small dispersion of the skilled-unskilled ratios for individual industries about the average for industry as a whole. This reflects the high degree of codification, centralized decision making, and consequent uniformity of wage relationships in the French case. If information were available on earnings, however, it would probably show less uniformity than the data on basic rates.

Occupational differentials have narrowed more sharply in the low-wage regions of the country than in the highest-wage regions. In the lowest-wage zone, for example, the average of men's skilled rates fell from 146 per cent of the common-laborers' average in 1947 to 122 per cent in 1954. In the highest-wage zone (Paris), the decrease was only from 145 per cent to 136 per cent. This difference can be attributed largely to the operation of the minimum wage system. The reduction in the total width of the geographical zones from the original 25 per cent to the present 12.5 per cent has meant that the legal minimum wage has risen fastest in the lowest-wage zones. This would not have affected occupational differentials if equal percentage increases had been given to higher skill grades as well. In practice, however, the increases in the minimum have not been fully reflected in the higher rates. Employers and government have followed a conservative policy in this respect, and the unions have been too weak to insist on fully proportional increases even if they had wished to.[20] As a result, the higher skill grades have been squeezed, and the squeeze has been most severe in the zones in which the minimum has risen most rapidly.

Table 8-5. Skilled-Unskilled Differentials (Men) in Various Industries, Paris Region, 1947, 1948, and 1954 (skilled rate as percentage of common-labor rate)

INDUSTRY	JAN. 1, 1947	INDUSTRY	MAY 1, 1948	JULY 1, 1954
Foodstuffs	138	Food & agriculture	130	128
Paper and boxes	143	Paper and boxes	138	143
Printing	153	Printing	148	146
Textiles	145	Textiles	149	138
Clothing	146	Clothing	144	136
Leather & furs	159	Leather & furs	143	144
Woodworking	153	Woodworking & furniture	139	139
Construction	141	Construction, public works	136	133
Transportation (excl. rail)	133	Transportation	128	131
Chemicals	132	Chemicals, rubber	124	123
Rubber	138			
Metallurgy	156	Metal production	134	144
Metalworking	149			
Fine Metals	175			
Stonecutting	140			
Pottery	150			
Miscellaneous	135			
		Mechanical, electrical	139	137
		Glass	144	136
		Ceramics, bldg. materials	137	119
		Misc. manufacturers	158	142
		Trade (grocery)	130	127
		Trade (exc. grocery)	130	129
		Banks, insurance, etc.	134	—
		Cinema	164	142
		Health	136	129
AVERAGE	145	AVERAGE	139	136

Source: Derived from Ministry of Labor, quarterly survey of wages and employment

The reduction in skill differentials since 1945 has been shaped mainly by government policy rather than by market forces. This raises the question of whether the movement of differentials has departed so far from

20. The CGT, much the most powerful group, has usually argued for flat-rate (equal francs per hour) increases for all grades. The CGT-FO has shown an ambiva-

market requirements as to create a shortage of labor in the skilled occupations. An answer to this question would require a more elaborate investigation than was made in this study. The predominant opinion of authorities consulted in Paris in 1951 was that no difficulties in skilled-labor supply had been created, but this should not be taken as conclusive. A shortage, being a hypothetical quantity which does not show up in the statistics of employment, is difficult to detect and measure. Moreover, because of the extended training period for the skilled occupations, there may be a considerable lag between the development of inadequate wage rates and the appearance of labor shortages.

The impact of narrower differentials on the supply of skilled labor has probably been reduced by the following factors:

1. French workers, particularly skilled workers, are reputed to be highly immobile.

2. Decisions about apprenticing oneself to a skilled trade are made at the school-leaving age of fourteen. Experienced observers assert that these choices are typically made without careful economic calculation, and that they are not closely related to the wage structure. In any event, all the places available in the government-sponsored apprenticeship programs have been filled in recent years.

3. Reduction of wage differentials leaves intact numerous other advantages of skilled employment, including the possibility of promotion to the supervisory ranks.

4. Where wage rates have been too low to attract an adequate number of workers, employers have probably adjusted to this situation in one of several standard ways. One hears a good deal about overclassification of workers in some industries—semiskilled workers become skilled, and skilled men become highly skilled. Incentive wage systems and individual premiums or bonuses can also raise earnings considerably above basic wage rates. Adequate data on earnings for carefully defined skill classifications would probably show that the reduction in *earnings* differentials has been considerably less than the reduction in *rate* differentials since 1945.

It is interesting in this connection that certain skilled, scarce, and strongly unionized groups have been able to maintain their differential in rates. In the Paris metalworking industries, for example, the percentage differential of the machinist over the common laborer remains almost the same as in 1945, while the molders have actually increased

---

lent tendency. On the one hand, it professes to want a return to the occupational relationships envisaged in the 1945 scale. On the other hand, it insists on an increase in the minimum wage to establish a national minimum standard of life for all. The two policies pull in opposite directions, and the latter has tended to predominate in practice.

their differential slightly.[21] The skilled groups in the printing industry have also been able to win equal percentage increases in wage rates and to maintain their premium over the unskilled.

One seems justified in concluding that the reduction of occupational differentials, for the most part, has not yet reached the point at which it interferes seriously with labor recruitment to the higher occupations. Where the shoe has begun to pinch, the market has reacted on the wage structure so as to maintain earnings at a satisfactory level, either through maintenance of differentials in base rates or through a progressive deviation of earnings above base rates.

INTERINDUSTRY DIFFERENTIALS

The postwar inflation has carried the wage levels of different industries upward at a remarkably uniform rate. When one computes the percentage increase in the average wage level in each industry from 1946 to 1954, the bulk of the indexes fall within a quite narrow range. The highest index (textiles) is only about 25 per cent above the lowest (building construction), and most of the indexes fall within a range of 10 per cent.[22]

Where an industry has deviated significantly from the average movement, this can usually be explained by the nature of the labor force. Building construction shows the smallest wage increase partly because laborers in this industry have since 1945 been recruited increasingly from North African immigrants, whose supply is highly elastic at a low wage level. Several of the industries which show the largest increase in wage level—textiles, clothing, foodstuffs, retail grocery trade—employ predominantly female workers. The relative rise in the wage levels of these industries reflects mainly the leveling up of women's wages relative to men's.

A different explanation must be sought for the book-printing industry. This industry, which stood at the top of the wage structure in 1946, has not merely maintained but increased its advantage in subsequent years. The explanation seems to lie in the long training period and high entrance requirements for the principal crafts, the guild-like structure of the industry, the unusual strength of union organization, and the domination of union policy by the most skilled and highest-paid workers.[23]

---

21. See on this point François Sellier, "Les Effets de l'inflation sur la structure des salaires," to be published in the forthcoming report of the International Economic Association conference on wage determination.

22. Calculated from data in quarterly surveys of wages and employment of the Ministry of Labor.

23. Sellier, "Les Effets de l'inflation sur la structure des salaires."

The best indication of the interindustry wage structure is obtained by comparing rates for the same grade of labor in the same geographical region. A comparison of this sort, covering rates for male common labor and male skilled labor in the Paris region, is shown in Table 8-6. Similar tables have been prepared and analyzed for female labor and for other geographical regions. These look quite similar to Table 8-6 and support the same general conclusions.

Table 8-6 suggests several observations:

1. Interindustry differentials are small even for skilled labor and are very small for common labor. In July 1954 the common-labor rates for all save four industries fell within a range of less than 8 francs, or about 6 per cent of the general average.

2. Interindustry differentials have been decreasing over the course of time. The quartile deviation of common-labor rates has decreased from .033 in 1947 to .017 in July 1954. For the more diversified skilled-labor category the reduction has been less, but even here the quartile deviation fell from .053 to .042. The gravitation of common-labor rates toward the median can be attributed mainly to the minimum wage system, which has had greatest impact on the rates at the bottom of the wage structure.

3. The ranking of different industries by skilled-labor rates is very similar to their ranking by common-labor rates, which amounts to saying that occupational differentials are quite similar from one industry to the next.

4. The ranking of industries did not change appreciably over the period 1947–54. Printing remained at the top and somewhat increased its advantage. Pottery, foodstuffs, leather, and chemicals remained near the bottom. Comparing only men with men (and women with women) in the same region, textiles, clothing, and foodstuffs have *not* advanced in the wage structure as they appear to have done if one compares broad industry averages.

These conclusions rest entirely on information concerning rates. Since 1949 the Ministry of Labor has collected earnings information as well, so that one can say something about the difference between the two measures.[24] In October 1953, average hourly earnings exceeded average hourly wage rates by as much as 32.5 per cent in the chemicals and rubber industry, and by as little as 0.3 per cent in the clothing industry.

24. See the mimeographed releases of earnings data by the Ministry of Labor, and the analysis of this material in the August 1954·issue of *Etudes et conjoncture.* The earnings information is unfortunately tabulated only by industry attachment and not by occupational level, sex, or geographical area. This makes it impossible to say anything about the difference between rates and earnings as regards these dimensions of wage structure.

Table 8-6. Rating of Industries in Order According to Level of Wages of 1. Common Labor and 2. Skilled Workers, Paris, January 1, 1947 and July 1, 1954 (Men)

| | JAN. 1, 1947 AV. HOURLY | | | JULY 1, 1954 AV. HOURLY | |
INDUSTRY	WAGE RATE	RANK	INDUSTRY	WAGE RATE	RANK
Common Labor					
Printing	39.6	1	Cinema	147.8	1
Stonecutting	36.7	2	Printing	126.6	2
Transportation			Mechanical, electrical	131.4	3
(excl. rail)	35.9	3	Trade (nonfood)	128.5	4
Clothing	34.7	4	Miscellaneous	127.5	5
Paper and boxes	34.7	5	Glass	126.7	6
Miscellaneous	34.1	6	Chemicals, rubber	125.7	7
Construction	34.1	7	Woodworking, furniture	125.6	8
Fine metals	33.9	8	Transportation (excl.		
Metalworking	33.9	9	rail)	125.5	9
Woodworking	33.9	10	Construction, public wks.	125.0	10
Textiles	33.9	11	Paper and boxes	124.3	11
Rubber	33.5	12	Health	124.0	12
Foodstuffs	32.5	13	Food & agriculture	123.6	13
Pottery	32.3	14	Trade (food & agriculture)	123.0	14
Chemicals	32.3	15	Clothing	122.9	15
Metallurgy	32.1	16	Textiles	122.6	16
Leather & furs	31.9	17	Leather and furs	121.5	17
			Metals production	121.1	18
			Ceramics, bldg. materials	117.5	19
Skilled Labor					
Printing	60.7	1	Printing	214.6	1
Fine metals	59.3	2	Cinema	209.3	2
Woodworking	51.9	3	Miscellaneous	181.6	3
Stonecutting	51.3	4	Mechanical, electrical	179.7	4
Clothing	50.8	5	Paper and boxes	177.2	5
Leather & furs	50.6	6	Leather and furs	175.2	6
Metalworking	50.5	7	Metals production	174.8	7
Metallurgy	50.2	8	Woodworking, furniture	174.0	8
Paper and boxes	49.7	9	Glass	172.9	9
Textiles	49.1	10	Textiles	169.3	10
Pottery	48.4	11	Clothing	167.6	11
Construction	48.0	12	Trade (nonfood)	166.4	12
Transportation			Construction, public wks.	165.8	13
(excl. rail)	47.7	13	Transportation (excl.		
Miscellaneous	46.1	14	rail)	164.6	14
Rubber	46.1	15	Health	159.9	15
Foodstuffs	44.8	16	Food & agriculture	157.9	16
Chemicals	42.7	17	Trade (food, agriculture)	155.8	17
			Chemicals, rubber	154.1	18
			Ceramics, bldg. material	140.0	19

Source: Derived from Ministry of Labor, quarterly survey of wages and employment

The average excess of earnings over rates for all industries was 12.7 per cent. The heavy industries, which have relatively high wage rates, had a larger excess of earnings over rates than did the low-paid soft-goods industries. The heavy industries in recent years have had a longer work week and larger overtime payments, a greater proportion of workers benefiting from production bonuses, and a lower proportion of young workers paid at less than standard rates. Interindustry wage dispersion is thus substantially greater in terms of earnings than in terms of base rates.

GEOGRAPHICAL DIFFERENTIALS

There is little information on geographical wage differences in the prewar years, but the most remote agricultural communities appear to have been something like 40 per cent below the Paris wage level. The official scale of 1945 provided for a number of geographical zones, with wage rates in the lowest zone set at 25 per cent below Paris rates. This probably reflected a considerable leveling of geographical differences during the war years. The limit of the lowest zone was raised by subsequent decrees to 20, 18, 15, 13.5, and eventually to 12.5 per cent below Paris.[25]

The actual wage level of several of the most important zones in 1947 and 1954 is shown in Table 8-7. It is clear that actual differentials have consistently been wider than those contemplated in the official scale. The

Table 8-7. Geographical Wage Differences, France, 1947–54 (per cent below Paris)

OFFICIAL ZONES		AVERAGE HOURLY WAGE RATES	
1947	1954	OCT. 1947	JULY 1954
5	3.5	10.2	13.0
10	7.5	17.5	17.6
15	11.25	20.6	21.2
20	13.50	23.9	23.5
25	—	28.7	—

Source: Ministry of Labor, quarterly survey of wages and employment

explanation is partly that the official scale is binding only as regards minimum rates for common labor. While actual wage rates for laborers in the lowest-wage zone are very close to the legal minimum, rates in the higher zones are farther above it. Moreover, occupational differen-

25. Quarterly surveys of wages and employment of the Ministry of Labor.

tials above the common-labor rate are considerably larger in Paris than in the rural areas (see above, pp. 213–18). In part, too, the geographical differential is really an interindustry differential. Paris has a more than average proportion of high-wage industries, while the rural areas have more 'than their share of low-wage industries.

The zone system seems to have had the effect of raising laborers' rates in the most rural areas relative to the Paris level. It has tidied up the lower fringe of the wage structure. The relation among wage levels in the higher zones, however, has remained relatively unaffected. Paris remains more than 10 per cent above the larger provincial cities, and from these cities wages descend by another 10 to 15 per cent as one passes to the most rural communities.

There is no reliable information on cost-of-living differences among the various regions. The prevalent opinion is that there has been a considerable leveling of living costs in different parts of the country since 1939. Rough estimates on this point must have been used in determining the width of the official zones. Trade union and other political pressures, however, were more directly responsible for the narrowing of the official differentials, and it would be rash to say that they correspond at all closely to living-cost differences.

The best guess at present is that geographical differences in living costs, while substantial, are not as great as the differences in wage levels, so that one descends in *real* wage rates as well as *money* wage rates in passing from Paris to the provinces. It is impossible to estimate the size of the differentials in real wages, however, or to say whether they are narrower today than in 1939.

OTHER DIFFERENTIALS

In January 1946 there was an average differential of about 15 per cent between men's and women's rates for comparable jobs. The official scale provided for a differential of 10 per cent in *minimum* rates, but differentials in actual rates remained somewhat wider, just as in the case of geographical differences. In July 1946 the legal differential was abolished and a policy of "equal pay for equal work" was proclaimed. This did not succeed in eliminating differentials in actual wage rates, for women's rates clung very close to the legal minimum while men's rates remained somewhat above it. The actual differential was sharply reduced, however, from an average of 15 per cent in January 1946 to about 8 per cent in January 1947. Since 1947 the difference between men's and women's wages has remained relatively stable. It has tended to widen somewhat in periods of price stability, reaching a peak of 9 per cent in 1950. It shrank back to 7 per cent in mid-1951 with the new wave of inflation set off by the Korean war, rose to slightly over 8 per cent in 1953, and was again 7.1 per cent in mid-1954.[26]

An interesting feature of the male-female differential is its variability among occupations and industries. It ranges from about 5 per cent for common laborers to more than 10 per cent for skilled workers. It varies from almost 20 per cent in the printing industry to less than 5 per cent in some branches of manufacturing,[27] these differences arising mainly from the skill composition of the different industries. In general, where the wage level is lowest the male-female differential is smallest. This phenomenon is obviously related to the operation of the minimum wage system, which has greatest impact on women's wages in the most poorly paid sectors.

We have already had occasion to mention the large role of social payments in the incomes of French workers. In addition to unemployment compensation, old age pensions, workmen's compensation, medical services, paid holidays, and vacations, the French system provides substantial family allowances.[28] The cost of these benefits is covered primarily by employer contributions, which have become a large proportion of labor costs. In 1950 social charges on employers averaged slightly more than 32 per cent of direct wage payments.[29]

In some industries the figure is considerably higher. In the metal and mechanical industries of the Paris region, for example, social charges of all sorts have risen from 15 per cent of direct wage payments in 1938 to 42 per cent at the end of 1951.[30] On the railroads, where an extensive system of employee benefits already existed before the war, social charges have risen from 41 per cent of wage payments in 1938 to 76 per cent in 1950. Almost half of both railroad labor costs and railroad workers' incomes now arise from various types of social payment.[31]

The effect of the family-allowance system is particularly interesting. Since this is a lump-sum addition to workers' incomes, it has the effect of reducing wage differentials considerably. In July 1952 a skilled worker in the foodstuffs industry in the Paris region, working normal hours, would have earned 6,634 francs per week. An unskilled worker

26. Quarterly surveys of wages and employment of the Ministry of Labor.

27. *Ibid.*

28. See Alvin, *Salaire et sécurité sociale,* in which he treats this subject in detail for the period 1935–46.

29. Raymond Lévy-Bruhl, "L'Evolution des salaires en 1951," *Revue d'économie politique, 62* (May–August 1952), 561. See also INSEE, "Les Salaires en France en 1953," p. 51.

30. Lévy-Bruhl, "L'Evolution des salaires en 1951," p. 562.

31. Ministry of Finance, Direction des Programmes Economiques, *Masses des dépenses de main d'oeuvre à la charge des entreprises et des revenus salariaux distribués* (Paris, 1951), Chap. 4, Section A, No. 1 "S.N.C.F., 1938–1950," p. 86.

in the same industry would have earned 5,047 francs, or about 76 per cent as much. If each worker was married, had two children, and was the sole support of his family, each would have received an additional 2,633 francs as family allowance. The *income* of the unskilled worker, then, would have been about 83 per cent of the skilled worker's income.[32] For families with four or five children the occupational differential would be still smaller.

A worker's income rises a good deal more rapidly with increasing numbers of children than with increasing degrees of skill. The cost of rearing the additional children must, of course, be considered at the same time. While calculations differ somewhat on this point, it appears that the French system approximately covers the marginal cost of additional children, so that a family with five or six children can enjoy about the same level of consumption as a family with one or two children.[33] While the larger family is not actually benefited, it is sheltered against a reduction in its standard of life. The father of a large family, in consequence, is not placed under pressure to increase his direct wage income by climbing the occupational ladder, working longer hours, or in other ways. Such a system should have important consequences for labor supply and mobility.

CONCLUDING OBSERVATIONS

The dominant feature of the French case is the unusual degree to which the determination of labor incomes has been "politicized" through the role of government as employer, through government intervention in the setting of private wage rates, and through the extensive development of social transfers. Growth in the wage-paying ability of the economy obviously raises the question of how increments in real labor income are to be distributed—as among workers of different occupational grades, different geographical areas, different degrees of family responsibility, and so on. This is treated increasingly in France as a matter of deliberate social policy and is a subject of acute political controversy.

French wage determination involves "politics" in the strict sense of governmental procedures. When American scholars refer to wage determination as a political matter, they typically have in mind the operation of trade union and management organizations—the so-called "politics of collective bargaining." These processes have in France a

32. Calculated from data in the Ministry of Labor quarterly surveys of wages and employment, and from a reprint of INSEE, "Les Salaires en France en 1952," p. 1.

33. On this point, see some interesting calculations in INSEE, "L'Economie française en 1950," *Etudes et conjoncture* (January–February 1951).

rather shadowy significance. The trade unions make their principal gains not through collective bargaining but through a kind of guerrilla warfare directed not so much against private employers as against the government. There is a menacing overture from the side of labor—a strike or threatened strike in some key industry, usually at the nerve center of French politics in the Paris region. The government responds not by engaging in collective bargaining over the issue but by announcing a new minimum wage scale, or a change in tax schedules or family allowances. At the tail end of a wage movement, the new wage structure is written into union-management agreements. It is questionable how far these agreements involve "bargaining" rather than mere imitation of government-established patterns. Most of the union-employer discussions have the character of an afterthought.

A second key feature of the French situation is the strong tendency toward "built-in inflation." The wage-price mechanism is such that a monetary expansion can run mainly to price increases. The minimum wage system provides a lever for effecting a rapid increase in the money wage level. Cartelization of industry, with controlled prices and profit margins, makes possible a rapid adjustment of wholesale prices. The tradition of fixed retail mark-ups passes these increases on to the retail level. The politically powerful peasant class makes sure that government-controlled farm prices keep pace with the general movement. A similar inflationary mechanism exists in many other countries, but the French system seems to operate with unusual vigor in raising prices with a minimum expansion of production and employment.

The marked leveling of every type of wage differential over the period 1939–54 has its main roots in the sharp wage-price inflation. It is a simple arithmetical proposition that general wage increases, unless applied on a uniform percentage basis to all wage earners, must lead to a reduction of relative wage differentials. In the French case, as indeed in most other countries during these years, the increases for the higher-paid groups have not been fully proportionate. If the compression of wage differentials has been greater in France than elsewhere, this is partly because the inflation has been much more severe.

Wage policy has been influenced by a combination of financial considerations and standard-of-living considerations. The policy of raising low wages more rapidly than higher wages, which enables one to bring up the low-paid workers while holding down the increase in the total wage bill, has suited the conservatism of employers and has also eased the budgetary problems of successive ministers of finance. Beyond this, however, lies a concern with the living standards of the poorest groups in the community, and an effort to outbid the CGT and the Communist party for the support of these groups. The limited resources available have been allocated deliberately in the direction of building dikes against the inroads of extreme poverty. Because of the slow increase in per capita output, this has perforce been done partly through income redistribution at the expense of higher-income groups.

While recognizing the importance of government action, one should not discount the influence of supply and demand forces operating in the labor market. If government policy were the only factor at work, one would expect to find the pattern of actual wage rates, at least for common labor, corresponding quite closely to the legal minimum rates. This is not, however, what one finds in actuality. Men's rates stand further above the legal minimum than do women's rates, rates in Paris stand further above the minimum than do rates in rural areas.

In the case of occupational differentials, too, one finds numerous indications of market influence. Instead of a rigid adherence to the échelle hiérarchique, one finds that occupational differentials are wider in Paris than in the provinces, and wider in certain industries than in others. In all industries, moreover, one finds that occupational differentials have widened substantially on an *absolute* (francs per hour) basis since 1945. This is contrary to the general tenor of government policy, which has tried to minimize increases in the higher wage rates as the lower rates are raised.

If adequate earnings data were available, the influence of market forces would be still more apparent. There is reason to think that occupational, geographical, and interindustry differentials are appreciably wider on an earnings basis than on a rate basis.

These signs all point in the same direction. Market forces have operated to pull the earnings of particular groups well above the levels specified or intended by government. The fact remains that differentials have been substantially reduced on a percentage basis. How is this phenomenon to be interpreted? Has the shrinkage been in accord with market tendencies or contrary to them? Is the 1955 situation one of rough equilibrium or of serious disequilibrium?

Three observations are pertinent in this connection. First, the actual shrinkage of differentials has not been as great as appears at first glance. Documentation of this point would require more detailed breakdowns of wage-rate data than are presently available, and above all collection of material on earnings. Second, the shrinkage which has occurred seems to be generally in accord with market tendencies. The phenomenon is not limited to France but exists in varying degree in each of the countries we have studied. There are good reasons, which will be developed in Chapter 13, for expecting a gradual narrowing of wage differentials in a mature industrial economy.

Third, to the extent that differentials have fallen below the level prescribed by market forces, the situation is unstable and potentially reversible. It is significant that wage differentials widened perceptibly during 1952 and 1953, years of high employment with stable prices. This suggests that wage leveling had gone too far during the previous inflationary period and that, when the compressing force of inflation was removed, differentials rebounded toward the equilibrium levels prescribed by the market. Before this process had gone very far, the minimum-wage increases of 1954–55 intervened and brought a new compression of differentials, but this may also prove to be temporary. Given a further period of price stability, the slow-moving forces of labor demand and supply will make themselves felt, and differentials may widen somewhat from the 1955 level.

CHAPTER 9 *Sweden*

INFLUENCES ON WAGE DETERMINATION

THE case of Sweden stands in sharp contrast to that of France. There is a minimum of government intervention in the setting of particular wage rates. Union and employer organizations are highly developed and exercise a strong influence on the year-to-year movement of wages. The major industries are covered by industry-wide agreements, often supplemented by more detailed bargaining at the local level. A still greater degree of centralization results from the powerful influence which the top union and employer federations exercise over the policies of their constituent groups. These top-level discussions are carried on with a close eye on the national economic situation, and are coordinated with recent and prospective actions of government. The movement of both the wage level and wage structure from year to year has a "planned" character such as exists in few other countries.

COLLECTIVE BARGAINING INSTITUTIONS [1]

Swedish employers are organized in forty-three industry associations. Each association employs a full-time, professional executive secretary, who plays a leading role in the annual contract negotiations and who keeps in close touch with the central office of the Swedish Employers Confederation (SAF). A single agreement is signed for the entire industry, though further adjustments within prescribed limits may be worked out by subsequent local negotiations. No employer may sign separately with the union, and all are obliged to stand together in the event of a work stoppage. In the large metal strike of 1945, for example, not a single plant in the industry attempted to operate, and each received strike benefits of 2 kroner per man per day from the central association.

The separate industry associations are bound together in a central confederation, the SAF. The constitution of the SAF provides that no labor agreement may be signed by an industry association until it has

1. See Walter Galenson, "Scandinavia," in *Comparative Labor Movements* (New York, Prentice-Hall, 1952); U. S. Department of Labor, Bulletin #1038, *Labor-Management Relations in Scandinavia* (1952); Charles A. Myers, *Industrial Relations in Sweden* (*Some Comparisons with American Experience*) (Cambridge, M.I.T. Press, 1951); and Paul H. Norgren, *The Swedish Collective Bargaining System* (Cambridge, Harvard University Press, 1941).

been approved by the executive board of SAF, and damages may be assessed for violation of this provision. It has not been necessary in practice to invoke this penalty provision, because the federation's influence operates quite effectively through informal channels. As bargaining proceeds in a particular industry, the executive secretary of the industry association refers major points to the president of SAF, a full-time executive of great experience and influence. The president may say, "Yes, I think that is all right," in which case he is bound to support it later before the executive board. Alternatively, if the industry appears to be deviating from general employer practice or from SAF policy in a particular year, he may say, "I will have to discuss that with the board." Key issues are thus discussed informally with the board while negotiations are proceeding, and the federation makes its influence felt *before* any agreement is drafted with the union. When the agreement comes before the executive board for formal approval, this is usually a foregone conclusion.

The influence of the SAF appears to operate in several main directions:

1. During the years of high prosperity since 1945, it has frequently had to hold back some of the most prosperous industries, which left to themselves might have been quite willing to raise wages disproportionately and disrupt the labor market. It has also on occasion had to prod certain industries which were lagging unduly behind the general advance of wages.

2. The federation discourages too close a relationship between current profit levels and wage changes in a particular industry. It favors a gradual but steady advance of wage rates, rather than a roller-coaster movement geared to year-to-year fluctuations in profits.

3. The federation also favors elimination of "unreasonable" differences in the wage levels of different industries—not full equality, but greater equality over the course of time. (The central trade union federation, as we shall see, also pursues a policy of "reasonable" or "equitable" interindustry differentials. The standard of reasonableness, however, differs somewhat as between the two bodies, which leaves something to bargain about!)

Trade union organization is powerful and typically follows industry lines. The many craft and multiple-craft unions which existed at an earlier time have gradually been merged, as a result of deliberate policy, into fewer and more inclusive groups. The forty-four national unions which exist at present are bound together in a central federation, the Landsorganisationen (LO).[2] While the power of LO over the affiliated unions is limited, it can influence their wage policies in a variety of ways. The central secretariat

2. Confederation of Swedish Trade Unions.

supervises the policies of the affiliated unions, and endeavors to have them planned and carried out in a uniform way. It also considers and settles disputes arising between the unions and encourages solid and trustful cooperation among them. It is incumbent upon the unions to keep the Secretariat informed of any major wage claims or labor disputes, irrespective of whether they have resulted in strikes or not. In questions of principle of major significance, or in questions of major practical importance, the unions are obliged to consult the Secretariat. . . . The Secretariat may, if it wishes, send one or several representatives to attend the unions' wage negotiations, and to submit proposals for a settlement, either during the negotiations, or to the union concerned.

No union may take strike action (including sympathy action) involving more than 3 per cent of its total membership, without the sanction of the Secretariat. . . . Finally, if a proposal to settle a dispute, submitted by the Secretariat has been rejected by the union concerned, the Representative Body of LO may decide to withdraw the economic subsidies which regularly are given to any union involved in a dispute (12 kroner a week per member).[3]

The LO cannot forbid a union to strike or expel it for so doing; but a union which chooses to strike for demands which the LO leadership considers unwise can be denied central support and thrown entirely on its own resources.

The strongest influence which the LO exerts over its affiliates is a moral one. Over the course of generations a strong feeling of solidarity has developed within the Swedish labor movement. The leaders of individual unions are reluctant to take positions which would embarrass either the LO or the Social Democratic party with which the unions are closely affiliated. This does not mean that a particular union will follow the advice of LO headquarters in every detail. It does mean that the leaders of one union are sensitive to the reactions of their colleagues in other unions, and that they will hesitate to deviate far from national policies.

The LO constitution also requires each affiliated national union to give its own executive council final responsibility for calling strikes and signing agreements. Membership votes are advisory only, and cannot override the judgment of the leadership. This strengthens the hand of union leaders in conforming to national policy even in the face of strong membership sentiment to the contrary. There have been cases in which an executive council signed an agreement despite a more than 90 per cent negative vote.

3. *Trade Unions and Full Employment* (Stockholm, Confederation of Swedish Trade Unions, 1952), p. 100.

It is not necessary to discuss the nature of LO wage policies at this point, because we shall have occasion to elaborate on them in later sections. Briefly, one can say that LO leaders have usually followed a moderate and even cautious strategy, which does not seek to extract the last possible kroner from each industry each year, which is sensitive to price-level considerations and oriented toward gains in *real* wages, and which is equalitarian in the sense of favoring gradual reduction of most types of wage differential.

THE COURSE OF WAGE MOVEMENTS

The majority of industry agreements run out between January 1 and April 1. The timing of negotiations, however, is not rigidly tied to these expiration dates. If either party is unready to begin negotiations by the expiration date, the contract is invariably extended with a provision that any changes shall be made retroactive. As a general rule, serious discussion begins in at least a few industries before January 1, and other industries come along later in the spring. Wage movements are concentrated almost entirely in the first half of each year.

Before negotiations begin there has of course been a long period of preparation. As early as the previous summer the Swedish cabinet may have organized a series of discussion meetings, at which leaders of the LO, SAF, and other economic groups are asked to present their views on wage policy for the coming year. Within the LO a wage-policy committee will have been at work, advising the secretariat as to proposals for submission to a meeting of the representative body of LO around September 1. These proposals are discussed at length, in some cases with the participation of the Minister of Finance, and eventually a policy recommendation is adopted which, while it does not bind individual unions, indicates how the LO leadership looks upon the situation and how far it is prepared to go in backing specific wage demands. In some years, however, there have been important deviations between the wording of the resolution and subsequent LO policy.

When the negotiating season opens, there is some jockeying for position. Each union is reluctant to be the first to sign, because others may come in later and sign for larger amounts. Insofar as LO and SAF leaders can influence the timing, they apparently try to expedite negotiations in those industries where pressure for wage increases is least, leaving the tougher cases until the end. Because of this, and sometimes because of the rising trend of prices, there has been a tendency for the later settlements to be larger than the earlier ones in each wage movement, and this in turn has accentuated the tendency toward maneuver and delay.

The leaders of the LO and SAF shepherd the negotiations in each industry as best they can. The individual settlements never conform precisely to the original policy statements of the top federations. (The LO policy statements, of course, frequently contemplate differing increases for·different groups, and are usually vague enough to leave latitude for later negotiation and compromise.) On the whole, however, national policy leaves a strong imprint on the specific settlements. Even on the union side, where formal instruments of control are weakest, the advice of LO representatives who participate in the industry negotiations carries much weight. In isolated cases where a union threatens to go seriously out of line, it may be necessary for LO to refuse strike support, and this is invariably effective.

Collective bargaining negotiations in Sweden appear to be generally amicable in tone. The union and industry officials who bear the brunt of the negotiations tend to regard each other as professional colleagues, sitting down to apply their expertise to a common problem. The level of economic literacy is high on both sides. This in no way prevents serious conflicts of economic interest; but bluff, deception, and sheer intransigence seem to play a smaller role than they do in the United States. The cultural homogeneity of the population and the long experience of collective bargaining probably have a good deal to do with this. Beyond this, the strength of both organizations and the fact that failure to agree will mean complete shutdown of the industry for an indefinite period leads all concerned to bend their best efforts toward a settlement. Large-scale strikes are rare and when they do occur are orderly and unspectacular, both sides settling down for a sheer test of economic endurance.

COLLECTIVE BARGAINING AND NATIONAL ECONOMIC POLICY

A key characteristic of Swedish collective bargaining is the extent to which the LO and SAF adapt their policies to the national economic situation and the economic strategy of the Swedish government. This again stems from the homogeneous background of Sweden's political and economic leaders, the high degree of economic literacy and the sharing of a common body of assumptions about cause-and-effect relationships, the limited size of the economy and the role of Stockholm as both economic and political capital, and the fact that the key people involved are accustomed to dealing with each other.

Another important element is the close relation existing between the trade unions and the Social Democratic party. The two movements share a common political orientation and a substantially common membership, about two-thirds of the party membership coming from direct affiliation of local unions.[4] The Social Democratic party has been in the government, either alone or as the dominant element in a coalition, continuously since 1932.[5] Trade union leaders, anxious that the government should succeed and continue in office, are sensitive to the necessities of economic policy and hesitant to take positions which would be embarrassing politically. The fact that this is *their* government gives them a feeling both of greater willingness and greater safety in cooperating with it than would be the case if the government had a different complexion.

This cooperative relationship does not mean a complete identity of outlook. For government leaders, wage policy is only one element in a complicated pattern which includes the value of the currency, the export-import balance, tax and subsidy policies, farm price policies, and numerous other things. Price stability has been a key problem throughout the postwar period, and the objective of stable prices has set limits to the wage increases which could safely be allowed in a particular year. Government leaders concerned with this problem have tended to set lower wage targets than union leaders, who must be responsive in some degree to the sentiments of their members. It has been difficult to explain to union members why wage demands should be limited at a time of great labor scarcity and maximum union strength. There have thus been repeated occasions on which the government has recommended a wage increase of, say 3 per cent, the LO leadership has plumped for 6 per cent, and the unions have actually gone out and gotten 8 per cent.

The government pulls back on the coattails of the LO, and the LO does the same for its affiliated unions, but these efforts have met with uneven success. In some years the LO has said to the government (or the unions have said to both): "We cannot accept what you propose." Government policy failed rather completely, for example, in 1948, 1952, and 1955. In 1942–44, 1949–50, and 1953–54, on the other hand, it was quite successful.

The union leaders themselves must and do look beyond the wage sector of the economy. Each year, for example, the Swedish government negotiates with the organized farmers of the country over the level of farm price guarantees. LO representatives sit on the committee which conducts these negotiations and, with an eye to the living costs of union members, tend naturally to favor price stability. At the same time, the unions are negotiating with employers over wages, and the prospective movement of living costs is a major factor in these negotiations. The situation is further complicated by a provision that the in-

4. Galenson, "Scandinavia," p. 156.
5. Tage Lindbom, *Sweden's Labor Program* (New York, League for Industrial Democracy, 1948), p. 26.

crease in the net income of farmers in a particular year should approximate the rate of wage increase for farm laborers. The farm laborers, however, are organized in a union affiliated with the LO and expect to receive at least the same increase as other LO unions. Thus the circle is complete, and what emerges is a complicated politico-economic bargain over the division of national income.

The impact of general economic considerations and of government policy on wage determination can be illustrated most graphically by a brief review of the past decade.[6] Sweden, along with most other countries, experienced a sharp wage-price inflation in the years just after World War II. By the end of 1948 the wage level (including both agreed increases and the "wage drift" outside the agreements) had risen by 30 per cent in three years. At this point the government embarked on a more rigorous stabilization policy. The public's purchasing power was reduced by a number of excise taxes, and the level of investment was reduced by administrative controls. LO contributed to the general program by recommending to its affiliates that they extend their 1948 agreements through 1949 without wage increases. Union members apparently accepted the argument that wage increases would lead only to price increases, and the "wage stop" was put into effect throughout the union movement.

The stabilization program was successful, and price increases virtually ceased in 1949. Plans were accordingly laid to continue the wage stop through 1950. Some difficulty was caused by the devaluation of the kroner in September 1949, which raised both the profits of export industries and the cost of imported goods. The government undertook to offset the latter factor, however, by subsidizing imports which entered importantly into consumption. Thus price increases were postponed, and the unions agreed to continue the wage stop during 1950.

Before the end of 1950 the Korean crisis had occurred, and it was clear that a substantial price increase was unavoidable. Apart from this, it would probably have been impossible to continue the wage stop beyond 1950 because of inequities which had accumulated during the previous three years. Some workers had benefited substantially from unofficial increases (wage drift). Others had not benefited at all and were demanding that their relative position be restored. The brakes were consequently removed, and large increases occurred during the spring of 1951, averaging 15 per cent.

In order to protect itself against further increases in living costs, the LO executive demanded in December 1951 that the SAF agree to a cost-of-living escalator system which would maintain real wages. In the absence of such a system it was expected that 1952 wage demands

6. For a fuller discussion see *Trade Unions and Full Employment,* pp. 49–72.

would be very large indeed. The SAF replied that it was opposed to escalator clauses in peacetime, but that it would nevertheless accept them provided the LO would accept a single central agreement covering the wage levels of all affiliated unions. The LO was not willing to move this rapidly toward complete centralization of wage bargaining and did not believe the affiliated unions would agree to it in any case. The eventual outcome was a central bargain, but with enough elasticity to allow a good deal of supplementary bargaining in individual industries.

The agreed wage increase was considerably larger than the government wished it to be. The government recommended that the increase in money earnings be held within 5 per cent, which would have allowed an increase of only about 3 per cent in base rates. The LO replied that this was too little in view of the high level of corporate profits, the very active demand for labor, and the lag of earnings behind both prices and national income since 1950. The central agreement provided a general wage increase of 8 per cent for men and 10 per cent for women. It was calculated that these wage increases would raise prices by 3 per cent, yielding a net gain in real wages (for men) of 5 per cent. In order to protect the real wage increase, it was provided that if prices rose by 6 per cent, wages should rise by an additional 3 per cent; if prices rose 7 per cent, wages should go up 4 per cent; and so on.

The agreement was so arranged as to be particularly beneficial to the lowest-wage groups. Women were increased more than men. A minimum increase of 25 ore per hour was set for everyone, which for some low-wage workers was higher than the 8 per cent figure. Further, a union in any industry whose hourly earnings had risen by less than 20 per cent during 1951 (the amount of the increase in the price level) could negotiate with its employers' association for an extra increase to make up for this lag. If a union had experienced an inequitable wage lag during any period before 1951, it could also negotiate separately on this issue. These elastic provisions made it possible to make necessary adjustments in particular industries without violating the terms of the central agreement.[7] Partly because of this flexibility, the agreement was generally accepted by the affiliated unions. Greatest difficulty was experienced in the paper industry, which had been earning very high profits because of a favorable export market and in which the union felt it could have obtained a much larger increase without LO interference. In order to bring the union into line the LO had to threaten to withdraw all moral and financial support in the event of a strike.

The 1952 agreement worked out favorably from the unions' standpoint. The earnings of manufacturing workers (including wage drift) rose by about 18 per cent while the cost-of-living index rose only 8

7. *Ibid.,* p. 68.

per cent, yielding a substantial increase in real wages. Despite this successful experience it was decided not to renew the central agreement in 1953. This seems to have been due partly to interunion frictions generated by the central agreement, partly to fears concerning the long-run effect of centralized bargaining on trade union democracy, but perhaps most of all to the change in the economic situation. The government, after the "deliberate, once-for-all inflation" of 1951 and 1952, took vigorous action to hold further inflation within bounds, and by the end of 1952 the economy had been brought into approximate balance. Conditions for money wage increases were not promising. In its September 1952 policy statement, therefore, the LO advised the affiliated unions to avoid general wage demands in 1953 and instead to concentrate on improvements for special cases and groups. This advice appears to have been followed, the average increase in wages through collective agreements being less than 1 per cent in 1953.

In 1955 the government failed signally to persuade the unions to restrain their wage demands. Individual unions filed demands ranging from 5 to 25 per cent; and it appears that the increase in wage level for the year, including wage drift, will be about 10 per cent. This posed the question of what anti-inflationary measures the government could adopt. Tax increases were rejected, because in an election campaign in the fall of 1954 the government had promised "tax reductions soon." Forced saving was given serious consideration but aroused intense public controversy and was also rejected. In the end, the government resorted to the orthodox expedient of a stiff increase in interest rates and a tightening of credit controls. Economic theorists have sometimes speculated that democratic governments, particularly prolabor ones, will not dare to counter money wage increases in this way but will instead resign themselves to price inflation. Swedish experience suggests that this hypothesis needs critical examination.

The year-to-year movement of wages from 1944 to 1953 is summarized in Table 9-1. Each year the economic research department of LO attempts to calculate the increase in hourly earnings which should result from the new agreements signed early in the year. These estimates cannot be exact because of the complicated nature of some of the wage adjustments, but are believed to be generally accurate. The results of this calculation appear in the left-hand column of Table 9-1. The right-hand "total" column shows the actual percentage increase in earnings over the previous year, as reported in government statistics. The center column gives a residual figure, and has been variously designated as "wage slide," "wage glide," or "wage drift." It is an attempt to measure increases in earnings over and above those required by the terms of collective agreements.

The source of the pronounced wage drift during the postwar years has been the tightness of the labor market, which has forced employers to resort to various expedients to attract and hold labor. "The wage drift has all forms: *sub rosa* agreements between employers and the local branch of a union, spontaneous employer action to make itself more attractive to workers (in spite of desperate warnings from the Employers' Associations), loose ways of interpreting contract clauses about skill etc., loose piece rates, *ex post facto* piece rates for what was really time work, non-reduction of piece rates in spite of technical improve-

Table 9-1. *Increase of Hourly Earnings for Men in Manufacturing Industries, Sweden, 1945–53 (per cent)*

YEAR	BY AGREEMENT	"WAGE DRIFT"	TOTAL
1945	4	0	4
1946	4	3	7
1947	11	3.5	14
1948	4	4	9
1949	0	3.5	3
1950	0	4	4
1951	15	5.5	21
1952	12	4.5	17
1953	1	2	3

Source: Adapted from G. Rehn, "Memorandum on the Wage Drift in Sweden" (mimeographed, LO, 1954), p. 3. Totals in last column do not add exactly because of rounding.

ments." [8] The increase in average hourly earnings has been about the same for timeworkers as for pieceworkers in manufacturing industries; but in the case of timework a larger proportion of the increase has come from contractual agreement, while for piecework a larger proportion has resulted from wage drift.

It will be noted that there was a substantial increase in earnings even during the wage stop of 1949 and 1950. The fact that this increase had been very uneven from one industry to the next was an important reason for union dissatisfaction and for abandonment of the wage stop in 1951. It is also significant, however, that there was a marked wage drift even in years when contractual increases were large—1947, 1951, 1952. The obvious interpretation of this phenomenon is that most unions have been underpricing their labor throughout the postwar period. The degree of latitude remaining to employers, however, is such that actual

8. Rehn, "Memorandum on the Wage Drift in Sweden," pp. 3–4.

earnings have diverged further and further from contractual rates. Earnings have raced ahead, propelled by an inflationary market situation, and bargained wage rates have come along behind, ratifying with some lag the wage level which the market permitted.

EVOLUTION OF THE NATIONAL WAGE STRUCTURE

THE ECONOMIC CONTEXT

The years since 1939 in Sweden have been years of high employment and substantial economic progress. Unemployment, which in 1938 was about 11 per cent of all union members, fell sharply during the war years and even more during the postwar period. During the late forties and early fifties it oscillated between 3 and 4 per cent of the members of unemployment-insurance funds (about half of all wage earners). A substantial part of this unemployment has been among seasonal and handicapped workers, and unemployment of regular year-round workers has been extremely low.[9] Thus employer competition for labor has been active, and conditions have been favorable for winning wage increases.

While it is difficult to make precise comparisons of gross national product for prewar and postwar years, it appears that gross national product rose by about 40 per cent in real terms between 1938 and 1947. Taking account of a population increase of almost 9 per cent, GNP in per capita terms rose about 29 per cent, or approximately 3 per cent per year. Since 1947 we have the careful calculations of the OEEC, which indicate that between 1947 and 1952 GNP per capita rose by 18.6 per cent,[10] again an annual rate of slightly more than 3 per cent. While part of this increase undoubtedly came from a transfer of labor out of agriculture and other sectors to the more productive industrial sector, there must have also been a substantial increase of per capita output *within* each sector.

The period in question was one of moderate inflation. Prices advanced substantially during 1939–42, were held almost completely stable from 1942–47, then began to creep up gradually, and advanced sharply once more in 1951–52. At the end of 1952, prices stood 93 per cent above the 1939 level—a percentage almost identical with that for the United States.

The course of money and real wages since 1939 is shown in Table

9. Swedish Central Bureau of Statistics, *Statistical Abstract of Sweden* (Stockholm, 1954), p. 220; and International Labour Office (ILO), *Yearbook of Labour Statistics* (Geneva, 1954), p. 93.
10. Organization for European Economic Cooperation (OEEC), *Statistics of National Product and Expenditure, 1938, 1947 to 1952* (Paris, 1954), p. 82.

9-2. These figures, which are based on average hourly earnings, reflect increases in piecework earnings, individual premiums and bonuses, paid vacations, and numerous other things in addition to agreed increases in base rates. They include, that is to say, the wage drift discussed in the preceding section. The substantial increase in real wages is apparent from the table. For male workers in manufacturing, the increase from

Table 9-2. Cost of Living, Money Wages, and Real Wages for Adult Workers, Sweden, 1939–54 (1939 = 100)

YEAR	COST OF LIVING *	MONEY WAGES †		REAL WAGES	
		MEN	WOMEN	MEN	WOMEN
1939	100	100	100	100	100
1940	113	109	110	96	97
1941	128	117	119	91	93
1942	138	128	130	93	94
1943	139	133	135	95	97
1944	139	137	141	99	102
1945	139	142	150	102	108
1946	139	153	163	110	117
1947	143	175	193	122	135
1948	150	190	213	127	142
1949	152	196	221	129	145
1950	154	204	229	132	149
1951	178	246	275	138	154
1952	193	293	325	152	168
1953	195	307	339	157	174
1954 ‡	197	319	351	162	178

* This index excludes direct taxes and differs, therefore, from the index of the Social Board which includes the effect of taxes. It concerns moderate-income families in cities.

† Manufacturing industries. This series differs only slightly from the saf "all-industries" series which has a somewhat broader coverage.

‡ Preliminary.

Source: Social Board statistics

1939 to 1952 was 62 per cent. It will be noted that the rate of increase was quite variable from year to year. Real wages fell slightly during the war period of wage restraint from 1940–44, rose substantially as wage restraint was relaxed and wages got ahead of prices in the immediate postwar years, then leveled off from 1948–50, and rose sharply once more during the "managed inflation" of 1951–52. The increase in real wages was also somewhat variable as among different categories of labor. Women's wages rose more rapidly than men's, partly because of deliberate trade union policy, partly because of the active demand for women workers in a tight labor market.

There may have been a slight increase in the proportion of national income going to wage and salary payments. It is estimated that in 1939 wages and salaries formed between 59 and 63 per cent of national income measured at factor cost, the difference in these figures being an admitted margin of error in the data. By 1949 wage and salary payments had risen to between 62 and 67 per cent of national income.[11] This increase is so slight as to be still within the margin of error in the estimates. About all that can be said, therefore, is that there was no drastic redistribution of income toward wage and salary earners. As a group they received approximately their pro rata share of the general increase in national output. *Within* the wage-salary sector there was some redistribution from salary earners to wage earners, as will appear later in this section.

We proceed now to consider the main dimensions of wage structure. In general, Sweden has experienced a reduction of most types of wage differential since 1939. The reduction has been less drastic than in the case of France, partly because many differentials were already quite small, partly because the price inflation was more moderate in Sweden, partly because the wage-equalization policy of the LO has been applied in a cautious and pragmatic way. It is noteworthy also that a number of occupations and industries have managed to swim against the tide and to increase their wage advantage over the period.

The reduction of differentials in Sweden has resulted partly from a high level of demand for all kinds of labor in a period of full employment, and partly from government and union policies of granting larger relative increases to lower-paid workers as a matter of principle. Even during periods of strong wage restraint, such as 1942–45, exceptions were permitted for the lowest-paid groups—women workers, workers in rural areas, workers in abnormally low-wage firms, and so on. During periods of wage advance, the unions have on occasion encouraged flat-rate increases for all or even flat-rate increases with "ceilings" which excluded the higher-wage workers in each industry. On other occasions equal percentage increases were the general rule. Over the period as a whole, however, union policy has operated in a leveling direction.

OCCUPATIONAL DIFFERENTIALS

There are strong indications that the earnings of the lower occupational strata have risen more rapidly than those of the top occupational

11. Social Board statistics.

groups. Some indication of the general tendency is provided by Table 9-3. Various occupational groups are here arranged from left to right in decreasing order of annual earnings in 1939. It will be noted that the percentage increase in annual earnings since 1939 rises steadily from left to right, being smallest for the high-wage engineers and greatest for the low-paid agricultural workers. Women's earnings have also risen more rapidly than men's earnings in the same occupational grade. There has thus been a general leveling tendency, rather moderate within manufacturing, quite marked as between manufacturing and agriculture.

On the narrower question of occupational differentials among manual workers in the same industry, there is unfortunately a great scarcity of information. The best material is that for the engineering (metalworking) industry. This large and important industry, a traditional wage leader, may give some indication of the occupational structure prevailing in Sweden. In the Stockholm area in 1953, the three top crafts (about 2 per cent of all workers) in the industry earned 45 per cent

Table 9-3. *Wage Developments for Selected Occupational Groups, Sweden, 1939–52* (*Kroner*)

	MANUFACTURING INDUSTRIES						AGRICULTURE
			CLERKS		WORKERS		
	ENGINEERS	FOREMEN	MEN	WOMEN	MEN	WOMEN	MEN
Annual earnings, 1939	6,546	4,947	4,569	2,367	3,056	1,872	1,602
Annual earnings, 1952	14,748	12,072	11,739	6,672	8,710	5,800	6,507
Percentage increase	225	244	257	282	285	310	406

Source: Social Board statistics

more than the lowest category of unskilled labor. The skilled group as a whole (40 per cent of all workers) averaged only 18 per cent above the lowest unskilled group. Percentage differentials declined moderately, i.e. by two or three points, between 1939 and 1949. Since 1949 there has been a slight reverse tendency toward a widening of the skilled workers' percentage advantage. This reflects a shortage of skilled labor, which may result partly from the fact that the drive for higher status through education is directed more toward white-collar jobs than toward skilled manual jobs. It may also reflect an enlarged use of piece rates for the skilled workers, and a reluctance by employers to adjust piece rates as technical improvements accumulate for fear of losing labor in a tight market.[12]

Drawing on this case and on scattered bits of information for other industries, one can say that occupational differentials in 1939 were already quite narrow, that they showed a slight tendency to shrink further during the next decade, but that since the late forties they have tended to widen once more. Over the period as a whole, differentials among manual workers in the same industry do not seem to have changed substantially.

INTERINDUSTRY DIFFERENTIALS

The average hourly earnings of male workers in the principal manufacturing industries in 1939 and 1952 are shown in Table 9-4. It is clear that there has been a considerable reduction in the dispersion of industry wage levels since 1939. Dispersion reached its lowest point in 1946 and has increased somewhat since that time, but it remains well below the 1939 level. The quartile deviation of the industry averages was .0916 in 1939, .0619 in 1952. The reduced dispersion is indicated also by the strong negative correlation between the wage level of an industry in 1939 and its rate of wage increase over the period 1939–52. In general, the lowest-wage industries at the beginning of this period have been the ones to gain ground most rapidly during the years 1939–52. This is true not only within manufacturing but also as between manufacturing and other branches of industry. The high-wage building construction industry, for example, has lost ground relatively since 1939. Average hourly earnings in building construction, almost 50 per cent above those of male manufacturing workers in 1939, are less than 30 per cent higher today. On the other hand, farm and forest wages, which were relatively depressed in earlier decades, have risen much faster than other wage rates. Farm workers in 1952 earned three-quarters as much as male manufacturing workers, compared to only half as much in 1939. The tendency toward leveling of interindustry differences has thus been consistent throughout the economy.

In addition to reduced dispersion, there have been considerable changes in the ranking of different industries in the wage structure. In most cases there appears a reasonable economic explanation for the changed position of particular industries. During the thirties, the export industries and those subject to severe import competition were in a depressed condition compared to sheltered home-market industries such as building, printing, and food processing. Wage levels in industries such as

12. See in this connection the comments of G. Rehn in "Unionism and the Wage Structure," to be published in the forthcoming report of the 1954 IEA conference on wage determination.

baking, brewing, meat packing, and flour milling appear to have been comparatively high relative to the skills required in these industries. Their lower ranking in 1952 may reflect a fairer valuation of these types of labor.

Table 9-4. Average Hourly Earnings of Adult Workers, 1939 and 1952, and Percentage Changes, Sweden, 1939–52 (men)

		1939	1952 (PRELIMINARY)		% INCREASE
BRANCH OF INDUSTRY	ORDER	KR. PER HR.	ORDER	KR. PER HR.	1939–52
Mines and ore-dressing plants	1	1.79	1	5.00	179
Breweries and soft drinks	2	1.62	—		—
Bakeries	3	1.57	11	3.62	130.6
Shipyards	4	1.48	2	4.27	188.5
Meat packing	5	1.47	13	3.51	138.8
Flour mills	6	1.45	18	3.38	133.1
Engineering works	7	1.41	3	4.05	187.2
Paint, oil, and perfume	8	1.36	7	3.79	178.7
Chocolate & confectionery	9	1.33	10	3.64	173.7
Metal manufacturing works	10	1.32	5	3.93	197.7
Clothing industries	11	1.32	16	3.41	158.3
Boot and shoe industries	12	1.32	14	3.51	165.9
Iron, steel, & copper works	13	1.31	4	4.01	206.1
Pulp mills	14	1.29	8	3.78	193.0
Rubber-goods industries	15	1.29	6	3.83	196.9
Paper and cardboard mills	16	1.24	15	3.51	183.1
Cement industries	17	1.23	9	3.73	203.3
Sugar industries	18	1.22	24	3.16	159.0
Hosiery industries	19	1.17	19	3.36	187.1
Brick works	20	1.14	17	3.39	197.4
China and tile industries	21	1.14	12	3.59	214.9
Glass works	22	1.14	20	3.33	192.1
Sawmills and planing mills	23	1.08	22	3.24	200.0
Cotton industry	24	1.04	21	3.33	220.2
Woolen industry	25	1.04	23	3.22	209.6

Source: Social Board statistics

Workers in the iron ore mines of central Sweden, on the other hand, have considerably increased their advantage over other industries, from 103 per cent of the average for all manufacturing industry in 1939 to 117 per cent in 1952. This probably indicates that under full employment it is necessary to pay a substantial premium to induce workers to perform arduous physical labor in remote locations. The rise in the standing of the rubber industry may be associated with the fact that employment in this industry has doubled since the prewar years. The higher standing of iron and steel, metal manufacturing, and engineering may be connected with the very high activity in heavy industry throughout the war and postwar periods.

The net effect of these cross-currents, as indicated earlier, has been to reduce the size of interindustry differentials. This stands out even more strikingly in the case of women's wages than in that of men. In 1952 average hourly earnings of adult women workers in eleven manufacturing industries varied from a low of 2.25 kroner per hour to a high of only 2.78 kroner, and the quartile deviation had the very low value of .0187. This is much smaller than the figure of .0619 for men in 1952 and .0467 for women in 1939. Rehn makes the following comment on this point:

> Whereas the interindustry wage dispersion of male workers shows many great exceptions from the general rule of narrowing toward the mean, the development of the interindustry structure of women's wages is very "unidirectional": levelling is general. Apparently this has its explanation in the high degree of uniformity of job content of female workers in different industries. Wages were distorted earlier, but the high fluidity of the labor market [under full employment], plus conscious efforts of the union movement under the guidance of the central secretariat based on the moral demands for justice put forth by low-wage groups, have been creating a more equitable wage structure, in this case simply implying similar wages in all industries.[13]

It is clear that the LO leaders have not followed a "monopolistic" policy of pressing for the greatest possible advantage in each industry, a policy which would produce substantial interindustry dispersion. On the contrary, they have followed a "solidaristic" wage policy aimed at developing equitable relationships among industries in the light of the work performed. This policy has been welcomed most warmly by unions in low-wage industries or in a weak bargaining position. Unions in industries such as food processing, which were formerly out of line on the high side and have suffered a decline in relative standing, have been less enthusiastic. The pulp and paper workers, who have been restrained from taking advantage of an unusually favorable bargaining position in the early fifties, have been especially restive. On the whole, however, the solidaristic policy has been accepted and applied with a unanimity scarcely conceivable in the United States. While it has meant a gradual leveling of interindustry differences, this has not been carried out in a doctrinaire fashion. Exceptions have been permitted, as in the case of the iron ore miners, where they seemed justified on the basis of the job conditions.

13. Rehn, "Unionism and the Wage Structure."

GEOGRAPHICAL DIFFERENTIALS

In 1939 Sweden was officially divided into nine cost-of-living zones. In 1946 the number was reduced to five on the basis of new investigations, and in 1953 the two lowest zones were merged, reducing the number to four.

The lowest zone consists of scattered areas, overwhelmingly rural, in the south of Sweden. The highest zone includes Stockholm and the remote areas of the north. Comparing the situation in 1939 and 1951, one finds that percentage differentials have been substantially reduced. In 1939 the earnings of male manufacturing workers in the highest

Table 9-5. *Differentials in Average Hourly Earnings in Various Cost-of-Living Zones, All Branches of Industry, Sweden, 1939 and 1951*

	1939			1951		
COST-OF-LIVING ZONE	AVERAGE HOURLY EARNINGS (KR. PER HR.)	ABSOLUTE DIFFER-ENCE OVER ZONE 1	PERCENT-AGE OF ZONE 1	AVERAGE HOURLY EARNINGS (KR. PER HR.)	ABSOLUTE DIFFER-ENCE OVER ZONE 1	PERCENT-AGE OF ZONE 1
Men						
1	1.07	—	100	2.85	—	100
2	1.17	.10	109	3.05	.20	107
3	1.31	.24	122	3.22	.37	113
4	1.46	.39	136	3.51	.66	123
5	1.80	.73	168	3.92	1.07	138
Women						
1	.69	—	100	2.04	—	100
2	.74	.05	107	2.16	.12	106
3	.80	.11	116	2.25	.21	110
4	.80	.11	116	2.39	.35	118
5	.89	.20	146	2.64	.60	129

Source: Social Board statistics. For 1939 the zoning is an *ex post* recalculation on the basis of the 1946 zone system. There were actually 9 geographical zones in 1939.

zone averaged 68 per cent above those in the lowest zone. By 1951 this advantage had been reduced to 38 per cent. In the case of women workers, the geographical spread was reduced from 46 to 29 per cent. The picture is not substantially changed when one examines data for individual industries. Within each industry, of course, the geographical spread is considerably less. The size of geographical differentials varies moderately among industries, but the shrinkage over the years 1939–51 is quite consistent.

The figures in Table 9-5 give an exaggerated impression of the size of geographical differentials in Sweden, because they combine three different things: "pure" zone differentials, differentials among industries with different levels of wages, and differentials among plants of varying size within· each industry. The three have an additive effect, because industries with low skill demands and other causes of low wages are concentrated in the more rural areas, and because the smaller plants in each industry also tend to be located in the lower-cost-of-living zones.

Concerning the relation between plant size and wage level, data are available for the engineering and woodworking industries. The indexes shown in Table 9-6 were calculated separately for each of the five cost-of-living zones and then combined, so that they are unaffected by the correlation between zone and plant size. The reduction in the range of plant wage levels in each industry is apparent. The remaining differences, at least in engineering, are largely a result of differing volumes of piecework in large and small firms.

Table 9-6. Relation Between Plant Size and Wage Level, Sweden, 1939 and 1950 *
(index)

NUMBER OF EMPLOYEES	ENGINEERING 1939	ENGINEERING 1950	WOODWORKING 1939	WOODWORKING 1950
500 and over	100	100	—	—
201–500	95	97	100	100
51–200	94	95	92	97
11–50	88	93	88	95
1–10	85	87	85	92

* Indexes have been calculated separately for each of the five cost-of-living zones and then combined.

Source: Rehn, "Unionism and the Wage Structure"

For other industries information is less complete. It appears, however, that interplant dispersion in a number of industries has been reduced to roughly half its prewar size. This reduction can be traced to union policies plus the full employment situation, which both strengthened the unions' bargaining position and tended to bring low-wage employers into line through the operation of market forces. Rehn says:

> During and after the war the ambition of the unions has been to bring the geographical wage structure to conform with the official cost-of-living geography, *i.e.*, to reduce inter-zone differences. The inter-zone equalization was stimulated by the increase of wages in agriculture

and the generally high incomes of farmers. The "zone dispersion" has been reduced from 30–40 per cent to 12–25 per cent, in most industries. At the same time the inter-plant differences in each zone and each industry have been systematically "hunted" by the unions in those many cases where such levelling was not brought about by the high employment and competition for workers and the resulting wage drift.[14]

The movement of agricultural incomes is important and has been operative in every country included in the present study. The low industrial wage rates in small towns and rural areas are based on a low level of agricultural wage rates and farm incomes. As agricultural incomes rise during prosperity periods, industry must pay more to draw labor from the land. This forces wage rates up most rapidly in the most rural areas and leads almost automatically to a telescoping of geographical differentials.

CONCLUDING OBSERVATIONS

The shifts in the Swedish wage structure since 1939 stem basically from events in the economy—shifts in the relative profitability of various industries, shifts in the relative supplies of skilled and unskilled labor, price inflation, changes in the level and structure of agricultural incomes, and a prolonged period of very high aggregate demand. Economic influences have been reinforced, however, and perhaps occasionally offset, by trade union policies. The LO has followed a generally egalitarian line, a policy of whittling away gradually at almost every sort of wage differential. There is no dogmatic attempt at wage leveling, but rather a presupposition that an inequality is inequitable unless specific justification for it can be shown.

We have already remarked on the relatively centralized character of Swedish wage determination. The degree of centralization should not be exaggerated. On the employer side, the more profitable firms in an industry find ways of paying more than the bargained wage level when it suits their purpose, and SAF warnings to the contrary tend to be brushed aside, particularly during inflationary periods. Similarly, individual unions do not docilely accept the advice received from LO headquarters. Wage demands often vary widely, and there turns out to be a large difference between official programs and actual behavior. One can say only that central influence is stronger than in most other countries and that it appears to be increasing over the course of time.

Union and management leaders deal with each other in a reasonable

14. *Ibid.*

and technically competent manner. Both sides consult with government, and there is at least the beginning of coordination between private wage-price policies and government monetary and budget policy. All parties concerned have highly competent economic advice.

In such an atmosphere of reasonableness, do not all problems of wage determination speedily resolve themselves? The answer is that they do not; and it is instructive to examine why they do not. In Sweden (and again in Britain, as we shall see in Chapter 10) one comes up against the hard core of problems which beset centralized wage determination, even in the most skillful hands. These problems can be sorted out into five categories:

1. The LO has tried to work toward more "reasonable" or "equitable" wage relationships among various occupational and industrial groups. But what is equity? Can different groups of workers ever be persuaded to construe equity in precisely the same way? Can differing management and union conceptions of equity be fully reconciled?

Up to now, equity has tended to mean a greater degree of equality. The leveling process has been gradual, and the ultimate limits to it have never been clearly visualized. At some point further leveling of occupational differentials, in particular, will begin to interfere with the supply of skilled labor. Can one assume that this danger will be perceived in time and that narrowing of differentials will halt at just the right point? Or does the possibility of employers paying more than the agreed rates provide enough flexibility to maintain the supply of skilled workers whatever may happen to contract rates?

If these problems could be resolved, one might arrive in time at an "equilibrium" wage structure, accepted as reasonable by all concerned. The labor movement would still have the function of ensuring that *all* wages rose by a proper percentage year after year, but the work of correcting specific inequities would be over. Does this not leave the labor movement, particularly the lower-level union leaders, with a rather prosaic task? It may be, of course, that job content will change fast enough so that established differentials will rapidly become obsolete and the unions will be kept busy with constant wage revisions; but this still seems rather poor cement for a strong labor movement.

2. Central emphasis on equity as the test of wage differentials implies that differentials should not be used to attract labor to expanding firms, industries, or regions. One can make a plausible case for this view. It can be argued that to create differentials large enough to attract labor to the constantly shifting points of excess demand would mean a constant whipsawing of the wage structure, which would conflict with any policy of restraining inflation. Differentials must always be established by raising specific rates, never by lowering them, and the result

must be a more rapid rise of the average wage level. If one ceases to rely on wage differentials, however, what other methods can be used to reallocate labor rapidly toward the growth points of the economy? Swedish economists and union leaders have clearly visualized this problem, but have not yet reached an agreed solution.

3. While the LO aims at equity and at a controlled movement of wage differentials, its efforts are hampered by the existence of wage drift. Profitable firms and industries, faced with a tight market, find ways of paying more than the contract rates and of widening their differentials over other employers. Advocates of the free market may find this a heartening phenomenon, for here is the market breaking through all efforts to restrain it. But it is clear that there are disadvantages in this degree of employer freedom. The wage drift is quite uneven from one part of the economy to the next, not only because of different levels of excess demand for labor, but also because of different technical conditions as between employees with strongly "normalized" weekly or monthly wages and piece-rate workers whose earnings show a persistent upward tendency. The workers whose wages are lagging behind quickly perceive this and demand that their unions take action to close the gap. The inevitable result is a whipsawing of wages which hampers any effort to stabilize the general wage level.

What is the answer? Should the possibility of a wage drift be removed by converting the contract rates into effective maxima as well as minima? Is this actually feasible? Would it be desirable if it could be accomplished?

4. Swedish union and management leaders have given much thought to the strategy of full employment and to the role of wage policy in this strategy.[15] The tendency of many countries (including Sweden) in the immediate postwar years was to maintain full employment through a condition of suppressed inflation. Fiscal and monetary policies were used to create an excess of aggregate demand, and inflation was held in check only through investment controls, subsidies, rationing, price controls, and wage limitations. This situation, tenable for a short time, creates serious difficulties and distortions over any extended period. On the wage side it means either direct government control of wages, which Swedish unions and employers reject as a matter of principle, or deliberate trade union restraint enforced by a high degree of centralization within the labor movement. Apart from the fact that a centralized "wage restraint" policy cannot be fully effective, because of wage drift as well as union deviations from the central policy, it tends

15. See particularly the analysis in the LO report, *Trade Unions and Full Employment*, pp. 73–105; also Ralph Turvey, ed., *Wages Policy under Full Employment* (London, W. Hodge, 1952).

to distort the purpose of the labor movement. Union members are apt to conclude that it is a queer kind of organization which works overtime year after year to *prevent* workers from getting higher wages.

LO leaders have become increasingly restive at being called on to take direct responsibility for the price level and have tended to emphasize that this is a responsibility which government must assume through monetary-fiscal policy.[16] While correct monetary measures would not guarantee a sensible wage policy by the trade unions, it is perhaps a pre-requisite for such a policy. Given a noninflationary government policy, it would be reasonable for the LO to try to hold the rate of increase in the money wage level to no more than the rate of increase in productivity. This should be regarded, of course, as only the average tendency. There should be freedom to bring up unduly low wages more rapidly than other wages and to work gradually toward an equitable system of differentials. Indeed, if this second objective is not actively pursued, the first will remain unattainable. Groups which feel themselves disadvantaged will demand outsize wage increases, these will tend to be imitated by other groups, and a competitive wage scramble will be on. An orderly and con-trolled advance of the whole wage structure becomes possible only when each group is reasonably content with its *relative* position.

5. Any over-all wage strategy raises serious internal problems for the labor movement. There seems a general disposition to move in the direction of greater centralization of wage policy and a stronger voice for LO officers in specific negotiations. How can this be reconciled with the traditional democratic control of each union by its members? What is likely to happen to the loyalty of local union members and officers as they find the important decisions concerning their economic status transferred increasingly to Stockholm? Is there not likely to be serious friction among the various national unions as LO leaders urge larger increases for some than for others in order to arrive at "equitable" relationships?

These problems are in no sense generically Swedish problems. They exist also in other countries with similar political and collective bargaining institutions, notably the other Scandinavian countries and Great Britain. They exist in embryo form in the United States. They are not problems of merely transient importance. On the contrary, they will almost cer-tainly be with us into the indefinite future.

16. See, for example, the discussion in *Trade Unions and Full Employment*, pp. 86–93.

CHAPTER 10 *Great Britain*

INFLUENCES ON WAGE DETERMINATION

THE case of Great Britain resembles that of Sweden in many ways, but there are also significant differences. To put the matter in a word, things are less "tidy" in Britain. The structure of the trade union movement is more complicated. Industry-wide bargaining is not so pervasive. The influence of the Trades Union Congress over individual unions is not so great. The rich variety of the wage structure has not been so completely harnessed by the collective bargaining system as is the case in Sweden. Anomalies abound, and there are many exceptions to any general statement. The tendency toward wage leveling, while strong, has not been so universal as in Sweden, and one finds numerous crosscurrents running in the opposite direction.

TRADE UNIONISM AND COLLECTIVE BARGAINING [1]

British trade unionism, like British industrialism, has a long tradition reaching back almost two centuries. Union membership by 1951 had reached a level of 9,480,000 persons, or almost half the gainfully employed population of 22,214,000.[2] Union organization is unevenly developed in different sectors of the economy. Coal mining, transport, and shipping are better than 80 per cent organized. In other mining and quarrying, building construction, public utilities, cotton and woolen textiles, metals and engineering, and the civil service, the proportion of union members is typically between 50 and 60 per cent. From this level the proportion runs down to about 20 per cent in the distributive and consumer service industries.[3] On the whole, however, the strength of the trade unions and their effectiveness in collective bargaining is matched in few other countries. Even in partially unionized industries

1. Selected references for this and the next sections are the following: *British Trade Unionism: Six Studies by PEP* (London, Political and Economic Planning, 1949); Allan Flanders, "Great Britain," in Galenson, ed., *Comparative Labor Movements;* Ministry of Labour and National Service, *Industrial Relations Handbook* (new ed. London, 1953); *Trade Union Structure and Closer Unity: Final Report* (London, Trades Union Congress, 1947); and Sidney and Beatrice Webb, *Industrial Democracy* (rev. ed. London, Longmans, 1920). ·
2. *Industrial Relations Handbook,* p. 9; and Central Statistical Office.
3. Flanders, "Great Britain," p. 28.

the wage levels set through collective bargaining tend to set the pace for nonunion firms.

Because of the long period over which unionism has developed, and because of the lack of central coordination, the structure of the union movement is remarkably complex. There are some seven hundred separate unions, though many of these are extremely small. In 1951 the seventeen largest unions included two-thirds of the total union membership.[4] Unions are of three principal types: 1. the early unions of *skilled* workers, many of which have now opened their membership to lower-skilled workers. Typical of this group are the Amalgamated Engineering Union and the Electrical Trades Union, which have members in many industries and occupations but are still dominated by the skilled and upper semiskilled groups. 2. *Industrial* unions, such as the National Union of Mineworkers and the National Union of Railwaymen, which include a large majority of the workers in their respective industries. 3. There are two huge *general* workers' unions: the Transport and General Workers' Union, which has a membership of a million and a quarter and includes the lower-skilled workers in a wide range of manufacturing and other industries; and the National Union of General and Municipal Workers with 800,000 members.

While meetings of the Trades Union Congress have occasionally paid lip service to the notion of simplifying trade union structure along industrial lines, it has not been possible to do much in this direction against the weight of union history and tradition. The TUC lacks power to assign exclusive jurisdiction over an industry or trade to a single union. Different unions compete for membership in the same firm and industry, but this competition is less virulent than in the United States and is restrained by a strong sense of solidarity within the labor movement.

The sprawling and overlapping character of union organization necessitates a great deal of interunion cooperation in collective bargaining. In the engineering, shipbuilding, building construction, and textile industries, for example, a considerable number of unions join together in federations for the purpose of negotiating with employers' associations. To the extent that different unions represent different occupational strata, there are differences of interest which must be reconciled in formulating wage demands. The importance of this will emerge more clearly when we come to consider trends in occupational wage differentials.

The trade union federations are typically matched by employer federations. In 1952 there were 1,800 employer associations for dealing with labor matters. Some of these are local, some cover particular sections of an industry, and some operate nationally.[5] While industry-wide bar-

4. *Industrial Relations Handbook,* p. 9.
5. *Ibid.,* p. 13.

gaining on a national scale is the commonest situation, this is a recent development in some industries and in others does not yet exist. Flanders reports that

> national negotiations are the main form of collective bargaining . . . today. Usually they are conducted through the medium of a permanent joint organization set up for this purpose, although engineering is an important exception. In many cases these joint bodies include all the trade unions with a substantial membership in the industry or complex of industries covered and they all become parties to the same agreements. Frequently there is some provision for arbitration or a third-party decision (by an independent chairman, for example) in the event of the two sides failing to agree. Some industries, for example coal mining, railways, and civil service, have their own arbitration tribunals; others agree to resort to the Industrial Court.[6]

This frequent acceptance of arbitration over new contract provisions as well as over contract interpretations differs sharply from American practice.

Variation in the form of collective bargaining procedures is accompanied by considerable variation in the things which are bargained about. In some industries, wage bargaining deals only with general increases rather than with the wage schedules themselves. In other cases the collective agreement sets only a national minimum, with or without regional variations. Rates above the minimum are set by custom or by local negotiation. In industries where piecework prevails, the national agreement may specify only a minimum time rate (a guaranteed or "fall-back" wage), and a percentage addition to this which a normal pieceworker is expected to attain. Piece rates and work loads are then negotiated separately in each plant.

The wage structures of British industries have come down from the past encrusted with tradition. The method of computing a worker's earnings is often extremely complex. The earnings of a pieceworker in the steel industry, for example, are calculated as follows: the starting point is a basic occupational rate, which dates from several decades ago and is now a small part of total earnings. To this is added the worker's "tonnage" earnings, computed from a piecework scale. The sum of these is multiplied by a percentage, at present 75 per cent, which is a remnant of the old sliding-scale arrangement based on steel prices. Finally a cost-of-living adjustment is added. This is a flat-rate addition of so many pence per day for each point increase in the consumer price index. These different components of earnings represent successive

6. Flanders, "Great Britain," p. 53. This article provides an excellent general review of trade unionism and collective bargaining in Britain.

geological strata in the development of wage-setting customs in the industry. Their combination produces a complicated movement of wage differentials over the course of time and poses an intricate task for union and management negotiators.

Because of the age of British industry, many wage-setting practices antedate the first appearance of collective bargaining. Firms in the same industry but in different areas may have developed quite different wage levels, wage structures, and methods of wage computation. Studies of industry wage structures, even after an extended experience of collective bargaining, often reveal a perplexing diversity of practice and wide variation of earnings for the same class of labor.

Collective bargaining attempts to mold this primeval diversity into some semblance of regularity. In Britain, however, this process has been extremely gradual and pragmatic. One does not find instances of union and employer federations agreeing to remodel the whole wage structure of an industry. The "going" structure is accepted as a starting point, and discussions go on from there. In the early stages of national negotiation, it is frequently agreed that certain amounts will be added to existing rates without the rates themselves being incorporated in the agreement. At some stage the union will typically try to win agreement to a national minimum for the industry. These minima, as we shall see, are frequently so far below actual earnings as to have little practical effect. They are important, however, in that a nationally agreed advance in the industry minimum tends to raise the earnings of everyone in the industry by at least that amount. It is equivalent to an order to "move three paces to the right from wherever you happen to be at the moment." Minimum rates for specific occupations are rare in manufacturing industry, though one frequently finds a base rate for skilled workers and a lower base for the unskilled. Detailed adjustment of occupational rates is typically done on a plant-by-plant basis, though frequently within the framework of a district agreement. Over the course of time the union may try also to insert in the agreement some general rules concerning the relative earnings of pieceworkers and timeworkers, men and women workers, and others.

Even after decades of bargaining the national agreements in most industries provide only a general framework, a basic platform above which rates and earnings are adjusted by regional and local negotiation. The individual employer also remains free to deviate upward from the bargained rates when he finds it advisable to do so. During the years of labor scarcity since 1940, such deviations have been common. Workers have been upgraded, actual wage rates have been raised above the basic rates, various kinds of premium and bonus have been added, piece-rate standards have been loosened. Earnings have drifted upward even without rate changes, and the gap between earnings and rates has steadily widened. National union officials admit frankly that they have no precise information on what their members are earning, job by job and area by area. They know what the scale provides, but actual practice is something else again. Since 1945, indeed, there has been a serious problem of raising the official scales fast enough to keep within sight of actual earnings and thus to reduce the employers' freedom to cut earnings in the event of depression.

Another important feature of British collective agreements is their indefinite duration. There is no expiration date and no necessity for annual negotiations. This means that "rounds" of wage increases occur less frequently than in Sweden or the United States and take a more leisurely course when they do develop, because there is no contract expiration date hanging over the heads of the negotiators. It means also that the phenomena of "wage patterns" and "wage leadership" are less prominent in the British case. The nearest thing to a consistent wage leader appears to be the Amalgamated Engineering Union. This union occupies a strategic position because of the size and wide geographical distribution of the engineering industry, because it has been since 1940 a prosperous and expanding industry, because it is linked with shipbuilding for negotiating purposes, and because AEU members are widely distributed as maintenance mechanics in railroad shops, manufacturing plants, and other sectors of the economy. A general wage movement in engineering, therefore, is likely to be felt widely in other industries. There is considerable variation, however, in the list of unions which spearhead a particular wage advance, and in the timing and size of their demands.

THE ROLE OF GOVERNMENT

The wages and conditions of the majority of the insured workers in Britain are now regulated by collective agreements, and the proportion is steadily growing. It is generally recognized that this method is preferable to direct regulation by government. Where union organization is weak or absent, it may be necessary for government to intervene and set minimum standards of employment. This is regarded, however, not as a permanent necessity but as a holding operation until voluntary wage-setting procedures are developed.

The British system of minimum wage regulation, first established by an Act of 1909, operates through wage councils for individual industries. In 1950 there were some sixty wage councils functioning, principally in such industries as clothing, textiles, food and drink, metal fabrication, distribution, and other services. The total number of workers, including agricultural workers, covered by minimum wage regulation was estimated at 4,500,000,[7] or about 20 per cent of the gainfully employed population.

The wage council for a particular industry is composed of an equal number of labor and employer members, plus a small number of independent members appointed by the Minister of Labour. The council is empowered to determine minimum wage standards which, after approval by the minister, are enforceable at law. Since 1945 the councils have been empowered to set "minimum remuneration" as well as minimum hourly rates, which may include payment for a guaranteed work week.[8] The council may also specify the number of paid holidays during the year, and it may advise the minister on such other problems as training, recruitment, and working conditions. The Act provides that whenever a majority of workers and employers in an industry decide that statutory protection is no longer necessary, they may ask the minister to abolish the council in their industry. This is designed to encourage the superseding of government regulation by collective bargaining, and has already been used in one industry (furniture manufacturing).

The procedure for regulating agricultural wages, while formally similar to that in industry, presents certain differences in practice. Minimum wages are set by two tripartite Agricultural Wages Boards, one for England and Wales and one for Scotland.[9] The decisions of these boards are final and not reviewable by the Minister of Labour. Wages' decisions are also closely linked to price decisions. The prices of most farm products are supported by government on what amounts to a cost-plus basis. Whenever the farmers can show that their costs have been raised by a wage increase, the government will normally make an appropriate price adjustment. This obviously reduces the employers' incentive to oppose wage increases.[10]

In addition to setting minimum wages where collective bargaining is absent or ineffective, the British government has tried in various ways to extend the terms arrived at through collective bargaining to all firms—union or nonunion—in the industry in question. One way of doing this

7. Flanders, "Great Britain," p. 57.
8. The Wages Councils Acts, 1945–48.
9. The Agricultural Wages Act, 1948, and the Agricultural Wages (Scotland) Act, 1949.
10. In one recent year, the agricultural wages board for England and Wales granted a wage increase, while the board for Scotland turned it down. When the farmers descended on the government for an offsetting price increase, government officials were hesitant to apply the price increase to Scotland where costs had not risen. The Scottish farmers then went back to the agricultural workers' union and said: "Please ask us again for a wage increase—right away. This time we'll give it to you."

is by "fair-wage" clauses in purchase contracts, requiring all government contractors to observe the "recognized" rates and conditions of the district in which they work. In any region where there is a union agreement this is usually interpreted to mean the bargained rates.

During World War II there was an important extension of this principle of reinforcing the terms arrived at through collective bargaining. The Conditions of Employment and National Arbitration Order of 1940 [11] set up a National Arbitration Tribunal to decide industrial disputes which could not be settled by other methods, and prohibited strikes and lockouts. It also made it compulsory for every employer in a trade or industry to observe the wages and conditions of employment recognized in that trade or industry in the district. "Recognized" was interpreted to mean terms agreed on by a substantial proportion of workers and employers in the district, or decided by a Joint Industrial Council or similar body, or awarded by voluntary arbitration or by the National Arbitration Tribunal. Enforcement was left to the trade unions, and there was no automatic inspection by the Ministry of Labour such as exists for minimum wage rates. If an employer appeared to be violating the regulation, he could be reported to the Minister of Labour. If the complaint was upheld his workers could sue him for the amount of the deficiency in their wages. This provision was useful to unions in bringing into line employers who had previously paid less than the union scale.

In 1951 the wartime order was replaced by a milder Industrial Disputes Order.[12] This created an Industrial Disputes Tribunal, with a tripartite composition similar to that of the National Arbitration Tribunal. Either party to an industrial dispute may report the dispute to the Minister of Labour and National Service. The minister must make sure that all voluntary-settlement machinery within the industry has been utilized, and he may not take jurisdiction if there has already been an agreement, decision, or award arrived at through joint machinery or through reference to voluntary arbitration. The minister is empowered to use conciliation, to urge voluntary arbitration, and to try in various ways to arrive at a private settlement of the dispute. If all other steps have failed, he is required to refer the case to the Industrial Disputes Tribunal for decision. Strikes and lockouts are not forbidden; but an award by the tribunal becomes an implied term of the employment contract.

Employers are not required automatically to observe the recognized (i.e. collectively bargained) terms of employment in their industry and area. A trade union or employers' organization, however, may report to the ministry an "issue" about whether a particular employer should be

11. Command Paper No. 1305.
12. The Industrial Disputes Order, 1951, Statutory Instruments 1951, No. 1376.

required to observe the recognized terms. Such an issue, unless otherwise settled, must be referred to the Industrial Disputes Tribunal and may become the subject of an award. It appears, therefore, that the unions still have an effective instrument by which to bring straggling employers into line.

The stronger unions rarely resort to the tribunal or to any other government procedure. They are able to protect their interests by direct action. The arbitration procedures are used mainly by the weaker unions, which find them a useful way of establishing recognized terms in an industry and then extending these terms to employers outside the scope of the original award.

The extent to which wage increases since World War II have been arrived at through direct union-management negotiation as against various types of government procedure is shown in Table 10-1. If one counts sliding scales (cost-of-living escalators) as part of normal collec-

Table 10-1. Percentage Distribution of Amounts Secured in Weekly Wage Increases, Great Britain, 1945–53

METHOD OF SETTLEMENT	1945	1946	1947	1948	1949	1950	1951	1952	1953
Voluntary negotiations	59	85	56	82	43	65	72	53	25
Sliding scales	3	1	1	6	11	8	6	15	19
Statutory bodies	10	10	30	9	33	19	17	19	36
Arbitration	28	4	13	3	13	8	5	13	20
Total amount secured (thousands of pounds)	1,774	2,860	1,786	1,021	1,074	2,040	6,547	4,426	2,397

Source: *Ministry of Labour Gazette,* monthly issues

tive bargaining procedure, and adds items 1 and 2, it is clear that private negotiation is the dominant method of bringing about wage increases. This is particularly true in years when the total wage movement is large, as in 1946, 1951, and 1952. Minimum wage increases awarded by statutory bodies seem to come in waves (1947, 1949, 1953), and to form a large percentage of the total only when the total itself is small.

Arbitration awards, excepting 1945 and 1953, were a small part of the total. Moreover, it appears that the National Arbitration Tribunal, the Industrial Disputes Tribunal, and other arbitration bodies have been mainly "wage followers" rather than "wage leaders." Their decisions seem to rest predominantly on the movement of wages in other sections of the economy, on what would in the United States be termed "inequities" and in Britain are often called "customary relativities." Arbitration awards thus tend, as Roberts suggests, to "confirm the pattern established by the free bargaining sector." [13]

In summary, the British government plays a greater role in wage determination than is the case in Sweden or the United States. Unlike the case of France, however, the British government concentrates mainly on supplementing collective bargaining procedures. Unions and employers in the principal industries take the lead in bringing about changes of wage level and wage structure. Government concentrates on filling gaps in the collective bargaining structure, bringing stragglers into line, and tidying up around the edges.

In addition to its influence on wage rates in private industry, government is a large employer of labor in its own right. In addition to the regular military and civil services the government owns and operates the coal mines, the electric power industry, rail and air transport, local transport, radio and other communications, and a variety of other enterprises. The nationalized industries are normally operated by quasi-autonomous public corporations. While they are ultimately responsible to Parliament through a cabinet minister, they are more effectively insulated against direct ministerial intervention than is the case in France. They are also placed under statutory obligation to cover their costs from the sale of their products, a circumstance which has a direct bearing on their wage policies.

The immediate impact of nationalization was less than many workers and union officers had anticipated. [14] Collective bargaining was in most cases a long-established custom and was continued with virtually the same personnel under national ownership. There was, however, some reinforcement of the tendency toward centralized wage determination and toward leveling of interplant differentials. It is possible for two private employers in an industry to argue with the union that their differing circumstances warrant different wage levels, but this becomes difficult when both enterprises form part of a single public corporation. Not only is there bound to be greater union pressure for wage equalization, but the public corporation is in a better position to accede to this

13. Ben C. Roberts, "Trade Union Behavior and Wage Determination," to be published in the forthcoming report of the 1954 IEA conference on wage determination.

14. One high union official commented: "My new agreement (the first since nationalization) was negotiated with exactly the same people I've always dealt with. Nationalization has been purely a financial operation. There is a new top board, but the underlying structure of the industry is the same as before and it could be denationalized without much trouble. Personally, I don't care very much one way or the other. But it's hard to explain to the men why the new heaven and the new earth didn't descend when the government took over. Our old propaganda is catching up with us."

pressure because of the possibility of offsetting losses on high-cost plants against profits on low-cost ones.

In coal mining, for example, the efficient and profitable fields have customarily paid higher wages than the less profitable ones. Partly on this account, collective bargaining was never able to rise above a district level. With nationalization, the National Union of Mineworkers was able to deal with the Coal Board for the industry as a whole. With all the earnings of the industry going into a common pool, it became possible to pay more nearly uniform wage rates and to use earnings of the profitable fields to offset losses in the poorer fields. Minimum hourly rates for both underground and aboveground workers have now been substantially equalized throughout the country. Most of the underground workers, however, are paid according to complicated piece-rate scales which have a long tradition. Even the national union officers do not know much about the detailed variation of piece scales and actual earnings from one coal field to another, but it is certain that earnings do still vary substantially.

Another consequence of nationalization has been at least a temporary retardation of wage decisions. Under private ownership, even where there was a national agreement there remained considerable scope for local adjustment of base rates, piece prices, premiums, and bonuses. The manager of one unit of a nationalized industry, however, knowing that concessions which he makes will speedily be used as precedents elsewhere, and fearing that his decisions may be overruled by higher echelons of management, is likely to avoid decisions and to pass the responsibility on to London. Clegg reports that "there has thus been a swollen volume of business for the higher stages of the bargaining machinery and, therefore, delay in settling claims and considerable discontent." [15]

An interesting question is whether nationalization of certain industries has increased or decreased the ability of the unions in those industries to win wage increases. In principle, the board of directors of a nationalized industry is responsible for carrying on collective bargaining and reaching a reasonable settlement in much the same manner as a private board of directors. In a public industry charged with covering its costs, however, a wage increase implies a price increase which in a key industry like coal or electricity or transport will have reper-

15. Hugh Clegg, *Industrial Democracy and Nationalization* (Oxford, Blackwell, 1951), pp. 82–3. See also Adolf Sturmthal, "Nationalization and Workers' Control in Britain and France," *Journal of Political Economy, 61* (February 1953), 43–79. A good article on the structure of nationalized industries is William A. Robson, "Nationalized Industries in Britain and France," *American Political Science Review, 40* (June 1950), 299–322.

cussions throughout the national economy. Moreover, a wage increase by a public corporation may be interpreted as a direct expression of government policy and may stimulate wage demands in private industry. In such circumstances the officers of the corporation are bound to consult the responsible minister, and discussion of an important wage dispute will probably reach the cabinet level. Considering the strong stand which British governments have taken in favor of price stability, it seems likely that the influence of cabinet members will be exerted in a restraining direction. Trade unions may well find that wage movements are more sluggish and increases harder to come by in public than in private industry.

In support of this view may be cited the experience of the regular civil services, which have lagged behind the general pace of wage and price advance. It may be pointed out on the other side that the Coal Board was quite liberal in raising miners' wages during the late forties and early fifties. This policy was directly connected with the coal shortage and the urgent necessity of recruiting more workers for the mines. It seems certain that wages would have risen rapidly even under private ownership. Experience with nationalization is still too limited to warrant a definitive judgment. Thus far, however, there seems little ground for fears that powerful unions in nationalized industries will make monopolistic raids on the public purse.

THE WAGE LEVEL AND NATIONAL ECONOMIC POLICY [16]

For Britain as for other countries, control of inflation remained a pressing problem throughout the late forties and early fifties. The problem was especially acute in Britain because of the importance of foreign trade in the national economy and the necessity of maintaining a domestic price level which would enable British exports to compete in world markets. The Labour government of 1945–51 found itself in much the same position as the Social Democratic government in Sweden. It was obliged to appeal to the trade unions, who form the base of its popular support, to restrain their wage demands in the face of a full-employment situation favorable to a rapid rise in money wages.

The most successful efforts at voluntary wage restraint were made during the years 1948–50. Pressure for wage restraint emanated from

16. There has been considerable literature on the wage level and national economic policy in Britain. Three good references are S. R. Dennison, "Wages in Full Employment," *Lloyds Bank Review* (April 1950), 18–37; Allan Flanders, "Wages Policy and Full Employment in Britain," *Bulletin of the Oxford University Institute of Statistics, 12* (July and August 1950), 225–42; and E. Henry Phelps Brown and Ben C. Roberts, "Wages Policy in Great Britain," *Lloyds Bank Review* (January 1952), 17–31.

the cabinet and particularly from the Chancellor of the Exchequer, Sir Stafford Cripps. TUC leaders were drawn into the discussions, and the restraint policy was eventually approved by the TUC council. The TUC leadership, while lacking formal control powers over the wage policies of affiliated unions, was successful in persuading the boards of the principal unions to support the policy. There was a certain amount of grumbling in the ranks, and a good deal of sniping at the established union leaders by Communists and other critics. On the whole the members seem to have gone along in a state of puzzled but loyal acceptance of their leaders' policies—"We don't understand why they want it, but they wouldn't ask us to do it if it wasn't right."

Wage restraint did not mean a complete "wage freeze." Cost-of-living escalators continued to operate, piece-rate earnings continued to creep up, employers made adjustments above the union scale, and union leaders under strong membership pressure sometimes discovered "special circumstances" warranting an exception to the general policy. The rate of wage increase nevertheless was appreciably retarded. Basic wage rates rose by only 11 per cent between 1947 and 1950, compared with a 14 per cent increase in living costs. The rate of increase in both rates and earnings was a good deal slower than in 1945–47 or 1951–52.

The wage-restraint policy would probably have had to be abandoned soon after 1950 because of the strains and inequities which had developed under it. In Britain as in Sweden wage increases were much more tightly restricted in some industries than in others. Unions whose members were paid on time rates and who had no cost-of-living escalator found their wage levels virtually frozen. Unions with an escalator clause were more favorably situated. Unions with a piece-rate basis of payment were even less affected by wage restraint and had little objection to the policy. Complaints of inequity accumulated, therefore, with the passage of time. The *coup de grâce* was administered by the rapid increase in the retail price index after mid-1950. Union acceptance of wage restraint had been conditioned on price stabilization, and when this failed the position became untenable. The TUC convention in September 1950 abandoned the policy. By late 1950 most unions were actively pressing wage claims, and by mid-1951 a complete round of wage increases had been accomplished.

The British experience of 1948–50 tends to confirm the conclusions reached from Swedish experience in the last chapter. Even with full employment and strong union organization, the rate of increase in money wages can be held to a moderate level by union-government collaboration. Wage advances can only be retarded and not stopped, however, and the policy cannot be applied successfully for more than two or three years at a time. Over any extended period the uneven advance of earnings in different sectors produces complaints of inequity and demands for loosening of restraints.

The success of the British venture in wage restraint depended on a happy combination of circumstances which might not be present at another time and place:

1. The episode occurred shortly after a major war. This meant on the one hand that the successful wartime experience with wage restraint and controlled prices was vividly in mind, while on the other hand the economic difficulties of the nation during postwar reconstruction could be dramatized as the basis of a popular appeal.

2. The policy was carried out under a Labour government. The trade unions were solidly behind the government, proud of having an absolute majority in Parliament for the first time, fearful of a return of Conservative rule, and anxious not to do anything to embarrass the government or endanger its success. There is elaborate machinery for consultation between TUC and Labour party leaders, so that policy decisions of a Labour government have the aspect of "family affairs" rather than of something imposed on the trade unions by alien authority.

3. The structure of British unions and the nature of bargaining procedures are also important. Authority is strongly centralized within most unions, the general secretary and other key officers having high security of tenure and great influence. Wage negotiations of national scope are carried on largely by these officers. While they must remain within the limits of what is acceptable to the membership, they have considerable discretion in directing the course of wage policy.

The fact that the contract is a continuing one is important. The typical union contract in the United States makes it certain that the wage issue will be raised at least once a year, and the members presume that this will mean some increase in wages. In Britain there is no such presumption, and if the economic climate is calm union officers may go along for several years without raising the wage issue.

British collective bargaining procedures tend to retard the pace of wage movements. Negotiations often consume a great deal of time, particularly where several unions and several employer groups are involved. After this stage there are frequently standing arbitration bodies or joint industrial councils to which resort can be had. If disagreement is serious the case may go on to a governmental court of inquiry or arbitration tribunal. After an award has been made there may be additional months of negotiation over its precise application to particular occupations and areas. It is not uncommon for twelve to eighteen months to elapse between the filing of a wage claim and the final settlement. One is tempted to advise any government concerned with inflation control to build as many lags as possible into the collective bargaining process,

The British wage lag is certainly longer than in Sweden, France, or the United States.

During the wage-restraint period the British system made it possible for union leaders to give the illusion of motion without actually doing much. Almost every union had a wage claim on file and sitting at some stage in the negotiating process. If members raised questions a union official could always say, "We have a proposal under discussion," but at the same time he could refrain from seeking quick action on the proposal. As one observer comments, "They ran very hard but managed to stay in the same place. Everyone jockeyed around so that he would be at the starting line when the gun finally went off," as it did in late 1950.

4. The fact that the government did an effective job of stabilizing retail prices and restraining nonwage incomes was important. Wage restraint was part of an effective over-all stabilization program and could not have operated by itself.

5. A further consideration was that wage restraint did not prevent higher earnings for many millions of workers. There was enough flexibility via piece-rate systems, cost-of-living adjustments, individual merit increases, and other payments to drain off much of the pressure for increases in base rates.

These qualifications must be kept in mind in any attempt to generalize from the British experience. It seems unlikely, for example, that a policy of voluntary wage restraint could have much success in the United States where most of these supporting conditions are absent.

EVOLUTION OF THE NATIONAL WAGE STRUCTURE

THE ECONOMIC CONTEXT

In Britain, as in other countries, the years from 1940 through the early fifties were years of full (or overfull) employment. Registered unemployment, which equaled 9.5 per cent of insured workers in 1938, fell to the remarkably low level of 0.3 per cent at the peak of war production in 1944. Except for the reconversion year of 1946, unemployment remained below 2 per cent through 1953.[17] There was a general shortage of labor, and in some industries and occupations an acute shortage, which led employers to bid up wages even without union pressure.

The productive apparatus of the country was disrupted, not merely by drastic shifting between peacetime and wartime products, but by bomb damage and by inability to make adequate repairs and replace-

17. Allan Flanders, "Great Britain," p. 71; and *Ministry of Labour Gazette,* monthly issues.

ments during the war years. By 1947, however, per capita gross national product measured in constant prices had recovered to 104 per cent of the 1938 level. By 1952 the index had risen to 115, a gain of almost 11 per cent in five years.[18] This seems to have been due partly to an increase in labor force greater than the increase in population, partly to the fact that the postwar boom was concentrated in the high productivity industrial sector of the economy. Industrial output rose by more than 30 per cent in the four years 1947–51 alone.

The price level, after a sharp jump at the outset of the war, was effectively stabilized by a combination of rigorous taxation, price controls, rationing, and subsidies to key cost-of-living items. From 1941 through mid-1947 the cost-of-living index fluctuated within the remarkably narrow range of 128 to 132 (October 1938 = 100). It is true that the official index, being based on a 1914 pattern of working-class expenditures, somewhat understated the actual increase in living costs. Dennison states that "A recalculation, taking account of the changed pattern of consumption, shows that by 1945 the cost of living of working class families had risen not by the 30 per cent of the official index but by about 50 per cent." [19] Most of this increase had taken place by 1941, however, and the stability of prices over the next six years in the face of full war mobilization was a considerable feat of economic engineering.

Prices rose almost 10 per cent between mid-1947 and mid-1948, and concern over this increase led to development of the wage-restraint policy and other anti-inflation measures. The rate of inflation was slowed down during the next two years, but prices again rose sharply in 1951 and 1952. The new cost-of-living index, on a June 1947 base, stood at 136 in 1952 and at 142 in April 1954. Over the entire period 1939-54, the retail price level rose by very nearly the same percentage as in Sweden and the United States.

The movement of money and real wage rates and earnings is shown in Table 10-2, where the greater rise in weekly earnings than in weekly wage rates stands out clearly. This is a general phenomenon of high employment, and can be traced in the statistics for Sweden, the United States, and other countries. It results from the movement of labor from lower-wage to higher-wage employments, upgrading of individual workers and even of whole job classifications, voluntary bidding up of rates above the official scale by employers eager to recruit labor, unchecked increase in piece-rate earnings with improved production methods, and

18. OEEC, *Statistics of National Product and Expenditure, 1938, 1947 to 1952* (Paris, 1954).

19. Dennison, "Wages in Full Employment," p. 21. R. G. D. Allen has estimated that the actual increase in living costs by June 1947 was upward of 60%, *London and Cambridge Economic Service Bulletin, 25* (August 11, 1947), 75.

a variety of other factors. The index of average *hourly* earnings moves somewhat differently from that of *weekly* earnings from year to year because of variations in the length of the work week.

Table 10-2. Indexes of Wages, Hours and

YEAR	INDEX OF WEEKLY WAGE RATES *	INDEX OF AVERAGE HOURLY EARNINGS †	INDEX OF AVERAGE WEEKLY EARNINGS †	AVERAGE HOURS PER WEEK †
	(SEPT. '39 = 100)	(OCT. '38 = 100)	(OCT. '38 = 100)	(IN OCT. '38-46.5 HOURS)
1943	136	—	171	(July) 50.0
1944	141	172	181	48.9
1945	149	176	178	47.2
1946	161	184	182	46.0
1947	168	205	199	45.1
	(June '47 = 100)	(Apr. '47 = 100)	(Apr. '47 = 100)	
1948	106	111	112	45.3
1949	109	116	117	45.4
1950	111	120	122	45.9
1951	120	131	135	46.2
1952	131	142	145	45.9
1953	136	150	154	46.3
April 1954	141	156	161	46.5

* This index is based on monthly computations of changes on recognized rates fixed by collective agreement or statutory order.

† Information on average hourly and weekly earnings and on average hours is based on Ministry of Labour biennial surveys of a sample of employees in industry.

‡ The cost-of-living index until 1947 was based on the 1914 expenditure pattern and thus cannot be depended upon to reflect changes accurately in the period covered by this table.

Source: Ministry of Labour and National Service

It is clear that there was a substantial increase in *real* hourly and weekly earnings over the period. Money earnings doubled between 1938 and 1947 and, even if the price index for 1947 should have stood at 150 as Dennison contends, this would still have meant an increase of one-third in real earnings in a single decade. In the years since 1947, for which we have a revised and more reliable cost-of-living index, real earnings have again increased substantially. Real weekly earnings appear to have risen by 13 per cent between 1947 and 1954, an increase of almost 2 per cent per year.

This increase in real earnings has resulted not only from a rising level of per capita national output, but also from a redistribution of national income in favor of wage earners. Phelps Brown has calculated

Cost of Living, Great Britain, 1938–54

INDEX OF COST-OF-LIVING ‡ (OCT. '38 ⎫ (SEPT. '39 ⎬ = 100)	REAL WEEKLY WAGE RATES	REAL WEEKLY EARNINGS	REAL HOURLY EARNINGS
	(SEPT. '39 = 100)	(OCT. '38 = 100)	(OCT. '38 = 100)
128	106	134	—
130	108	139	132
131	114	136	134
132	122	138	139
(June) 131	128	152	156
(June '47 = 100)	(June '47 = 100)	(Apr.–June '47 = 100)	(Apr.–June '47 = 100)
108	98	104	103
111	98	105	105
114	97	107	105
124	97	109	106
136	96	107	104
140	97	110	107
142	99	113	110

that average real income per wage earner relative to the average real income of all occupied persons (which he terms the "wage-income ratio") rose from slightly less than 100 per cent in 1939 to around 115 per cent in the early fifties.[20] Seers estimates that wages as a proportion of private income before taxes rose from 33.2 per cent in 1938 to 37.8 per cent in 1949 (Table 10-3). This result is due partly to shifting of labor into industrial employments where wages form a higher percentage of gross value of output than is the case in the agricultural, trade, and service sectors. Beyond this it is due to a moderate decline in the share of salaries and a rather sharp decline in the share of fixed income from rentals and interest payments. There does not seem to have been any appreciable redistribution from profits to wages within particular enterprises or industries. Profit margins have been well maintained and the share of corporate profits in national income has risen sharply.

The redistribution of income in favor of wage earners has been inten-

20. Phelps Brown, "The Long-Term Movement of Real Wages," to be published in the forthcoming report of the 1954 IEA conference on wage determination.

sified by the tax system. It will be noted from Table 10-3 that the wage share of posttax income has risen from 35.5 per cent in 1938 to 42.0 per cent in 1949.[21] To this should be added a considerable share of the

Table 10-3. Distribution of Private Income before and after Taxes, Great Britain, 1938–49 * (percentage)

	PRETAX			POSTTAX		
	1938	1946	1949	1938	1946	1949
Undistributed property income	21.3	14.5	12.9	—	—	—
Undistributed corporate profits	6.4	9.3	10.4	—	—	—
TOTAL PROPERTY INCOME	27.6	23.8	23.4	—	—	—
Professional earnings	1.6	1.4	1.5	—	—	—
Income from farming	1.1	2.0	2.4	—	—	—
Sole traders' profits	8.4	7.1	6.4	—	—	—
TOTAL MIXED INCOME	11.2	10.5	10.4	—	—	—
PROPERTY INCOME AND MIXED INCOME	38.8	34.3	33.8	34.9	—	27.1
Wages	33.2	32.6	37.8	35.5	—	42.0
Salaries	21.3	18.4	19.9	22.2	—	20.7
H. M. Forces' pay	1.5	5.5	2.2	1.6	—	2.4
TOTAL WORK INCOME	56.0	56.5	59.8	59.3	—	65.1
Social Security benefits	4.4	3.6	5.2			
War gratuities & pensions, etc.	0.8	5.7	1.2			
SOCIAL INCOME	5.2	9.2	6.4	5.7	—	7.8
TOTAL PRIVATE INCOME	100.0	100.0	100.0	100.0	—	100.0

* Net of depreciation at replacement cost. Gains made by merely holding capital, including inventory gains, have been excluded.

Source: Dudley Seers, The Levelling of Incomes since 1938 (Oxford, Blackwell, 1951)

"social income," amounting in 1949 to 7.8 per cent of the total. While most of the British social security and social consumption plans cover the entire population, they yield the largest percentage addition to the incomes of the poorest groups.[22]

21. On this point see Seers, The Levelling of Incomes since 1938, p. 48. Within industry, wages as a per cent of gross value of output (gross of depreciation and excluding inventory gains), fell slightly from 47.4% in 1938 to 46.5% in 1949. In agriculture also, the wage ratio fell from 37.4% to 36.7%. In the service industries, on the other hand, wages rose from 25.1% to 31.1%.

22. On this range of issues see Allan M. Cartter, The Redistribution of Income in Postwar Britain (New Haven, Yale University Press, 1955); see also Seers, The Levelling of Incomes since 1938.

OCCUPATIONAL DIFFERENTIALS

There are no over-all measures of occupational differentials in British industry, only limited data for individual industries. The most intensive analysis of these data has been made by Knowles and others at the Oxford University Institute of Statistics,[23] and we shall rely heavily on their studies in the present section.

Most of the data relate to occupational *wage rates* rather than to *earnings*. It is important to point out, therefore, that the two measures yield rather different results. This is clear from Tables 10-4, 10-5, and 10-6, which present data drawn from the shipbuilding, engineering, and

Table 10-4. *Average Weekly Rates and Average Weekly Earnings of Skilled and Unskilled Timeworkers: Shipbuilding, Great Britain, 1949–50*
(*in shillings*)

YEAR	AV. WEEKLY RATES			AV. WEEKLY EARNINGS		
	SKILLED	UNSKILLED	% DIFF.	SKILLED	UNSKILLED	% DIFF.
1940 (June)	75.0	56.0	74.7	105	82	78
1941 (Sept.)	78.5	59.5	75.8	114	91	80
1942 (Oct.)	83.5	64.5	77.2	128	102	80
1943 (Nov.)	89.5	70.5	78.7	135	109	81
1944 (Nov.)	93.5	74.5	79.6	136	115	85
1946 (Jan.)	98.0	79.0	80.6	117	98	84
1948 (Apr.)	104.0	85.0	81.8	137	112	82
1950 (Jan.)	109.0	92.0	84.4	146	117	80

Source: Knowles and Robertson, "Earnings in Shipbuilding"

railway industries. In every case the skilled-unskilled differential in earnings is greater than the differential in rates, i.e. the position of the skilled man is more favorable when computed on an earnings basis. The difference is most marked where, as in the case of engineering, a substantial proportion of the skilled workers are on piece rates. Even where time work prevails, however, as in shipbuilding and on the rail-

23. See the following articles in *Bulletin of the Oxford University Institute of Statistics:* K. G. J. C. Knowles and D. J. Robertson. "Differences between the Wages of Skilled and Unskilled Workers, 1880–1950," *13* (April 1951) 109–27; Knowles and Robertson, "Earnings in Engineering, 1926–1948," *13* (June 1951), 179–200; Knowles and Robertson, "Earnings in Shipbuilding," *13* (Nov. and Dec. 1951), 357–65; Knowles and A. Romanis, "Dockworkers' Earnings (Great Britain)," *14* (Sept. and Oct. 1952), 327–65; Knowles and H. J. D. Cole, "Rates and Earnings in London-Transport," *15* (August 1953), 261–94; Knowles and Monica Verry, "Earnings in the Boot and Shoe Industry," *16* (Feb. and March 1954), 29–72.

ways, the skilled men fare somewhat better on an earnings basis. This probably indicates that employers bid rates further above the official scale in the case of skilled workers than in the case of unskilled men. The range of job requirements and individual capacities being greater in skilled employment, the range of individual earnings might be expected to be correspondingly greater.

Table 10-5. Average Rates for Timeworkers and Average Earnings of Timeworkers and Pieceworkers: Engineering Industry, Great Britain, 1938–53
(in shillings)

YEAR AND MONTH	WEEKLY RATES *			WEEKLY EARNINGS †		
	SKILLED	UNSKILLED	% DIFF.	SKILLED	UNSKILLED	% DIFF.
1938 (July)	66.0	50.0	75.8	88.8	61.1	68.8
1939 (Oct.)	68.0	52.0	76.5	(104.1)	69.4	(66.6)
1942 (July)	81.5	65.5	80.4	148.8	100.4	67.5
1948 (Jan.)	102.0	87.0	85.3	146.6	115.8	79.1
1952 (May)	129.0	111.0	86.0	205.2	157.3	76.6
1953 (June)	136.3	118.3	86.8	219.9	166.6	75.8

* Timeworkers.

† Timeworkers and P. by R. workers combined.

Source: Knowles and Robertson, "Earnings in Engineering"; and Engineering and Allied Employers National Federation

Table 10-6. Comparison of Rates and Earnings in Railways, Great Britain, 1938–49

YEAR	AVERAGE WEEKLY WAGE			AVERAGE WEEKLY PAYMENT		
	ENGINE DRIVERS	GOODS PORTERS	% DIFF.	ENGINE DRIVERS	GOODS PORTERS	% DIFF.
1938	86.6	45.1	52	100.8	51.3	51
1939	87.2	46.8	54	101.7	57.3	56
1949	135.8	93.1	68	165.7	109.9	66

Source: Knowles and Robertson, "Differences between the Wages of Skilled and Unskilled Workers, 1880–1950"

It will be noted, however, that the *trend* in the skilled-unskilled differential since 1940 has been the same whether we look at rates or at earnings. The rate differential has narrowed sharply in each case. The earnings differential has narrowed sharply in engineering and on the railways, only slightly in shipbuilding. If we are concerned not so much with the size of differentials at a particular time as with the direction of movement over time, rates provide a fairly reliable guide. We must use them in any case because for most industries and most years we have nothing else.

Knowles and Robertson have traced the movement of rate differentials in four industries over the years 1880–1950. While this reaches back far beyond the period with which we are concerned here, the results are sufficiently interesting that they have been reproduced in Table 10-7. In all four cases, the ratio of unskilled to skilled wage rates remained virtually constant from 1880 to 1914. During the inflation of World War I there was a sharp narrowing of differentials in all cases. In the postwar deflation differentials widened once more but stopped well short of the prewar level, settling down on a new plateau at around 70–75 per cent instead of the old 55–65 per cent (in the case of railways, at around 60 per cent instead of 50 per cent).

The situation remained stable until the late thirties and was then upset by World War II, which brought a further sharp narrowing of differentials. Unlike the previous experience, the narrowing has continued during the postwar period. There has been (as yet!) no postwar deflation, and unskilled rates remain in the range of 80 to 85 per cent of skilled rates. Scattered evidence from other manufacturing industries indicates a rather remarkable clustering of unskilled-skilled ratios in the neighborhood of 80 per cent, which appears to be becoming a norm for this postwar period. The differential in earnings is doubtless somewhat greater, for reasons already noted. Skill differentials are now remarkably narrow, however, by the standards of a generation or two ago.

How can one account for the sharp narrowing of differentials since 1939? The main long-run influence at work has been the extension of public education, which tends to reduce the supply of unskilled labor and to increase the supply of skilled and clerical workers. Added to this have been two important short-term influences. The unusually high level of labor demand during 1939–55 tended to pull up laborers' rates more sharply than craftsmen's rates. The tripling of wage levels also had a compressing effect on relative wage rates because of the way in which wage increases were calculated.

From 1939 until 1950 or so, most wage increases in British industries were made on a flat-rate basis yielding the same amount to all grades of labor. We have already referred to the complex structure of national bargaining in many industries. Formulation of wage demands and settlements involves complicated negotiations among the various unions having a foothold in the industry. Flat-rate increases seem to emerge as a compromise which yields something for everybody, is easy to rationalize and explain, and is also easy to apply to existing rate schedules.

*Table 10-7. Skill Differentials in Four Industries and the Police Force,
Great Britain, 1880–1950*

TIME RATE OF UNSKILLED AS PERCENTAGE OF THAT OF SKILLED *

YEAR	BUILDING	SHIPBUILDING	ENGINEERING	RAILWAYS	POLICE
1880	63.9	54	60		
1885	63.6	54	60	50.5 †	81.6 †
1890	65.6	51	59		
1895	67.1	53	60		
1900	66.7	52	58		
1904	65.6	53	59		
1907	64.9			50.9	
1910	65.2				
1913	66.9			51.4	
1914	66.5	55.2	58.6	54.3	
1915	69.3	59.2	61.8	59.3	
1916	72.2	62.0	64.4	63.4	
1917	75.4	69.9	72.4	69.9	
1918	80.1	73.6	75.7	74.8	
1919	83.1	75.3	77.2	74.3	70.0
1920	81.0	77.2	78.9	81.2	70.0
1921	80.1	75.3	74.4	79.4	70.0
1922	74.8	74.5	71.7	71.5	70.0
1923	74.7	78.6	72.8	68.1	70.0
1924	75.6	68.8	70.9	68.1	70.0
1925	75.6	68.8	70.9	69.4	70.0
1926	75.6	68.8	70.8	68.1	70.0
1927	75.4	68.8	71.7	66.7	70.0
1928	74.8	68.0	71.3	66.7	70.0
1929	74.7	68.0	71.3	65.2	70.0
1930	74.5	68.5	71.2	63.9	70.0
1931	75.0	68.3	71.2	61.6	70.0
1932	74.6	68.3	71.2	61.6	62.0
1933	75.2	68.3	71.2	61.6	62.0
1934	75.3	68.3	71.2	61.6	62.0
1935	74.9	68.3	71.9	61.1	62.0
1936	75.2	69.3	72.8	61.1	62.0
1937	75.0	71.2	74.1	61.0	62.0
1938	75.6	72.1	74.9	61.0	62.0
1939	76.3	73.4	75.6	61.5	62.0
1940	77.9	75.3	77.2	64.7	67.3
1941	78.9	77.7	79.6	66.3	69.4
1942	79.3	79.2	79.6	72.8	69.8
1943	79.2	79.2	80.9	74.1	67.7
1944	79.0	80.1	80.9	75.4	68.7
1945	80.8	81.0	81.9	76.0	70.3
1946	80.0	81.8	84.4	74.9	70.0
1947	80.3	81.8	84.4	76.5	70.0
1948	80.4	81.8	85.3	74.6	70.0
1949	81.6	82.6	86.0	74.6	75.6
1950	84.1	83.4	84.7	77.4	75.6

* The occupations chosen for comparison in each industry are given in the Appendix of the article by Knowles and Robertson cited below.

† 1886.

Source: Knowles and Robertson, "Differences between the Wages of Skilled and Unskilled Workers, 1880–1950," p. 111

During the war, when flat-rate increases were almost the universal rule, they were generally referred to as "bonuses" or "cost-of-living bonuses," and the idea of the same bonus for everyone seemed natural. The cost-of-living adjustment clauses which have been a prominent feature of collective bargaining agreements since the war are set up on a uniform pence per hour basis for all. Employers like flat-rate adjustments, which are frequently kept separate from the prewar basic scales, perhaps in the hope that the inflationary tide may some day be reversed and the bonuses removed. (Some of the flat-rate bonuses granted during and after World War I were not finally absorbed into the basic wage structure of the industry until 1950 or so, a striking indication of the long memories of British unions and employers and the long lag between actual wage developments and their codification into collective agreements.) A minor point which may be of some importance is that percentages are difficult to apply to the British currency system. Percentage wage increases in the strict sense are very rare in Britain, though one does find adjustments which give larger absolute amounts to the skilled men.

By 1950, however, the skilled men in a number of industries were becoming restive at the nibbling away of their relative standing and were beginning to demand differentiated increases once more. In the substantial "round" of 1951 wage increases which followed abandonment of the wage-restraint policy the higher-paid workers received larger cash increases than the lower-paid ones in mining, railways, road passenger transport, printing, iron and steel, and textile manufacture. There are indications that the leveling tendency has reached its peak for the time being and that differentials are settling down on a new plateau similar to that of the twenties.

The new emphasis is well expressed in a statement of the engineering unions in connection with a 1953 wage demand:

On every occasion for many years past when we have found it necessary to make an application for a wage increase we have asked for a uniform advance for all adult male workers. This time, however, as you will note, we are asking for an increase on a percentage basis. The reason for this change is that we consider . . . that existing differentials in the Industry have tended to get out of line, and need to be adjusted to existing conditions.

Before the war, for instance, the skilled man's rate was about 28 per cent above that of the labourer. . . . Today, however, the skilled man's rate is only about 15 per cent above the labourer's rate. We have striven for a long time to secure this improvement in the position of the unskilled man, and we are very glad that it has been achieved. But we consider now that it would not be in the best interests of the Industry were the gap between the skilled and the unskilled rates to narrow still further, as would be the case if the practice of uniform increases for all grades were continued.

We should also note several cases first pointed out by Turner,[24] in which occupational differentials shrank little if any during the war and postwar period. These are: faceworkers as compared with other workers in coal mines; senior over less senior process workers in basic steel, particularly melters relative to second, third, and fourth assistants; and mule spinners over their assistants in cotton textiles. These cases have several common characteristics. In each case all workers concerned belong to a single industrial union. The union, moreover, is confined to a single industry, so that interindustry complications do not arise. Perhaps most important, the lower-skilled workers stand in a learner relation to the skilled men and can expect in time to work up to the top job. This probably makes them more willing to accept a substantial differential. The assistant spinner, who is a semiskilled man, gets about 60 per cent of the spinner's wage. The underground haulage collier gets rather less than 60 per cent of the faceworker's earnings. The laborer in steel smelting gets only about half as much as the melter. These differentials are substantially wider than the 80 per cent ratio which we have seen to exist in many industries.

One might expect that the general reduction of differentials would have reduced the number of young people willing to train for skilled trades. This expectation is not borne out by the evidence. Officials of the Ministry of Labour and National Service report that there is an over-all deficiency in the intake of apprentices in building construction, but here the main difficulty lies on the employer side. Because of the contract character of the industry, employers cannot predict their volume of activity very far in advance and are reluctant to take on a five-year apprenticeship agreement, which in Britain is legally binding. It has also proven difficult to get people into molding and foundry work and into certain shipyard occupations such as riveting. The conditions of work in these occupations are basically unattractive, and people are unwilling to enter them when so many alternative opportunities are available.

In most of the crafts, however, there are still more boys wanting to start apprenticeships than can be accepted. Skilled work has a long tradition and great prestige. Apprenticeship also has indirect advantages, including exemption from military service during the training period. Many boys reason, "This will take care of me for five years anyway, and perhaps by that time there won't be any more army." Apprenticeships have been made more attractive recently by raising the apprentice's

24. H. A. Turner, "Trade Unions, Differentials, and the Levelling of Wages," *Manchester School Economic and Social Studies,* 20 (September 1952), 227–82.

starting rate from the prewar 25–30 per cent of the journeyman's rate to a substantially higher percentage. The apprentice still typically earns less than a laborer, however, until he reaches the fourth year of apprenticeship.

The apparent lack of any strong impact of reduced differentials on recruitment of skilled craftsmen is an interesting phenomenon. It may be that the response has only been delayed and will show up more clearly a decade or two hence. A more likely explanation, however, is that the recent narrowing of occupational differentials is in accord with shifts in labor supply. The mechanism of the shrinkage in differentials has been the widespread use of cost-of-living bonuses and other flat-rate adjustments; but the market accepts the narrowing because the relative supply of skilled labor has increased. If this is correct, we should not say that the supply of craftsmen is high despite a lower wage premium, but rather that the premium is lower because the supply is high.

INTERINDUSTRY DIFFERENTIALS

There has been a substantial reduction of interindustry wage differences since 1939. Analysis of the average hourly earnings of male workers in the 104 industrial categories reported currently by the Ministry of Labour shows that the quartile deviation decreased from .069 in October 1938 to .065 in April 1948. For women workers in these same industries the quartile deviation fell from .073 to .063. Another significant calculation relates to minimum wage rates for the sixty or so industries whose wages are regulated by wage councils or special statutory boards. These rates approximate the earnings of common labor in the industries in question and this is a better measure of interindustry dispersions than average hourly earnings for all workers. If we compare February 1939 with February 1951, we find that the quartile deviation of male minimum hourly wage rates fell from .0588 to .0363. For female minima, the quartile deviation fell from .0690 to .0529.

The tendency for skilled and unskilled workers within an industry to receive the same absolute amounts during the war and postwar inflation seems to have extended also to the interindustry wage structure. When one examines the absolute increase in average hourly earnings between 1938 and 1948 for male workers in the 104 reported industries, one finds a remarkable tendency for the increases to cluster in the vicinity of 16d. to 18d. per hour. In very few cases does the increase lie outside the range of 15d. to 20d. This is true despite the great variation of industry wage levels in the 1938 base period, from a low of 12.4d. per hour in jute spinning and weaving to a high of 25.4d. per hour in tin plate and sheet manufacture. Something close to a uniform economy-wide wage increase was superimposed on the interindustry differences which existed in prewar years.

This result seems to have been due to a combination of collective bargaining pressures, market forces, and governmental wage policies. The tendency of unionists to seek maintenance of fixed cash differentials is effective across industry lines as well as within each industry. Once certain large and powerful unions had won increases of a certain size at a particular time, it was natural for these to be embodied in wage claims by other unions. Where these claims ended up before the National Arbitration Tribunal, the tribunal seems to have given heavy weight to "established relativities" in arriving at its decisions. This tendency of the collective bargaining mechanism worked in the same direction as the pressures of the labor market. In a tight market, the lowest-wage industries were under pressure to raise their wage levels by at least the same amount as the high-wage industries in order to retain their workers.

Government wage policy also contributed to the leveling of interindustry differences. The policy of wage restraint followed during the war, and again from 1948–50, included a provision that abnormally low wages would be permitted to rise. Indeed, the lowest wages were not merely encouraged but forced to rise through increases in the statutory minimum wage rates. Although the wage councils in the various industries covered by minimum wage regulation are separate from each other, each naturally takes into account the minima which have been established in other industries. In any event the dispersion of minimum wage rates has been much reduced since 1939.

In addition to a reduction of dispersion there have been considerable shifts in the ranking of individual industries. Over half the industries which ranked among the twenty lowest in 1938 were no longer in that group by 1948, and of the twenty industries which ranked highest in 1938, nine were no longer in the highest bracket in 1948. While the reasons for these shifts have not been thoroughly explored, there are indications that the rate of increase in employment had an important effect. Average hourly earnings have increased relatively fast, for example, in the rapidly expanding electrical and nonferrous metal manufacturing industries. At the other extreme there has been a relative decline of earnings in the lace industry, boot and shoe repairing, sawmilling, and machined woodwork.

The most spectacular leaps from "rags to riches" have occurred in three industries: cotton textiles, coal mining, and agriculture. Earnings in cotton rose between 1938 and 1948 by 154 per cent, and in agriculture and coal mining by about 170 per cent, compared with an average increase of about 100 per cent in the economy as a whole. Agriculture, traditionally a low-wage industry, now pays its laborers approximately the wage received by an engineering laborer. The explanation is partly that agriculture had to raise wages rapidly to hold labor in competition with urban employments; partly that war and postwar agricultural prosperity permitted payment of these higher rates; and partly that the system of government wage and price regulation in agriculture is conducive to a rapid advance of wages with minimum resistance by employers.

Cotton was a depressed export industry during the twenties and thirties. It stood near the bottom of the manufacturing wage structure and, partly on this account, suffered a heavy loss of labor during the war years. The labor force of the industry, which numbered some 300,-000 in 1939, had shrunk to 172,000 by mid-1945. When it became necessary to rebuild the labor force of the industry after the war to meet export targets, earnings were encouraged to rise as one means of attracting labor. By 1948 earnings of female cotton operatives had pulled ahead of those in noncotton industries competing for the same labor supply, and earnings of male operatives, while not equal to those elsewhere, were within a few shillings a week of equality. This probably had something to do with the fact that employment in the industry recovered to 325,000 by mid-1949.[25]

Coal mining also suffered from a severe labor shortage in the postwar years, combined with unattractive working conditions which made it difficult to attract and retain workers. The National Coal Board consequently followed a liberal wage policy in addition to reducing the work week and improving other terms of employment. It seems likely that coal wages would have risen relative to other wages for reasons of labor supply even had the industry remained in private hands.

It should be added that manipulation of wage differentials has not been the sole or even the main method used to recruit labor for the undermanned industries. If reliance had been placed on wages alone it would have been necessary to raise wages in certain industries even more sharply. The actual shifts in differentials have been moderate and they have been accompanied not only by improvement of other terms of employment but by a variety of administrative devices. The public employment exchanges are more widely used in Britain than in the United States, and perhaps half of all new jobs are found through the exchanges. Each local office is provided with a list of industries of national importance which are lacking manpower at the moment, and the interviewers are instructed to urge registrants in the direction of these industries. If the registrant has a strong preference for a particular type of work the interviewer will not try to persuade him otherwise. If

25. For comments on this experience see Sidney Rolfe, "Manpower Allocation under British Planning," *American Economic Review,* *44* (June 1954), 354–68.

he is vague in his intentions, however, as so many workers are, the interviewer may tell him that there are well-paid vacancies in coal mining. An effort is thus made to tap the normal turnover of labor flowing through the employment exchanges and to divert it in the desired directions. The registrants coming in from day to day include workers from every occupational stratum and wage level, and there are bound to be some for whom the wage levels of cotton or coal mining will prove attractive when called to their attention.[26]

The government also makes various types of cash grant to stimulate mobility. It will pay a worker's fare to a priority job. If the worker is married and must leave his family behind for the time being, he is given a lodging allowance to offset the extra cost of maintaining two residences. When he succeeds in finding a home for his family in the new location he receives an allowance to cover the cost of moving his family and household effects. The greatest obstacle to free movement of labor during the postwar period has been the unavailability or expensiveness of housing, particularly in remote areas such as the coalfields, and this is only gradually being overcome by new house building.

Another important program is the Youth Employment Service, which is administered by local education authorities under standards and procedures set up by the Ministry of Labour. The program includes provision of occupational information through lectures and by other means; individual interviews with students and their parents; provision of placement services, through which about half of the young people leaving school are placed in their first jobs; and a systematic follow up on the student's progress during his early years in employment. This procedure, like the employment exchange procedure for adult workers, is used to push people gently in the direction of work of national importance provided it seems in line with the youngster's interests and abilities.

GEOGRAPHICAL DIFFERENTIALS

The regular wage reports of the Ministry of Labour are not broken down by region. One is thrown back therefore on an inspection of rate structures, which may diverge quite widely from earnings, and on scattered earnings' data from private sources. It is virtually certain that there has been a reduction of regional differences since 1938, but the extent of the reduction cannot be measured precisely and one can find some exceptions to the general tendency.

26. This describes the procedures since March 1950. During the war years, and again from October 1947 to March 1950, employment service officials had powers of compulsory direction to work as a last resort. These powers had to be used very sparingly, however, and in effect the process was one of persuasion which did not differ too greatly from present practice.

A major force working in this direction has been the establishment of national minimum rates for an industry, either through collective bargaining or through the legal minimum-wage system. These rates are usually set so as to exert pressure on the lowest-wage districts and force them closer to the higher districts.[27] The pressure toward equalization is still stronger where a collective agreement sets national minima for skilled workers as well as for common labor.

In many industries the first national agreements simply recognized and codified existing regional differences by establishing a number of "wage zones," each with its own minimum rate. Over the course of time there has been a tendency to reduce both the number of zones and the range of variation among them. Turner comments on this point: "Building's original seventeen district rates, for instance, have been steadily reduced by merging to six under the current agreement, and their range of difference is much narrowed. The various district rates for engineering fitters and labourers were practically eliminated by absorption in the national minima of 1950. Some contemporary agreements—like that for railways—maintain London's advantage only. Agreements providing for more than three local rates for the same class of worker are increasingly rare."[28] Other observers have also commented that there is a tendency toward development of a "three-tiered wage structure"—one rate for London, another for the larger provincial cities, and a third for the remainder of the country.

Industry-wide flat-rate increases, which were the general rule during the war and postwar years, have reduced geographical differences on a percentage basis. Government wage policies—permitting low wages to rise faster than high wages during periods of wage restraint, strengthening the minimum wage system, evening out area differences in the nationalized industries—have worked in the same direction.

If one takes as a measure of geographical variation the percentage by which the lowest regional rate falls short of the highest, this has declined as follows: skilled building workers, 39 per cent in 1913, 6 per cent in 1946, and 2 per cent in 1951; skilled engineering workers, 47 per cent in 1913, 12 per cent in 1946, and 6 per cent in 1951; printing (hand compositors, job shops), 36 per cent in 1913, 17 per cent in

27. It must constantly be borne in mind, however, that national uniformity of rates may permit wide variation of earnings. Knowles and Verry found, for example, that actual rates of male timeworkers in the boot and shoe industry in 1949 averaged 130% of the national minimum in London, but only 112% in the Midlands, and only 105% in Norwich. This is an industry in which a uniform national minimum rate has existed since 1919. Knowles and Verry, "Earnings in the Boot and Shoe Industry," p. 38.

28. H. W. Turner, "Trade Unions, Differentials, and the Levelling of Wages," pp. 271–2.

1946, and 10 per cent in 1951; baking (single hands), 37 per cent in 1914, 7 per cent in 1946, and 5 per cent in 1951.[29]

These data relate to rates rather than to earnings but geographical variation of earnings has certainly diminished as well. The general tendency is illustrated by Table 10-8, which presents data on the earnings of skilled fitters and laborers in the engineering industry in 1938 and 1952. Regional dispersion of earnings has been considerably reduced for both occupations. The low-wage areas of Ireland, Scotland, and northern England have pulled up much closer to the London level. The Midlands area, which has a heavy concentration of the newer automobile and aircraft plants, has pulled ahead of London to become the highest-wage region in the industry.

Table 10-8. Geographical Differences in Earnings for Skilled Fitters and Laborers, Great Britain, July 1938 and May 1952 (London and home counties = 100)

	LABORERS		SKILLED FITTERS	
	JULY 1938	MAY 1952	JULY 1938	MAY 1952
Scotland	90.4	93.8	87.6	88.4
Northeast coast	91.0	94.4	88.4	92.7
Lancashire and Cheshire	87.8	94.4	90.3	94.6
Yorkshire	91.7	95.9	84.5	91.4
Midlands	92.3	100.8	102.2	105.8
London and Home Counties	100.0	100.0	100.0	100.0
West of England & So. Wales	89.7	94.6	95.6	96.4
Northern Ireland	87.2	89.4	91.2	100.6
Federation as a whole	91.7	96.7	93.8	97.9

Source: Engineering and Allied Employers Federation

There have, to be sure, been exceptions to the general leveling tendency. Knowles and Verry found that geographical variation of earnings in the boot and shoe industry has increased since 1939, both for timeworkers and for pieceworkers, primarily through London pulling farther ahead of other areas. There appears to have been a similar increase in the case of shipbuilding because the south of England, which works mainly on ship repairing rather than on new construction. has pulled further ahead of the other regions. The exceptions, however, are not numerous enough to upset the general conclusion that regional differences have diminished.

29. Data supplied by K. G. J. C. Knowles.

OTHER DIFFERENTIALS

There has been a substantial narrowing of the earnings differential between men and women workers. The course of events in this respect is indicated in Table 10-9. Women's hourly earnings, which averaged 51.8 per cent of men's in 1938, had risen to 60.3 per cent by the end of the war and edged upward to 61.7 per cent in 1952. There is considerable variation in this respect from one industry to another. In 1948, for example, women's hourly earnings were 81.4 per cent of men's in transport (excluding rail transport), but only 54.2 per cent in paper, printing, and stationery manufacture. These variations can be traced to the nature of the work performed and to other special circumstances in each industry. The case of transport, for example, is explained by the small proportion of women workers and by trade union insistence on equal pay for equal work.

Table 10-9. *Differentials between Average Hourly Earnings of Men and Women, Great Britain, 1938–54*

YEAR	MEN 21 AND OVER (IN PENCE)	WOMEN 18 AND OVER (IN PENCE)	WOMEN AS A PERCENTAGE OF MEN
1938	17.4d.	9.0	51.8%
July 1943	27.5	16.3	59.3
July 1944	29.1	17.3	59.5
July 1945	29.3	17.5	59.7
Oct. 1946	30.4	18.4	60.5
Oct. 1947	33.0	20.1	60.9
Oct. 1948	35.4	21.5	60.7
Oct. 1949	36.6	22.7	62.0
Oct. 1950	37.9	23.6	62.3
Oct. 1951	41.7	26.0	62.4
Oct. 1952	44.9	27.7	61.7
Oct. 1953	47.4	29.3	61.8
Oct. 1954	50.6	31.0	61.1

Source: Ministry of Labour and National Service

The narrowing of differentials may be seen from another point of view in Table 10-10, which shows the indexes of average hourly earnings for men, boys, women, and girls over the years 1938–52. Women's earnings have risen faster than men's throughout the period, and within each sex group the earnings of young people have risen faster than those of adult workers.

This behavior of earnings can probably be attributed mainly to shifts in demand and supply for the various categories of labor involved. The market for women's and juveniles' work was considerably widened by the high labor demand during the war and postwar years. At the same time the supply of women workers is limited by household responsibilities, and it tended to shrink after the war because of high marriage and birth rates. The supply of juvenile labor was considerably reduced by low depression birth rates and by the increase in the school-leaving age from fourteen to fifteen years.

Table 10–10. Index of Average Hourly Earnings in Great Britain, 1938–52
(October 1938 = 100)

YEAR	MEN 21+	YOUTHS	WOMEN 18+	GIRLS	ALL WORKERS
July 1943	158	174	181	181	163
July 1944	158	180	193	190	174
July 1945	169	177	195	194	177
Oct. 1946	175	184	205	219	191
Oct. 1947	190	208	224	250	209
Oct. 1948	204	236	240	282	226
Oct. 1949	210	241	252	292	235
Oct. 1950	218	253	262	300	243
Oct. 1951	240	274	289	330	268
Oct. 1952	258	297	308	342	288
Oct. 1953	272	312	326	364	303
Oct. 1954	291	337	344	390	322

Source: Ministry of Labour and National Service

We are fortunately able to document the influence of market forces, for a large proportion of labor turnover in Britain flows through the employment exchanges, and placings and vacancies at the employment exchanges are reported by age and sex categories. The situation during a sample month in 1947 and another month in 1954 is shown in Table 10-11.[30] The consistency of the data is striking. There was a scarcity of labor in both periods, though rather less acute in 1954 than in 1947. In each period, the shortage was more serious for women workers than for men, and more serious for young people than for adult workers. There seems merit in Dennison's comment that, "Here, behind the many complications and cross-currents of policy and negotiation, is the essential fact in the changed wage structure." [31]

30. This idea was suggested by Dennison's article on "Wages in Full Employment." Data for 1947 are taken from this article, p. 30.
31. *Ibid.*

Table 10–11. Placings and Vacancies at the Employment Exchange, Great Britain, 1947 and 1954 (in 000's)

	FOUR WEEKS ENDING SEPT. 3, 1947			FOUR WEEKS ENDING JULY 28, 1954		
	A. PLACINGS	B. UNFILLED VACANCIES	A AS PER CENT OF B	A. PLACINGS	B. UNFILLED VACANCIES	A AS PER CENT OF B
Men	135	251	54%	126	151	83%
Women	54	211	25	61	105	58
Youths	17	59	29	16	57	28
Girls	13	84	15	18	70	26
TOTAL	219	605	36	221	383	58

Source: Calculated from data published in the *Ministry of Labour Gazette*

CONCLUDING OBSERVATIONS

We may now summarize briefly the main lessons of British experience.

1. There has been a marked tendency toward leveling of every type of wage differential. This has not resulted, however, from deliberate policy decisions taken at a central point. It is partly the unintended, almost accidental, result of inflation of the price level. Large flat-rate wage increases superimposed on the irregularities of the prewar wage structure have reduced the relative size of those irregularities. A second factor has been the existence since 1939 of a high demand for labor, which has forced up wages in low-wage firms, occupations, and industries. The persistent pressure of trade unions for "the standard rate" has doubtless been of considerable importance, as have the minimum wage system and other lines of government policy. The British case presents a more nearly equal balance, and a more intricate combination, of these various forces than either the French or the Swedish cases.

2. The British case is characterized by a high degree of voluntarism, gradualism, and localism. The attachment of workers to a local community and work place, and the existence of customary differences in wages and other terms of employment among localities, are deep rooted and resistant to change. Collective bargaining has developed gradually and in many cases quite recently from a local or district basis to a national basis. The network of controls established by national agreement rests only lightly on the shoulders of local unions and employers. Looking beyond the national unions to the Trades Union Congress, one does not find the degree of centralized authority which exists under the LO in Sweden. The notion of a central "wages policy" which has been advanced by certain economists and others in Britain has been rejected as impractical and undesirable by most trade union officials. Nor has the

British government set out to plan the national wage structure from Whitehall. On the contrary, the government has consistently taken the line that its function is to reinforce voluntary methods of wage determination.

This pragmatic and undoctrinaire approach doubtless accounts for the many anomalies in the British wage structure. It may be that we simply have more information about Britain, and that if we knew as much about the detailed pattern of wages in France, Sweden, and other countries their wage structures would appear equally ragged and anomalous. Taking this consideration into account, however, it seems likely that the British structure actually is more irregular.

3. We may note next the continued prominence of market forces in spite of, or at any rate along with, the growth of collective bargaining and other wage-regulating institutions. This shows up in a variety of ways: in the rapid rise of earnings in agriculture, cotton textiles, and coal mining as a response to acute manpower shortages; in the relative rise in earnings for women workers and young people as a result of relatively greater scarcity of labor in those categories; in the bidding up of rates for skilled workers above the official scale, and the upward drift of earnings for many pieceworkers, as a result of employer efforts to attract and retain labor; in the variation of rates and earnings from region to region in response to local availability of labor.

To a considerable extent, indeed, the "growth points" of the wage structure since 1939 seem to have been dictated by market pressures, and the increase of earnings at these points has run ahead of bargained wage rates. Collective bargaining has come along behind, regularizing and codifying the gains, trying to reduce the gap between rate schedules and actual earnings and to set up dykes against a relapse of earnings in the event of depression. This relatively free and open-ended development of the earnings structure, this continued responsiveness to supply and demand forces, has been a source of strength to the British wage system.

4. The frequently expressed fear that collective bargaining may produce a wage structure which will prevent desirable movements of labor between industries and occupations does not seem justified on the basis of British experience to date. On the one hand it has proven possible to encourage movement of labor in desirable directions by administrative devices. On the other hand, when wage differentials have proven a barrier to recruitment the wage structure has typically been modified. The earnings of the scarce categories of labor have been raised, either openly by adjustment of agreed rates, or informally by payment over the official scale. What seems to be emerging is a combined use of

(moderate) wage differentials in the "right" direction, plus reinforcement of wage incentives by administrative techniques.

5. British experience casts doubt on the technique of voluntary wage restraint as a means of controlling the money wage level. The experiment of 1948–50 was carried out under unusually favorable circumstances: the balance of payments crisis was obvious to all, a Labour government was in office, and wage restraint was supported by an effective over-all policy of inflation control. Even so, the rise in the money wage level was retarded rather than stopped. The policy proved workable for only two years or so, and even this breathing spell was due partly to the time-consuming nature of British collective bargaining procedures.

CHAPTER 11 *Canada*

INFLUENCES ON WAGE DETERMINATION

THE economic institutions of Canada bear a marked resemblance to those of the United States. Canada is a relatively young country which has experienced a rapid rate of population growth and economic expansion. It is a nation of continental scope, exhibiting the same diversity of terrain, population elements, and economic activities which one finds in the United States. Each region of Canada, indeed, bears a stronger resemblance to the adjacent region of the United States than to other regions within Canada itself. British Columbia and the Pacific Northwest, the Prairie Provinces and the Plains States, Ontario and New York State, the Maritime Provinces and New England—the similarities are striking in each case and extend to the geographical structure of wages. Many leading Canadian corporations are either subsidiaries of, or closely affiliated with, corresponding companies in the United States. This is true particularly in automobiles, tires, electrical equipment, oil refining, metal mining and refining, and other branches of heavy industry. Most of the trade unions, too, are branches of parent organizations located in the United States. In Canada, as in the United States, the United Automobile Workers bargains with the "big three" auto companies, the United Rubber Workers bargains with the four major tire producers, the Electrical Workers bargains with General Electric and Westinghouse.

These similarities should not be allowed to obscure the substantial differences between the two economies. The Canadian economy is in an earlier stage of development, a stage showing an even more rapid rate of expansion than prevails in the United States. The rapid development of Canada's mineral and oil resources since 1940 has tended to distract attention from the equally spectacular growth of manufacturing industry. Many Canadian industries suffered virtually no drop in employment at the end of World War II and immediately took off on a sustained rise in output which has lasted to the present time. Despite this rapid rate of growth the Canadian economy is still much smaller in absolute terms, both population and national output being less than 10 per cent of the American total. Adam Smith's dictum that "the division of labor is limited by the extent of the market" helps to explain why man-hour output and real wage levels in Canada are somewhat below the level of the United States.

Canadian industry is concentrated in a relatively small area of the country. A heavy preponderance of all manufacturing is located along the Windsor-Toronto-Montreal axis. The western provinces and the maritime provinces are isolated from the economic heart of the country by distance and transportation costs to an even greater degree than is true in the United States.

TRADE UNIONISM AND COLLECTIVE BARGAINING

The upsurge of union organization in the United States during the thirties left Canada largely unaffected. The outbreak of war in 1939, however, brought a sharp rise in employment and increased government protection for unionism under wartime labor disputes regulations. Union membership climbed steeply from 359,000 in 1939 to 1,268,000 in 1954.[1] This is about one-quarter of the nonagricultural labor force, compared with a ratio of about one-third in the United States in the same year. Union organization is rather uneven geographically—strongest in British Columbia, moderately strong in Ontario, relatively weak in Quebec, strong again in coal mining, steel, construction, and railway occupations in the Maritime Provinces. Industry for industry, the percentage of workers covered by union contract usually runs somewhat below that in the United States.

Most unions are affiliated with the Trades and Labour Congress of Canada or the Canadian Congress of Labour, which correspond roughly to the AFL and CIO in the United States, and are to be merged into one federation by the end of 1955. In addition, there is a Confederation of Catholic Workers of Canada with a substantial membership in the Province of Quebec, plus a considerable scattering of independent unions. At the beginning of 1954, some 600,000 workers were in unions affiliated with the Trades and Labour Congress, 360,000 were affiliated with the Canadian Congress of Labour, 100,000 with the Confederation of Catholic Workers, and about 200,000 were in unions not affiliated with any central federation.[2] In most industries, then, one finds some establishments organized by one union and some by another, plus a certain number of nonunion establishments. Interunion collaboration on wage policy is hampered by the fact that the unions involved are typically rivals for membership. One does find cases of informal cooperation and mutual support, but this is scarcely the prevailing pattern.

1. Canadian Department of Labour, *Labour Organization in Canada 1954*, Forty-third Annual Report (Ottawa, 1954), p. 4.
2. *Ibid.*, p. 6.

There are nonetheless certain industries in which collective bargaining has an important influence on the pattern of wages. The list includes the transportation and communication industries, pulp and paper, basic steel, automobiles, rubber tires, heavy electrical equipment, meat packing, printing and publishing, and building construction. Outside this central core the influence of unionism tapers off rather rapidly. While there is a substantial union membership in textiles, clothing, boots and shoes, and other branches of light manufacturing, union influence on wages is limited by actual and potential nonunion competition.

Local unions in Canada, except for the Catholic unions, are typically affiliated with an international union whose headquarters and most of whose members are located in the United States. While the Canadian locals have a large measure of autonomy and formulate their own wage policies, they are somewhat influenced by their international affiliation. The fact that U.S. wages are typically higher than Canadian wages in the same industry is sometimes used as an argument in negotiations. The Steelworkers locals in Canada succeeded for a brief period in establishing the same common-labor rate as in the United States, though rates for higher jobs were graduated less steeply so that average plant wage levels remained lower in Canada. Even the parity in labor rates was lost after a year or two, and the union has not been able to reestablish it. The packinghouse workers, who are strongly organized in Canada, have also made a serious effort to establish wages at parity with the United States, though they have not entirely succeeded. For the most part, however, the parity concept is a talking point to support demands formulated on other grounds.

The Canadian unions are somewhat influenced by their American colleagues in the size of wage demands from year to year. This is particularly true in heavy manufacturing where the "pattern" concept has been popularized on both sides of the border. If the Steelworkers or Auto Workers make large demands on American employers in a particular year there are likely to be large—though not necessarily identical—demands on Canadian employers. This is not sheer imitation but in part a response to similar economic conditions. Business fluctuations in the two countries are sufficiently similar so that the wage-paying ability of employers on both sides of the border is likely to be moving in the same direction at the same time.

THE ROLE OF GOVERNMENT

Government has little influence on the Canadian wage structure. Wartime wage controls left some imprint on occupational and interindustry differentials. These controls lapsed at the end of the war, leaving only:

1. Minimum wage standards established under provincial legislation for particular industries and categories of labor. There is no national minimum wage, and the provincial standards have been rendered less effective by the inflation of the past decade. In 1953 the minimum rates for male factory workers ranged from 40 cents to 60 cents per hour at a time when the average hourly earnings of all manufacturing workers stood at $1.36.

2. In Quebec, a Collective Agreement Act permits rates set through collective bargaining in certain establishments to be extended through the remainder of the industry by government decree. Several other provinces have "industrial standards acts" under which minimum rates are set at a conference called by the Minister of Labour at the request of employers and employees in an industry. The schedule of minimum wages agreed to may be declared legally binding on the entire industry in the district concerned. These potentially powerful statutes are little used in practice. Where unionism is strong the unions prefer to set rates through direct negotiation, and where the unions are weak they can usually not persuade the provincial government to take action.

3. Government contracts contain "fair wage" provisions similar to those in the United States, and these may have some supporting effect on wages in construction and a limited number of other industries.

The fact that the Dominion government plays such a limited role in wage determination is partly a matter of constitutional structure, under which regulation of labor conditions (except for interprovincial transportation and communication and a few other cases) falls within provincial jurisdiction. Beyond this, however, it is a matter of political outlook. Ever since 1921, except for the years 1930–35, the Dominion government has been in the hands of the Liberal party. The outlook of this party is liberal in the historic sense of relying on private industry and commerce for economic progress, emphasizing the role of free competition and free pricing, and holding government controls to a minimum. In this view, direct control of wages by government beyond establishing certain minimum standards is both unwise and unnecessary.

Canada, like the United States, comes closer than any of the European countries to the free-market economy of economic theory. It has also experienced during the past fifteen years an extremely rapid rate of economic expansion and marked shifts in the composition of employment. Here, if anywhere, one would expect to find wages behaving in an "economic" fashion and playing their traditional role of allocating labor among areas, occupations, and industries. How far is this expectation confirmed by the actual behavior of wages over the past fifteen years? This central question should be borne in mind as we examine wage developments in Canada since 1939.

EVOLUTION OF THE NATIONAL WAGE STRUCTURE

THE ECONOMIC CONTEXT

The past fifteen years have witnessed a striking increase in the output of the Canadian economy. Between 1938 and 1952, gross national product in real terms rose by 121 per cent, an average rate of increase of 5.8 per cent per year. Even on a per capita basis gross national product came close to doubling during this period.[3]

This expansion was due partly to a sharp reduction in unemployment. One-eighth of the civilian labor force was totally unemployed in 1938, and, if one excludes people engaged in agriculture, the proportion of the *industrial* labor force unemployed was 20 per cent. This situation changed rapidly after the outbreak of war. Most of the unemployed had been absorbed by 1941, and by 1943 unemployment had fallen to 1.7 per cent of the labor force. Canada suffered no serious reconversion unemployment, the expansion of peacetime industries picking up rapidly as war production fell off. Unemployment was only 3 per cent of the labor force in 1946, and the annual average fluctuated between 1.5 and 3 per cent from 1946 through 1953.[4] Considering the geographical diversity of the country and the large shifts in the composition of employment this is a remarkably low level. Wage developments have thus occurred in the context of a tight market for most kinds of labor in most areas.

High employment has been reinforced by a rapid rate of increase in productivity. Unpublished estimates prepared in Ottawa indicate that, in the nonagricultural sector of the economy, output per man-hour rose by 51 per cent between 1939 and 1951, or a compound annual rate of 3.5 per cent. An extraordinarily rapid rate of increase during the war years was followed by a tapering off in the late forties, and then by a renewed rise of productivity beginning in 1950. In agriculture, man-hour output rose by 84 per cent over the period 1939–51, or an average of 5.2 per cent per year, due mainly to increased farm mechanization over the period and also to fuller utilization of the farm labor force in 1951.

This rising volume of output was sold at higher and higher prices. The retail price level rose only 17 per cent between 1939 and 1945 due to a rigorous program of wartime price control. After the war prices rose rapidly from 1946–49 and, after leveling off for a brief period, shot up again with the outbreak of the Korean war. In 1952 retail prices

3. OEEC, *Statistics of National Product and Expenditure, 1938, 1947 to 1952*, pp. 89–90.

4. International Labour Office, *Yearbook of Labour Statistics* (Geneva, 1954), p. 90.

stood 82 per cent above the 1939 level, only slightly below the corresponding index in the United States.

The progress of real and money wages in manufacturing industries over the years 1939–53 is traced in Table 11-1. Wage rates rose sharply

Table 11-1. Movement of Money and Real Wage Rates and Earnings in Manufacturing, Canada, 1939–53 (1939 = 100)

		MONEY WAGES			REAL WAGES		
YEAR	COST OF LIVING *	HOURLY WAGE RATES †	AVERAGE HOURLY EARNINGS ‡	AVERAGE WEEKLY EARNINGS ‡	HOURLY WAGE RATES	AVERAGE HOURLY EARNINGS	AVERAGE WEEKLY EARNINGS
1939	100.0	100.0	100.0	100.0	100.0	100.0	100.0
1940	104.1	104.3	105.0	110.6	100.3	100.9	106.3
1941	110.0	115.2	115.4	123.1	104.7	104.9	111.9
1942	115.3	125.2	131.5	139.1	108.8	114.1	120.6
1943	116.7	136.8	143.1	147.6	117.2	122.6	126.5
1944	117.1	141.4	152.8	153.2	120.8	130.5	130.8
1945	117.7	146.5	164.5 §	152.6 **	124.5	139.8	129.7
1946	121.8	161.5	165.9	148.2	132.6	136.2	121.7
1947	133.5	183.3	190.2	169.4	137.3	142.5	126.9
1948	152.7	205.9	216.4	191.2	134.8	141.7	125.2
1949	158.4	217.9	233.6	207.0	137.6	147.5	130.7
1950	162.8	230.7	245.5	217.5	141.7	150.8	133.6
1951	179.9	261.6	276.8	242.2	145.4	153.9	134.6
1952	184.3	277.6	306.2	266.1	150.6	166.1	144.4
1953	182.8	291.1	321.8	278.4	159.2	176.0	152.3

* The cost-of-living index for 1939 to 1949 is based on the years 1935–39; the consumers price index for 1950 to 1953 is based on the year 1949.

† Hourly wage rates in selected manufacturing industries. From 1944 on, the index includes piece rates for many occupations.

‡ Weighted average of earnings of male and female hourly-rated employees. For the years 1939 to 1944 the data are for the month of highest employment in each firm. For the years 1945 to 1953 the data are based on monthly surveys of earnings and hours.

§ For the year 1945 part of the apparent sharp rise in average hourly earnings is accounted for by the change in method of survey. The index of average hourly earnings for the month of highest employment (the basis for the 1939–44 series) was only 157.8. The average 12-months index was 164.5.

** The change in method of survey affected average weekly earnings in the opposite direction from hourly earnings. The index for the month of highest employment was 154.3, whereas the 12-months index was 152.6.

Source: Dominion Bureau of Statistics, Annual Review of Man-Hours and Hourly Earnings, 1945–1953; Canadian Department of Labour, Economics and Research Branch, annual reports on wage rates and hours of labor

during the early years of the war, and the methods of wage control were sufficiently flexible to permit substantial increases. At the outset wages were allowed to rise to their 1926–29 level, or any higher level attained during the thirties (an academic provision in most cases), before controls were applied. This was designed to remedy wage distortions and inequities which had developed during the Great Depression. In November 1941 a firmer control system was established under the supervision of a National War Labour Board and regional boards in each province. Wage increases were now permitted on only two counts: 1. a flat-rate cost-of-living bonus was established, the amount to increase with each rise in the cost-of-living index; 2. special adjustments could be made to bring rates in an establishment up to those prevailing for comparable jobs elsewhere in the locality. Under this system wage rates continued to rise at about 10 per cent per year during 1942 and 1943.

Earnings rose somewhat faster than *rates,* for the usual reasons. The average weekly earnings of manufacturing workers rose 48 per cent between 1939 and 1943, compared with a rise of 37 per cent in hourly rates. The price index having risen only 17 per cent, there was a substantial gain in real earnings.

By 1943 the continued advance of wages and prices was giving rise to considerable concern, and firmer measures were adopted to deal with it. Under a Wartime Wages Control Order issued at the end of 1943, all cost-of-living bonuses being paid as of February 15, 1944 were to be consolidated with basic wage rates, and no further bonuses were to be paid. Wage increases were to be authorized only where it could be shown that a "gross injustice or gross inequality" existed. The National War Labour Board was also given appellate power over the regional boards to secure greater uniformity of policy throughout the country. This tightening of wage controls was predicated on a similar tightening of price policies. Price ceilings were to be held unchanged, and government subsidies were to be used where necessary to absorb unavoidable increases in costs. The objective was a genuine price freeze—not a retardation of inflation, but a full stop. There was an understanding that, if the cost-of-living index rose by as much as three points, the whole wage policy would be reconsidered.[5]

The success of this strategy is apparent from Table 11-1. The cost-of-living index rose by only one point between 1943 and 1945. At the end of the war it was actually lower than it had been in October 1943 when the tighter price controls were introduced. The advance of wage rates, while not stopped, was much retarded. Manufacturing wage rates, which had risen by 9.0 per cent between 1942 and 1943, rose by only

5. R. E. Moffat, "Canadian Price Control since 1939," *The Annals of the American Academy of Political and Social Science,* 253 (Sept. 1947), 128–9.

3.4 per cent in 1943–44 and 3.6 per cent in 1944–45. The corresponding figures for industry generally (manufacturing, mining, logging, transportation, communication, services) are 9.1 per cent, 3.1 per cent, and 2.8 per cent.[6] Because of price stability these moderate gains in money wages meant an equivalent gain in real wages. By the end of the war the real wage rates of industrial workers stood about 20 per cent above the 1939 level, while real hourly earnings had risen by 30 per cent.

The course of events since the end of the war has been similar to that in the United States. Wage controls were relaxed in February 1946 and abandoned entirely in November 1946. Decontrol of prices proceeded more gradually but had been substantially completed by the spring of 1947. Prices rose sharply after the removal of controls, the cost-of-living index rising twenty-six points during 1946–48. Wage rates rose even faster, however, and real hourly wages moved up continuously throughout the postwar period. Weekly earnings fell in money terms, and even more in real terms, during 1945–46 as working hours were cut back and overtime payments diminished. Not until 1949 did real weekly earnings regain the 1945 level. From this point on, however, the advance was continuous, and by 1953 real weekly earnings stood 18 per cent above 1945 and 52.3 per cent above 1939. Real hourly earnings in 1953 were 76 per cent above the 1939 level. The rate of increase in both productivity and real wages since 1939 has been unusually rapid in comparison with other countries.

OCCUPATIONAL DIFFERENTIALS

A gradual decline in occupational differentials seems to have been in progress in Canada for at least several decades. Data for selected industries in 1930 and 1939 are shown in Table 11-2a. With a few exceptions, such as the strongly unionized compositors in the printing industry, the skilled workers lost ground relative to the unskilled over this period. The fact that absolute as well as percentage differentials declined in many cases reflects the substantial drop in the money wage level during the thirties.

The course of events over the years 1943–52 is suggested by Table 11-2b, which compares rates for typical semiskilled and skilled occupations in selected industries with rates for common labor in the same industry. The data are not comparable with those for earlier years, and Table 11-2b cannot be linked up directly with Table 11-2a. The 1943–52 data are of very good quality, however, and both occupational categories used and the method of collection appear to be quite comparable over

6. Canadian Department of Labour, Economics and Research Branch, annual reports on wage rates and hours of labor.

the period. The figures used exclude overtime but include straight-time piecework earnings. They also exclude special payments such as night shift premiums, Christmas bonuses, profit-sharing arrangements, and fringe benefits.

Table 11-2a. Occupational Wage Differences in Selected Industries, Canada, 1930–39 *

INDUSTRY	1930		1939	
	$ ABOVE LABORER	% ABOVE LABORER	$ ABOVE LABORER	% ABOVE LABORER
Agricultural implements				
Patternmaker	.25	68	.16	41
Machinist	.23	62	.13	33
Building trades				
Bricklayer and mason	.90	200	.60	150
Carpenter	.55	122	.30	75
Coal mining, Alberta				
Contract miners	3.50 †	82	2.79	69
Driver	.77 †	18	.31	7
Coal mining, Nova Scotia				
Contract miners	3.29 †	97	3.31	99
Driver	.20 †	6	0	0
Cotton yarn and broad woven goods				
Loom fixer, male (above female twisters)	.29	132	.24	96
Ring spinner, female (")	.08	36	.03	12
Electrical apparatus, etc.				
Tool makers	n.a.	n.a.	.28	70
Coilwinder (male)	n.a.	n.a.	.05	13
Electric street railway				
Linemen	.23	44	.27	56
Shop and barn men	.16	31	.20	42
Foundry and machine shop				
Coremaker	.20	67	.17	45
Chippers and grinders	n.a.	n.a.	.08	21
Logging, Br. Columbia				
Donkey engineers (above roadmen)	n.a.	n.a.	2.50	63
Fallers and buckers (")	n.a.	n.a.	3.00	75
Printing trade				
Compositors, machine & hand, news	30.10 ‡	173	30.05	194
Pulp				
Digester cook (above woodhandler)	.45	129	.39	91
Grinderman (")	.11	31	.10	23
Newsprint				
Machine tender (above beaterman)	n.a.	n.a.	.94	184
Backtender (")	n.a.	n.a.	.74	145
Sheet metal products				
Blacksmith	20	55	.29	76

Table 11-2a. Occupational Wage Differences in Selected Industries, Canada, 1930–39 * (Continued)

INDUSTRY	1930		1939	
	$ ABOVE LABORER	% ABOVE LABORER	$ ABOVE LABORER	% ABOVE LABORER
Shipbuilding				
Shipwright, carpenter	.27	71	.23	62
Caulker	.22	58	.30	81
Automobile parts				
Tool makers	.34	83	.32	80
Assemblers (male)	.02	5	.08	20

* The data in this table give a rough approximation only of wage differentials, since the wage reports prior to 1943 contained only a "representative" selection of wages rather than a good sample. The criteria for the selection are not clearly explained in the reports nor are they necessarily consistent from year to year.

† Daily.

‡ Weekly.

Source: Canadian Department of Labour, Wages and Hours of Labour in Canada, 1930, 1939

It is clear from Table 11-2b that the premium for skilled labor was still substantial in 1952. It was in the neighborhood of 40 to 50 per cent in many industries and rose to more than 100 per cent in a few cases. The cases of unusually large differentials, such as printing, pulp and paper, and building construction, can be attributed to the degree of skill required by the top crafts and the strength of union organization among these crafts.[7]

The skilled-unskilled differential varies not only from industry to industry but also among regions of the country. In Canada, as in the United States, the high-wage Pacific Coast region tends to show smaller skill differentials than other parts of the country.

In most industries the cents-per-hour differential between skilled men and laborers widened considerably during the period 1943–52. On a percentage basis there was a moderate narrowing of the differential in most cases, though not so sharp a reduction as in most other countries. The course of events was intermediate between what would have resulted from uniform cents-per-hour increases on the one hand and uniform percentage increases on the other.

There has been a marked tendency toward uniform flat-rate increases for much the same reasons as in other countries. An important factor

7. See, for example, the discussion of papermakers' earnings in Chap. 5.

has been the general wage and price inflation. There was a tendency after 1939 to adjust to inflation by uniform cents-per-hour increases for all workers in the plant. The new industrial unions in steel, automobiles, electrical manufacturing, and other industries typically demanded this sort of increase in Canada as in the United States.

*Table 11-2b. Occupational Wage Differences in Selected Industries, Canada, 1943–52 ***

INDUSTRY AND OCCUPATION †	ABSOLUTE DIFFERENCES (ABOVE LABORER)		PERCENTAGE DIFFERENCES (LABORER = 100)	
	1943	1952	1943	1952
Agricultural implements				
Patternmaker	$ .28	$ .57	149	147
Machine operator	.19	.41	133	134
Coal mining (Alberta)				
Miners, contract	3.51	5.34	163	144
Driver	.67	.56	112	105
Coal mining (Nova Scotia)				
Miners, contract	3.03	5.06	165	151
Driver	.04	.54	101	106
Construction (selected cities)				
Bricklayer (Montreal)	.45	.75	175	165
Bricklayer (Toronto)	.56	1.25	190	214
Cotton yarn and broad woven goods				
Loom fixer, male	.30	.40	183	144
Spinner (ring), female	.05	.14	112	116
Electrical machinery and apparatus				
Tool and die maker	.41	.58	169	146
Coil winder, male	.22	.14	137	111
Iron castings and machine-shop products				
Coremaker	.16	.29 ‡	127	133 ‡
Chippers and grinders	.05	.15 ‡	108	117 ‡
Logging (British Columbia)				
Donkey engineer	1.92	2.81	131	121
Fallers and buckers	3.04	10.44	149	179
Rigging slinger	1.57	1.74	125	113
Primary iron and steel				
Blacksmith	.21	.25	137	118
Printing and publishing (Toronto)				
Compositor, hand & machine, news	31.94 §	1.41	270	240
Pulp and paper products (pulp & newsprint)				
Pulp				
Digester cook	.39	.54	171	142
Grinderman	.06	.10	111	108

Table 11-2b. *Occupational Wage Differences in Selected Industries, Canada,*
1943–52 * (Continued)

| | ABSOLUTE DIFFERENCES (ABOVE LABORER) | | PERCENTAGE DIFFERENCES (LABORER = 100) | |
INDUSTRY AND OCCUPATION †	1943	1952	1943	1952
Newsprint				
Machine tender	1.01	1.34	262	199
Backtender	.82	1.12	232	183
Steel shipbuilding				
Shipwright, carpenter, & joiner	.38	.35	166	130˙
Chipper and caulker	.39	.26	167	123

* The "wage rate" of this table is considerably broader than the ordinary concept of wage rate. It is 1. inclusive of piecework earnings, and 2. exclusive of overtime. It also excludes certain special payments such as night shift payments, Christmas or profit-sharing bonuses, and fringe benefits.

† In selecting occupations three criteria have been used: 1. the availability of data for both 1943 and 1952; 2. the classification of the occupation as skilled or semi-skilled in the occupational schedules attached to wage survey questionnaires; and 3. the numerical importance of the occupation in the particular industry concerned.

‡ 1949.

§ Per week.

Source: Canadian Department of Labour, Economics and Research Branch, annual reports on wage rates and hours of labor in Canada

The government's wage-stabilization policies also contributed to flat-rate increases during the war years. Under the cost-of-living bonus instituted in 1941, workers received a flat bonus of so many cents per hour for each point increase in the consumer price index. This policy of automatic escalation was abandoned at the end of 1943 as part of a general tightening of wage and price controls, but the bonuses being paid at that time were consolidated into the rate structure. The other main basis for granting wage increases was to bring an employer's rates up to those being paid by other firms for comparable work in the locality. Where adjustments were granted on this ground the National War Labour Board typically required that they be applied on a uniform cents-per-hour basis, and requests for percentage adjustments were resisted. The general drift of board policies, in short, was in a wage-leveling direction.

In recent years there has been some tendency in Canada, as in the United States, to abandon flat-rate increases and provide larger wage adjustments for the skilled employees. One factor working in this direction is the fragility of many of the new unions and the ease with which craft groups can secede and join another organization. It frequently seems expedient to demand larger increases for the skilled men in order to maintain their loyalty to the union and to ward off appeals from rival groups. A more basic factor, however, has been the continuing shortage of many types of skilled labor during the postwar years. They have included, among others, skilled metalworkers, hard rock miners, coal miners (in the early postwar years), members of the trowel trades in building construction, operating engineers, and technicians of every description.[8] There does not seem to have been a corresponding scarcity of low-skilled factory labor, though there has been a chronic shortage of farm workers and of domestic servants. In a relatively free labor market one would expect this situation to produce a widening of cents-per-hour differentials between skilled and unskilled occupations, and this is what has actually occurred.

It will be noted also from Table 11-2b that in most industries the semiskilled workers have gained ground on the skilled in percentage terms. This has been true particularly in industries where the semiskilled are paid on an incentive basis and the skilled workers on a time basis. The normal growth of machine efficiency tends to reflect itself in a rapid rise of incentive earnings which, in a tight labor market, is unlikely to be checked by piece-rate reductions. A striking case in point is the British Columbia logging industry. The principal semiskilled jobs are those of fallers and buckers. These are hazardous jobs, usually paid by the piece, and earnings have always been high relative to skilled jobs of the traditional craft type. During and just after the war, the power saw was introduced in felling trees. Piece rates were not adjusted to offset this sharp rise in output, and the earnings of the fallers relative to those of laborers rose from 149 per cent in 1943 to 202 per cent in 1947. Their position has declined somewhat since that time but is still remarkably high relative to that of skilled classifications in the industry. The same thing seems to have happened to a lesser extent with chippers and grinders in the production of iron castings, and there are indications of a similar development in primary iron and steel though the data do not admit of precise comparisons. These cases may indicate a broader tendency for jobs which are still classified as semiskilled to become of central importance in production, while the traditional skilled jobs decline to a minor position.

8. This cannot be verified from Employment Service data because rather less than one-quarter of job vacancies in Canada are filled through the Employment Service, and this percentage is quite variable as among localities, industries, and skill levels. Other types of data, however, leave little doubt that the observation is correct.

INTERINDUSTRY DIFFERENTIALS

The war years 1939–45 brought sharp shifts in employment [9] which were bound to have repercussions on the interindustry wage structure: absorption of the large-scale unemployment which existed in 1939; movement into urban industry of large numbers of farmworkers and of people previously outside the labor force; movement of workers from civilian industries to war industries; and withdrawal of large numbers of men for military service.

A sample survey conducted in 1944 indicated that there had been a net movement of 450,000 workers into war industry between 1940 and 1944, undoubtedly the residue of a much larger gross movement. Of these workers, 300,000 had come from other industries and 150,000 were people previously outside the labor force. Seventeen per cent of those employed in civilian manufacturing in 1940, 32 per cent of those in building construction, and 10 per cent of those in finance had shifted to war manufacturing by 1944. The outflow from agriculture is indicated by the fact that 160,000 of those employed in industry in 1944 had been in agriculture in 1940. In addition an estimated 100,000 had moved from agriculture to industry and thence to the armed services.[10] Despite natural increase, the agricultural labor force declined by some 20 per cent between 1939 and 1943.

Under these conditions one would have expected a sharp increase in the relative earnings of farmworkers. Farm wage rates tripled between 1939 and 1945 while manufacturing wage rates rose less than 50 per cent. Farm wages, unlike industrial wages, were not subjected to wage controls during the war years. Farm rates were of course starting from a very low base and in 1945 were still well below manufacturing wages on an absolute basis. The average monthly wage of Canadian farm laborers, without board, in August 1945 was $97.00.[11] This compares with an average of $35.00 per week, or upward of $150.00 per month, for all workers in manufacturing. Compared with *unskilled* labor in industry, however, farm laborers had achieved approximate parity in 1945 —a parity which was short lived and was lost once more during the postwar years.

Wage developments in the manufacturing sector of the economy from 1939 to 1945 are shown in Table 11-3. The most detailed material available for this period unfortunately relates to weekly earnings rather

9. Department of Labour, Research and Statistics Branch, *Changes in Population and the Labour Force* (Ottawa, 1946).

10. *Ibid.*, pp. 16–23.

11. *Idem., Wage Rates and Hours of Labour, October, 1948* (Ottawa, 1949), p. 103.

Table 11-3. Wage Changes in Selected Manufacturing Industries, Canada, 1939–45 (men)

*INDUSTRY	AVERAGE WEEKLY EARNINGS 1939	1945	INCREASE 1939–45 $	%	INCREASE IN EMPLOYMENT 1939–45	RANK 1939	1945	% OF MANUFACTURING AVERAGE 1939	1945
Coke and gas products	$29.67	$34.99	5.32	18	⎱ 33%	1	24	133%	100%
Petroleum products	28.95	36.95	8.00	28	⎰	2	16	130	105
Automobiles	28.99	48.53	19.54	67	72	3	1	130	139
Machinery	28.59	36.09	7.50	26	115	4	19	129	103
Nonferrous metal smelting and refining	27.92	37.76	9.84	35	31	5	11	126	108
Primary iron and steel	27.75	39.50	11.75	42	80	6	6	125	113
Printing and publishing	27.55	37.31	9.76	35	16	7	13	124	106
Railway & rolling stock	27.20	39.51	12.31	45	67	8	5	122	113
Pulp and paper	26.93	37.05	10.12	38	32	9	15	121	106
Agricultural implements	26.61	37.49	10.88	41	148	10	12	120	107
Shipbuilding and repairs	26.30	39.54	13.24	50	1200	11	4	118	113
Scientific and professional equipment	26.15	41.95	16.80	60	n.a.	12	3	118	120
Aircraft	26.13	44.13	18.00	69	1203	13	2	118	126
[Iron and its products]	[26.11]	[38.86]	[12.75]	[49]	[121]	—	—	[117]	[111]
Automobile supplies	25.58	39.14	13.56	53	127	14	8	115	112
Acids, alkalis, and salts	25.29	37.16	11.87	47	130	15	14	114	106
[Nonferrous metal products]	[25.24]	[36.64]	[11.40]	[45]	[109]	—	—	[114]	[105]
Brass and copper products	24.63	38.50	13.87	56	175	16	9	111	110
Iron and steel products, miscellaneous	24.21	39.20	14.99	62	n.a.	17	7	109	112
[Nonmetallic mineral products]	[23.89]	[33.46]	[9.57]	[40]	[58]	—	—	[107]	[95]
Slaughtering and meat packing	23.80	32.74	8.94	38	75	18	29	107	93
Breweries	23.55	34.64	11.09	47	n.a.	19	25	106	99
Electrical apparatus and supplies	23.54	35.83	12.29	52	114	20	22	106	102
Clothing, women's factory	23.17	38.15	14.96	65	19	21	10	104	109
Printing and bookbinding	23.02	33.52	10.50	46	n.a.	22	28	104	96
Castings, iron	22.65	36.31	13.66	60	114	23	17	102	104
Rubber goods, including rubber footwear	22.39	36.05	13.66	61	55	24	20	101	103

Table 11-3. Wage Changes in Selected Manufacturing Industries, Canada, 1939–45 (men) (Continued)

*INDUSTRY	AVERAGE WEEKLY EARNINGS		INCREASE 1939–45		INCREASE IN EMPLOYMENT 1939–45	RANK		% OF MANUFACTURING AVERAGE	
	1939	1945	$	%		1939	1945	1939	1945
[Chemicals and allied products]	[22.25]	[33.83]	[11.58]	[52]	[194]	—	—	[100]	[97]
Clothing, men's factory	22.09	35.12	13.03	59	28	25	23	99	100
Hardware and tools	21.64	36.00	14.36	66	99	26	21	97	103
Miscellaneous chemical products	21.55	34.23	12.68	59	n.a.	27	26	97	98
Aluminum products	21.50	36.23	14.73	69	275	28	18	97	103
Sheet-metal products	21.47	33.65	12.18	57	94	29	27	97	96
Hoisery and knitted goods	20.77	28.98	8.21	40	n.a.	30	33	93	83
[Wood and paper products]	[20.59]	[32.34]	[11.75]	[57]	"	—	—	[93]	[92]
[Animal products]	[20.18]	[30.73]	[10.55]	[52]	"	—	—	[91]	[88]
[Textiles and textile products]	[19.96]	[30.25]	[10.29]	[52]	[28]	—	—	[90]	[86]
Foods, miscellaneous	19.90	27.34	7.44	37	26	31	36	90	78
[Vegetable products]	[19.75]	[30.49]	[10.74]	[54]	n.a.	—	—	[89]	[87]
[Miscellaneous industries]	[19.44]	[32.70]	[13.26]	[68]	[97]	—	—	[87]	[93]
Foods, stock, and poultry	19.35	29.99	10.64	55	"	32	31	87	86
Flour and feed mills	19.33	28.46	9.13	47	"	33	34	87	81
Bread and other bakery products	19.32	29.65	10.33	53	"	34	32	87	85
Biscuits, confectionery, cocoa, etc.	18.93	26.84	7.91	42	"	35	39	85	77
Woolen cloth	18.90	28.06	9.16	48	"	36	35	80	80
Tobacco, cigars, and cigarettes	17.83	30.71	12.88	72	"	37	30	80	88
Cotton yarn and cloth	17.58	27.11	9.53	54	"	38	38	79	77
Boots and shoes, leather	17.43	27.17	9.74	56	11	39	37	78	78
Sawmills	16.01	—	—	—	n.a.	40	—	72	—
Fruits and vegetable preparations	15.58	25.69	10.11	65	50	41	40	70	73
AVERAGE ALL INDUSTRIES	22.23	35.04	12.81	58	76	—	—	100	100

* The industries in brackets are large categories, some of whose subgroups are in the list.

Source: Dominion Bureau of Statistics, Weekly Earnings and Hours of Work of Male and Female Wage-earners Employed in Manufacturing (1945), pp. 12–15

than hourly rates. Differing amounts of overtime work in 1945 may thus affect the results for some industries. A table using hourly rates, however, would probably not yield very different conclusions.

There is no simple explanation for differences in the rate of wage increase from industry to industry. There is only a slight relationship, for example, between rate of increase in wages and rate of increase in employment. Some industries with very large increases in employment showed above-average wage increases (aircraft, hardware and tools, aluminum products); but others showed less than average increases in earnings (basic iron and steel, shipbuilding, brass and copper products, electrical apparatus, chemicals). Again there is little relation between the 1939 wage level and the rate of wage increase from 1939 to 1945. The industries with low wage levels in 1939 do not typically show larger *percentage* increases over the subsequent period as might have been expected. These results are apparently due to the character of the wartime industrial expansion. A transformation occurred in industrial structure and in wage structure which has to be explained in terms of the changing character of product markets and the changing demand for particular types of labor.

The largest percentage increases in weekly earnings were in aircraft, automobiles, hardware and tools, and aluminum products. These increases are explained not just by the large wartime expansion of production in these industries but by other attendant circumstances. The aircraft labor force was built up from almost nothing at the outbreak of war. The lack of a firmly established wage structure dating from prewar days made wage controls difficult to apply, and the fact that virtually the entire output was for war use encouraged generosity in developing whatever wage scales seemed necessary to recruit labor. The automobile industry, while not itself new, was converted to a completely new set of military products during the war. This meant new piece-rate schedules, long production runs on identical items, and consequent high piece-rate earnings. Relatively long hours and high overtime payments also swelled earnings in the automobile and aircraft industries.

Average weekly earnings rose relatively little in meat packing, certain other foodstuffs, hosiery and knitted goods, pulp and paper, printing and publishing, and coke and gas products. These were peacetime industries whose relative importance in the economy declined during the war. In some cases, such as meat and other foodstuffs, price controls were unusually tight because of the importance of these items in living costs, and this helped to retard wage increases. In other cases cutbacks in production and employment may help to account for the sluggishness of wages. The printing and paper industries had their production restricted during the war and in addition had relatively high wage levels at the outset. The exceptionally small wage increase in coke and gas products is clearly related to the decline of this industry during the war period.

The most puzzling feature of the period is the moderate decline in the relative wage position of such industries as primary iron and steel, railway rolling stock, shipbuilding (despite a phenomenal expansion of employment), electrical apparatus and supplies, petroleum products, and nonferrous smelting and refining. These industries were all linked to the war effort, had substantial increases in employment, and might have been expected to show above-average increases in wages. Yet their increases were below average on a percentage basis and in most cases on an absolute basis as well. The explanation is partly that at the beginning of the war these were high-wage industries which were able to draw labor away from lower-wage industries simply by announcing the existence of vacancies. Large wage increases were not essential for recruitment purposes. Another part of the explanation may lie in the employment of a larger proportion of unskilled and semiskilled labor, including women in some cases, as a result of the shift to mass production during the war. This dilution of skills would lead average hourly earnings to rise less rapidly than basic wage rates.

These divergent rates of wage increase led to a considerable reranking of manufacturing industries. The last two columns of Table 11-3 indicate that there was also a moderate decline in interindustry dispersion of wage levels. The quartile deviation fell from .118 in 1939 to .107 in 1945. The leveling of interindustry differences was more moderate, however, than in most other countries.

The end of the war brought renewed shifts in the composition of employment. Civilian industries whose output had been restricted during the war now experienced a sharp upsurge. Industries geared to war production, such as aircraft and parts, shipbuilding, certain iron and steel products, nonferrous metals, and chemical products, experienced a sharp drop in employment during 1945–46. After 1946 most of these industries regained and even passed their wartime peaks as a consequence of the general boom in manufacturing. By 1951 only aircraft, shipbuilding, chemical products, and coal mining showed employment levels below those of 1945.

The increase in average hourly earnings in selected industries between 1945 and 1953 is shown in Table 11-4. Once more there is no marked correlation between the rate of wage increase and either the rate of employment increase or the 1945 wage level of the industry. The factors at work have obviously been complicated and some sort of composite and almost individualized explanation is necessary for each industry. The nearest one can come to generalization is to note that

Table 11-4. Wage Changes in Selected Industries, Canada, 1945–53

*INDUSTRY	AVERAGE HOURLY EARNINGS 1945	AVERAGE HOURLY EARNINGS 1953	INCREASE 1945–53 ¢	INCREASE 1945–53 %	INCREASE IN EMPLOYMENT 1945–53	RANK 1945	RANK 1953	% OF MANUFACTURING AVERAGE 1945	% OF MANUFACTURING AVERAGE 1953
Mining	85.0¢	153.8¢	68.8	81	36%	—	—	—	—
Metal mining	85.0	156.5	71.5	84	51	—	—	—	—
Coal	93.8	150.4	56.6	60	–19	—	—	—	—
Construction	73.5	143.7	70.2	96	120	—	—	—	—
Buildings and structures	80.9	156.8	75.9	94	193	—	—	—	—
Highways, bridges, and streets	63.2	112.8	49.6	78	41	—	—	—	—
Electric and motor transportation	n.a.	135.1	—	—	n.a.	—	—	—	—
Services	43.0	78.2	35.2	82	34	—	—	—	—
Hotels and restaurants	41.3	77.8	36.5	88	29	—	—	—	—
Laundries and dry-cleaning plants	46.9	75.1	28.2	60	17	—	—	—	—
Manufacturing	69.4	135.8	66.4	96	13	—	—	—	—
Durable goods	76.7	147.1	70.4	92	n.a.	—	—	—	—
Nondurable goods	60.7	122.9	62.2	102	n.a.	—	—	—	—
[Transportation equipment]	[86.9]	[156.9]	[70.0]	[81]	[–5]	—	—	[125]	[116]
Railroad and rolling-stock equipment	86.3	157.1	70.8	82	16	1	7	124	116
Shipbuilding and repairing	86.3	145.3	59.0	68	–54	2	9	124	107
Aircraft and parts	85.2	157.7	72.5	85	–6	3	6	123	116
Products of petroleum and coal	83.8	180.9	97.1	116	37	4	1	121	133
Smelting and refining	77.5	165.1	87.6	113	65	5	2	112	122
Printing, publishing, and allied industries	75.8	157.9	82.1	108	39	6	5	109	116
[Iron and steel products]	[75.1]	[152.9]	[77.8]	[104]	[11]	—	—	[108]	[113]
Agricultural implements	75.0	160.7	85.7	114	18	7	4	108	118
Aluminum products	74.9	141.4	66.5	89	45	8	15	108	104
[Nonferrous metal products]	[73.8]	[152.0]	[78.2]	[106]	[16]	—	—	[105]	[112]
Machinery manufacture	72.1	145.4	73.3	102	30	9	8	104	107
Rubber products	71.9	142.6	70.7	98	2	10	14	104	105
Pulp and paper mills	71.8	161.6	89.8	125	35	11	3	103	119
Electrical apparatus and supplies	70.5	143.2	72.7	103	69	12	13	102	105

Table 114. Wage Changes in Selected Industries, Canada, 1945–53 (Continued)

*INDUSTRY	AVERAGE HOURLY EARNINGS		INCREASE 1945–53		INCREASE IN EMPLOYMENT 1945–53	RANK		% OF MANUFACTURING AVERAGE	
	1945	1953	¢	%		1945	1953	1945	1953
Chemical products	68.4	138.0	73.2	102	−16	13	16	99	102
Meat products	67.9	144.3	76.4	113	−2	14	10	98	106
Distilled and malt products	67.8	143.6	75.8	111	30	15	11.5	98	106
[Paper products]	[67.7]	[151.2]	[83.5]	[123]	[34]	—	—	[98]	[111]
Sheet-metal products	66.7	143.6	76.9	115	15	16	11.5	96	106
[Nonmetallic mineral products]	[65.6]	[135.0]	[69.4]	[106]	[56]	—	—	[95]	[99]
Grain-mill products	62.6	127.7	65.1	104	22	17	20	90	94
Saw and planing mills	62.0	128.8	66.8	108	32	18	19	89	95
Glass and glass products	61.1	131.3	70.2	115	46	19	17	88	97
[Wood products]	[60.5]	[120.7]	[60.2]	[100]	[22]	—	—	[87]	[89]
[Food and beverages]	[59.0]	[115.5]	[56.5]	[96]	[16]	—	—	[85]	[85]
Furniture	57.9	109.9	52.0	90	28	20	24	83	81
Medicinal and pharmaceutical preparations	56.5	113.7	57.2	101	13	21	22	81	84
Other paper products	55.3	119.9	64.6	117	31	22	21	80	88
Bread and other bakery products	53.1	103.9	50.8	96	20	23	26	77	77
[Clothing (textile and fur)]	[53.0]	[95.3]	[42.3]	[80]	[21]	—	—	[76]	[70]
[Leather products]	[52.2]	[96.4]	[44.2]	[85]	[1]	—	—	[75]	[71]
Tobacco and tobacco products	51.3	129.4	78.1	152	−15	24	18	74	95
Canned and preserved fruits & vegetables	50.1	98.1	48.0	96	5	25	28	72	72
Boots and shoes (except rubber)	49.8	92.6	42.8	86	8	26	30	72	68
[Textile products (except clothing)]	[49.7]	[107.5]	[57.8]	[116]	[9]	—	—	[72]	[79]
Synthetic textiles and silk	49.6	109.8	60.2	121	36	27	25	71	81
Woolen goods	49.2	102.1	52.9	107	−2	28	27	71	75
Cotton yarn and broad-woven goods	48.5	110.1	61.6	127	2	29	23	70	81
Knit goods	47.4	95.3	47.9	101	2	30	29	68	70

* The industries in brackets are broad categories, some of whose subgroups are also included in the list.

Source: Dominion Bureau of Statistics. Annual Review of Man-Hours and Hourly Earnings, 1945–1953, p. 10

the industries showing unusually large increases during the postwar period have tended to be highly concentrated and quasi-monopolistic, and also strongly unionized. We may note particularly the high degree of union organization in basic steel, farm machinery, pulp and paper, meat packing, and tobacco. These industries show wage increases for 1945–53 which are well above average, and tobacco is the only manufacturing industry in which Canadian wage levels appear to be fully equivalent to those in the United States. The petroleum products industry, which also show a wage increase well above average, is not strongly unionized, but the leading producer is reputed to follow a high-wage policy in part as a means of forestalling union organization. There are also a considerable number of civilian industries whose output and employment were curtailed during the war and whose wage increases lagged behind the general average. During the postwar years these industries experienced a sudden expansion of their markets, production and employment rebounded, and it was natural to expect that their wage levels would make up some of the losses of the war years. Industries in this category include printing and publishing, pulp and paper, liquors, cotton yarn and cloth, and synthetic textiles.

The industries showing the smallest percentage increase in hourly earnings during the postwar period were, reading up from the bottom, coal mining, metal mining, shipbuilding and repairing, clothing, railroad rolling stock and equipment, leather products, aircraft, and aluminum products. In the case of coal mining natural resources are of key importance. The quality of Canadian coal is not high, being limited largely to the softer bituminous and subbituminous coals, and the principal deposits (in Alberta, British Columbia, and Nova Scotia) are located far from the main industrial centers. Production and transport costs of coal are sufficiently high that Canadian industry has tended to shift to hydroelectric power wherever possible and has also turned increasingly to imported coal. Employment in Canadian coal mining dropped by one-quarter between 1946 and 1953, the industry was in serious financial difficulties, and the United Mine Workers was able to make only limited progress on wages despite an aggressive policy and severe strikes.

The figures for metal mining reflect the declining position of the gold mining industry, which stood at the bottom of the labor priorities list during the war, lost a large part of its labor force, and made no comeback in the postwar period.[12] The small wage increases in shipbuilding,

12. Copper, nickel, lead, and zinc mining, on the other hand, improved their relative position in the postwar period. See Alex Shelton, "The Canadian Mining Industry Today," in *The Annals of the American Academy of Political and Social Science,* 253 (Sept. 1947), 66–80.

aircraft, and aluminum seem adequately explained by the sharp contraction of production in these industries after the war.

In most cases, then, one can find a reasonable economic explanation for divergent wage developments over the years 1945 to 1953. The developments of this period were in part a reversal of developments during the war years. Peacetime industries which had lagged during the war now shot ahead, while a considerable number of "war babies" dropped back. Certain industries, however, lagged behind in both periods (gold mining, leather products), and a few gained in both periods.

The change in the relative ranking of industries between 1945 and 1953 is shown in columns 7 and 8 of Table 11-4. The reshuffling of rankings was accompanied by a further moderate drop in interindustry dispersion, the quartile deviation falling from .153 in 1945 to .122 in 1953.

Looking beyond manufacturing to other sectors of the economy one finds a similar tendency for wartime developments to be reversed and for the wage structure to shift back in the direction of the prewar relationships. The most striking case is that of agriculture. Farm wage rates rose by only 50 per cent between 1945 and 1953, compared with an increase of 96 per cent in manufacturing industry. The gap between farm and factory labor, which had been almost closed by 1945, opened out once more.

A similar development occurred in the service industries. These industries, which typically stand near the bottom of the wage structure, had been forced during the war to raise wages in competition with manufacturing industry and had come close to matching the rate of wage increase in manufacturing. With the relative loosening of the labor market after the war, these industries once more lagged behind. Average hourly earnings of service workers rose only 82 per cent between 1945 and 1953, compared with an increase of 96 per cent in manufacturing.

REGIONAL DIFFERENTIALS

In Canada, as in the United States, there are well-established regional differences in wages. The Pacific Coast stands at the top of the wage structure. Taking the average wage level of manufacturing in all Canada as 100, the index for British Columbia fluctuates between 110 and 120. Ontario, the manufacturing heart of the country, comes next with an index of 105 to 110. Quebec, the other principal manufacturing province, stands substantially below Ontario with an index in the neighborhood of 90. The Maritime Provinces of New Brunswick and Nova Scotia stand somewhat below Quebec. These relationships hold good whether one looks at 1939 or at 1953. The industrial wage structure, in short, slopes downward steadily from west to east, without the additional north-south dimension which complicates the pattern in the United States.

The reasons for these differences are known in a general way. British Columbia is, economically speaking, similar to the U.S. Pacific Northwest, and the reasons for the wage superiority of the two areas are much the same. British Columbia has built up its labor force mainly by immigration from other parts of Canada and from abroad. There is no large surplus of rural population which can be tapped to meet the needs of expanding industries. The region is rich in natural resources, which has made it a center for high-productivity industries such as metal mining, smelting and refining, logging, pulp and paper. Trade unionism is stronger than in any other part of the country. Comparisons with the high wage levels prevailing in lumbering, paper, and other industries in Washington and Oregon may have some influence on British Columbia levels. The B.C. differential is partly due to the heavy concentration of industry in the Vancouver metropolitan area, so that there is a size-of-community factor at work. After adjusting for this, however, one still finds a net differential in favor of the Pacific Coast.

The most important and troublesome differential is that between the major manufacturing provinces of Ontario and Quebec.[13] In many industries plants located in Ontario compete directly with plants in Quebec, and the existence of wage differentials of 10 to 20 per cent has been a source of concern to both employers and union leaders. The sources of Quebec's wage inferiority are similar to the sources of low wages in the southern United States. It is scarcely pressing the analogy too far to say that Quebec is "the South" as far as Canada is concerned.

The Quebec differential, like the B.C. differential, is due partly to differences in community size. The Montreal metropolitan area is the only large manufacturing city in Quebec, while Ontario has Toronto, Hamilton, Windsor, London, Oshawa, Kitchener, and a number of other centers. Quebec's industrial composition also tends to produce a lower average wage level because it is lacking in basic steel, automobiles, automotive equipment, and a number of other durable-goods industries.

Correcting for these things, Quebec still stands lower industry by industry and community by community. How can this be explained? Surplus labor is certainly part of the answer. The high rate of natural increase among the French Canadian population produces a chronic

13. See Gilles Beausoleil, *Wages in Quebec and Ontario* (Montreal, the Canadian Congress of Labour and the Canadian and Catholic Confederation of Labour, 1954).

surplus of population beyond what can be absorbed in agriculture. Migration out of Quebec is a possible solution, and there has been considerable expansion into adjacent areas of Ontario, the Maritimes, and New England. There is reluctance, however, to migrate long distances to communities with a different language, religion, and cultural background. Excess labor supply accumulates and has a depressing effect on wage levels similar to that in the American South.

Other factors are operative. Data on output per worker suggest that there is a productivity differential adverse to Quebec. The relative weakness of union organization in Quebec may also help to account for its lower wage level. The French Canadian culture appears resistant to aggressive trade unionism.

The Ontario-Quebec differential, like the North-South differential in the United States, varies markedly among industries and occupations. In 1953 average hourly earnings in Ontario exceeded those in Quebec by only 6.7 per cent in cotton textiles and 9.5 per cent in pulp and paper. At the other extreme the differential in favor of Ontario was 18.4 per cent in chemical products, 22.8 per cent in metal mining, and 31.4 per cent in highway, bridge, and street construction.[14] While we have not made a detailed analysis by occupational level, it seems clear that Ontario's superiority is considerably greater for common labor than for skilled workers.

The Maritime Provinces, which stand even below Quebec in the wage structure, are also an area of chronic population surplus. Mobility out of the area is low. In earlier days there was considerable migration to the New England states, as well as to western Canada. With the relative decline of the New England economy and the settlement of the Prairie Provinces, the possibilities in these directions have diminished. Industrial development in the Maritimes is hampered by geographical remoteness and consequent high transportation costs to other regions, by the limited size of the local market, and by other cost disadvantages vis-à-vis central Canada. The traditional industries of the region—agriculture, fishing, coal mining—have shown little expansion in recent years or have actually declined. This combination of circumstances tends to produce downward pressure on wage levels.

The war years brought important shifts in interregional wage relationships. This was due partly to the fact that war industry was heavily concentrated in certain provinces. Over three-quarters of those employed in war manufacturing in July 1944 were in Quebec and Ontario. The percentage of employees in each province who were engaged in war manufacturing was as follows: Prince Edward Island, 7.2 per cent; New Brunswick, 13.8 per cent; Nova Scotia, 26.5 per cent; Quebec, 31.5

14. *Ibid.*

per cent; Ontario, 34.3 per cent, Manitoba, 18.6 per cent; Saskatchewan, 5.9 per cent; Alberta, 9.3 per cent; and British Columbia, 31.2 per cent.[15]

The shifts in the relative position of the various provinces between 1939 and 1945 are shown in Table 11-5. Ontario, a high-wage area before the war, fell slightly in relative standing. British Columbia, the other traditional high-wage area, just maintained its position. At the bottom of the wage structure, the three Maritime Provinces rose sharply.

Table 11-5. Average Hourly Earnings * in Manufacturing, by Province as Per Cent of Canadian Average, 1939, 1945, and 1953 (men)

	% of all Canada Average		
	1939	1945	1953 †
Prince Edward Island	56	81	—
Newfoundland	—	—	94
Nova Scotia	81	99	87
New Brunswick	78	86	85
Quebec	88	93	91
Ontario	108	105	105
Manitoba	114	97	97
Saskatchewan	93	94	96
Alberta	103	96	100
British Columbia	112	113	116
ALL CANADA	100	100	100

* Hourly rated wage earners.

† The figures for 1953 are not, strictly speaking, comparable to those for 1939 and 1945, since both the classification of industries and method of wage survey were changed between 1945 and 1953. However, these changes are probably of minor importance where we are only comparing broad provincial averages.

Source: Dominion Bureau of Statistics

The fact that Nova Scotia pulled up more rapidly than New Brunswick was doubtless due to the fact that Nova Scotia had twice as large a percentage of its workers engaged in war industry. Quebec, which had a heavy concentration of war industry, also pulled up substantially, and the Ontario-Quebec differential was cut almost in half. The Prairie Provinces had little war industry. The drain of population from these provinces and the tripling of farm wage rates put upward pressure on industrial wages. These factors were nevertheless insufficient to prevent

15. Calculated from Table 6 in *Changes in Population and in the Labour Force*, p. 26.

a decline in the relative standing of Alberta and Manitoba,[16] while Saskatchewan about held its own.

During the postwar period there was a tendency for interregional differences to widen and for traditional relationships to reassert themselves. Between 1945 and 1953 the standing of Nova Scotia dropped sharply while that of New Brunswick and Quebec fell moderately. One reason is that well over half of the war industry employment in Quebec and Nova Scotia was in munitions, shipbuilding, and aircraft. These industries were difficult to reconvert to peacetime use and suffered a spectacular drop in employment after the war. The curtailment of these industries produced a greater labor surplus in Quebec and the Maritimes, where they employed over one-half of the war industry labor force, than in Ontario, where only one-third of war manufacturing employment was in these sectors. The high rate of natural increase in Quebec and the Maritimes also came back into play as the possibilities for migration which had existed during the war were removed. Since 1945 the industrial centers of Quebec and the Maritimes have shown up among the looser labor-market areas in the classification maintained and published regularly by the Dominion Department of Labour.

In Ontario and British Columbia, on the other hand, local labor markets have consistently been tighter than in other parts of the country. It is not surprising, therefore, that the relative wage position of these provinces rose between 1945 and 1953. The Prairie Provinces maintained their position in the middle of the wage structure without substantial change, indicating a continued high level of agricultural wages and a rapid expansion of nonagricultural employment, particularly in Alberta.

Over the whole period 1939–53 the geographical wage structure shows an accordion-like movement, narrowing appreciably during the war years, widening again since the war. This phenomenon seems attributable basically to economic forces. The differentials existing in 1939 have an economic rationale, the wartime narrowing is understandable in terms of labor force and employment shifts, and the course of events since the war can also be related to the relative tightness of different labor markets. Wage relationships changed approximately as they "should" have changed on economic grounds.

Trade unionism has not as yet had a marked leveling effect on regional

16. The high index for Manitoba in 1939 is partially spurious. It is heavily weighted by the inclusion of the high-wage CPR and CNR main repair shops in Winnipeg and St. Boniface. A comparison limited strictly to manufacturing would show Manitoba in a considerably lower position. This distortion does not exist to the same extent in 1945 because by that time other branches of manufacturing had expanded sufficiently to have greater weight in the over-all index.

differentials. A union can operate on geographical wage differences only within a particular industry. In many Canadian industries one can scarcely speak of a geographical wage structure because production is so highly concentrated. They are usually limited to part of a province or at most two or three provinces. Where production covers both Ontario and Quebec, this usually means that at least two unions are involved in the industry, which makes it difficult to secure a coordinated policy. The only cases in which collective bargaining has brought any approach to wage uniformity are basic steel and meat packing. In basic steel there are only three plants, one in Nova Scotia and two in Ontario, and the United Steelworkers have succeeded in bringing these plants to approximately the same wage level. The meatpacking industry is unionized throughout the country by the Packinghouse Workers Union. In 1954 the highest base rate in the country, $1.41 per hour in British Columbia, was only slightly above the lowest rate of $1.31 in the Maritimes, with Toronto standing at $1.37. Regional differences have not been completely eliminated, but they have been reduced to a more moderate level than prevails in manufacturing generally. These two cases are the exception; regional wage diversity is still the general rule.

OTHER TYPES OF DIFFERENTIAL

Data on the relative earnings of men and women workers relate only to manufacturing, but it seems likely that trends in nonmanufacturing industries have been similar. In 1939 women's average hourly earnings in manufacturing were 61 per cent of men's earnings. During the war this ratio rose to a peak of 67 per cent in 1944, dropped to 62 per cent with the demobilization of war industries in 1945–46, and has remained at about this level ever since. Once again we find an accordion-like movement, a narrowing of differentials during the war followed by an expansion after the war.

This movement does not seem to have been due mainly to changes in women's rates relative to men's rates in the same occupation, but rather to changes in the range of occupations open to women. The proportion of manufacturing work performed by women rose during the war from 22.0 per cent in 1939 to 28.6 per cent in 1944, as more and more men were withdrawn for military service. This meant that many women were admitted to traditionally male occupations which were more skilled and better paid than the general run of women's work. Once admitted to these occupations and working in them alongside the men, women normally had to be paid the men's rate both as a matter of good personnel practice and of War Labour Board regulations which prescribed equal pay for equal work. Even where women entirely took over a previously male occupation, it was usually not feasible to reduce the customary position of the occupation in the wage hierarchy. The upgrading of women in terms of work done thus meant an upgrading in wage level and a closer approach to the level of men's earnings.

Table 11-6. Trends in Women's Wages and Employment, Canada, 1939–53

YEAR	AVERAGE HOURLY EARNINGS IN MANUFACTURING * (¢ PER HOUR)		DIFFERENCE A-B ¢ PER HOUR	RATIO OF FEMALE TO MALE	FEMALE WORKERS AS % OF ALL MANUFACTURING WORKERS
	A. MALE	B. FEMALE			
1939	46.2	28.3	17.9	61%	22.0%
1940	48.7	28.5	19.8	59	21.8
1941	53.8	31.6	22.2	59	22.6
1942	61.9	37.1	24.8	60	26.0
1943	67.1	43.1	24.0	64	28.2
1944	71.2	47.9	23.3	67	28.6
1945	73.6	46.5	27.1	63	26.3
1946	80.7	50.2	30.5	62	23.4
1947	92.1	58.2	33.9	63	22.3
1948	102.3	65.1	37.2	64	22.0
1949	106.6	68.3	38.3	64	22.4
1950	114.2	72.5	41.7	63	22.5
1951	131.3	82.5	48.8	63	22.0
1952	140.2	86.3	53.9	62	21.7
1953	147.1	91.0	56.1	62	22.1

* Hourly rated wage earners.

Source: Dominion Bureau of Statistics, Earnings and Hours of Work in Manufacturing, annual surveys; Annual Review of Employment and Payrolls, 1953, p. 5; "Prices and Wages," Report of the Royal Commission on Prices, 2 (Ottawa, 1949), 183

At the end of the war these processes were thrown into reverse. As women withdrew from the labor force because of layoffs, marriage, and other reasons, the proportion of women workers in manufacturing quickly dropped back to the prewar level. Some of the high-wage jobs on which women had been employed during the war simply disappeared. Other jobs were taken back by male workers who had customarily done them in the past. Thus the level of work done by women fell and this was reflected in an increased gap between male and female earnings.

The difference between male and female earnings varies considerably from industry to industry, reflecting mainly the division of duties in each case. In 1952, women earned only half as much as men in printing and publishing, where the men are high-skilled craftsmen while women are admitted only to low-skilled jobs such as bindery work. In tobacco manufacturing, on the other hand, where women form a high proportion of the production workers, women earned 80 per cent as much as men in 1952.

CONCLUDING OBSERVATIONS

The most striking feature of the Canadian case is the extent to which the developments of the war years were either reversed or arrested after the war. Interregional differences narrowed during the war but widened again after 1945. The same is true of differences in the earnings of male and female workers. Agricultural earnings approached more closely to industrial earnings from 1939 to 1945, then fell away again after 1945. In the case of interindustry differentials within manufacturing, there is a similar breaking point at the end of the war. After 1939 many armament industries, though not all, surged ahead of the general average, and many civilian-goods industries were left behind. After the war the civilian industries surged ahead of some of the "war babies" dropped back to a lower rank. Only in the case of occupational differentials does movement seem to have continued in the same direction throughout the entire period. Even here, the shrinkage of differentials was appreciably retarded after 1945.

Canadian wage differentials as of 1953 remain quite wide relative to those in other countries. The highest-wage region in Canada stands about 40 per cent above the lowest-wage region (excluding Prince Edward Island, a small and predominantly agricultural province with little industrial development). Men earn on the average about 60 per cent more than women in manufacturing industries. Average hourly earnings in the highest-paid manufacturing industry are approximately double those in the lowest. Skilled workers typically earn about 50 per cent more, and in some cases 100 per cent more, than unskilled workers in the same industry. These differentials are extremely wide by European standards and are even wider at some points than those prevailing in the United States.

Canadian wage developments over the past fifteen years can be explained mainly as a natural response to economic impulses. We noted at the beginning of the chapter that collective bargaining is still imperfectly developed in Canada, and that government has little influence on the wage structure. One might expect to find the course of wages dominated by market forces, and this expectation is well sustained by the evidence. Repeatedly we have found labor demand and supply concepts helpful in interpreting shifts in differentials.

The Canadian case is one of a young and rapidly expanding economy, with large shifts occurring in the composition of labor demand and an unusual degree of decentralization and freedom in wage determination. One would expect to find substantial wage differentials of every type, and one would also expect rapid shifting of differentials prompted mainly by labor demand and supply developments. The fact that events seem to accord closely with these a priori expectations suggests that economic theories of wage determination retain a high degree of usefulness in analyzing liberal economies of the Canadian sort.

CHAPTER 12 *United States*

INFLUENCES ON WAGE DETERMINATION

MOST readers will already be familiar with wage-setting institutions in the United States. It will suffice here to recapitulate briefly some of the ways in which the American milieu differs from that of other countries, notably Great Britain and Sweden.

First, collective bargaining is less extensive than in Britain or the Scandinavian countries. Only about one-quarter of the national labor force, and perhaps one-half of urban manual workers, are union members. There is a considerable list of industries in which almost all employees are covered by collective agreements: coal mining, railroading, other branches of transportation, metal mining, longshoring, basic steel, automobile and aircraft manufacture, clothing manufacture, and numerous others. The commonest situation, however, is the partially unionized industry, where 40, 60, or 80 per cent of the workers are covered by collective agreements with a substantial nonunion sector remaining. In such industries the competition of nonunion firms at lower wage levels, plus the possibility that new firms may be established in nonunion areas, serves as a significant restraint on union wage policy. There are numerous instances in which a union, well established at one time, gradually lost its grip on the industry because of the growth of nonunion competition.

Second, bargaining units are more narrowly defined in the United States than in Britain or Scandinavia. The commonest situation is one in which a national union bargains with a single employer. The next commonest pattern finds a national union bargaining with local associations of employers. This is the typical situation in printing, building construction, longshoring, trucking and warehousing, men's and women's clothing manufacture, and most of the service industries. National bargaining exists, in effect though not in form, in railroad transportation and coal mining. It is found also in a few minor manufacturing industries (pottery, stoves, wallpaper, certain types of glassware). It is still rare, however, and there is no clear tendency for it to increase. Employers in the United States have typically opposed industry-wide bargaining, and many of the strongest unions seem quite content to deal with employers one at a time.

The great majority of collective agreements in the United States, unlike those in Britain, expire annually and must be renewed. There is no presumption that the old agreement will be extended until a new one is reached. On the contrary, negotiations are typically conducted with a strike deadline hanging over the heads of the parties. This imparts a certain nervousness and haste to American wage movements, and an expectation on the part of workers that wage increases will be forthcoming at least once a year. Unlike the case of Sweden, there is no regular "negotiating season." The expiration dates of certain key agreements—basic steel, automobiles, bituminous coal—tend to be watched rather closely and may lead to some bunching of negotiations in other industries at about the same time. During any month of the year, however, one will find hundreds of agreements running out and many important negotiations in progress. It is not possible to separate successive rounds of wage increases with any precision. The process is a continuous one, and the curve of average hourly earnings rises rather smoothly over the course of time.

Third, American collective bargaining is decentralized in the sense that each national union charts its own course. There is a certain amount of informal consultation, emulation, and rivalry among unions in the same or neighboring industries. A pattern established by one union in a particular year may be virtually binding on another union, especially if the two are rivals for the same clientele. Apart from competitive emulation, however, there is no central coordination of wage policy by the top federations. The tradition of autonomous action by each national union is very strong, and the federations have only such limited authority as will enable them to establish clear demarcation lines among unions and to further labors legislative objectives. Any effort to influence the wage policy of a particular union would certainly fail.

Fourth, the government plays a smaller role in wage determination in the United States than in most other countries. During World War II, the government intervened actively through the National War Labor Board, which had what amounted to powers of compulsory arbitration in industrial disputes and also power to control voluntary wage increases. The operations of the NWLB not merely restrained the rise of the general wage level but also affected wage structure in a variety of ways. The Wage Stabilization Board, which operated during the Korean war, had similar but rather milder effects.

During peacetime the influence of government is felt mainly through: 1. minimum wage rates set by federal and state legislation, which since 1940 have tended to lag behind the actual progress of wages. The federal minimum wage of 75 cents per hour in 1954 was so far below the level of earnings in most industries as to have little coercive effect; 2. "prevailing-wage" clauses in government contracts. The prevailing wage tends to be interpreted as the union scale where one exists, and this reinforces the wage levels set through collective bargaining; 3. the wage and salary scales paid to government employees who now number several millions. These tend also to be adjusted to those prevailing in private employment in the locality in question. In each of these respects government tends to be a wage follower rather than a wage leader, accommodating itself to the movement of rates in the private economy.

EVOLUTION OF THE NATIONAL WAGE STRUCTURE

In this as in previous chapters we shall concentrate primarily on the period 1939–54; but we shall occasionally refer to earlier periods where adequate evidence is available.

THE ECONOMIC CONTEXT

Throughout the thirties the United States had an unemployment rate considerably higher than that of other countries. In 1938 more than ten million people, or about 20 per cent of the civilian labor force, were totally unemployed. With the beginning of military production in 1940 unemployment shrank rapidly and fell to about 1 per cent of the labor force at the peak of war activity. The years 1945–54 were years of almost continuous high employment and economic expansion. Unemployment fluctuated between two and three million, which means between 3 and 5 per cent of the labor force, rising above the upper figure only during the mild recessions of 1949–50 and 1953–54. The labor market from 1945 to 1954 was almost continuously a tight market, and conditions were favorable for money wage increases.

Between 1938 and 1952 the civilian labor force increased by 15 per cent, employment by 39 per cent, and industrial output by 147 per cent. A more reliable indication of the increase in total production is provided by gross national product, measured in constant prices, which rose by 110 per cent between 1938 and 1952. Even after adjusting for the substantial increase in population, GNP per capita increased by 73 per cent. A considerable part of this increase went for military purposes and for capital formation, but per capita private consumption rose by 43 per cent, making possible a substantial advance in living standards.[1]

The degree of inflation was almost precisely the same as in Britain and Sweden. The retail price level in 1954 stood about 93 per cent above the 1939 level. The movement of average hourly earnings in

1. OEEC, *Statistics of National Product and Expenditure, 1938, 1947 to 1952,* p. 94.

manufacturing, the consumer price index, and real hourly earnings from 1939 to 1954 are shown in Table 12-1. The money wage level roughly tripled while the price level doubled, so that real hourly earnings advanced by some 50 per cent.

Table 12-1. *Average Hourly Earnings, Cost of Living, and Average Real Hourly Earnings in Manufacturing, United States, 1929–54 (1939 = 100)*

	AVERAGE HOURLY EARNINGS	COST OF LIVING	REAL AVERAGE HOURLY EARNINGS
1929	89	123	72
1930	87	120	73
1931	81	110	74
1932	71	99	72
1933	70	93	75
1934	84	96	88
1935	87	99	88
1936	87	100	88
1937	98	104	95
1938	99	101	98
1939	100	100	100
1940	104	101	104
1941	115	106	109
1942	135	117	115
1943	152	125	122
1944	161	127	127
1945	162	130	125
1946	171	141	122
1947	196	160	122
1948	213	173	124
1949	221	172	129
1950	231	173	134
1951	252	188	135
1952	264	191	138
1953	279	193	145
1954 (Aug.)	283	193	147

Source: BLS *Monthly Labor Review*, 76 (March 1953), 345 for cost of living; *Handbook of Labor Statistics, 1950*, p. 59 for average hourly earnings

OCCUPATIONAL DIFFERENTIALS

A major development of the years since 1939 has been the rise in the earnings of manual workers relative to those of white-collar workers. This trend is generally recognized to have occurred, but since our statistics of salaries are less abundant and regular than those for wages it is difficult to document satisfactorily.

A study of data for 1939 concluded that the annual earnings of white-collar workers in that year were 38 per cent above those of manual workers.[2] McCaffree also found that the premium for white-collar work had been falling for fifty years or so prior to 1939, mainly because of a rapid increase in the number of high school graduates, most of whom aspire to white-collar work, and the taking over of an increasing proportion of office work by women.

The shrinkage of the differential in favor of white-collar employment continued at an accelerated rate after 1939. Between 1940 and 1943, average weekly earnings in manufacturing establishments covered by the state unemployment compensation systems increased by 71 per cent, while weekly earnings in the industries containing a predominance of white-collar workers (retail trade, banking, insurance) rose by only 21 per cent. In the federal government, white-collar workers in the executive branch gained only 15 per cent between 1939 and 1943, while manual workers increased their earnings by some 75 per cent.[3] Since the end of the war, white-collar workers seem about to have held their own; but they have been unable to recover the losses of the war years. Average annual earnings per full-time employee in finance, insurance, and real estate stood at 129 per cent of the manufacturing average in 1939 but had fallen to 99 per cent by 1950. Employees in public education earned 103 per cent as much as manufacturing workers in 1939 but only 89 per cent as much in 1950. For retail trade and automobile services the ratio fell from 90 per cent in 1939 to 85 per cent in 1950.[4]

One additional piece of evidence may be cited. The Sample Survey of Consumer Finances conducted annually for the Federal Reserve Board found that the median annual income in 1952 was $3,850 for people in the "clerical and sales" category, and $4,000 for those in the "skilled and semi-skilled category." [5] This suggests that most skilled workers and a substantial proportion of the semiskilled have now pulled ahead of the white-collar group. It is interesting also that the 1952 relationship between the two groups is almost exactly the same as that shown by the first survey conducted in 1946. The white-collar workers do not appear to have made up any of their wartime losses during the postwar years,

2. K. M. McCaffree, "The Earnings Differential between White Collar and Manual Occupations," *Review of Economics and Statistics, 25* (February 1953) 20–30.

3. BLS, Bulletin 783 (Washington, 1944). This bulletin contains further details on the period.

4. U. S. Department of Commerce, *Survey of Current Business, National Income Supplement, 1951* (Washington, 1951) pp. 184–5.

5. Board of Governors of the Federal Reserve System, *1953 Survey of Consumer Finances* (reprinted from the *Federal Reserve Bulletin*, March–Sept. 1953), p. 9.

which suggests that we have to deal with a permanent shift in differentials rather than a mere lag in adjustment.

Turning to wage relationships within the manual occupations, we find once more a substantial decline in differentials over the course of time. The most intensive study of this subject is that of Harry Ober, covering selected manufacturing industries over the period 1907–47.[6] The technique used was to calculate, for a particular industry in a particular year, an average wage rate for a representative group of skilled occupations and a similar average for typical unskilled occupations. The skilled rate was then reduced to a percentage of the unskilled rate, yielding what Ober terms an "occupational index." After this had been done for all industries for which data were available, a frequency distribution of the occupational indexes for each year was prepared and analyzed. Both the basic data and the method of analysis are defective in certain respects. The industries included, for example, differ from one time period to the next depending on availability of material. The fact that the years chosen for scrutiny are in different cycle phases (e.g. 1918–19, a year of war boom, and 1931–32, a year of deep depression) has some distorting effect on the results.[7] The trends which appear from the study are so clearly marked, however, that they can probably be taken as roughly reliable.

A compact summary of Ober's results appears in Table 12-2. It is clear that occupational differentials in 1907 were strikingly wide. On the average the skilled wage level stood at 205 per cent of the unskilled. In one quarter of the industries studied the occupational index of the skilled workers was 280 per cent or more. Moreover, these figures do not show the full range between the lowest-paid and highest-paid jobs in each industry. The occupational index shows the difference between the average wage for a group of skilled jobs and the average wage for a group of unskilled jobs. The distance between highest and lowest job would obviously be greater than this.

Over the years since 1907 there has been a continued shrinkage of differentials, region by region, and for the country as a whole. By 1945–47 the average occupational index had fallen to 155, a decline of about one-half in the skilled worker's premium as compared with forty years earlier. The dispersion of occupational indexes has also been sharply reduced, the quartile deviation in 1945–47 being only

6. Harry Ober, "Occupational Wage Differentials, 1907–1947," *Monthly Labor Review*, 67 (August 1948), 127–34.

7. For critical comments on the Ober study and some original contributions to the problem see Philip W. Bell, "Cyclical Variations and Trends in Occupational Wage Differentials in American Industry since 1914," *Review of Economics and Statistics*, 33 (November 1951), 329–37.

8.1 per cent compared with 24.4 per cent in 1907. Manufacturing industries now conform more closely to a standard size of skill differential, and industries with much larger differentials are rare. The variation in occupational differentials from region to region, which also stands out clearly from Table 12-2, will be examined below.

Table 12-2. *Relationship between Earnings of Skilled and Unskilled Occupations in Manufacturing, Selected Periods, United States, 1907–47, by Region* *

	OCCUPATIONAL INDEX	
	MEDIAN	RANGE (MIDDLE HALF ALL INDEXES)
United States		
1907	205	180–280
1918–19	175	150–225
1931–32	180	160–220
1937–40	165	150–190
1945–47	155	145–170
Northeast		
1907	200	175–245
1918–19	165	150–235
1931–32	175	155–215
1945–47	155	145–175
South		
1907	215	195–235
1918–19	195	175–230
1931–32	190	165–235
1945–47	170	150–195
Middle West		
1907	190	170–250
1918–19	175	145–235
1931–32	170	150–215
1945–47	150	140–165
Far West		
1907	185	165–200
1918–19	170	160–195
1931–32	160	145–170
1945–47	145	140–165

* See article for list of states in each region. Data for 1937–40 are inadequate to warrant presentation of separate regional indexes.

Source: Ober, "Occupational Wage Differentials, 1907–1947," p. 130

Data for nonmanufacturing industries are less plentiful, but Ober presents an interesting series for building construction. The movement of differentials in this industry is similar to that in the British industries

Table 12-3. Relationships between Union Wage Scales of Journeymen and Laborers and Helpers in the Building Trades, United States, 1907–52

YEAR	INDEX *	CENTS PER HOUR DIFFERENCE
1907	185	20
1908	188	21
1909	191	23
1910	192	25
1911	195	25
1912	197	26
1913	197	26
1914	199	27
1915	199	28
1916	199	29
1917	191	29
1918	183	30
1919	180	34
1920	166	41
1921	168	42
1922	174	42
1923	180	49
1924	180	53
1925	181	54
1926	177	56
1927	180	60
1928	179	60
1929	179	60
1930	177	62
1931	179	64
1932	179	54
1933	182	54
1934	178	52
1935	179	54
1936	175	53
1937	172	56
1938	170	60
1939	170	60
1940	169	61
1941	167	61
1942	160	61
1943	159	61
1944	158	61
1945	154	59
1946	147	59
1947	143	64
1948	140	67
1949	141	71
1950	139	71
1951	138	75
1952	138	79

* Average for laborers and helpers = 100.

Source: 1907–47: Ober, "Occupational Wage Differentials, 1907–47," p. 130; 1948–52: data from H. M. Douty, Chief, Division of Wages and Industrial Relations, Bureau of Labor Statistics

studied by Knowles and Robertson. Differentials shrank markedly during World War I, widened just after the war, and then settled down on a new plateau for most of the twenties and thirties. Differentials began to decline again in the late thirties, and the decline was accelerated during World War II and the postwar years. By 1947 the skilled man's premium stood at only 43 per cent, or considerably less than half the 1914 level. It is interesting also that the absolute differential between building craftsmen and laborers remained almost unchanged at around 60 cents an hour over the twenty years 1927–47,[8] again resembling the behavior found in many British industries.

There has been no equally intensive study of developments since 1947. Douty, however, has stated: [9]

> Recent studies by the Bureau indicate that by early 1953, further compression had taken place in relative occupational differentials. For example, the wages of skilled maintenance workers in manufacturing averaged only about 37 per cent above the level for male janitors in 20 large labor markets surveyed during late 1952 and early 1953. While this figure is not strictly comparable with the figure of 55 per cent given earlier for 1947, it unquestionably is illustrative of the general tendency. . . . In the building trades, the average union scale for journeymen in 1952 stood 38 per cent above the level for laborers and helpers as compared with 43 per cent in 1947.

It should be emphasized that the tendency toward reduction of skilled differentials has operated much more strongly in some industries than in others. In railway repair shops, machinists earned 107 per cent more than laborers in 1936. In 1953 they earned only 29 per cent more.[10] The advantage of the building-trades craftsmen dropped from 79 per cent in 1935 to 38 per cent in 1952.[11] In the printing industry, on the other hand, there was only a moderate drop in differentials. In 1938 the average union scale for hand compositors exceeded the average scale for bindery women by 127 per cent. In 1952 this differential stood at 101 per cent.[12]

Turning from craft industries to mass-production industries, one finds a striking contrast between basic steel and automobiles, which

8. Ober, "Occupational Wage Differences, 1907–1947," p. 130.

9. Harry M. Douty, "Union Impact on Wage Structures," *Proceedings of the Sixth Annual Meeting, Industrial Relations Research Association . . . 1953*, pp. 61–76.

10. Carriers' Exhibit 11, submitted to Board of Arbitration, 1954 Engineers' wage case.

11. See Table 12-3.

12. Douty, "Union Impact on Wage Structures," p. 71.

might have been expected to show similar tendencies. In 1922 automobile tool and die makers averaged about 55 per cent more than laborers; by early 1950 this advantage had fallen to 33 per cent.[13] In basic steel, on the other hand, occupational differentials have been remarkably well maintained. Blowers, for example, earned in 1920 about 83 per cent more than laborers in blast furnace departments. In 1951 they earned 80 per cent more.[14] These variations, which probably reflect differences in occupational structure and occupational trends in each industry as well as differences in union and management policies, could be explained only by careful industry case studies.

By the early fifties the tendency toward shrinkage of differentials had slowed down, and a new plateau period appeared to be developing. The differential in building construction did not narrow appreciably after 1950. Numerous other industries which had become accustomed to uniform cents-per-hour increases during the thirties and forties began to show increased concern for the skilled worker, and changed over either to percentage increases or to graduated cents-per-hour increases giving larger absolute amounts to the higher-paid groups. In 1949 and 1950, only about 20 per cent of the wage settlements reported to the Bureau of Labor Statistics provided larger increases for the skilled workers. By 1953 about 40 per cent of the settlements contained such provisions.[15] The United Automobile Workers have sought several special increases for the highly skilled tool and die makers. The United Steel Workers have made a deliberate and successful effort to maintain differentials during the postwar years. In 1953 for the first time skilled workers in the machinery industry actually increased their percentage differential over the unskilled.[16]

The marked decline of occupational differentials in recent decades has resulted from a variety of factors,[17] which were described in Chapter 7 and need only be recapitulated here: the cutting off of mass immigration after the early twenties; the diffusion of educational opportunities throughout the population, which has swelled the labor supply for skilled and white-collar occupations while depleting the supply of laborers; the fact that many skilled occupations are becoming less

13. *Ibid.,* p. 74.
14. *Ibid.,* p. 73.
15. Computed from BLS, *Monthly Report on Current Wage Developments* (mimeographed).
16. During the calendar year 1953, average hourly earnings of tool and die makers and production machinists advanced by 6.1% and 6.6% respectively, compared with 4.8% for laborers. BLS, Bulletin 1160 (*Wages and Related Benefits in the Machinery Industries,* Washington, 1954), p. 3.
17. For an illuminating discussion of this matter, see Douty, "Union Impact on Wage Structures."

skilled, arduous, and responsible than they used to be; the very high level of employment since 1940, which tends to raise low wages more rapidly than high wages; and the sharp rise in the money wage level, accomplished partly through flat-rate increases which have the necessary effect of compressing occupational differentials on a percentage basis.

It is an interesting question how far trade union wage policies have been an independent factor contributing to the shrinkage of occupational differentials. Clark Kerr concludes that the influence of unionism in this respect has been minor.[18] We would be inclined to give somewhat greater weight to union influence for reasons outlined in Chapter 7; but certainly most of the shrinkage is readily explicable on economic grounds.

We may conclude this section with a word about the pattern of occupational differentials at the present time. The last comprehensive study, that of Harry Ober, found that in 1945–47 workers in skilled occupations requiring an extensive learning period were earning on the average about 55 per cent more than people on light unskilled jobs. Semiskilled occupations involving some judgment and considerable experience were yielding about 35 per cent more than light unskilled work, while repetitive semiskilled work requiring little training yielded about 15 per cent more. Heavy unskilled workers also earned about 15 per cent more, on the average, than light unskilled workers.[19] If comparable data were available for 1954 it would undoubtedly appear that these differentials have diminished further since 1947. A study limited to certain occupations in manufacturing industries in late 1952 and early 1953 found that skilled maintenance workers averaged about 37 per cent more than men janitors at that time. Tool and die workers were the only workers studied whose earnings averaged more than 50 per cent above the janitor level.[20]

These averages present an extremely condensed and correspondingly inaccurate impression of the occupational wage structure. There is great variation of skill differentials from industry to industry, region to region, and even from plant to plant in the same city. It will be recalled from Table 12-3 that one-quarter of the industries studied by Ober had occupational indexes of less than 145 in 1945–47 while an-

18. See his paper to be published in the forthcoming report of the 1954 IEA conference on wage determination.

19. Ober, "Occupational Wage Differentials, 1907–47," p. 128. See also, by the same author, "Occupational Wage Differentials in Industry," in W. S. Woytinsky and Associates, *Employment and Wages in the United States* (New York, Twentieth Century Fund, 1953), pp. 466–74.

20. Toivo P. Kanninen, "Occupational Wage Relationships in Manufacturing, 1952–53," *Monthly Labor Review*, 76 (November 1953), 1171–8.

other one quarter had indexes above 170. The three highest indexes were for women's suits and coats (293), women's dresses (268), and precious jewelry (230). The three lowest were for leather tanning and finishing (134), mechanical rubber goods (134), and soap and glycerine (134).[21] Such differences reflect characteristics of the occupational structure in different industries. In industries where the unskilled work is difficult and unpleasant, or in which there are no highly skilled operations, the range of wage rates is considerably narrower than in industries marked by unskilled work of a light and undemanding nature.

There is also a systematic regional variation of skill differentials, which are largest in the Deep South and smallest in the Far West. Ober found in 1945-47 that the median percentage by which skilled rates exceeded the unskilled was 70 in the South, 55 in the Northeast, and 45 on the Pacific Coast. Kanninen's study in 1952-53 yielded generally similar results. Three of the four cities with largest skill differentials were southern cities, the other being New York. Four of the eight cities with lowest differentials were in the Far West. This results from the fact that earnings of skilled workers in the South compare fairly well with those of skilled workers in other regions, while rates for common labor are substantially lower in the South then elsewhere. The reasons for this will be examined in a later section on geographical differentials.

Even within the same city there is great variation in the size of skill differentials in different establishments. Kanninen found that the highest establishment percentage for maintenance electricians over unskilled labor exceeded the lowest establishment percentage by more than seventy-five points in each area studied. This illustrates the familiar phenomenon that employers in a city pay widely differing wage rates for any given job. Laborers' rates vary widely from plant to plant and electricians' rates also vary widely. This could still be consistent with uniformity of occupational differentials provided the pattern of interplant variation were the same for the two jobs. In practice this is not the case and skill differentials also vary widely from plant to plant.

INTERINDUSTRY DIFFERENTIALS

Before examining wage differences among urban industries it will be useful to say a word about one of the most striking differentials in the American economy, that between the urban wage level and the rural wage level. Tables 12-4 and 12-5 present information on the relative movement of rural and urban wage rates from 1914 to 1948. There is

21. Woytinsky and Associates, *Employment and Wages in the United States*, p. 759. This data, previously unpublished, was the basis of Table 2 in Ober, "Occupational Wage Differentials, 1907-1947," p. 129.

a marked difference in the behavior of the agricultural series and the urban series. The agricultural wage level is more flexible downward and is highly responsive to fluctuations in farm prices and incomes. During World War I farm wages rose at almost exactly the same rate as factory wages. When farm prices collapsed after the war, however, farm wage

Table 12-4. Index Numbers of Wage Rates of Farm Laborers and Factory Laborers, United States, 1914–29 (1914 = 100)

YEAR	FARM LABORERS' DAILY WAGE RATES, NO BOARD *	FACTORY LABORERS' HOURLY WAGES †
1914	100	100
1915	101	104
1916	110	118
1917	138	134
1918	178	175
1919	212	216
1920	242	255
1921	148	215
1922	144	198
1923	157	218
1924	160	225
1925	160	224
1926	162	227
1927	159	232
1928	159	233
1929	157	239

* Bureau of Agricultural Economics, Farm Wage Rates, Farm Employment and Related Data (1943), pp. 4–5.

† Data for 1914–20 from Federal Reserve Bank; data refer to hiring wage rates per hour paid to male unskilled laborers in N.Y. Data for 1921–29 refer to average hourly earnings of male unskilled laborers in manufacturing, base July 1914 is 100; see Wages, Hours and Employment in the U.S., 1914–1936, Table 4, pp. 52–6.

Source: David J. Ahearn, Jr., The Wages of Farm and Factory Laborers, 1914–1944 (New York, Columbia University Press, 1945), p. 227

rates fell much more sharply than those in industry. The decline between 1920 and 1922 was about 40 per cent in agriculture compared with only 20 per cent in manufacturing. Agriculture remained relatively depressed throughout the twenties and farm wages were virtually stationary, while the urban wage level rose gradually. The great depression of the 1930's brought a new collapse of farm prices, and farm wage rates once more fell drastically. They were cut in half between 1929 and 1932, compared with a drop of less than 20 per cent for factory laborers. There was some recovery in the late thirties, but it was sluggish compared with that in urban industry. In 1939 the money wages of farm laborers were only slightly above the 1914 level, and real wages were somewhat below 1914. Farm workers had made no progress dur-

Table 12-5. Average Hourly Cash Earnings of Farm Laborers, Workers in Manufacturing Industries, and Common Labor in Road Building, United States, 1929–54 *

	AVERAGE HOURLY EARNINGS DOLLARS PER HOUR			HOURLY EARNINGS OF FARM WORKERS AS PERCENTAGE OF	
YEAR	FARM LABORERS	WORKERS IN MANUFACTURING	COMMON LABOR IN ROAD BUILDING	WORKERS IN MANUFACTURING	COMMON LABOR IN ROAD BUILDING
1929	.239	.566	.39	42	61
1930	.222	.552	.39	40	57
1931	.173	.515	.36	34	48
1932	.128	.446	.32	29	40
1933	.113	.442	.38	26	30
1934	.126	.532	.42	24	30
1935	.137	.550	.41	25	33
1936	.148	.556	.40	27	37
1937	.168	.624	.40	27	42
1938	.166	.627	.40	26	41
1939	.164	.633	.42	26	39
1940	.168	.661	.46	25	36
1941	.205	.729	.48	28	43
1942	.267	.853	.58	31	46
1943	.351	.961	.71	37	49
1944	.419	1.019	.74	41	57
1945	.466	1.023	.78	46	60
1946	.503	1.086	.83	46	61
1947	.543	1.237	.91	44	60
1948	.580	1.350	1.02	43	56
1949	.559	1.401	1.13	40	49
1950	.561	1.465	1.19	38	47
1951	.625	1.59	1.27	39	49
1952	.661	1.67	1.41	40	47
1953	.672	1.77	1.49	38	45
1954	.661	1.80 †	1.53 †	37	43

* Earnings of farm laborers from the Division of Agricultural Economics. Earnings in manufacturing industries from the Bureau of Labor Statistics. Earnings of common labor in road building from the Public Roads Administration.

† Simple average of first 11 months of the year.

Source: Louis J. Ducoff, "Wages in Agriculture," in Woytinsky and Associates, Employment and Wages in the United States. Brought up to date and revised by Mr. Ducoff and the Division of Agricultural Economics, U. S. Department of Agriculture

ing an entire generation while the real wage level of factory workers had doubled.

Agricultural labor was rescued temporarily from this depressed condition by the high demand for farm products during World War II and the consequent rapid increase in agricultural prices and farm incomes. The farm wage level more than tripled between 1939 and 1946. The rise in urban industries was less rapid and the farm-city gap was considerably diminished. The average hourly earnings of farm workers rose from 26 per cent of the average for all manufacturing workers in 1939 to 46 per cent in 1946. A more relevant comparison with common labor in road building shows farm laborers rising from 39 per cent of road laborers in 1939 to 61 per cent in 1946. After 1946 the rate of increase in farm wages leveled off and the gap between farm and factory wage levels widened once more.[22]

Apart from the greater volatility of farm wage movements, the most striking fact which appears from the statistics is the chronic depression of farm wages relative to urban wages over the last several decades. It is difficult to judge just what kind of comparison is appropriate. It can be argued that most farm labor is relatively unskilled and that the appropriate comparison is with road labor, railway labor, or heavy unskilled work in manufacturing rather than with the full range of manufacturing occupations. It is also true that farm laborers work a longer week than factory workers, and regular farm laborers (as distinct from seasonal workers) probably get more weeks of work during the year, so that farm earnings compare more favorably on a monthly or annual basis than on an hourly basis. These things, however, affect only the size of the differential rather than its existence. Even if one chooses the basis of comparison most favorable to agriculture and takes the most favorable year in modern times (1946), the adverse differential remains strikingly large.

Several explanations of the differential can be dismissed as having little validity. It might be that farm laborers are simply less capable, on the average, than factory laborers. Gale Johnson, however, after a careful analysis of this question, concludes that there is no evidence of any substantial difference in natural ability.[23] It can also be pointed out that the rate of productivity increase has been slower in agriculture than

22. The best discussions of the rural-urban differential and its source are to be found in Ducoff, "Wages in Agriculture"; H. L. Parsons, *The Impact of Fluctuations in National Income on Agricultural Wages and Employment* (Cambridge, Harvard University Press, 1952); Ahearn, *The Wages of Farm and Factory Laborers, 1914–1944;* and Theodore W. Schultz, *The Economic Organization of Agriculture* (New York, McGraw-Hill, 1953).

23. D. Gale Johnson, "Comparability of Labor Capacities of Farm and Nonfarm Labor," *American Economic Review, 53* (June 1953), 296–313.

in industry. Ahearn estimates the increase in output per adult worker in agriculture from 1914 to 1939 at 43 per cent, compared with an increase of 129 per cent in output per man-hour in manufacturing.[24] In a fully competitive economy, however, there is no reason why the wage level of a particular industry should move parallel to the rate of productivity change in that industry. On the contrary, one would expect wages for a specified category of labor in different industries to move roughly parallel with each other at a rate determined by the rate of productivity increase *for the economy as a whole*.

The true reasons for the large rural-urban differential are rooted in the nature of the agricultural industry. On the one hand domestic demand for farm products has been rising only slowly for several decades, being dependent mainly on the rate of population increase. On the other hand, rural birth rates are relatively high and there is a constant tendency toward accumulation of excess population on the land. These divergent trends of demand and rural population mean that agriculture finds itself chronically overexpanded, a result which produces downward pressure on the incomes of farm operators and laborers alike.

Agriculture has twice been rescued from this dilemma by a wartime upsurge of economic activity, from 1914 to 1920 and 1939 to 1945. During these periods the high demand for labor in urban industries drew millions of people from farm to city, while farm prices and incomes rose at a spectacular rate. Thus a larger income was available to be divided among fewer people. With the return of peacetime conditions the chronic depression of agriculture has also returned. The "agricultural problem," as Schultz has argued persuasively,[25] is not really an agricultural problem at all but an urban problem. The problem is to maintain continuous high employment and a rapid rate of growth in the urban economy, which will at once strengthen the demand for farm products and draw excess population from the land at an adequate rate. Even a spectacularly large differential between urban and rural incomes is not by itself adequate to induce large-scale migration to the cities. Most people will refuse to exchange a low-income farm situation for unemployment in the city. Only an obvious abundance of employment opportunities in the city—accompanied, to be sure, by favorable income differentials—is adequate to induce migration on an adequate scale.

Turning to wage differences among nonagricultural industries, the most important source of information is the average hourly earnings data published regularly by the Bureau of Labor Statistics. The move-

24. Ahearn, *The Wages of Farm and Factory Laborers, 1914–1944*, p. 213.
25. Theodore W. Schultz, *Agriculture in an Unstable Economy* (New York, McGraw-Hill, 1945).

Table 12-6a. Comparison of Hourly Earnings in Selected Manufacturing Industries, United States, 1939-54 *

INDUSTRY	1939 EARNINGS	1939 RANK	1954 * EARNINGS	1954 * RANK	INCREASE, 1939–1954 ¢ PER HOUR	INCREASE, 1939–1954 %
Petroleum refining	.97	1	3.46	1	1.39	143
Tires and inner tubes	.96	2	2.29	3	1.33	139
Automobiles	.93	3	2.20	6	1.27	137
[All petroleum and coal products]	[.89]	—	[2.27]	—	[1.38]	[155]
All printing, publishing, and allied products	.87	4	2.27	4	1.40	161
Blast furnaces, steel works, rolling mills	.85	5	2.21	5	1.36	160
Aircraft engines and parts	.84	6.5	2.10	10	1.26	150
Tractors	.84	6.5	2.05	12	1.21	144
Computing machines, cash registers	.82	8	2.16	7	1.34	163
[All transportation equipment]	[.79]	—	[2.13]	—	[1.34]	[170]
Machine-tool accessories	.78	9	2.31	2	1.53	196
Engines and turbines	.77	10.5	2.13	9	1.36	177
Locomotives and parts	.77	10.5	2.15	8	1.38	179
Steel foundries	.76	12	1.99	13	1.23	162
[All rubber products]	[.75]	—	[1.95]	—	[1.20]	[160]
[All nonelectrical machinery]	[.75]	—	[2.01]	—	[1.26]	[168]
Machine tools	.75	13.5	2.08	11	1.33	177
Communication equipment	.75	13.5	1.73	30.5	.98	131
[All primary metal industries]	[.74]	—	[2.10]	—	[1.36]	[184]
Structural steel and ornamental metal work	.73	15	1.93	16	1.20	164
Glass and glass products	.72	16.5	1.81	25.5	1.09	151
Agricultural machinery (exc. tractors)	.72	16.5	1.90	19	1.18	164
Fur-felt hats and hat bodies	.71	18	1.74	29	1.03	145
[Durable goods]	[.70]	—	[1.91]	—	—	—
Gray iron foundries	.70	19.5	1.87	20	1.17	167

Table 12-6a. Comparison of Hourly Earnings in Selected Manufacturing Industries, United States, 1939–54 * (Continued)

INDUSTRY	1939		1954 *		INCREASE, 1939–1954	
	EARNINGS	RANK	EARNINGS	RANK	¢ PER HOUR	%
Primary nonferrous metals	.70	19.5	1.98	14	1.28	183
[All electrical machinery]	[.70]	—	[1.81]	—	[1.11]	[159]
Meat products	.69	21	1.86	21	1.17	170
Nonelectrical heating, cooking	.67	22.5	1.82	23.5	1.15	172
Malleable iron foundries	.67	22.5	1.92	17	1.25	187
Jewelry and findings	.66	24	1.53	42	.87	132
[All chemicals and allied products]	[.65]	—	[1.93]	—	[1.28]	[197]
Synthetic fibers	.65	25	1.82	23.5	1.17	180
Wool carpets, rugs, carpet yarn	.64	27.5	1.73	30.5	1.09	170
Millinery	.64	27.5	1.66	36	1.02	159
Silverware and plateware	.64	27.5	1.81	25.5	1.17	183
[All stone, clay, and glass products]	[.64]	—	[1.77]	—	[1.13]	[177]
Typewriters	.64	27.5	1.84	22	1.20	188
[Total manufacturing]	[.63]	—	[1.79]	—	—	—
Pottery and related products	.63	30.5	1.69	33	1.06	168
Leather products	.63	30.5	1.76	27.5	1.13	179
Bakery products	.62	32	1.67	34	1.05	169
[All food and kindred products]	[.61]	—	[1.64]	—	[1.03]	[169]
Rubber footwear	.61	33.5	1.66	36	1.05	172
Tin cans and other tinware	.61	33.5	1.97	15	1.36	223
Cutlery and edge tools	.60	35	1.65	38	1.05	175
Hardware	.59	37	1.91	18	1.32	224
Watches and clocks	.59	37	1.66	36	1.07	181
All paper and allied products	.59	37	1.76	27.5	1.17	198
[Nondurable goods]	[.58]	—	[1.65]	—	—	—

Table 12-6a. Comparison of Hourly Earnings in Selected Manufacturing Industries, United States, 1939–54 * (Continued)

INDUSTRY	1939		1954 *		INCREASE, 1939–1954	
	EARNINGS	RANK	EARNINGS	RANK	¢ PER HOUR	%
Radio, phonograph, TV sets and equipments	.58	39	1.70	32	1.12	193
Cigarettes	.56	40	1.63	39	1.07	191
Dyeing and finishing textiles	.54	41	1.51	43	.97	180
[All leather and leather products]	[.53]	—	[1.37]	—	[.84]	[158]
[All apparel and other finished textiles]	[.53]	—	[1.35]	—	[.82]	[155]
All furniture and fixtures	.52	42	1.57	41	1.05	202
Tobacco and snuff	.51	43	1.42	45	.91	178
All lumber and wood products (exc. furniture)	.49	44.5	1.58	40	1.09	222
Confectionery	.49	44.5	1.37	47	.88	180
[All tobacco manufactures]	[.48]	—	[1.29]	—	[.81]	[169]
Knitting mills	.47	46	1.30	48	.83	177
[All textile mill products]	[.46]	—	[1.36]	—	[.90]	[196]
Canning and preserving	.46	47	1.38	46	.92	200
Cigars	.42	48	1.15	49	.73	174
Fertilizers	.41	49	1.47	44	1.06	259
Shirts, collars, and nightwear	.40	50	1.13	50	.73	183

* August. The industries in brackets are broad categories. Some of their subgroups are also included in the list.

Source: BLS, Bulletin 916, Handbook of Labor Statistics 1948; and Monthly Labor Review, 77 (December 1954), 1393–1408.

ment of average hourly earnings in selected industries between 1939 and 1954 is summarized in Tables 12-6a and 12-6b. A more reliable basis for interindustry comparisons within manufacturing, however, is

Table 12-6b. Comparison of Average Hourly Earnings in Major Branches of Industry, United States, 1939 and 1954

	AVERAGE HOURLY EARNINGS		INCREASE, 1939–54	
INDUSTRY	1939	1954 *	¢ PER HOUR	PER CENT
Manufacturing				
Total	.63	1.79	1.16	183
Durable	.70	1.91	1.21	173
Nondurable	.58	1.65	1.07	184
Mining				
Metal				
Total	.71	2.05	1.34	189
Iron	.74	2.16	1.42	192
Copper	.68	2.01	1.33	196
Lead and zinc	.68	1.88	1.20	176
Coal				
Anthracite	.92	2.50	1.58	172
Bituminous	.89	2.48	1.59	179
Crude petroleum and natural gas	.87	2.27	1.40	161
Nonmetallic mining and quarrying	.55	1.77	1.22	222
Contract construction				
Building construction, total	.93	2.60	1.67	180
Trade				
Wholesale trade, total	.71	1.84	1.13	159
Retail trade				
General merchandise stores	.45	1.16	.71	158
Transportation and public utilities				
Class I railways	.71	1.92	1.21	170
Local railways and bus lines	.71	1.82	1.11	156
Telephone	.82	1.74	.92	112
Service				
Hotels, year-round	.32	.96	.64	200
Cleaning and dyeing plants	.49	1.19	.70	143

* August

Source: BLS, Bulletin 916, Handbook of Labor Statistics 1948; and Monthly Labor Review, 77 (December 1954), 1393–1408

the data on common-labor rates which were collected for many years by the National Industrial Conference Board. The movement of these rates from 1923 to 1946 is summarized in Table 12-6c.

Several conclusions can be drawn from this material. First, there has been some reduction of interindustry dispersion within manufacturing, though not such a sharp reduction as has occurred in France or Sweden. In the case of the average hourly earnings data, the quartile deviation fell from .12 in 1939 to .09 in 1953. The data on common labor rates show a fall in quartile deviation from .200 in 1939 to .140 in 1946.

Table 12-6c. Comparison of Average Hourly Earnings of Male Unskilled Labor at Selected Dates, United States

	1923		1939		1946	
INDUSTRY	EARNINGS	RK	EARNINGS	RK	EARNINGS	RK
Printing, newspapers and magazines	.540	1	.623	10	1.005	9
Rubber	.522	2	.673	3	1.222	1
Automobile	.496	3	.797	1	1.161	2
Paint and varnish	.494	4	.627	8	.959	11
Iron and steel	.484	5	.638	6	1.080	4
Chemical	.477	6	.694	2	1.082	3
Wool	.470	7	.524	16	.956	12
Foundry and machine shops	.469	8	.629	7	1.068	5
Agricultural implements	.450	9	.654	5	1.055	6
Leather and tanning	.442	10	.557	11	.935	15
Paper and pulp	.442	11	.540	13	.939	14
Printing, book and job	.442	12	.543	12	.998	10
Paper products	.435	13	.531	15	.868	19
Electrical manufacturing	.428	14.5	.669	4	1.036	7
Meat packing	.428	14.5	.624	9	1.021	8
Cotton (North)	.403	16	.494	17	.890	17
Furniture	.390	17	.536	14	.900	16
Lumber and mill	.369	18	.479	18	.948	13
Boot and shoe	.367	19	.434	20	.577	20
Hosiery and knit goods	.356	20	.458	19	.872	18

Source: Sumner H. Slichter, "Notes on the Structure of Wages," *Review of Economics and Statistics, 32* (February 1950), 85

Second, the relative ranking of various industries has not changed drastically particularly as measured by common-labor rates. The rankings shown in Table 12-6c show a rank correlation coefficient of .911 for 1939–46 and even over the longer period 1923–46 there is a coefficient of .710, indicating a considerable degree of stability in the interindustry wage structure. The rankings in terms of average hourly earnings might be expected to have shifted more drastically because of changes in the occupational structure and labor-force composition of each industry. Even here, Table 12-6a yields a rank correlation co-efficient of .897.

Third, despite this general stability there were certain industries whose wage levels rose much more or much less than the general average. It is interesting that the industries whose wage levels rose un-usually fast in Britain after 1939—coal mining, cotton textiles, and agriculture—showed the same tendency in the United States and for much the same reasons. Cotton textiles, long a low-wage industry, tended to lose labor during the war to industries with much higher wage levels and was forced to raise its own level to maintain a labor force. Coal mining also proved unattractive to the rising generation when there was an abundance of alternative opportunities, and higher wages were necessary to hold people in the coal fields. Starting from a relatively high level in 1939, coal wages achieved about the same percentage increase as did manufacturing wages, and their absolute increase was among the largest in the economy. Union pressure was present in both industries, but the indications are that it did not raise the industry wage level by any substantial amount.[26] In the case of agriculture, which we have al-ready examined, union pressure was entirely absent.

The industries showing a relatively low percentage increase in wage level from 1939 to 1954 were of two types: 1. industries whose wage level in 1939 was relatively high and whose increases, while they matched or exceeded those of other industries in absolute terms, fell short on a percentage basis. Examples are automobiles, tires and tubes, and petroleum refining; 2. industries with a preponderance of white-collar workers whose wage changes reflect the decline of white-collar salaries relative to the wage rates of manual workers. Examples are whole-sale and retail trade and telephone service.

There have been numerous efforts in recent years to develop a com-prehensive explanation of differential rates of increase in industry wage levels, particularly within manufacturing. This was stimulated in part by the attempt of Arthur Ross to discover whether the degree of union organization in an industry has had an appreciable effect on its rate of wage increase. Other writers have explored the influence of productivity trends, profit levels, degree of industrial concentration, and other features of industrial structure.[27] All of these studies, except that by Slichter,

26. The case of cotton textiles is examined in Chap. 4. For a careful study of bituminous coal wage levels, see Albert Rees, "The Economic Impact of Collective Bargaining in the Steel and Coal Industries during the Postwar Period," *Proceed-ings of the Third Annual Meeting, Industrial Relations Research Association . . . 1950*, pp. 203–212.

27. See in this connection Arthur M. Ross, "The Influence of Unionism upon Earnings," *Quarterly Journal of Economics, 62* (February 1948), 263–86; John T. Dunlop, "Productivity and the Wage Structure," in *Income, Employment and Public*

have been based on average hourly earnings data. It is not feasible here to review each study in detail and to do full justice to the ingenuity of individual authors, but an examination of them yields several general impressions:

1. There appears to be a marked relation, at least within manufacturing, between the rate of increase of average hourly earnings in each industry and the rate of increase in output per man-hour. The studies of Dunlop and Garbarino, using somewhat different industries and time periods, both yielded high correlation coefficients.

2. A similar relation appears to exist between the rate of increase in earnings and the degree to which output is concentrated in a few firms. Garbarino's analysis of data for 1923–40 yielded a "Z" of 0.7702.[28]

3. When account has been taken of these two factors, there is probably some net relation between rate of increase of earnings and degree of unionization. This relation is not so strong or clear cut as in the first two cases. To the extent that it does exist, it appears to be an effect of new rather than of continuing unionism.[29] Lester and Robie, after a study of seven industries characterized by high unionization and regional or national collective bargaining, conclude: "Generally speaking, wage and earning levels do not appear to have risen more rapidly under national and regional bargaining than for manufacturing as a whole." [30]

4. There is marked intercorrelation among the variables of rate of increase in man-hour output, degree of concentration, and extent of unionization, and particularly between the last two. Garbarino obtained a "Z" of 0.893 for the relation between unionization and concentration, which was within the 1 per cent level of significance. This relation is not surprising, for once the core of employer resistance has been penetrated, full unionization of a highly concentrated industry is simpler than union-

Policy, Essays in Honor of Alvin H. Hansen (New York, Norton, 1948); Joseph Garbarino, "A Theory of Inter-Industry Wage Structure Variation," Quarterly Journal of Economics, 44 (May 1950), 283–305; Stanley Lebergott, "Wage Structures," Review of Economics and Statistics, 29 (November 1947), 274–85; Rees, "The Economic Impact of Collective Bargaining in the Steel and Coal Industries during the Postwar Period"; Arthur M. Ross and William Goldner, "Forces Affecting the Inter-Industry Wage Structure," Quarterly Journal of Economics, 64 (May 1950), 254–81; Slichter, "Notes on the Structure of Wages," pp. 80–91; and Stephen P. Sobotka, "Union Influence on Wages: the Construction Industry," Journal of Political Economy, 61 (April 1953), 127–43.

28. Garbarino, "A Theory of Inter-Industry Wage Structure Variation," p. 302.

29. Ross and Goldner, "Forces Affecting the Inter-Industry Wage Structure," p. 267. Note, however, that their conclusion that new unionism has been a source of wage advantage is based on an analysis of absolute rather than percentage wage increases; in percentage terms, the presumed advantage disappears.

30. Richard A. Lester and Edward A. Robie, Wages under National and Regional Collective Bargaining, p. 93.

ization of an industry containing scores or hundreds of small concerns. Many industries of the latter sort in the United States are less than half organized after thirty or forty years of union effort. The association of unionism with concentration seems mainly responsible for the fact that a simple correlation between rate of increase of earnings and degree of unionization yields a high positive coefficient. High concentration, in other words, tends to accompany *both* high unionization and a rapid rate of increase in earnings.

5. These facts seem to be compatible with a model of the following sort: a rapid rate of increase in man-hour output in an industry is likely [31] to be accompanied by a rapid reduction in total cost per unit of output. The benefits accruing in this way are available for division among purchasers of the product, employees, owners, and other factor suppliers. A high degree of concentration, with the accompanying control over prices, tends to reduce the extent to which cost reductions are passed on to purchasers of the product. It tends to insulate the industry against pressure from consumers, and to protect productivity gains on behalf of factor suppliers. A high degree (or a rapid rate) of unionization, in turn, may mean that more of the gains are passed on to workers and less to owners than would otherwise be the case.[32] It should be emphasized, however, that large, oligopolistic, and progressive firms seem in any event to follow a high-wage policy. Unionism has only an incremental, and probably a minor, effect on the outcome.

It seems reasonable to conclude that definitive findings are not yet available on the sources of change in the interindustry wage structure. They are indications that the influence of unionism has been weak relative to that of market forces. This conclusion may apply more strongly to manufacturing than to industries in which skilled-craft organization plays a more dominant role. Manufacturing has been almost overstudied in recent years, and it would be worth while to devote more attention to the various branches of transportation, communications, building construction, and some of the service industries.

GEOGRAPHICAL DIFFERENTIALS

There are long-standing differences in the wage levels of various regions of the United States. The southern states have traditionally been below the northeastern and midwestern states, while the Pacific Coast

31. This is only a probable, not a necessary, relationship. The usual man-hour output data reflect *gross physical productivity* rather than *net value productivity*, i.e. they do not take account of the added capital inputs which may be necessary to secure lower labor inputs per unit of product.

32. This view is similar to that developed in the interesting article by Joseph Garbarino to which reference has already been made.

has been substantially above any other part of the country. These regional differentials vary from one occupation and industry to another. It is therefore difficult and perhaps unwise to attempt any summary measure of their size. In agriculture, for example, wage rates in the southwestern states are about half of those in the Northeast, the precise differential varying with the type of farming in question and the method of wage payment. In manufacturing, a BLS study in 1945–46 found that the median relation of southern to northeastern wages for corresponding occupations was 85 per cent.[33] In book and newspaper printing and in the building trades, however, the difference is less than 10 per cent, and in bituminous coal mining there is scarcely any differential in earnings for corresponding work.[34] If forced to summarize, one could say that the urban wage level in the South averages out at something like 15 per cent under the Northeast, while the Pacific Coast is perhaps 15 per cent above the Northeast. The severe limitations of any summary figure, however, should be clearly realized.

It is also important to note that differences in wage rates or earnings among geographical regions are not necessarily due to "regional" influences. The North-South differential is largely a differential in rates of return to agriculture ånd to low-skilled urban occupations, and is much less important for skilled and white-collar work. It is also in part a white-Negro differential. The gap between rates for northern workers and white southern workers is considerably less than the gap for all northern and southern workers. The differential is influenced further by the smaller average size of city in the southern states. There is a marked positive relation within each region between wage level and community size. The fact that a larger proportion of southern industry is concentrated in relatively small communities makes for a lower average level of earnings in the South.

Any average statement about regional differentials reveals only a small part of the story. The significant fact is the wide variation of regional differentials among occupations and industries. Lester, who has done more work on the North-South differential than anyone else, notes that "Wage differentials between the South and the North and within both regions vary widely and irrationally from industry to industry and locality to locality." [35] On an occupational basis,

33. Joseph W. Bloch, "Regional Wage Differentials," *Monthly Labor Review,* 66 (April 1948), 375.

34. Harry Ober and Carrie Glasser, "Regional Wage Differentials," in BLS, *Trends in Wage Differentials, 1907–1947* (Washington, 1949), pp. 29, 31.

35. Richard A. Lester, "Trends in Southern Wage Differentials since 1890," *Southern Economic Journal, 11* (April 1945), 337. See also Lester's excellent summary article, "Southern Wage Differentials: Developments, Analysis, and Implications," *Southern Economic Journal, 13* (April 1947), 386–94.

it is clear that regional differentials widen as one goes down the occupational ladder. The BLS manufacturing study found that rates for skilled male occupations in the South averaged 91 per cent of those in the Northeast in 1945–46. For common labor, however, southern rates were less than 80 per cent of those in the Northeast.[36] In building construction, journeymen's rates in the South in 1945 varied from 90 to 100 per cent of those in the North, depending on the size of city. Rates for helpers and laborers, however, ranged from 69 per cent of northern rates in the larger cities to 87 per cent in small cities. In department stores, skilled work in the South paid 96 per cent as much as in the North. For unskilled work the percentage was only 77 per cent.[37] This confirms our observation in a previous section that occupational differentials are considerably wider in the South than in the North, and that this is due to the relatively depressed level of laborer's rates.

These conclusions based on hourly earnings data are in general agreement with information on annual earnings from census sources. The census indicates that, in 1939, median family incomes from wages and salaries for white families in the South relative to families in the Northeast were 91 per cent for families whose head was an independent proprietor, 89 per cent for professional families; 88 per cent for sales and clerical workers; 100 per cent for craftsmen and foremen; 84 per cent for operatives (semiskilled), 73 per cent for service workers (excluding domestic service), and 61 per cent for laborers, including farm laborers.[38] These figures are not adjusted for differences in community size between the two regions, which would raise all the percentages somewhat but would not destroy the gradation from higher to lower occupations.

The size of the North-South differential also varies widely from one industry to another. Studies made by the BLS in 1945 and 1946 showed that the ratio of average hourly earnings in the southern states to those in the Middle Atlantic states ranged from more than 95 per cent in some industries to less than 65 per cent in others. Among the industries showing largest differentials were upholstered furniture (63 per cent), structural clay products (67 per cent), sheet-metal work (61 per cent), footwear (68 per cent), and iron foundries (73 per cent). Industries showing very high ratios included cigars (100 per cent), pulp and paper mills (98 per cent), integrated cotton textile mills (92 per cent),

36. Bloch, "Regional Wage Differentials," pp. 371–7.
37. Ober and Glasser, "Regional Wage Differentials," p. 33.
38. Data cited in D. Gale Johnson, "Some Effects of Region, Community Size, Color, and Occupation on Family and Individual Income," in *Studies in Income and Wealth, 15* (New York, National Bureau of Economic Research, 1952), p. 59.

and seamless hosiery (93 per cent).[39] Examination of data on common-labor rates yields similar results. In 1942 the ratio of southern to northern common-labor rates was only 56.5 per cent in sawmills, 63.8 per cent in brick and tile works, 64.7 per cent in chemical plants, and 65.1 per cent in fertilizer plants. But the ratio was 82.5 per cent of the northern average in the glass industry, 86.1 per cent in leather, and 89.7 per cent in pulp and paper.[40]

Lester summarizes the situation as follows:

> The average North-South wage differential varies widely and irrationally from industry to industry. Such a differential is practically nonexistent in the various branches of the glass industry, aircraft production, rayon, bituminous coal, seamless hosiery, pulp and paper (excluding the west), and in many skilled trades. The average North-South differential is only 5 or 10 per cent of Northern rates in such industries as automobiles, oil, printing, work clothes, railroad transportation, men's shirts, and cotton textiles. Yet for furniture, full fashioned hosiery, rubber tires and tubes, and food products, the average southern wage is between 20 and 30 per cent below the average northern wage for all comparable jobs.[41]

There appear to be several reasons for these interindustry differences. First, the size of the North-South differential is inversely related to the wage level of the industry, i.e. the differential is largest in industries which are low-wage industries, throughout the country. In high-wage industries, on the other hand, the regional differential tends to be small. This distinction corresponds fairly closely with the distinction between hard-goods industries and soft-goods industries. Most of the soft-goods industries are characterized by numerous small producers, vigorous price competition, and a high ratio of labor cost to total cost. Wages are always under pressure, and in the South, with its chronic labor surplus and weak unionization, the downward pressure breaks through more readily than in the North.

Second, there is some tendency for the differentials to be small and to diminish over time in industries where the South is the dominant producer. Examples are cotton textiles and seamless hosiery, in both of which the South has around 80 per cent of total employment. In industries where only a minor part of total employment is in the South, differentials tend to be larger.

Third, collective bargaining has had a leveling effect on regional

39. BLS, *Trends in Wage Differentials, 1907–1947*, p. 27.

40. Richard A. Lester, "Diversity in North-South Wage Differentials," *Southern Economic Journal*, 12 (January 1946), 242.

41. Lester, "Southern Wage Differentials: Developments, Analysis and Implications," p. 387.

differentials in some cases, including cotton textiles, bituminous coal, pulp and paper, and basic steel. Nonunion industries tend to show larger differences between South and North. In some industries, finally, large wage differentials reflect basic differences in the type of product made and consequent differences in skill requirements. In the women's and

Table 12-7. *Median Regional Differences in Occupational Wage Rates in Manufacturing Industries, United States, by Skill and Sex, Selected Periods (wage rates for corresponding occupations in Northeast = 100)*

OCCUPATIONAL CATEGORY AND PERIOD	MEDIAN RELATION TO NORTHEAST (IN PER CENT)		
	SOUTH	MIDDLE WEST	FAR WEST
All Occupations			
1907	86	100	130
1919	87	97	115
1931–32	74	97	113
1945–46	85	101	115
Men's Occupations			
1907	88	100	131
1919	88	98	117
1931–32	74	97	114
1945–46	84	102	115
Men's Skilled Occupations			
1907	93	99	131
1919	95	98	*
1931–32	83	96	*
1945–46	91	101	113
Women's Occupations			
1907	*	*	*
1919	81	92	*
1931–32	73	*	*
1945–46	87	98	114

* Number of occupations covered too small to justify selection of median.

Source: Bloch, "Regional Wage Differentials"

misses' dress industry, for example, earnings in the Middle Atlantic states are more than double those in the South. The explanation lies partly in the difference between the highly styled and high-priced garments made in New York and the house dresses and other cotton garments which predominate in the South.

Have geographical wage differentials remained relatively constant, or have they tended to diminish over the course of time? Table 12-7 suggests that for manufacturing occupations the North-South differential in 1945–46 was considerably narrower than in 1931–32, but about

Table 12-8. Ratio of Southern to Northern Wages, United States, 1890–1944

YEAR	FOUNDRY & MACH. SHOP TRADES	BUILDING TRADES	COTTON TEXTILES	FARM WAGES	BLAST FURNACES	LUMBER	FURNITURE	HOSIERY SEAMLESS	HOSIERY FULL-FASHIONED
1890	114.3	94.9	59.6	78.1	74.6	71.3			
1891	113.1	94.1	58.4	76.1	68.3	73.7			
1892	111.9	89.4	55.4		65.5	71.0			
1893	110.8	89.1	52.0	71.9	64.3	71.8			
1894	114.9	87.9	56.3	72.2	78.7	77.0			
1895	113.0	87.9	54.9	69.4	68.4	76.6			
1896	112.7	89.9	55.3	—	68.7	76.0			
1897	113.3	90.9	56.6	69.9	70.9	76.1			
1898	114.3	91.7	58.8	68.5	68.4	73.8			
1899	113.9	91.0	58.0	—	62.8	70.9			
1900	113.0	92.4	53.2		68.7	69.5			
1901	112.2	95.0	55.4	—	67.6	69.1			
1902	112.5	93.5	54.6	70.2	68.3	69.0			
1903	111.1	95.1	59.7	—	61.7	68.8			
1904	110.9	94.8	62.3		72.1	69.0 [i] / 89.1 [j]			
1905	109.8	93.5	64.9		76.0	89.7			
1906	109.7	95.2	64.0	77.5	78.5	94.0			
1907	113.8 [h] / 106.1 [h]	94.8	68.0		75.1 / 70.9 [f]	95.1 / 84.9 [g]			
1908	106.5	94.3	—		70.2	89.3 [g]			
1909	108.7	95.2	72.3	72.5	71.7	88.0 [g]			
1910	107.7	93.4	75.3	73.6	76.8	79.5 [e]			
1911	108.0	94.4	74.0	74.1	75.0	78.8			
1912	106.5	94.2	74.6	72.8	74.4	80.6			
1913	105.4	92.6	72.8	73.2	74.4	81.6			
1914	103.4	92.7	72.8	70.4	74.0	—			
1915	103.1	91.6	72.8	69.2	72.7	78.7			
1916	102.1	90.3	—	68.4	—	—			
1917	99.3	86.9	63.0	70.6	—	—			
1918	105.2	90.9	—	72.9	—	—			
1919	108.2	93.6	63.5	74.4	68.0	76.9			
1920	101.3	89.9	78.7	72.9	68.3	—			

Year									
1921	97.7	89.5	—	67.5	—	69.3	—	—	—
1922	96.8	92.0	63.7	69.5	74.4	70.7	—	—	—
1923	—	85.4	60.9	64.5	66.0	—	—	—	—
1924	—	88.9	—	68.3	—	75.3	—	—	—
1925	—	88.2	65.9	69.6	62.5	—	—	—	—
1926	—	91.7	—	69.9	—	—	—	—	—
1927	—	89.5	69.3	67.5	—	71.2	—	—	—
1928	—	85.7	—	67.0	58.2	—	—	—	—
1929	—	82.9	70.8	67.2	—	69.3	65.9	—	—
1930	—	80.6	—	65.5	67.8	—	—	—	—
1931	—	80.0	74.0	63.0	—	—	65.5	76.4[n]	71.6[n]
1932	—	82.5	82.0[a]	62.9	77.5[d]	62.3	—	—	—
1933	—	85.3	84.4[a]	65.4	—	—	—	—	—
1934	—	86.8	82.5[b]	68.3	78.8	—	—	—	—
1935	—	83.8	82.7[b]	66.7	—	—	—	—	—
1936	—	84.2	80.6[b]	65.5	—	—	—	—	—
1937	—	84.0	82.0[b]	64.2	—	—	71.9[k]	—	—
1938	—	82.3	82.0	63.6	—	—	67.6[k]	80.3[o]	83.5[o]
1939	—	84.8	83.3	66.1	—	—	69.8[e]	—	—
1940	—	86.4	83.4	65.7	—	—	69.1[k]	90.7[o]	—
1941	—	88.6	82.9	62.5	—	—	76.1[l]	—	—
1942	—	87.9	83.3	63.2	—	—	73.8[l]	90.4[p]	77.4[p]
1943	—	—	—	61.9	—	—	—	89.1	74.5
1944	—	—	83.1[c]	63.3	—	—	69.0[m]	89.8[q]	75.4[q]

a. August.
b. Averages for last 6 months of 1936, first 6 months of 1937 and last 6 months of 1938.
c. Average for first 9 months.
d. Average of date for first and second half of March.
e. Basis of calculation different from 1910 on.
f. A change in occupational basis from 1907 on.
g. Based on laborers only.
h. Shift from average hourly earnings to average of union wage rates.
i. Figure calculated on basis of % change from 1903 to 1904 according to data in BLS, *Bull. No. 59*, pp. 43–4.

j. Not comparable with preceding figures as number of employees covered in 1904 in both North and South more than double the number in 1903.
k. July.
l. November.
m. January.
n. Early months.
o. September.
p. Last quarter.
q. Nine months.

Source: Lester, R. A., "Trends in Southern Wage Differentials since 1890." *Southern Economic Journal, 11* (April 1945), 335, 339–41.

the same as in 1919 or in 1907. The premium enjoyed by the Pacific Coast over the remainder of the country declined considerably between 1907 and 1919 but has not changed markedly since that time.

When one examines data for individual industries one finds, as always, a great diversity of experience. Data assembled by Lester for eight industries over a considerable period of time are shown in Table 12-8. In the building trades, and in the metal trades up to 1922, southern wages have tended to fall relative to northern wages over the course of time. One may surmise that, at the beginning of the period, the shortage of skilled labor in these industries in the South was sufficiently great that these trades were very highly paid relative to unskilled work. As a more adequate supply of skilled labor was developed, however, wages in these trades tended to fall both relative to similar trades in the North and to unskilled labor in the South. The North-South differential in farm wage rates has also grown somewhat larger over the course of time.

In the cotton textile industry, on the other hand, the North-South differential decreased considerably over the period 1890–1944. The reasons for this were examined in some detail in Chapter 4. One reason was certainly the rapid expansion of the southern industry and the decline of textiles in the North. The two periods of sharp increase in the South-North wage ratio coincided with a sharp rise in the percentage of active cotton spindles located in the South. During the thirties and forties government wage policies and trade union pressure were also of considerable importance.

The limited data on blast furnaces and lumber show no long-run tendency for the North-South differential to increase or decrease. In both industries the South's share of U.S. production has remained approximately constant over the period. In the furniture industry, however, there has also been no tendency for the differential to increase or decrease although the South's share of total output has been rising. In the hosiery industry the only marked decrease in differentials occurred between 1938 and 1940 and was probably due to installation of the federal minimum wage during that period.

On the whole, then, the tendencies have been quite mixed, and the narrowing of North-South differentials has not been nearly so marked as one might judge by looking only at certain industries or at short periods of time. To the extent that differentials have narrowed, Lester concludes that this has been due to some combination of:

> (a) relative expansion of the industry in the South . . . (b) minimum wages under the NRA, the Fair Labor Standards Act, and the National War Labor Board, which particularly affected certain low-wage industries . . . (c) company wage policies, particularly in

those higher-wage industries in which firms pay practically the same wage scale in the South as in the North (e.g., glass, rayon, autos, aircraft, and federal civil service employees), (d) unions and union policies (e.g., . . . in cotton textiles . . . and bituminous coal mining), and (e) wartime and postwar "full" employment, which underlies the relative rise in the wage rates for less skilled workers, especially in the South.

The relative, over-all importance of each of these five factors is difficult to assess, since the situation varies from industry to industry. Nevertheless studies seem to indicate that government policies, including wage minima, have been less significant in narrowing South-North wage differentials than has commonly been assumed, and that basic economic factors, such as relative expansion of the industry in the South, full employment, and the relative rate of population growth in the South, have been more effective influences than is generally realized.[42]

Information about wage differentials *within* each region, particularly among communities of different size, is rather meagre. Gale Johnson has made estimates of hypothetical mean family incomes for a standardized occupational distribution, by region and community size, for 1935–36.[43] In New England, village units with less than 2,500 people had incomes 83 per cent as large as those of cities with 100,000 population and over. In the Pacific states the ratio was 87 per cent, and in the South 81 per cent. From a different body of data, Sufrin has calculated average annual wages in manufacturing, by region and community size, in 1939. In the North, average earnings in communities of less than 40,000 population were 87 per cent as large as those in communities of 500,000 to 1,000,000. In the South the corresponding ratio was 72 per cent.[44]

Do geographical differentials in money wages reflect differences in living costs, or are they real wage differentials as well? The answer seems to be that the differences are mainly, though not entirely, differences in real wages. A study of the larger cities by the Bureau of Labor Statistics in 1946 found that average hourly earnings of factory workers in the highest city (New York) were about 45 per cent above those in

42. Lester, "Southern Wage Differentials: Developments, Analysis, and Implications," pp. 386–7.

43. Johnson, "Some Effects of Region . . . on Family and Individual Income," p. 55. The data include property income as well as labor income, of course, and are thus affected by the (probable) greater concentration of property incomes in the larger communities.

44. Sidney C. Suffrin, Alfred W. Swinyard, and Francis M. Stephenson, "The North-South Differential—a Different View," *Southern Economic Journal, 15* (October 1948), 186.

the lowest city (Memphis). The difference between these two cities in the cost of the standard "city worker's family budget," however, was only 3 per cent. The total range in living costs from the lowest city studied (Houston) to the highest (Seattle) was only 15 per cent, indicating a greater standardization of prices than of hourly wages throughout the country.[45]

Geographical wage differences are substantial, then, and they are accompanied by substantial differences in consumption levels. What are the reasons for this? The answer has sometimes been sought in efficiency differences among workers in different areas. In particular it has been asserted that southern workers are less capable than those in the North and that this justifies a considerable differential in wages. This is a difficult matter to investigate, but the best opinion seems to be that southern workers, given equivalent training, supervision, and mechanical equipment, produce about as much as workers in the same occupations elsewhere.[46] Certainly the difference is not great enough to warrant any considerable difference in wage levels.

The clue to a true explanation, as has been indicated in Chapter 7, lies in regional differences in population pressure and in regional variations in the value productivity of agricultural labor. The North-South differential has gradually been whittled down as workers migrated to the North and as industrial investment grew in volume in the South. However, the immobility of Southern labor and rapid population growth in the South have slowed the narrowing process. The result is that differentials in some industries have remained larger than one would expect under conditions of perfect mobility of labor and capital.

DIFFERENTIALS BY AGE, SEX, AND RACE

There are no regular statistics of hourly wage rates or earnings classified by age, sex, race, and other personal characteristics of the wage earner. Data are available on quarterly and annual earnings of workers covered by the Old Age and Survivors' Insurance system (OASI), but the limitations of these data should be clearly understood. The differences in earnings revealed by these tabulations do not result mainly from differing rates of pay on the same job, but rather from the fact that different categories of workers have unequal access to occupational opportunities. Adult, male, white workers typically enjoy first claim

45. Lily Mary David and Harry Ober, "Intercity Wage Differences, 1945–1946," *Monthly Labor Review*, 66 (June 1948).

46. On this point see Lester, "Effectiveness of Factory Labor—South-North Comparisons," *Journal of Political Economy*, 54 (February 1946), 60–75.

to the highest-paid and most desirable occupations, while young people, women, and Negro workers are concentrated more heavily in the lower-paid jobs. The annual earnings data are also affected by irregularity of employment within the year, which again is likely to be least for the white adult males. The effect of this factor can be reduced, however, by confining one's comparisons to workers for whom some earnings were reported in each of the four calendar quarters (referred to hereafter as "four-quarter workers").[47]

There is a definite tendency for earnings to vary with age. An analysis of OASI data for male four-quarter workers in 1946 shows median annual earnings of $845 for workers under 20, $2,805 for those aged 40–44 (the highest group), and $2,165 for those aged 65–69. The pattern for women is similar, except that the general level is much lower and the rise and decline from one age group to the next is smaller. Woytinsky remarks that "the low earnings of young workers reflect not only their lack of skill and experience but also their higher rate of job turnover. At the other end of the age span, earnings tend to taper off somewhat because diminished speed and vitality lower the efficiency and employability of older people and disability increasingly deprives them of working days."[48]

Regularly employed (four-quarter) male workers in 1938 had median earnings 1.6 times as large as the median for four-quarter women workers. This ratio rose to a peak of 1.9 times in the years 1942–44, then fell back to 1.6 times in 1946. There does not seem, then, to have been any marked change in sex differentials since prewar days. The explanation for the differential lies partly in the restriction of occupations open to women, and partly in the greater discontinuity of employment for women. It is probably not due in any significant measure to differing rates of payment on identical jobs.

In the case of Negro workers, the main source of inequality in earnings is the fact that they have a narrower choice of occupations than white workers. In 1937 the ratio between median annual earnings of whites and Negroes was 3.0 for men and 2.9 for women. By 1946, however, these ratios had fallen to 1.9 for men and 2.1 for women, indicating a sharp reduction in the Negro-white differential. The high demand for labor during the war and immediate postwar years opened up to Negroes many types of work which were not open to them in earlier periods. The increasingly strong sentiment against racial dis-

47. The best available summary of these OASI data is contained in Woytinsky and Associates, *Employment and Wages in the United States,* Chaps. 37–8. The statements made in this section are based on Woytinsky's tabulations.

48. *Ibid.,* p. 444.

crimination in employment, and the enactment of anti-discrimination statutes in a considerable number of states, probably had some effect as well; but main credit must be given to the favorable economic environment arising from full employment.

There is a substantial variation in the Negro-white differential among industries and among regions of the country. In 1946 Negro male workers earned 41.2 per cent as much as white workers in South Carolina but 83.6 per cent as much in Michigan. By industry divisions, Negro male workers earned 39.7 per cent as much as white workers in wholesale trade, 55.2 per cent as much in manufacturing, and 83.9 per cent as much in mining. These differences reflect partly the geographical distribution of various industries, partly the range of occupations open to Negroes within each industry.

CONCLUDING OBSERVATIONS

We may conclude this chapter with a brief restatement of a few cardinal points. Wage differentials of every kind—occupational, interfirm, interregional, interindustry—are considerably wider in the United States than in the European countries. They are also more varied from one industry or region to the next, and the whole wage structure has a more untidy and haphazard air. This greater diversity is perhaps inherent in the continental sweep of the United States, the uneven development of union organization, and the balance of political forces which limits the scope of government intervention in wage matters. The American wage structure may be viewed, on the one hand, as regrettably untidy, filled with anomalies and inequities, and awaiting the pruning shears of union organization and government authority to bring it into better order. Alternatively, it may be viewed as a desirable outcome of private initiative operating in a relatively new environment, establishing such differentials as are necessary to allocate labor effectively among occupations and areas.

While there has been some tendency toward narrowing of differentials since 1939, this tendency has been considerably weaker than in the European countries, and also less consistent as among different types of differential. The reduction in occupational differentials has been rather marked. Interindustry and geographical differentials, on the other hand, have shown only a slight tendency to diminish over the course of time. Male-female differentials have changed scarcely at all. Compression and systematization of the wage structure, in short, has not proceeded so rapidly as in Britain or Sweden even though the level of employment and the rate of inflation since 1939 has been roughly comparable in the three countries.

In all these ways the United States wage structure reflects the turbulence of a market economy as yet only partially harnessed by collective bargaining and other types of deliberate control. Whether and how fast the American wage structure will move in the direction of the European countries, whether it is desirable or undesirable that it should move in this direction, will undoubtedly be a major issue for decades to come.

CHAPTER 13 *The Dynamics of Wage Structure*

THIS book has been concerned with a level of wage analysis midway between the individual firm and the general level of money wage rates. The general wage level has been disaggregated along occupational, industrial, and geographical lines, and we have inquired how these components move relative to each other over the course of time. This is the classic problem of relative wage rates, whose lineage can be traced through two centuries of economic thought. There is a natural temptation to reduce the data presented in Chapters 8–12 to a few summary tables, which could be used to compare the size of wage differentials in various countries at the present time and the rate of change in differentials since the prewar period. Such tables were prepared at one stage of the analysis, but were subsequently discarded because they seemed likely to mislead the reader by a spurious appearance of precision. Any summary measure for an entire country involves a high degree of aggregation and does violence to the complexity of actual wage structure. Moreover, the data for different countries contain serious discrepancies in coverage by industries and time periods, in the concept of wages being measured, and in methods of sampling and analysis. To select and adjust these data for purposes of precise international comparison would be a major enterprise in itself.[1]

Making allowance for these deficiencies in the data, they do suggest the following hypotheses:

1. Most types of differential in most countries have declined in percentage terms since 1939. The shrinkage has been particularly marked in the case of occupational and interindustry differentials, less striking in the case of geographical and male-female differentials.

2. Differentials seem to have declined most in France and Sweden, least in Canada and the United States, with Britain occupying an intermediate position. It is suggestive that the decline in differentials was greatest in those countries where wage determination is most highly centralized, and

---

1. John T. Dunlop and Melvin Rothbaum are presently engaged in a study oriented specifically toward international comparisons of the size of wage differentials and their movement over time. Some preliminary findings were reported in their article "International Comparisons of Wage Structures," *International Labor Review* (April 1955).

least in those countries where wage decisions are very decentralized. Britain is intermediate both in degree of centralized wage determination and rate of shrinkage of differentials.

3. When one compares the present size of wage differentials, the ranking of countries is roughly the same. Differentials are widest in Canada and the United States, narrowest in France.[2] Britain and Sweden are in an intermediate position but rather closer to the French level.

The main purpose of this chapter, however, is not to make a factual summary. The object is rather to explore what we have learned about the determination of relative wage rates by examining a variety of institutional situations in different economies. The central issue is the one pursued throughout the book, the extent to which wage structures are shaped by individual responses in the market as against the influence of collective bargaining and government regulation. This is something which must be judged on the basis of quantitative and qualitative evidence, experience, and intuition. One is in a better position to make such judgments if one has felt one's way into the heart of the wage mechanism in a number of economies which differ as regards stage of industrialization, rapidity of economic progress, strength of trade unionism, and extent of government intervention. Only in this way can one work toward a general economics rather than an economics geared to the institutions of a single country.

WHAT ARE THE IMPORTANT QUESTIONS?

A sketch map of the ground to be covered may help the reader to follow the argument of succeeding sections. The key questions can be sorted out into five boxes:

1. Are there natural economic tendencies in the evolution of national wage structures? What happens to wage differentials in a country as industrialization reaches its zenith and levels off? Does the gradual growth of man-hour output and real wages have an appreciable effect on wage structure? What is the effect of sharp bursts of price inflation? How do fluctuations in the level of employment affect the size of wage differentials?

2. How does the growth of collective bargaining affect the various dimensions of wage structure? Does strong unionism make for a general leveling of wage differentials? How do the conclusions which were

2. It must always be borne in mind, however, that the data for France relate to wage *rates*, whereas for the other four countries they relate to *earnings*. Earnings data for France would undoubtedly show wider differentials than the rate data, and the difference between France and Britain or Sweden would be considerably less marked.

reached for the United States in Chapter 7 stand up in the light of experience in other countries?

A similar range of questions arises with respect to government intervention. Have the governments of the western democracies typically worked in the direction of wage equalization? If so, what are the mainsprings of this policy?

3. To what extent is wage structure shaped by individual worker and employer decisions, and to what extent by group decisions reached through collective bargaining and governmental procedures? This problem takes a different form in different types of economy. In economies such as those of Canada or the United States, the issue is best phrased in this way: to what extent is the existing wage structure a determinate result of individual responses? To what extent is it indeterminate on these grounds, and thus potentially malleable with the growth of collective bargaining and government intervention?

In the more highly regulated economies of Western Europe, the question is how much power government and trade unions already have over wage structure. Is their influence as great as it seems to be? Are structural changes which appear to result from group decisions actually a response to more deep-seated economic tendencies? What happens when wage differentials are set out of line with market requirements? What are the limits to the compressibility of differentials through group action?

In Western Europe one faces the influence of unions and government on wage structure, while in Canada and the United States the question is still mainly one of potential influence. The theoretical issues are the same in both cases, and the same kinds of factual evidence are relevant.

4. What kind of wage theory is implied in the answers to the foregoing questions? Must we choose between "economic" and "political" models of wage determination? Can a synthetic theory be developed which will give adequate weight to both individual choice and group decision making? Is the same kind of wage theory adequate for every type of national economy, or is it necessary to develop tailor-made theories for various institutional settings?

5. What are the implications of the findings for national economic policy? Should the growth of collective wage determination through unions and government be viewed with alarm or with general approval? Is it feasible to resist this tendency even if one might wish to do so?

This is an ambitious agenda. Definitive answers cannot be reached from the few countries and the short span of time examined in this book. If the wage series analyzed in previous chapters are continued on a comparable basis for another twenty or thirty years, many things may become clear which now can only be surmised. The statements made below are not intended as dogma, though the necessity of brief statements may sometimes give them a dogmatic air. They seem reasonable on the basis of information now available, but they require much additional testing and revision.

THE NATURAL HISTORY OF WAGE STRUCTURES

What would one expect to see happening to wage differentials over long periods in a liberal capitalist economy untouched by union organization and government regulation? Is the gradual leveling of differentials observed in Chapters 8–12 enforced arbitrarily by unions and government against the "normal" course of events? Or is it something which has deep roots in the economic process and which is at most reinforced by union and governmental pressures?

INDUSTRIALIZATION AND WAGE STRUCTURE

Industrialism takes off from the agricultural wage level as a base. What happens when a new industry, arising from a Schumpeterian innovation, comes into a previously agricultural environment? The first plants in the industry will reap the rewards of innovation. Labor in these plants will have a high value productivity and a correspondingly high demand curve. Not only can they afford to pay, but it will be necessary for them to pay a wage premium in order to overcome the inertia of the labor force and set it moving in new directions. It takes some time for workers to become aware of new employment opportunities and favorable wage differentials. Additional time is required for workers to shift in substantial numbers, particularly where geographical movement is involved. Training of workers to full proficiency in the new skills also requires time.

Initial inelasticity of labor supply combined with high demand will produce wages in the new industry which are considerably above the previous level in agriculture. This premium is both an interindustry and an occupational differential, since the new industry will give rise to occupations which did not previously exist. To the extent that the industry is concentrated in certain areas of the country, it will give rise to geographical differences as well.

After the initial impact the wage premium offered by the new industry should fall gradually. On the demand side, entrance of additional producers attracted by high profits will lower the value productivity of labor. On the other side, labor supply to the new industry will become increasingly elastic with the passage of time.

The decline of wage differentials may be postponed if demand for the products of the new industry, instead of remaining stationary, continues to rise at a rapid rate. The effect of a rising labor demand curve may for a time outweigh the growing elasticity of supply, and the industry's wage premium may actually increase during the phase of rapid expansion.

Most industries, however, seem to pass through a characteristic life cycle. Rapid expansion is followed by a slower rate of growth, then by stability, and finally by decline as demand shifts to newer products.[3] The labor force of the industry will therefore reach a maximum and then decline. Growing elasticity of labor supply is no longer offset by rising demand, and the wage level of the industry will fall relative to the agricultural base.

Long before this cycle has been completed, however, additional industries will have appeared on the scene and entered on their expansion phase. How will this affect the interindustry wage structure? One hypothesis would be that each new industry will be forced to establish a wage level higher than the maximum reached by previous industries, in order to divert labor in its direction. If this were true, the range of wages from the agricultural base to the highest-paid urban industry would widen steadily over time.

New industries, however, do not expand solely by detaching workers already employed in other industries. They rely partly on newcomers to the labor force who have not yet formed a regular attachment. Agriculture also continues to provide a mobile labor reserve, generation after generation, because of the high level of rural birth rates. On these grounds it can be reasoned that each new industry, during its period of rapid expansion, will be obliged to offer a wage premium no larger than that offered by earlier industries at their peak. There will be no tendency for interindustry differentials to widen indefinitely. Indeed, interindustry dispersion can remain constant only if new industries appear at a regular rate. If the pattern of production were ever to become frozen in a static circular flow, and if no industry had a problem of expanding its labor force, one might expect interindustry differentials to diminish.

One can thus argue that interindustry wage dispersion tends to reach a maximum some time during the early stages of industrialization and to diminish gradually after that point. The decline of differentials can be postponed, however, by a high rate of technical change, leading to rapid shifts of labor demand and continual churning up of new industries to the surface of the wage structure. The persistence of large differentials in countries like Canada and the United States can perhaps be rationalized on these grounds. Industrial output in real terms doubled

3. For an analysis of this phenomenon in manufacturing industries, see Arthur F. Burns, *Production Trends in the United States since 1870* (New York, National Bureau of Economic Research, 1934).

in Canada and the United States between 1939 and 1952, compared with increases of about 40 per cent in France and Britain and 50 per cent in Sweden. This greater rate of expansion may help to explain the persistence of wider wage differentials in the North American countries.

One might expect also that the ranking of industries in the wage structure would be inversely related to the date of their appearance on the industrial scene, the oldest industries lying nearest the bottom. The tables in Chapters 8–12 seem at first glance to provide strong support for this hypothesis. Many of the older industries, such as textiles, clothing manufacture, boots and shoes, and food processing, typically lie near the bottom of the wage structure. Steel, nonferrous metals, automobile production, electrical equipment, chemicals, petroleum refining, and other relatively new industries stand near the top in all countries. One cannot be certain, however, whether the low position of industries in the former group is due to the fact that they are: 1. old industries which have passed their expansion peak and have a low rate of technical progress; or 2. small-scale and highly competitive industries with little control over prices and output rates; or 3. industries which employ relatively light and low-skilled labor, including a considerable proportion of women workers. Factors other than age alone certainly contribute to the relative ranking of industries.

Is there similarly a natural history of occupational differentials? We have noted that in Britain and the United States, where our data go back before 1900, occupational differentials have been shrinking throughout the recorded period. This may reflect partly a change in the content of the "skilled" and "unskilled" categories. There are indications that many skilled occupations are becoming less skilled, arduous, and responsible with the improvement of mechanical equipment and working conditions. The locomotive fireman and engineer ride comfortably on foam rubber seats, with a clear view ahead through the windshield of their diesel locomotive, protected from many of the traditional hazards by automatic signal systems, and with a crew of maintenance specialists ready to diagnose and repair any ailments which the locomotive may develop. The machinist has become in many cases a machine operator, running automatic or semiautomatic equipment on a single specialized operation. At the other end of the ladder there are fewer and fewer jobs which are entirely unskilled. Laborers now work with an increasing amount of mechanical equipment, which both lends some element of skill to their work and raises their productivity. Narrowing of the differential in job content between skilled and unskilled work may be partly responsible for, or at any rate may help to legitimize, a narrower differential in wage rates.

Beyond this, however, there has certainly been a genuine shrinkage in (strictly defined) occupational differentials. A major factor working in this direction is the diffusion of educational opportunities throughout the population. At the beginning of the twentieth century, the high school graduation certificate was the prerogative of a small minority. Today a majority of young people in the United States complete the twelfth grade and the proportion is increasing year by year. We have carried over from an earlier day, however, the tradition that high school graduation provides a guarantee of skilled or white-collar employment. A high level of occupational aspiration is set up during the years of schooling, and the high school graduate considers it incongruous that he should turn to unskilled labor. The result is to swell the labor supply for the higher occupations and to deplete the supply of laborers. An increase in manual wages relative to white-collar salaries, and in laborer's wages relative to craftsmen's wages, is a natural consequence.

Clark Kerr has argued persuasively that occupational differentials tend naturally to decline with maturing industrialism:

> The absolute demand for skilled workers is certainly larger in an advanced industrial state than in one entering industrialization; but the need for skilled workers is much more critical in a nation undergoing industrialization, and particularly in one where the process is rapid. Percentagewise, the additional need for skilled men is much reduced as industrial societies mature. . . . Concurrently with the smaller increase in demand for skilled workers, as industrialization becomes well established, the supply of skilled workers greatly increases through the effects of public education, and perhaps also a concomitant reduction of class or social discrimination; while the supply of unskilled workers dries up as agriculture becomes a smaller segment of the economy, as income and the level of education rise, as technology increases mobility, as the growth of the trade and service industries draws also on the ranks of the unskilled. . . . We may be witnessing a great social phenomenon of occupational differentials being turned partly on their heads. . . . If this is the social process at work, then we should not be surprised that the narrowing of differentials has not caused a shortage of skilled workers, for their comparative plenitude has, in fact, caused the narrowing.[4]

These tendencies seem to be largely independent of forms of economic organization. Russia appears to have occupational differentials somewhat wider than those in the United States and much wider than those prevail-

4. Clark Kerr, "Trade Unionism and Wage Structures," to be published in the forthcoming report of the 1954 IEA conference on wage determination.

ing in Western Europe.[5] The explanation is partly that Russia is in an early and very rapid phase of industrial expansion, which has produced critical shortages of skilled workers and technicians. The practical necessity of inducing large numbers of people to train for the higher occupations has overriden an ideological preference for wage equalization.

The case of geographical differentials is complicated, and it is difficult to form any general expectation concerning their long-run movement. The course of events will depend on such things as: the rate of population growth relative to the rate of industrial expansion; the changing economic fortunes of agriculture relative to industry; the geographical distribution of new births relative to the distribution of new jobs; and the responsiveness of labor and capital migration to wage differentials. The strong presumption which we have found in favor of a shrinkage of occupational and interindustry differentials does not seem to exist in this case, and it would not be surprising to find geographical differentials maintained intact for long periods. This would presumably mean that labor and capital migration was not occurring rapidly enough to outweigh the effect of differential rates of population increase in various regions, a hypothesis which seems to be roughly correct for the United States over the last several decades.

The differential between male and female workers might be expected to decline with the progress of industrialization. A century ago there was still a strong prejudice against employment of women. The restricted demand for women workers, plus the fact that many women are only supplementary wage earners, tended to depress their wages below the male level. This gave women a competitive advantage which helped them to penetrate occupations previously reserved to men. The obvious profitability of employing women in many occupations, together with changes in attitudes and living habits resulting from industrialization and urbanization, gradually widened the market for women's services. The great expansion of clerical and sales occupations in recent decades has further increased the demand for women workers. The supply of women workers cannot be increased indefinitely, for it eventually reaches a limit set by the necessity of withdrawal from the labor market during the child-rearing period. Rising demand faced with an inelastic supply tends to raise women's wages relative to men's wages *in the same type of employment*. The average hourly earnings of *all* women workers relative to those of *all* male workers—a quite different ratio—also increases as women penetrate more of the high-wage occupations.

There is good reason, then, to expect every type of wage differential,

5. See on this matter A. Bergson, *The Structure of Soviet Wages* (Cambridge, Harvard University Press, 1946).

with the possible exception of geographical differentials, to decline as part of the normal evolution of an industrial economy. This presumption is strengthened by several other considerations, to which we now turn.

SECULAR INCREASE IN MONEY AND REAL
WAGE LEVELS

The appearance of new industries and the decline of older ones brings an expansion of per capita output in the economy, for the value productivity of labor in the new industries is typically above that for industry in general. One also finds a secular increase of output per man-hour even in long established industries. These tendencies together provide the possibility of a steady increase in real wages and living standards. This could conceivably occur through a secular decline in price levels. In practice, over the past two centuries or so it has occurred through a secular increase in the level of money wage rates.

Under competitive conditions, and with no change in demand and supply functions for labor of each occupational grade, this would mean an equal percentage increase in all wage rates and would leave wage differentials unaffected. This is not, however, what typically happens in practice. In some plants and industries one finds that all workers receive equal cents-per-hour increases, in others graduated cents-per-hour increases, in others equal percentage increases, and in others even more complicated types of adjustment. The outcome is that the higher wages in the system rise less rapidly, on a percentage basis, than the lower wages, and wage differentials become narrower.

This suggests that a rise in the money wage level is not a neutral phenomenon which can be disregarded in theorizing about the determination of relative wage rates. It appears to change some of the parameters of the system, most plausibly the shapes of labor supply functions. This could happen in at least two ways. Suppose that workers, in making occupational wage comparisons, think in terms of fixed money differentials rather than fixed percentage relationships. Labor supply to an occupation then becomes a function of the cents-per-hour differential between this occupation and other occupations which workers regard as related or comparable. So long as all wage rates rise by the same absolute amount, labor supply to each occupation will remain unchanged, even though percentage differentials are diminishing.

Another possibility is that workers may judge the adequacy of their wages on an absolute basis rather than on any kind of relative basis. Is the wage level adequate to maintain the worker's household at the standard of living to which it aspires? Are wages rising rapidly enough to permit a visible improvement in living standards over the course of time? So long as the higher-paid groups feel that their absolute position is improving, they may not be concerned about a decline in relative position. This would mean that supply curves to the higher occupations would flatten out as the money wage level rose, and percentage wage differentials would necessarily diminish.

It is not contended that either of these possibilities is a dominant feature of workers' behavior. But to the extent that they enter at all into workers' behavior, they will affect labor supply functions in such a way as to narrow percentage differentials. Nor is it necessary to assume that workers will continue to hold these types of "money illusion" indefinitely, but merely that they will hold them long enough at a time to permit an appreciable narrowing of percentage wage relationships.

Management officials also frequently prefer a uniform cents-per-hour increase to a uniform percentage increase. If it is considered necessary to add so many cents-per-hour to the bottom of the plant wage structure, it costs the company less to extend this to the higher occupations on an equal cents-per-hour basis than on an equal percentage basis. Further, equal cents-per-hour increases are administratively convenient. It is easy to estimate the cost of such an increase, easy to apply it to the wage structure, easy to explain and justify it to the workers, and easy to use it for interplant and interindustry comparisons. Finally, flat-rate increases provide an attractive way of reconciling (apparently) equal treatment for all with the egalitarian urge which employers along with other groups regard as the modern temper. All workers receive the same amount in each wage movement, yet real differences in living standards are gradually reduced.

To the extent that wage adjustments depart from percentage equality, the secular rise in the money wage level necessarily brings a reduction in every sort of wage differential. Fortunately, this is in accord with the long-run tendencies described in the previous section. Otherwise, flat-rate increases would soon produce an impasse and would have to be abandoned.

THE IMPACT OF INFLATION

During certain periods, usually associated with major wars, the normal increase in the money wage level is sharply accelerated as part of a general inflation. Since a gradual increase in the wage level produces a shrinkage of differentials, one might expect that a burst of inflation would produce a much sharper shrinkage. Most differentials in fact declined at an accelerated rate from 1914 to 1920 and from 1939 to the early fifties.

The impact of inflation, however, is not as decisive as might have been expected. In four of the countries studied (Canada, United States, Sweden, and Britain), the degree of inflation over the period 1939–54 was almost identical, the price level doubling and the wage level tripling in each country.[6] Yet the rate of decline in wage differentials was substantially different from one country to the next. Britain and Sweden show a marked decline in most types of differential, while Canada and the United States show a moderate shrinkage in occupational differentials and little change in other types. This suggests that differences in the wage setting institutions of these countries may have had more influence than inflation per se. It is also significant that in no country has the shrinkage of differentials been at all proportionate to the degree of inflation. A tripling of the wage level, if accomplished entirely through flat-rate increases, would reduce all wage differentials by two-thirds. Actually the shrinkage of differentials was much less than this in most cases, and was negligible in a fair number.

The most striking instance is that of France, where the wage level has increased more than twenty times since 1939. If flat-rate increases had been used consistently, wage differentials would have been virtually eliminated by 1954. In fact, differentials in wage rates seem to have fallen by roughly one-half, and differentials in earnings by somewhat less than this.

Why does inflation not produce the results which might be predicted from simple arithmetical calculations? The first onset of inflation does seem to have a strong leveling effect. Rapid increases in living costs obviously bear hardest on the poorest groups, and wage increases are arranged for these groups to keep their heads above water. Increases tend to be extended to higher groups on a flat-rate rather than a percentage basis, which is cheapest for employers, produces least inflationary pressure, and accords with the egalitarian outlook of most democratic governments. Cost-of-living escalator clauses, which tend to be adopted at the outset of inflation, have the same effect.

After some years of sustained inflation, however, countervailing forces are set in motion. The higher-paid groups begin to realize what is happening and to demand that their relative position be at least partially restored. Employers in need of skilled labor begin to bid up wage rates, going above the official scales where necessary. There is a tendency for

6. One must exercise caution in using price-level changes as a measure of inflationary pressure, since this pressure may be suppressed for considerable periods. This would be a serious objection to any international comparison using 1945 as the terminal date. By 1954, however, the suppressed inflation of World War II had been substantially released in all the countries studied, and actual price-level changes are a reasonably reliable guide.

the shrinkage of percentage differentials to cease or even be reversed. It is at this stage that institutional differences among national economies may have considerable effect. If union wage policy is centralized and has a strong egalitarian bent, if government intervenes strongly in the same direction, if workers themselves are persuaded that wage leveling is desirable, then creeping equalization may continue even after the first rush of inflation is past. In a predominantly market economy, with workers and employers following a more individualistic course, differentials are likely to rebound more vigorously and to return at least part way toward their previous level.

The shrinkage of differentials during inflation is fortunately in the same direction as the secular development of wage structure. There is a tendency to overshoot the mark during inflation, however, and to narrow differentials more sharply than is warranted by the stage of economic development. To the extent that this happens, the movement will be reversed after inflation has passed and differentials will return to the proper point on the curve of secular decline. From a long-range viewpoint, one can say that inflation has more effect on the *timing* of declines in wage differentials than on the average rate of decline. Instead of differentials shrinking slowly but steadily, as might happen with constant price levels, they follow a zig-zag course, now falling sharply, then stabilizing on a new plateau or moving upward for a time.

FLUCTUATIONS IN THE LEVEL OF EMPLOYMENT

It seems reasonable to expect that wage differentials will widen during a period of serious unemployment. Workers dislodged from higher occupations swell the supply of common labor, and new entrants to the labor force are restricted to low-skilled work. Laborers' wages are also less effectively protected through collective bargaining than are skilled wage rates. Occupational differentials might therefore be expected to increase.

The industrial incidence of depression is also uneven. Those industries which are hard hit may be forced to cut wages, while those which are faring better will probably try to maintain their wage levels. Inter-industry dispersion of wage levels is thus likely to increase. Geographical differentials will be affected by the fact that agricultural prices and incomes drop particularly sharply during depression. This pulls down farm wage rates, which in turn tends to depress common-labor rates in rural areas, leading to a widening of geographical differences.

Wage cuts are becoming rarer even during depression. To the extent that cuts are made, however, they will widen wage differentials unless they are applied on a uniform percentage basis to all groups. Flat-rate cuts widen wage differentials just as flat-rate increases tend to reduce them.

During prosperous periods these tendencies are thrown into reverse, and wage differentials narrow once more. The case of occupational differentials is particularly interesting. During a period such as the 1940's every kind of labor appears scarce, and one might think that this would have a neutral effect on occupational differentials. This is not the case, however, because the scarcity of different grades of labor arises from different causes. Shortages of skilled and semiskilled workers are temporary shortages which can be made good by recruiting additional workers from lower grades. In the case of common labor, on the other hand, one may encounter an absolute and continuing shortage. As workers are promoted to higher occupations, the supply of laborers can be replenished only through growth of the labor force. A point is eventually reached beyond which the supply of unskilled labor is completely inelastic with respect to wages or any other inducement, something which is not true of the higher occupations. This causes laborers' wages to be bid up at an unusually rapid rate and produces a shrinkage of occupational differentials.

Fluctuations in employment, like bursts of inflation, cause a zig-zag movement of wage differentials around the trend line of secular decline, but probably do not affect the slope of the trend line appreciably. The pure, or ceteris paribus, effect of employment fluctuations is difficult to distinguish empirically because it is always intermingled with the effects of other factors. Statistical measurements of wage differentials may thus show no clear relation to changes in the level of employment.[7]

THE CONJUNCTURE OF 1939-54

We have now examined two long-run and two shorter-run tendencies in wage structure. The long-run tendencies are the process of industrialization itself and the secular increase in the money wage level, both making for a shrinkage of wage differentials. Within this long-term movement, cyclical fluctuations in aggregate demand produce an alternating dilation and contraction of the wage structure. Occasional bursts of inflation, usually associated with war periods, produce an unusually sharp shrinkage of differentials at certain times, followed by a partial reversal after the inflation has passed.

7. For an analysis of the cyclical behavior of occupational differentials in the United States, see Philip Bell, "Cyclical Variations and Trends in Occupational Wage Differentials in American Industry Since 1914," *Review of Economics and Statistics, 33* (November 1951), 329-37.

The key to interpreting the years 1939–54 lies in the fact that for the time being all these influences were operating in the same direction. The long-run tendency toward a shrinkage of differentials was reinforced by inflation and by an unusually long period of high employment. In some countries these economic influences were further reinforced by the operation of collective bargaining and by government wage policies, to which we turn in the next section. Economic developments alone, however, are adequate to account for most of the decline in differentials.

The unusual conjuncture of events during 1939–54 makes it quite unsafe to project the tendencies of this period into the future. Indeed, the period of sharp contraction of differentials ended not in 1954 but at the latest in 1952. By 1952 the suppressed inflation of World War II and the secondary wave of inflation generated by the Korean war had run their course. Prices had stabilized in most countries, the tendency toward compression of wage differentials had been arrested, and occupational differentials in particular were tending to widen once more. It seems likely that differentials may now settle down on a plateau similar to that of the interwar period, assuming reasonable stability of prices and employment.

THE ROLE OF GROUP DECISION MAKING

COLLECTIVE BARGAINING

The impact of collective bargaining on wage structure in the United States was examined in Chapter 7. This section will be confined to a brief recapitulation and to inquiring whether the conclusions drawn from United States experience are applicable to other countries as well.

Unionism clearly makes for a reduction of *personal* differentials among members of the same occupational group. Unionism also makes for a sharp reduction of *interplant* differentials among firms competing in the same product market. In neither of these respects is there any reason to change the conclusions reached from American experience.

Union efforts to reduce interplant differences involve a reduction of *geographical* differentials within particular industries. The behavior of British and Swedish unions is quite consistent with that of American unions on this point. Moreover, the strong unionization of agricultural labor in most of the European countries seems to have made for reduction of geographical differentials. Leveling of regional differences in farm wages, and the raising of the farm wage level relative to the urban level, tends to undercut the strongest source of geographical wage variation.

Union influence on *occupational* differentials is less clear and direct. To the extent that unionism has been influential, however, it has made for a narrowing of occupational differentials. In the United States, at least, unions have demanded flat-rate increases in some situations where employers would have preferred percentage increases, while one finds few cases of the opposite sort. The Swedish unions have also favored reduction of occupational differentials on principle. Unions in some countries have demanded substantial fringe benefits which, to the extent that they apply uniformly to all workers regardless of wage level, tend to narrow differentials in income. Cost-of-living escalator arrangements, usually introduced at the instance of the union, also have a leveling tendency.

Only in the case of *interindustry* differentials is it necessary to modify appreciably the conclusions reached in Chapter 7. In the United States, under partial unionization, it appears that collective bargaining has as yet had little effect on the interindustry wage structure. Experience in Britain and the Scandinavian countries, however, suggests that a higher degree of unionization may lead to a narrowing of interindustry differentials. When unionism comes to include farm laborers, service workers, and other low-skilled groups, these groups may be able to overhaul the higher-paid industries more rapidly than they could do on a free market basis. It is significant, for example, that the unionized farm laborers in Britain and Denmark suffered much smaller wage cuts during the 1929–32 depression than did the unorganized farm workers in Canada and the United States, and that the differential between farm and factory wages is much less in the former countries. Moreover, when most industries are unionized and these unions are united in a central federation, the federation is likely to feel some responsibility for the interindustry wage structure. As federation leaders begin to search for principles of wage determination, the concept of equality for work requiring comparable skill and effort is bound to commend itself to them. Federation influence is likely to be directed, therefore, toward elimination of interindustry differences which cannot be justified on grounds of job content. The LO has followed this policy in Sweden and has achieved a considerable narrowing of interindustry differentials. In the other Scandinavian countries, in Holland, and in Britain the central federations have worked in the same direction within the limits of their authority.

The influence of collective bargaining is thus in the direction of reducing every kind of wage differential. Pressure for wage equalization is greatest in the case of personal and interplant differentials, less strong but still of some importance in the case of geographical, occupational, and interindustry differences. Collective bargaining works in the same general direction as the economic forces outlined in the previous section. This suggests the possibility that changes in wage structure may be wrongly attributed to collective bargaining, when in fact collective bargaining is merely ratifying the normal operation of economic tendencies.

GOVERNMENT WAGE REGULATION

The wage policies of democratic governments in recent decades have been dominated by a concern for the position of the lowest-income groups. This is clearly the inspiration of minimum wage legislation. Wartime wage controls, too, are typically applied in such a way as to freeze the highest wages most firmly, while the bottom of the wage structure is allowed to rise moderately. This is in part an anti-inflationary policy, but it is prompted also by egalitarian thinking. Government has also been responsible for adding various types of social benefit to the income structure—family allowances, old age pensions, unemployment compensation, various other health and welfare services. Since these benefits often apply equally to all workers regardless of wage level, and since they form a substantial part of total income, the result is to make incomes more nearly equal than hourly wage rates.

The wage activities of government thus work in a leveling direction. This is partly incidental to the pursuit of other objectives, but it is partly a matter of deliberate policy. An explanation of this general tendency lies in the realm of political history. It reflects the decline of political and economic conservatism throughout the democratic world, and the growing predominance of parties of the moderate left. The origins of wage leveling are the same as those of progressive income taxation, high inheritance taxes, and other egalitarian policies.

It is interesting that social benefits form the largest percentage of labor income in countries like France and Italy, which are economically less able to support them than Canada or the United States. But one cannot think about these matters primarily in economic terms. The key factors in France and Italy are the impotence of collective bargaining, which causes workers and union leaders to look for progress through political channels; the strength of left-wing parties, which forces the parties of the center and moderate right to compete strenuously for working class support; and the influence of Catholic emphasis on the family unit, which is mainly responsible for the generous family allowance systems in these countries.

ORGANIZATIONAL BEHAVIOR VERSUS INDIVIDUAL DECISIONS

We come now to the central issue of the relative importance of organizational behavior and individual decisions in wage determination. Within what limits, if at all, can wage relationships be manipulated by collective

bargaining or government decree? Are the efforts of unions and governments to manipulate wages actually effective or do individual decisions
in the market limit or even cancel out the intended results? Does collective bargaining perhaps provide only the mechanism, the "how" of wage
determination, with market decisions providing the "why"?

It is sometimes argued that organized "intervention" in wage determination is. bound to be either futile or harmful. This implies that the
unregulated wage structure reflects the working of a highly competitive
market and has, therefore, some special welfare significance. This may
be so, but it is only one of numerous possibilities. It may be that the wage
structure, while in equilibrium, is not in perfectly competitive equilibrium, but is distorted by employers' monopsony power arising from
peculiarities of labor supply. It may be that the existing wage structure
is only one of several potential equilibrium positions, each of which, if
attained, would be equally stable. This might be the case, for example,
if workers' conceptions of proper wage relationships were purely customary or conventional. Or it may be that the wage structure, while
potentially determinate on economic grounds, is never able to achieve
equilibrium because of rapid shifts in labor demand, additions to the
labor force, and labor and capital migration. We may have nothing but
a series of disequilibrium positions, which cannot be taken as having any
normative significance.

This is a complicated terrain, on which one must move with due
caution. It would certainly be wrong to underrate the strength of economic motivation and the vigor of the market mechanism. Wage differentials are an important factor in attracting workers to expanding
industries and occupations, and differentials are usually in the right
direction for this purpose. One does not find large numbers of workers
moving deliberately from higher-paid to lower-paid work. Conversely,
the wage structure itself is responsive to economic forces and particularly to shifts in labor demand. Sharp increases in demand at certain
points in the economy tend to raise relative wage rates at those points.
Particularly good examples of this tendency were found in the recent
development of the Canadian wage structure. Nor is there any reason
to doubt that a substantial wage increase for a certain kind of labor,
other things equal, will tend to result in less employment of that kind
of labor. With a little ingenuity, one can introduce various kinds of kinks
and discontinuities into the labor demand curve, but this is important
mainly for small changes in wages and for short periods of time. Over
any extended period it is difficult to deny the reality of a negatively
sloped demand curve for labor.

When due account has been taken of economic forces, one must still
conclude that the going structure of wages in Canada or the United

States does not represent anything approaching a perfectly competitive equilibrium. This conclusion is unoriginal and rather uninteresting. It is the reasons for the conclusion which are important, and of these, three appear to be of major significance.

First, there can be no doubt of employers' monopsony power over wages under nonunion conditions. The ordinary textbook demonstrations of labor market monopsony are unrealistic, and it is difficult to capture the essence of the matter in diagrammatic form. The reality of employer power is adequately demonstrated, however, by the prevalence of wide differences in wage rates for the same category of labor in the same local market. These differences are not offset by opposite variations in other terms of employment or in working conditions. High wages, large fringe benefits, and good conditions tend to be positively correlated. Nor does it seem that wage differences are fully offset by differences in the quality of the labor hired, though this is difficult to test. There appear to be substantial interfirm differences in efficiency wages, and these persist over long periods of time. This phenomenon is rooted in a willingness of the more profitable firms to pay higher wages than the minimum at which they could "get by." Important also is the failure of workers to seek out higher wage firms aggressively, partly because of inertia and ignorance, partly because of a sensible concern with security of tenure and the other benefits which come from long employment in the same enterprise.[8]

Second, there seems to be a strong conventional element in workers' judgment of an adequate wage rate. Workers in a particular occupation have an impression that their job ranks below certain occupations and above others. But how much above? Certainly not a fixed percentage amount, but rather the amount to which they have become accustomed over the years. A sharp change in wage relationships will at first seem strange and unreasonable, but if it is maintained for some time it may come to seem as natural as the earlier relation. Skilled workers in Britain at present may regard their 25 per cent premium over the laborer as quite as reasonable as their fathers considered the wider differential of 1925, or their grandfathers considered the still wider differential of 1900.

Third, an important consideration is that the wage structure never gets a chance to approach static equilibrium. A growing economy is constantly being jolted by the appearance of new industries, technical developments which create new skills and eliminate old ones, development of new areas of the country, growth of urban centers, shifting of population, and other types of change. Long before one set of changes has worked out its full effects, these effects are swamped by a new wave

8. A fuller discussion of this matter will be found in Reynolds, *The Structure of Labor Markets*, Chap. 8.

of change, which keeps the economy perpetually off balance. It is thus possible for a wage differential to remain consistently larger than it would be under static equilibrium, always tending to shrink toward the equilibrium level but never succeeding because of the rapid sweep of economic events. It was suggested in Chapter 12 that the failure of regional differentials in the United States to shrink substantially over the past fifty years may be explained in this way. The rate of population growth in the South, and the rate of industrial expansion in the North and West, have been large enough to offset the eroding effect of labor and capital migration on regional wage differences. If regional differences were narrowed by fiat, however, the new set of differentials might turn out to be perfectly stable.

Each of these three considerations works in the same direction, toward making wage differentials somewhat wider than they need be. To this extent the wage structure is potentially malleable, and wage differentials can be narrowed without disrupting the supply of labor to particular occupations and industries. This provides some latitude for readjustment of relative wage rates through collective bargaining and government regulation.

If deliberate wage regulation can be influential, however, it is far from being all powerful. This appears most clearly from an examination of experience in what we have termed the "regulated economies." In France, Sweden, and Britain, most types of wage differential have been reduced substantially since 1939—nominally, at least, through collective bargaining agreements and government wage decrees. Yet there seems to be no unusual shortage of labor in the areas, industries, and occupations which have been leveled down toward the general average. How can this be? Does it indicate that wages can be manipulated at will with no visible consequences? Or does it indicate something quite different from this?

Part of the explanation has already been suggested. Since 1939 economic tendencies have been favorable to a substantial narrowing of wage differentials. Union and government wage policies oriented in this same direction have thus been riding a flood tide. If economic developments had been in the direction of wider differentials, the situation would have been very different, and one may surmise that union and government efforts to narrow differentials would have been largely frustrated.

Another part of the explanation is that collective bargaining and government regulation typically set minimum wage standards only. Local unions and individual employers remain free to establish higher rates or earnings, and workers remain free to demand and accept these higher wages. So long as this remains true, not too much harm can be done by pushing upward on the bottom of the wage structure. This will at first cause all differentials to shrink; but as certain differentials become inadequate, the top of the wage structure will begin to move upward to restore differentials to a proper level. This reaction will go on through both individual responses and organizational behavior. Employers who find that differentials are no longer adequate to secure the kinds of labor they require will take steps to increase earnings where necessary. Workers will agitate for restoration of differentials, and their feelings will find expression in the kind of wage demands made in collective bargaining.

One must note also that unions and governments are not obstinate in pursuing wage-leveling policies. If government finds that the wage level of an industry is impeding labor recruitment, steps will be taken to raise the wage level even if this means putting the industry further out of line with other industries. If a union finds that bringing all wages in an industry to a common level will put certain firms out of business, it is likely to make concessions to those firms rather than throw its members out of work.

In Chapters 8–10 numerous instances were encountered of the rebound of wage differentials under the influence of market forces: the fact that wage differentials between Paris and the provinces have remained well above the official variation in minimum wage scales; the fact that there continue to be differentials between men's and women's rates in France despite the official policy of wage equality; the fact that occupational differentials in some French industries have been well maintained in the face of the general tendency to the contrary; the willingness and ability of many Swedish employers to pay more than the bargained wage scales in spite of contrary instructions from employers' associations; the tendency toward a widening of occupational differentials in Sweden after 1950 or so, reversing the trend of the previous decade; the substantial excess of earnings over bargained wage scales in many British industries; the fact that occupational differences in earnings are typically greater than the corresponding differentials in rates; and the extraordinary increase in the wage levels of certain undermanned industries in Britain, particularly coal mining, cotton textiles, and agriculture.

Wage differentials, then, are still heavily influenced by market pressures even in the regulated economies of Western Europe. The contrast between these economies and Canada or the United States is one of degree only. Collective bargaining and government intervention have tightened up the wage structure in various ways and have whittled down differentials closer to the essential minimum; but they have in no way set aside the pre-existing forces of employer and employee self-interest. Adjustments which have occurred in differentials have been within outer limits set by individual worker and employer responses.

Fifteen years is a short span of economic history, and it would be rash to assert that the differentials existing in 1955 indicate the minimum stable level of differentials over the long run. Some differentials may have been compressed unduly in the rush of wartime and postwar inflation, and may gradually creep upward over the next decade or two. Other differentials may still be above the necessary minimum level, and further compression may be possible in the future. The variation in the size of a particular type of differential from country to country suggests either that the minimum has not yet been reached in many cases, or that the minimum itself varies substantially from one country to the next.

As a matter of rough judgment, one may surmise that French differentials now stand close to the minimum and cannot shrink much more, whatever may happen in the way of further inflation or government controls. This is a point of practical importance, for French governments in 1955 were still trying to raise minimum wage rates while hoping to avoid proportionate increases in higher rates. Such efforts seem doomed to become less and less successful in future, and a government which raises the minimum wage will have to reckon on a proportionate rise in the whole wage structure.

In Canada and the United States, at the other extreme, most differentials are probably still above the necessary minimum and there is room for considerable shrinkage in future decades. Britain and Sweden occupy an intermediate position, rather closer to the French than to the American end of the scale.

WHAT KIND OF WAGE THEORY?

The analysis in previous sections suggests that it is possible to develop a general theory of relative wage rates which will have descriptive value for a wide variety of national economies. Variations in worker attitudes and behavior, in union structure and policies, and in other relevant factors from country to country are no greater than economic theory has customarily taken into account.

It also seems possible, indeed essential, to develop a unified theory which will take adequate account both of worker and employer responses in the market and of the behavior of trade unions and other organized groups. It is a mistake to think that the deficiencies of previous economic theorizing about wages can be corrected by jettisoning economic concepts and substituting some quite different political or organizational theory of wage determination. The development of collective bargaining and government wage determination does not remove the necessity of worker and employer decision, though it does alter the context in which these decisions are reached. Wage determination is a unified process in which individual and group decisions, decisions expressed directly in the market and indirectly through organizational behavior, interact constantly on each other. This calls for an integrated theory in which collective bargaining and government action are accepted as part of the central mechanism rather than as outside agencies intervening in an otherwise economic process.

Such a theory must start from a realistic view of the preunion labor market. It should take account of such things as: 1. the permissive and indeterminate behavior of labor supply, under which different firms, industries, and areas can offer quite different rates for the same category of labor, yet all can maintain their position in the market; 2. the tendency for substantial wage differentials to arise with the growth of modern industry, and the subsequent tendency for differentials to shrink gradually as industrialism matures; 3. the great importance of dynamic change, which may postpone indefinitely the appearance of the wage relationships appropriate to static equilibrium; 4. the feasibility of marked reduction of wage differentials over the course of time, both because differentials are typically above the equilibrium level and because the equilibrium relationships themselves tend to narrow over time.

We must next realize that the development of union organization and collective bargaining does not transform the labor market as drastically as has sometimes been supposed. Workers continue to choose among alternative jobs on the basis of relative wage rates and other inducements. Unionism may impose new restrictions and strengthen existing ones on labor mobility; but this is not of major importance, since nonunion labor markets are already highly segmented. Nor do recent studies in the United States suggest that there is much difference in the outlook and market behavior of union members as compared with nonunion workers in the same industry and occupational level.

The rise of unionism compels employers to bargain over wage adjustments instead of reaching unilateral decisions. Employer resistance to "uneconomic" demands remains powerful, however, and in most cases bargained wage changes do not depart far from what was "in the cards" on economic grounds. Each employer also remains free to decide how much labor and what kind of labor to employ at the bargained wage rates, to set up his own hiring specifications, and to use his own methods of labor recruitment. Collective bargaining, while it professes to determine the wage structure, leaves relatively unchanged the processes through which the wage structure was determined in preunion days. The old market forces and the new wage-setting procedures continue to operate alongside each other.

This raises the possibility that market tendencies and organizational decisions may conflict with one another. The situation is eased, however, by the fact that market forces allow considerable indeterminacy in the movement of wage differentials, and by the fact that both management and union officials give heavy weight to economic considerations. It is eased also by the natural tendency toward narrowing of wage differentials over the long run, which happens to be in accord with the main drift of both trade union and governmental wage policies. Further, there is a built-in safeguard against excess zeal on the part of unions or governments, for when wage differentials are reduced below the minimum tolerable level, organizational decisions appear to lose their effectiveness. The market takes over once more and pulls up the higher wage rates sufficiently to restore differentials to an adequate level.

It is arguable that to avoid the wage-distortion horn of the dilemma in this fashion lands one squarely on the opposite horn of chronic inflation. At the least, however, it is comforting to know that the wage-distortion horn does not seem formidable on the basis of experience to date. The sharpness of the chronic-inflation horn has probably also been exaggerated in recent discussion; but to argue this point would carry us far from our present purpose.

A NATIONAL WAGE POLICY?

The question of whether increased regulation of wages through collective bargaining and government control is beneficial or harmful has long been a central issue in political controversy. The analysis thus far suggests a conclusion generally favorable to wage regulation. We have argued that wage regulation tends to supplement and reinforce market tendencies rather than to work against them. When wage control does come into conflict with market requirements, its effectiveness is lost. Wage regulation, in short, does some good and can do little harm.

Additional reflection, however, leads one to qualify this optimistic conclusion. First, partial unionization may have a more disruptive effect than complete unionization. If the higher-paid groups organize first, as is typically the case, they may in the first instance widen interindustry and occupational differentials and pull them farther away from their natural level. This may have occurred, for example, in the United States between 1880 and 1930.

Second, the argument that wage regulation cannot conflict seriously with market requirements depends partly on employer freedom to set earnings above the levels specified by collective agreements or by government. Any attempt to enforce wage maxima as well as wage minima would remove this possibility and could have disruptive effects.

Third, we have argued that, if wage regulation overshoots the mark and unduly narrows a particular differential, the market will enforce a subsequent widening of the differential; but this process takes time.

Labor supply is sluggish and slow to respond to changed conditions. An inadequate differential may not cut down recruitment for a considerable period, during which the differential may shrink still further below its proper level. When recruitment does slacken off, it may take considerable time and a widening of the differential above its equilibrium level to get the flow started again. Meanwhile there may be serious labor shortages extending over a period of years.

Fourth, the freedom of maneuver which unions and governments have enjoyed in the past is diminishing as the size of wage differentials diminishes. One can envisage a time when, at least in some countries, all wage differentials will be near their equilibrium levels. In a growing and changing economy, however, the equilibrium level of differentials will continue to change over the course of time. There is serious question whether wages set through collective bargaining and government decree will be sufficiently flexible in the face of changing market requirements, and whether necessary adjustments in wage differentials will be made fast enough to prevent labor shortages at various points in the economy.

These dangers are real and important; but they are not sufficiently serious to justify the radical proposals sometimes advanced in the United States for prohibiting national collective bargaining. Nor does there seem much merit in the suggestion that bargained wage schedules be made subject to review and possible modification by a public authority. This would clearly undercut the freedom and spontaneity of private bargaining, and would cause all important wage issues to be passed on to the government tribunal for decision. A central organization of government employees would not necessarily reach wiser wage decisions than union and management officials directly involved in the industry. Even during wartime the wage control systems of Canada, the United States, and particularly Great Britain continued to rely mainly on union-management negotiation and voluntary wage settlements.

The growth of centralized authority and responsibility within the trade union federations contains greater possibilities of progress. Centralization may present some danger of unduly rapid advance in the general wage level, but the effects on wage structure can scarcely be anything but favorable. Federation leaders tend to think in terms of equitable wage relationships across industry lines as well as within each industry. Their influence is likely to be exerted to hold back the stronger groups and to bring up the groups in a weaker position.

This approach carries its own difficulties and dangers, which are clearly demonstrated by Swedish experience. Undue centralization threatens the basis for worker support of union organizations. A certain amount of autonomy in wage policy, both at the national and local union levels, seems to be part of the price of viable and democratic unionism.

It is also desirable on economic grounds in order to facilitate rapid adjustment to changing circumstances in particular industries and localities. The union movement must attempt to steer a middle course between complete and sterilizing conformity to central decisions and a policy of each union seizing as much as possible for itself.

It may seem premature to speak in this vein in the United States, where national union autonomy is deeply entrenched and federation influence has never been strong. But with the reunion of the CIO and AFL into a single body, with the increasing coverage of union organization, and with the growing acceptance of unionism as a permanent feature of the economic scene, it will be surprising if the next decade or two does not bring greater coordination of wage policy among the major unions. It would be naive to regard this as an unmixed blessing; but the experience of other countries suggests that it contains greater possibilities of good than of harm.

It is not very profitable for economists to spend their time deploring the course of events and advocating an atomistic system of wage determination—a concept which never had and never can have historical substance. The constructive course is to accept administered wage structures as inevitable; to work away at developing improved criteria for wage administration; to learn from, and occasionally to instruct, the private and public administrators through whom—and only through whom—economic wisdom can be made effective.

Notes on Sources

CHAPTER 2. RAILROAD TRANSPORTATION

The chief source of wage statistics for railroad employees is the reports of the Interstate Commerce Commission which cover all employees on Class I railways. ICC data go back as far as 1913 for the principal classes of train operating employees, and from 1922 to the present wage series are complete for nonoperating groups as well.

The ICC Statement M-300 publishes monthly the total compensation paid to each class of employees, the total number of hours on duty or held for duty by all the members of each class, and the total number of employees in each class (mid-month average).

The average hourly earnings of train-operating employees, as calculated by the Brotherhood of Locomotive Engineers in Table 2-2, and as calculated by the Bureau of Information of the Eastern Railways in Table 2-5, differ somewhat because of the complicated method of payment of these employees. In Table 2-2 total compensation has been divided by a larger number of "hours" than in Table 2-5 due to inclusions of the hour equivalent of "constructive allowances" in the divisor. The difference is not important, however, where we are concerned with a study of relative wages within railroad transportation.

The average weekly earnings of train-operating employees include daily rates, mileage payments, overtime payments, and constructive allowances, and have been arrived at by dividing total compensation by the average number of employees (mid-month).

The average weekly earnings of nonoperating employees given in Table 2-4 reflect largely the basic rates of pay and are not affected by working rules and practices to the same degree as with operating employees. They include any overtime payments and regular special allowances.

Wage statistics on railroad employees are the most comprehensive statistics studied in this book in terms of number of employees and occupations covered.

CHAPTER 3. IRON AND STEEL

The principal sources of data on occupational wages in the iron and steel industry are wage surveys made by the Bureau of Labor Statistics going as far back as 1907. The surveys made prior to the first World War were limited in scope with respect to number of plants and occupations covered. Gradually throughout the twenties the scope of the biannual surveys was widened until in 1931 some 213 plants or departments including 66,865 wage earners were covered, largely through personal visits of agents of the Bureau of Labor Statistics. The greater part of the data for the years through 1931 are contained in BLS Bulletins 442 (Washington, 1927), 513 (Washington, 1930), and 567 (Washington, 1932).

The BLS surveys of April 1938 and January 1951, the only ones made since 1933, are the chief ones used in this chapter. Both of these surveys covered practically all branches of the "basic" group of the iron and steel industry: blast furnaces, steel works, and rolling mills, as well as processing departments closely connected with rolling mills. The 1951 survey differed from the 1938 one in that it specifically excluded establishments employing less than 101 employees. The 1951 survey covered considerably more workers, 418,957 compared with 81,217 in 1938.

The difficulty in comparing the 1938 and 1951 occupational data stems chiefly from changes in job content over these years and lack of comparability of job titles. Data have been selected for Table 3-2 by choosing occupations where these changes have not been of primary importance.

The method of wage survey was the same in 1938 and in 1951. Data were obtained directly by BLS field representatives using job descriptions drawn up in the Bureau. In 1951 the job descriptions were based on the agreed classifications of the industry's Cooperative Wage Study.

The concept of "average hourly earnings" was somewhat different in 1938 and 1951. In 1938 average hourly earnings included shift differentials, production bonuses, special bonuses, and incentive earnings, while excluding overtime premiums. In 1951 not only overtime premiums but also special nonproduction bonuses not a regular part of the workers' pay were excluded from the calculation of average hourly earnings.

There are two sources of information on the general level of wages in the iron and steel industry. One is the BLS survey of hours and gross earnings of production workers in manufacturing, which includes a classification for "Blast furnaces, steel works, and rolling mills." The other is a series published by the American Iron and Steel Institute covering 93% of employees engaged in the production and sale of iron and steel products. It is also a series of gross earnings excluding only social security, pension, and insurance payments.

CHAPTER 4. COTTON TEXTILES

The source of data on occupational wages found in this chapter for the years 1937, 1940, 1943, 1946, 1952, and 1954 is surveys made by the Bureau of Labor Statistics in those years.

The definition of the cotton textile industry has varied in some details over the years. The "cotton goods" industry of April 1937, September 1940, and July 1943 wage surveys included 1. establishments primarily engaged in the manufacture of cotton broad-woven goods (over 12″ in width) and 2. establishments manufacturing cotton yarn and thread. Excluded were cotton narrow fabrics (less than 12″ in width) and establishments or departments engaged primarily in dyeing and finishing. The principal difference in the coverage of the April–May 1946 and the March 1952 wage surveys is that they *included* the dyeing and finishing departments of cotton broad-woven goods and cotton yarn establishments. These were subsequently excluded again in November 1954. These changes have had little effect on the comparability of occupational averages.

In all of these surveys the samples were chosen so that they would be representative with respect to geographical location, size of city, type of product, etc. The geographical coverage has been gradually extended until in the last two surveys all states with plants of any importance were included. The number of workers covered has gradually increased from 91,970 or about 20% of the industry in 1937 to 235,822 workers or about 56% of the wage earners in the industry in 1952. While the earlier surveys generally included samples of all sizes of establishments, the recent ones specifically excluded mills with less than 21 workers.

The "average hourly earnings" of the 1937 and 1940 surveys, while excluding overtime premiums, included production bonuses, shift differentials, and special bonuses such as Christmas bonuses. All the later surveys differed in that they excluded both shift differentials and special nonincentive payments. The recent series are thus genuine average straight-time hourly earnings.

There have been a number of minor changes in the coverage of the classifications "North" and "South" in the various surveys. The "North" and "South" of the 1937 and 1940 surveys have been compared in a number of tables in this chapter with "New England" and the "Southeast" of the 1946, 1952, and 1954 surveys. The reason that comparability is not greatly affected is that New England and the Southeast together include some 95% of the industry.

CHAPTERS 5 AND 6. PULP AND PAPER

The principal source of wage statistics for this study is the wage surveys conducted by the American Paper and Pulp Association. These surveys, which date from the period of the depression, provide a comprehensive record of hourly wage rates for key occupations in individual plants throughout the industry. In the prewar and war periods, wage information was reported annually (as of November 1) by approximately 270 plants—about one-third of the industry total, but representing perhaps two-thirds or more of industry output—and published in the Association's Survey of Occupational Wage Rates. Beginning in 1946, however, the annual survey was replaced by the Association's *Current Wage Survey,* which maintains a continuing and up-to-date record of occupational wage rates in 210 of the industry's plants. The coverage of this latter survey is somewhat smaller, but the great majority of plants included in it also reported wage data in the earlier surveys. The information contained in the *Current Wage Survey* for the postwar period is superior to that for earlier periods in that each member plant reports its current position following each change in wage rates. This makes possible the study of wage patterns and of differences among plants in the amount and timing of wage changes, and thereby enables the analyst to identify (and make allowance for) those wage differentials which represent merely temporary deviations from established patterns and trends.

While the Association's surveys were the primary source of wage data for the study, certain supplementary sources were relied upon to augment the basic series. The most important of these were the wage records of individual companies and the wage statistics collected by the principal unions in the industry. In addition, limited reference was made to the U. S. Bureau of Labor Statistics, "Pulp, Paper and Paperboard," *Wage Structure*, Series 2, No. 34 (Washington, 1946) and No. 91 (Washington, 1952); and to the American Paper and Pulp Association's *Quarterly Labor Review, Labor and Operating Statistics* (published monthly), and *Monthly Statistical Summary*. These latter sources contain only summary statistics (gross and straight-time average hourly earnings) of fairly wide coverage; consequently they were used sparingly in the study and only when more adequate data were not available.

Finally, the most valuable references for general industry statistics are the following: U. S. Pulp Producers' Association, *Wood Pulp Statistics* (New York, 1952); American Paper and Pulp Association, *The Statistics of Paper, 1951* (New York, 1952); and Lockwood's *Directory of the Paper and Allied Trades* (New York, Lockwood Trade Journal Co., Inc., published annually).

CHAPTER 8. FRANCE

The source of the wage data for all of the tables of this chapter is the quarterly survey of wages and employment of the French Ministry of Labor. This is the most comprehensive wage survey in France, and in its present form was begun early in 1946. No dependable data either on occupational wages or on the general level of wages exist for the prewar and war years.

The coverage of the survey was originally limited to those sectors of the economy subject to inspection by labor inspectors under the social security laws. Agriculture, mines, transport, and government services were thus excluded. However since 1946 some transport and mines have been included. At present the survey includes all economic activities except agriculture, water, gas, electricity, and government services.

In principle, since 1945 all establishments with over 50 workers were included and very few with under 10 employees. Although the survey was reorganized in 1951 to get better coverage of small establishments, the percentage return of questionnaires among small enterprises remains relatively small. Of the 40,000 to 45,000 establishments questioned, some 30,000 were giving usable answers in 1951; the usable answers included 90 to 95% of enterprises having over 50 employees.

The questionnaire asks for the hourly wage of five professional categories (men and women separately) in all industrial and commercial sectors except mines, railroads, and transport. However, there are no uniform job descriptions in use, and the decision as to what constitutes a skilled, unskilled, or highly skilled worker in each plant and industry rests largely with the individual employer.

The "average hourly wage" of all French wage data from the Ministry of Labor survey includes the basic wage, cost-of-living bonuses, and special or production bonuses granted to all the workers in the establishment. Excluded are overtime payments and special personal bonuses such as those for night work, Sunday work, or transport.

The general level of average hourly wages is calculated as follows: The arithmetic mean of hourly wages in each branch of industry and each wage zone is taken. These are then weighted according to the proportion of employees in the relevant categories as estimated in a special annual survey of the distribution of employees according to professional category.

For further details on wage statistics in France, see A. Aboughanem, "L'Organisation et le développement des statistiques sociales en France," *Revue française du travail*, 6 (July–Aug.–Sept. 1951), pp. 405–36.

CHAPTER 9. SWEDEN

The greater part of the wage data in this chapter comes from surveys by the Swedish Social Board of wages in mining and manufacturing in Sweden. Wage statistics are also collected separately for transportation, construction, forestry, public service, and public works sectors of the economy, but have not been analyzed in this chapter.

The Social Board survey of manufacturing and mining covered in 1952 about 80% of the total number of manual workers included in the Board of Trade's industrial statistics. In 1939 the same survey covered about 75% of them. The coverage of larger establishments has generally been better than that of smaller ones.

The method of survey is that of questionnaires. They are sent to all firms in manufacturing industries for which addresses can be obtained, and answering is voluntary. The information relates to total hours worked and total compensation for certain types of work (time work, piece work, overtime, shift work, etc.), and it is demanded separately for men, women, and juveniles. No information is obtained on occupational wage rates.

The "average hourly earnings" of the Social Board series for manual workers includes overtime and shift payments, holiday and sick payments, and some payments in kind—everything in the annual payroll divided by the number of hours worked.

The only important changes in the scope of the Social Board survey relate to statistics on white-collar wages (see Table 9-3). In 1946–47 the basis of the survey was altered from annual earnings to earnings in the month of September. As a result subsequent statistics understate considerably the increase in white-collar earnings over the whole period 1939–52. The only other changes in the scope of survey relate to variations in the identity and numbers of firms reporting. These are of varying importance according to the branch of industry.

The general level of average hourly earnings in manufacturing is calculated by weighting the various branches of industry according to the number of workers in the branches in each year as reported in surveys of employment of that year.

For further information, see the notes (with English summary) published each year in *Löner* (previously *Lönestatistisk Årsbok*) by the Social Board.

CHAPTER 10. GREAT BRITAIN

The source of the data on average hourly earnings and weekly wage rates in industry as a whole (Tables 10-2, 10-9, and 10-10) is the Ministry of Labour and National Service.

The index of weekly wage rates (Table 10-2) is based on weighted averages of minimum or standard rates as found in collective agreements, arbitration awards, or statutory regulations. Official indexes of wage rates exist as far back as 1880 but the coverage and method of calculation have changed a number of times. The series based on 1939 was revised and extended in June 1947 until it now covers agricultural workers, government workers, railroad workers, shop assistants, in fact all sectors of the economy covered by collective agreements or statutory arrangements. The method of calculation of the present series is explained in the *Ministry of Labour Gazette* (February 1948).

Surveys by the Ministry of Labour of actual earnings and hours worked exist for the years 1886, 1906, 1924, 1928, 1931, 1935, 1938, 1940, and from July 1941 for two different months out of each year. Since 1924 the surveys have included manufacturing industries and a number of nonmanufacturing industries and services. Agriculture, railroads, shipping, trade, domestic service, coal mining, docks, and entertainment are excluded. The present index is based on October 1938 and is weighted according to the estimated number of firms in the various branches of industry at that date. The method of survey is that of questionnaires with voluntary answers. In principle, questionnaires are sent to all establishments with over ten workers taking part in the 1938 survey plus a number of smaller and additional firms and important recently formed ones. The survey covers some 55,000 establishments employing about 6,000,000 workers.

The "average hourly earnings" of the Ministry of Labour survey includes all wage payments, personal and production bonuses, and excludes only employers' contributions to National Insurance and holiday funds.

No occupational earnings data are collected by the Ministry of Labour and National Service. The data in Tables 10-4 through 10-7 are taken from studies made at the Oxford University Institute of Statistics. They are based on wage files of various employers' federations. Further details may be obtained from the articles in the *Bulletin of the Oxford University Institute of Statistics* cited in this chapter.

For further details on official Ministry of Labour statistics, see the *Guides to Official Sources No. 1. Labour Statistics* published by the Ministry of Labour and National Service and R. B. Ainsworth, "United Kingdom Labour Statistics," *Journal of the Royal Statistical Society* (1950).

CHAPTER 11. CANADA

There are two principal sources of wage data on Canada: monthly statistics of average earnings collected by the Dominion Bureau of Statistics and occupational wages collected by the Economics and Research Branch of the Department of Labour.

The average hourly earnings, average weekly earnings, and average hours of the Dominion Bureau of Statistics relate to hourly rated wage earners or production workers employed full time or part time. The data for manufacturing (Tables 11-1, 11-4 and 11-5) relate to over 74% of all employees of firms cooperating in monthly surveys of employment and payrolls. In

1951 wage earners on whom man-hours (and thus average hourly earnings) information was obtained formed over 81% of wage earners in manufacturing reported to the Annual Census of Manufactures. In mining and construction the percentages were 82% and 54% respectively.

The "average hourly earnings" of the DBS is gross earnings before deduction of taxes and insurance contributions including overtime, incentive, and cost-of-living payments where regularly given. Excluded are bonuses paid at infrequent intervals, retroactive pay, and the value of any board and lodging given.

There have been two important changes in the DBS average hourly earnings series between 1939 and the present. The data for 1939 to 1945 refer to the month of highest employment for each firm reporting. The data for 1945 on refer to monthly surveys of hours and earnings. Furthermore in 1946 a considerable number of changes were made in the classification of industries within manufacturing. The general averages in Table 11-1, 11-5, and 11-6 cover the periods both before and after these changes were made, and it must be kept in mind that the figures are not strictly comparable.

The Economics and Research Branch of the Department of Labour has conducted an annual survey of wages and working conditions since 1943. Earlier surveys on a limited scale exist as far back as 1901. Prior to 1943 wage reports contained only a "representative" selection of wage rates (Table 11-2a) for a number of occupations in various industries and can only be used to give a rough indication of wage differentials. Furthermore incentive earnings were generally not included except where laid out in collective agreements. The survey has been gradually extended in scope since 1943 until it at present covers some 16,000 establishments. (Table 11-2b.)

The method of survey in the early years combined questionnaires with data from collective agreements, but gradually resort has been made only to survey questionnaire forms. From 1947 on, occupational schedules were included with the forms in an effort to get greater accuracy of reported occupational wages.

The "wage rates" of the occupational wage surveys have in fact been since 1943 straight-time average hourly earnings. Included are piece work, production and cost-of-living bonuses, mileage and other incentive payments, and value of meals and rooms where given. Excluded are overtime premiums, insurance and sick benefits, night shift payments, and special intermittent bonuses.

CHAPTER 12. UNITED STATES

For details on the method, scope, and history of wage statistics of the Bureau of Labor Statistics, as well as a bibliography on the subject, see BLS, *Techniques of Preparing Major BLS Statistical Series*, Bulletin 1168 (Washington, 1955).

Selected Bibliography

CHAPTER 2. RAILROAD TRANSPORTATION

Brotherhood of Locomotive Engineers. *The Wage Differentials of Railroad Engineers*. Submitted to the Board of Arbitration, 1953 wage movement. Mimeographed.

Interstate Commerce Commission, Bureau of Transport Economics and Statistics. *Wage Statistics of Class I Steam Railways in the United States*. Statement M-300. Monthly reports.

Jones, Harry E. *Railroad Wages and Labor Relations, 1900–1952*. Rev. ed. Washington, Bureau of Information of the Eastern Railways, 1953.

Kaufman, Jacob J. *Collective Bargaining in the Railroad Industry*. New York, King's Crown Press, 1954.

Kaufman, Jacob J. "Wage Criteria in the Railroad Industry," *Industrial and Labor Relations Review, 6* (Oct. 1952).

Monroe, J. Elmer. *Railroad Men and Wages*. Washington, Bureau of Railway Economics, Association of American Railroads, 1947.

Northrup, Herbert R. "Emergency Disputes under the Railway Labor Act," *Proceedings of the First Annual Meeting, Industrial Relations Research Association . . . 1948*, pp. 78–88.

Wolf, Harry D. "Railroads" in Harry A. Millis, ed., *How Collective Bargaining Works* (New York, Twentieth Century Fund, 1942), pp. 318–80.

CHAPTER 3. IRON AND STEEL

American Iron and Steel Institute. *Annual Statistical Report*, containing earnings and hours data.

Bureau of Labor Statistics:

"Earnings and Hours in the Iron and Steel Industry, April 1938, Part I, Hourly Earnings, and Part II, Occupational Differences," *Monthly Labor Review, 51* (Aug. and Sept. 1940), 421–42 and 709–26.

"Structural Steel Fabrication: Earnings, 1949 and 1950," *Monthly Labor Review, 72* (May 1951), 564–5.

United States Steel Corporation, Wage Chronology. Series 4, No. 3, with supplements 1–5. Serial Reprint.

Wage Structure, Basic Iron and Steel, January 1951. Series 2, No. 81. Processed, Washington, 1951.

Harbison, Frederick H. "Steel" in Harry A. Millis, ed., *How Collective Bargaining Works* (New York, Twentieth Century Fund, 1942), pp. 508–70.

Rees, Albert E. "The Economic Impact of Collective Bargaining in the

Steel and Coal Industries during the Postwar Period," *Proceedings of the Third Annual Meeting, Industrial Relations Research Association . . . , 1950*, pp. 203–12.

Rees, Albert E. "Postwar Wage Determination in the Basic Steel Industry," *American Economic Review, 41* (June 1951), 389–404.

Seltzer, George. "Pattern Bargaining and the United Steelworkers," *Journal of Political Economy, 59* (Aug. 1951), 319–31.

Stephens, John A. "Statement Regarding the Emergence of Patterns in the Steel Industry." Submitted to the President's Steel Board by the U. S. Steel Corporation, Aug. 30, 1949.

Tilove, Robert. *Collective Bargaining in the Steel Industry.* Philadelphia, University of Pennsylvania Press, 1948. Industry-wide Collective Bargaining Series.

Tilove, Robert. "The Wage Rationalization Program in United States Steel," *Monthly Labor Review, 64* (June 1947), 967–82.

CHAPTER 4. COTTON TEXTILES

Barkin, Solomon. "The Regional Significance of the Integration Movement in the Southern Textile Industry," *Southern Economic Journal, 15* (April 1949), 395–411.

Bureau of Labor Statistics:

"Average Hourly Earnings in Cotton-Goods Industry, 1937," *Monthly Labor Review, 46* (April 1938). Serial Reprint 747. Washington, 1938.

"Hours and Earnings in Manufacture of Cotton Goods, September 1940 and April 1941," *Monthly Labor Review, 53* (Dec. 1941). Serial Reprint 1414. Washington, 1942.

"Earnings in Cotton-Goods Manufacture during the War Years," *Monthly Labor Review, 59* (Oct. 1944), 823–35.

Wage Structure in Cotton Textiles, 1946. Series 2, No. 37. Processed, Washington, 1947.

Occupational Wage Relationships, Cotton Textiles, 1946. Series 1, No. 9. Processed, Washington, 1947.

Wage Structure, Cotton and Synthetic Textiles, March, 1952. Series 2, No. 89. Processed, Washington, 1952.

Earnings of Cotton Textile Workers, November 1954. Processed, Washington, 1955.

Northern Cotton Textile Association, Wage Chronology. Series 4, No. 2, with supplements.

Hinrichs, A. F., and Clem, Ruth. "Historical Review of Wage Rates in the Cotton-Textile Industry," *Monthly Labor Review, 40* (May 1935), 1170–80.

Lahne, Herbert J. *The Cotton Mill Worker.* New York, Rinehart, 1944.

Reynolds, Lloyd G. "Cutthroat Competition," *American Economic Review, 30* (Dec. 1940), 736–47.

Shapiro, Solomon, and Rubenstein, Charles. "Economic Problems and

Wage Structure in Cotton Textiles," *Monthly Labor Review, 75* (Aug. 1952), 140–9.

Tolles, N. Arnold. "Regional Differences in Cotton-Textile Wages, 1928 to 1937," *Monthly Labor Review, 46* (Jan. 1938), 36–47.

CHAPTERS 5 AND 6. PULP AND PAPER

American Paper and Pulp Association. *Presentation of the United States Pulp and Paper Manufacturers before the Senate Subcommittee on Trade Policies.* New York, Nov. 30, 1948.

American Paper and Pulp Association. "Some Economic Aspects of the Paper and Pulp Industry: Report of Industry Activities in 1934," *Monthly Review,* Vol. 2, Nos. 3, 4, and 5 (March, April, May, 1935).

Armstrong, Geo. S., & Co., Inc. "The Pulp, Paper and Board Industry," *An Engineering Interpretation of the Economic and Financial Aspects of American Industry, 9.* New York, Geo. S. Armstrong and Co., 1951.

Fleming, R. W., and Witte, Edwin E. "Marathon Corporation and Seven Labor Unions," *Causes of Industrial Peace under Collective Bargaining,* Case Study No. 8. Washington, National Planning Association, 1950.

Greening, A. E. *Paper Makers in Canada: A Record of Fifty Years' Achievement.* Cornwall, Ontario, International Brotherhood of Paper Makers, 1952.

Guthrie, John A. *The Economics of Pulp and Paper.* Pullman, Washington, State College of Washington Press, 1950.

Guthrie, John A. "Price Regulation in the Paper Industry," *Quarterly Journal of Economics, 60* (Feb. 1946), 194–218.

International Brotherhood of Paper Makers. *Labor Unrest and Dissatisfaction.* Albany, N.Y., International Brotherhood of Paper Makers, June 15, 1944.

Kerr, Clark, and Randall, Roger. "Crown Zellerbach and the Pacific Coast Pulp and Paper Industry," *Causes of Industrial Peace under Collective Bargaining,* Case Study No. 1. Washington, National Planning Association, 1948.

Maclaurin, W. Rupert. "Wages and Profits in the Paper Industry, 1929–39," *Quarterly Journal of Economics, 58* (Feb. 1944), 196–228.

Organization for European Economic Cooperation. *The Pulp and Paper Industry of the U.S.A.* A report by a Mission of European Experts. Paris, Organization for European Economic Cooperation, 1951.

Stevenson, Louis T. *The Background and Economics of American Papermaking.* New York, Harper, 1940.

U. S. Department of Commerce. *Transportation Factors in the Marketing of Newsprint, Transportation Series No. 2.* Washington, Government Printing Office, 1952.

U. S. Department of Labor. *Prevailing Minimum Wage for the Paper and Pulp Industry.* Official Report of Proceedings under Walsh-Healey Public Contracts Act, July 11, 1951. Washington, Alderson Reporting Company, 1951.

U. S. Department of Labor, Wage and Hour Division. *Report on the Pulp and Primary Paper Industry*. Mimeographed. Washington, March 18, 1940.

CHAPTER 8. FRANCE

Alvin, Louis. *Salaire et sécurité sociale*. Paris, Presses Universitaires de France, 1947.

Guglielmi, J.-L., and Perrot, M. *Salaires et revendications sociales en France, 1944–1952*. Paris, Librairie Armand Colin, 1953.

Institut National de la Statistique et des Etudes Economiques. *Etudes et conjoncture: Economie française*. Published monthly and frequently containing articles on wages in France.

Lévy-Bruhl, Raymond. "L'Evolution des salaires," *Revue d'économie politique, 63* (July–Oct. 1953), 735–51.

Lévy-Bruhl, Raymond. "L'Evolution des salaires de 1948 à 1950," *Revue d'économie politique, 61* (March–June 1951), 521–42.

Lévy-Bruhl, Raymond. "L'Evolution des salaires en 1951," *Revue d'économie politique, 62* (May–Aug. 1952), pp. 553–71.

Lorwin, Val. R. "France," in Walter Galenson, ed., *Comparative Labor Movements*. New York, Prentice-Hall, 1952.

Lorwin, Val. R. *The French Labor Movement*. Cambridge, Harvard University Press, 1954.

Ministère du Travail et de la Sécurité Sociale. *Revue française du travail*. Published quarterly and containing data on wages and social security.

Sauvy, Alfred. "Les Salaires français," *Revue économique* (Dec. 1950), 513–22.

Sellier, François. "Les Effets de l'inflation sur la structure des salaires," to be published in the forthcoming report of the 1954 International Economic Association conference on wage determination.

Sturmthal, Adolf. "Collective Bargaining in France," *Industrial and Labor Relations Review, 4* (Jan. 1951), 236–48.

Sturmthal, Adolf. "The Structure of Nationalized Enterprises in France," *Political Science Quarterly, 67* (Sept. 1952), 357–77.

CHAPTER 9. SWEDEN

Allen, G. R. "Relative Real Wages in Swedish Agriculture and Industry, 1930–1950," *Bulletin of the Oxford University Institute of Statistics, 15* (Dec. 1953), 436–52.

Galenson, Walter. "Scandinavia" in Walter Galenson, ed., *Comparative Labor Movements*. New York, Prentice-Hall, 1952.

Myers, Charles A. *Industrial Relations in Sweden (Some Comparisons with American Experience)*. Cambridge, Massachusetts Institute of Technology Press, 1951.

Norgren, Paul H. *The Swedish Collective Bargaining System*. Cambridge, Harvard University Press, 1941.

Rehn, Gösta. "Memorandum on the Wage Drift in Sweden." Stockholm, Confederation of Swedish Trade Unions. Mimeographed. 1954.

Rehn, Gösta. "Unionism and the Wage Structure," to be published in the forthcoming report of the 1954 International Economic Association conference on wage determination.

Social Board statistics published annually in the *Lönestatistisk Årsbok för Sverige* (since 1952 *Löner*).

Swedish Central Bureau of Statistics. *Statistical Abstract of Sweden*. Published yearly and containing principal wage series.

Trade Unions and Full Employment. Stockholm, Confederation of Swedish Trade Unions, 1952.

U. S. Department of Labor. *Labor-Management Relations in Scandinavia*. Bulletin 1038. Washington, 1952.

CHAPTER 10. GREAT BRITAIN

British Trade Unionism: Six Studies by PEP. London, Political and Economic Planning, 1949.

Dennison, S. R. "Wages in Full Employment," *Lloyds Bank Review* (April 1950), 18–37.

Flanders, Allan. "Great Britain," in Walter Galenson, ed., *Comparative Labor Movements*. New York, Prentice-Hall, 1952.

Flanders, Allan. "Wages Policy and Full Employment in Britain," *Bulletin of the Oxford University Institute of Statistics, 12* (July and Aug. 1950), 225–42.

Knowles, K. G. J. C., and Cole, H. J. D. "Rates and Earnings in London Transport," *ibid., 15* (Aug. 1953), 261–94.

Knowles, K. G. J. C, and Hill, T. P. "The Structure of Engineering Earnings," *ibid., 16* (Sept. and Oct. 1954), 271–328.

Knowles, K. G. J. C., and Robertson, D. J. "Differences between the Wages of Skilled and Unskilled Workers, 1880–1950," *ibid., 13* (April 1951), 109–127.

Knowles, K. G. J. C., and Robertson, D. J. "Earnings in Engineering, 1926–1948," *ibid., 13* (June 1951), 179–200.

Knowles, K. G. J. C., and Robertson, D. J. "Earnings in Shipbuilding," *ibid., 13* (Nov. and Dec. 1951), 357–65.

Knowles, K. G. J. C., and Romanis, A. "Dockworkers' Earnings (Great Britain)," *ibid., 14* (Sept. and Oct. 1952), 327–65.

Knowles, K. G. J. C., and Verry, Monica. "Earnings in the Boot and Shoe Industry," *ibid., 16* (Feb. and March 1954), 29–72.

Ministry of Labour Gazette. Published monthly and containing data on wages.

Ministry of Labour and National Service. *Industrial Relations Handbook*. New ed., London, 1953.

Ministry of Labour and National Service. *Time Rates of Wages and Hours of Labour*. Published yearly with data on wage rates as established in collective agreements.

Phelps Brown, E. Henry. "The Long-Term Movement of Real Wages," to be published in the forthcoming report of the 1954 International Economic Association conference on wage determination.

Phelps Brown, E. Henry, and Roberts, Ben. C. "Wages Policy in Great Britain," *Lloyds Bank Review* (Jan. 1952), 17–31.

Roberts, Ben C. "Trade Union Behavior and Wage Determination," to be published in the forthcoming report of the 1954 International Economic Association conference on wage determination.

Turner, H. A. "Trade Unions, Differentials and the Levelling of Wages," *Manchester School of Economic and Social Studies, 20* (Sept. 1952), 227–82.

CHAPTER 11. CANADA

Beausoleil, Gilles. *Wages in Quebec and Ontario.* Montreal, Canadian Congress of Labour and the Canadian and Catholic Confederation of Labour, 1954.

Coats, Robert H., ed. *Features of Present-day Canada.* Philadelphia, American Academy of Political and Social Science, 1947 (*Annals,* Vol. *253*).

Department of Labour. *Labour Gazette.* Published monthly.

Department of Labour, Economics and Research Branch. *Wage Rates and Hours of Labour in Canada.* Reports for October of each year, published annually.

Dominion Bureau of Statistics. *Annual Review of Man-Hours and Hourly Earnings, 1945–1953,* Ottawa, 1954.

Dominion Bureau of Statistics. *Earnings and Hours of Work in Manufacturing.* Published annually.

Logan, Harold A. *Trade Unions in Canada, Their Development and Functioning.* Toronto, Macmillan Company of Canada, 1948.

Royal Commission on Prices, "Prices and Wages," *Report of the . . . Commission,* Vol. *2.* Ottawa, 1949.

CHAPTER 12. UNITED STATES

Woytinsky, W. S., and Associates. *Employment and Wages in the United States,* New York, Twentieth Century Fund, 1953.

Occupational Differentials

Bell, Philipp W. "Cyclical Variations and Trends in Occupational Wage Differentials in American Industry since 1914," *Review of Economics and Statistics, 23* (Nov. 1951), 329–37.

Kanninen, Toivo P. "Occupational Relationships in Manufacturing, 1952–53," *Monthly Labor Review, 76* (Nov. 1953), 1171–8.

Ober, Harry. "Occupational Wage Differentials, 1907–1947," *Monthly Labor Review, 67* (Aug. 1948), 127–34.

Ober, Harry. "Occupational Wage Differentials in Industry," in W. S. Woytinsky and Associates, *Employment and Wages in the United States,* chap. 40.

Interindustry Differentials (Including Union Impact)

Dunlop, John T. "Productivity and the Wage Structure," in *Income, Employment and Public Policy* (Essays in Honor of Alvin H. Hansen), New York, Norton, 1948.

Garbarino, Joseph. "A Theory of Inter-Industry Wage Structure Variation," *Quarterly Journal of Economics, 64* (May 1950), 283–305.

Lebergott, Stanley. "Wage Structures," *Review of Economics and Statistics, 29* (Nov. 1947), 274–85.

Rees, Albert E. "The Economic Impact of Collective Bargaining in the Steel and Coal Industries during the Postwar Period," *Proceedings of the Third Annual Meeting, Industrial Relations Research Association . . . 1950,* pp. 203–13.

Ross, Arthur M., and Goldner, William. "Forces Affecting the Inter-Industry Wage Structure," *Quarterly Journal of Economics, 64* (May 1950), 254–81.

Slichter, Sumner H. "Notes on the Structure of Wages," *Review of Economics and Statistics, 32* (Feb. 1950), 80–91.

Regional Differentials

Bloch, Joseph W. "Regional Wage Differentials," *Monthly Labor Review, 66* (April 1948), 371–7.

Lester, Richard A. "Diversity in North-South Wage Differentials," *Southern Economic Journal, 12* (Jan. 1946), 238–62.

Lester, Richard A. "Southern Wage Differentials: Developments, Analysis, and Implications," *Southern Economic Journal, 13* (April 1947), 386–94.

Lester, Richard A. "Trends in Southern Wage Differentials since 1890," *Southern Economic Journal, 11* (April 1945), 317–44.

Lewis, L. Earl. "City Comparisons of Wage Levels and Skill Differentials," *Monthly Labor Review, 74* (June 1952), 643–7.

Ober, Harry, and Glasser, Carrie. "Regional Wage Differentials," *Monthly Labor Review, 63* (Oct. 1946), 511–25.

Suffrin, Sidney C., and others. "The North-South Differential—a Different View," *Southern Economic Journal, 15* (Oct. 1948), 184–90.

Union Influence on Occupational, Regional, Interplant Differentials

Douty, Harry M. "Union Impact on Wage Structures," *Proceedings of the Sixth Annual Meeting, Industrial Relations Research Association . . . 1953,* pp. 61–76.

Douty, Harry M. "Union and Nonunion Wages," in W. S. Woytinsky and Associates, *Employment and Wages in the United States,* chap. 43.

Kerr, Clark. "Unions and Wage Structures," to be published in the forthcoming report of the International Economic Association conference on wage determination.

Sobel, Irvin. "Collective Bargaining and Decentralization in the Rubber-Tire Industry," *Journal of Political Economy, 62* (Feb. 1954), 12–25.

Sobotka, Stephen P. "Union Influence on Wages: the Construction Industry," *Journal of Political Economy, 61* (April 1953), 127–43.

Local Wage Diversity
Lester, Richard A. "Wage Diversity and Its Theoretical Implications," *Review of Economic Statistics, 28* (Aug. 1946), 152–9.

Agricultural Wages
Ahearn, David J. *The Wages of Farm and Factory Laborers, 1914–1944,* New York, Columbia University Press, 1945.
Ducoff, Louis J. "Wages in Agriculture," in W. S. Woytinsky and Associates, *Employment and Wages in the United States,* chap. 42.

Bureau of Labor Statistics
Bulletin 1135. *Wage Differentials and Rate Structures among 40 Labor Markets, 1951–52,* Washington, 1953.
Bulletin 1116. *Wages and Related Benefits, 20 Labor Markets, 1952–53,* Washington, 1954.
Bulletin 1157. *Wages and Related Benefits, Major Labor Markets, 1953–1954* (Pts. I, II, and III), Washington, 1954 and 1955.
Bulletin 1160. *Wages and Related Benefits in the Machinery Industries. Postwar Wage Trends. Survey of 20 Labor Markets, 1953–54,* Washington, 1954.

Index